C++

How-To

Jan Walter
Danny Kalev
Michael J. Tobler
Paul Snaith
Andrei Kossoroukov
Scott Roberts

SAMS

A Division of Macmillan Computer Publishing
201 West 103rd St., Indianapolis, Indiana, 46290 USA

The Waite Group's C++ How-To

Copyright © 1999 by Sams Publishing

International Standard Book Number: 1-57169-159-6

Library of Congress Catalog Card Number: 98-86976

Printed in the United States of America

First Printing: January, 1999

02   01   00   99   4   3   2   1

Trademarks

Warning and Disclaimer

EXECUTIVE EDITOR
Tracy Dunkelberger

ACQUISITIONS EDITOR
Michelle Newcomb

DEVELOPMENT EDITOR
Bryan Morgan

MANAGING EDITOR
Jodi Jensen

PROJECT EDITOR
Dana Rhodes Lesh

COPY EDITOR
Mike Henry

INDEXER
Johnna VanHoose

PROOFREADER
Eddie Lushbaugh

TECHNICAL EDITORS
Darralyn McCall
Jeramie Hicks
Vincent Mayfield

SOFTWARE DEVELOPMENT SPECIALIST
Dan Scherf

TEAM COORDINATOR
Michelle Newcomb

INTERIOR DESIGNER
Gary Adair

COVER DESIGNER
Karen Ruggles

LAYOUT TECHNICIANS
Brandon Allen
Timothy Osborn
Staci Somers
Mark Walchle

CONTENTS AT A GLANCE

INTRODUCTION   **1**

Part I   Language Topics

CHAPTER 1:   A QUICK INTRODUCTION TO THE LANGUAGE . .7

CHAPTER 2:   OBJECT ORIENTATION—THEORY AND
             PRACTICE .51

CHAPTER 3:   OBJECT ORIENTATION—C++ SPECIFICS 69

Part II   Data Structures

CHAPTER 4:   STRUCTURES VERSUS CLASSES 105

CHAPTER 5:   COMMON MISTAKES MADE WITH CLASSES . .157

CHAPTER 6:   TEMPLATE CLASSES 217

CHAPTER 7:   THE STANDARD TEMPLATE LIBRARY'S
             CONTAINER CLASSES 245

Part III   Algorithms

CHAPTER 8:   THE STANDARD C LIBRARY'S INCLUDED
             ALGORITHMS 285

CHAPTER 9:   THE STANDARD TEMPLATE LIBRARY'S
             INCLUDED ALGORITHMS 313

Part IV   Error Handling

CHAPTER 10:   C-STYLE ERROR HANDLING 371

CHAPTER 11:   EXCEPTION HANDLING IN C++ 407

Part V   Memory Management

CHAPTER 12:   NEW AND DELETE VERSUS MALLOC()
              AND FREE() .441

CHAPTER 13:   MEMORY MANAGEMENT TECHNIQUES USING
              CLASSES 471

Part VI   I/O

CHAPTER 14:   UNDERSTANDING THE I/O STREAMS
              LIBRARY 497

CHAPTER 15:   FILE I/O 523

Part VII   Appendixes

APPENDIX A: NAMESPACES 549

APPENDIX B: RUNTIME TYPE INFORMATION 559

INDEX   **569**

TABLE OF CONTENTS

INTRODUCTION **1**

PART I
Language Topics

CHAPTER 1

A QUICK INTRODUCTION TO THE LANGUAGE **9**

1.1 Write the simplest C++ program without knowing the language 12
1.2 Create a program to perform calculations 17
1.3 Use the various loop statements that are available in C++ 21
1.4 Create a program that uses one or more functions 25
1.5 Use the derived data types such as arrays and pointers 29
1.6 Create data when the program is running 37
1.7 Create a program to perform error handling, specifically
exception handling 41

CHAPTER 2

OBJECT ORIENTATION—THEORY AND PRACTICE **53**

2.1 Understand the object-oriented paradigm 55
2.2 Learn the concept of inheritance so that I can apply it
programmatically 57
2.3 Learn the concept of encapsulation 62
2.4 Learn the concept of polymorphism 64

CHAPTER 3

OBJECT ORIENTATION—C++ SPECIFICS **71**

3.1 Create a simple class in C++ 72
3.2 Implement the use of inheritance in C++ 80
3.3 Apply the use of encapsulation in a C++ program 87
3.4 Implement polymorphism in C++ 91
3.5 Implement static members of a class 97

PART II
Data Structures

CHAPTER 4

STRUCTURES VERSUS CLASSES **107**

4.1 Create my own data type 110
4.2 Hide my data from external programs 118
4.3 Use encapsulation? What steps are required to encapsulate data? 129

4.4   Create my own operators 134
4.5   Overload relational and equality operators 139
4.6   Provide access to encapsulated data to certain classes 144
4.7   Maintain global data in my program 148
4.8   Know when I should use structures and when I should use classes 151

CHAPTER 5
COMMON MISTAKES MADE WITH CLASSES 159

5.1   Know when to take an object-oriented approach or a procedural approach . . .162
5.2   Use and access a class's data members 169
5.3   Use the scope resolution operator 175
5.4   Use dot notation to access the member functions of an object 181
5.5   Know which constructor to use when there are several to choose from 186
5.6   Implement function overloading 191
5.7   Correctly make use of inheritance 194
5.8   Pass parameters back through the C++ inheritance mechanism
      to parent classes 200
5.9   Distinguish between virtual classes and nonvirtual classes? How do I know
      when to use virtual classes and what does the word *virtual* mean in C++? 206

CHAPTER 6
TEMPLATE CLASSES 219

6.1   Create a template class to represent any simple data type and understand
      how to use the template in a working C++ program 221
6.2   Create a template class to represent any simple data type and extend it
      to read in data to a variable of any data type 225
6.3   Create a template class to represent a compound data type and understand
      how to use the template in a working C++ program 228
6.4   Write a template class that has two undefined data types that can be resolved
      at a later time 233
6.5   Use a template class to handle a structure 238

CHAPTER 7
THE STANDARD TEMPLATE LIBRARY'S CONTAINER CLASSES 247

7.1   Create a container object that automatically grows or shrinks as needed 250
7.2   Read a single element of a container 254
7.3   Modify a single element of a container 257
7.4   Use a generic LIFO data model 261
7.5   Prevent automatic reallocation of a container 268
7.6   Traverse through a container's elements 273
7.7   Implement a queue data model 278

PART III
Algorithms

CHAPTER 8

THE STANDARD C LIBRARY'S INCLUDED ALGORITHMS **287**

8.1   Sort an array 289
8.2   Find an element in an array 298
8.3   Locate an element in a nonsorted array 302
8.4   Choose between `_lfind` and `_lsearch` 305
8.5   Generate a sequence of random numbers 309

CHAPTER 9

THE STANDARD TEMPLATE LIBRARY'S INCLUDED ALGORITHMS . . .**315**

9.1   Create classes for sequential containers 320
9.2   Use predicates with sequence operations 328
9.3   Repeat an action with all elements in a container range 333
9.4   Compare two sequences 337
9.5   Search for a sequence of values in a container 341
9.6   Accumulate all container elements and create a sequence
         of accumulated sums 345
9.7   Sort elements in a container using different sorting indexes 351
9.8   Change the order of the container elements 362

PART IV
Error Handling

CHAPTER 10

C-STYLE ERROR HANDLING **373**

10.1   Handle runtime errors in my programs 376
10.2   Use the standard C library functions `perror` and `strerror` and the
          predefined C macros to report runtime errors in my programs 381
10.3   Use `assert` to catch errors in my code when running in debug mode 385
10.4   Use `raise` and `signal` to indicate errors in my programs 387
10.5   Use `abort` to terminate my application if a serious error occurs 391
10.6   Use `exit` and `atexit` together to perform some action when my program
          terminates normally 393
10.7   Detect errors that occur when reading from or writing to a file using the
          file functions provided with the Standard C Library 395
10.8   Use `setjmp` and `longjmp` to maintain state when handling errors 397
10.9   Use a C++ class to handle runtime errors in a more maintainable fashion 400

CHAPTER 11

EXCEPTION HANDLING IN C++ 409

11.1 Utilize the exception handling mechanism to process potential
      error conditions 411
11.2 Use the various catch constructs such as multiple catch clauses,
      catch ordering, and the rethrowing of exceptions 419
11.3 Implement and use an exception class .425
11.4 Specify exceptions that a function will throw 430
11.5 Handle exceptions that are not caught or not expected 434

PART V
Memory Management

CHAPTER 12

NEW AND DELETE VERSUS MALLOC() AND FREE() 443

12.1 Use new and delete with the C malloc() and free() routines 445
12.2 Use other C mem... routines on objects allocated with new 446
12.3 Find out how much memory my structures and classes really take 447
12.4 Prevent memory leaks caused by not using delete[] to delete arrays 450
12.5 Override the new or delete operators for my classes 451
12.6 Overload the new and delete functions for arrays 455

CHAPTER 13

MEMORY MANAGEMENT TECHNIQUES USING CLASSES 473

13.1 Make a simple class to clean up dynamically allocated memory
      automatically 475
13.2 Make a class that automatically cleans up objects allocated with new 479
13.3 Make an object that deallocates itself when there is no more
      code referencing it 483

PART VI
I/O

CHAPTER 14

UNDERSTANDING THE I/O STREAMS LIBRARY 499

14.1 Use the C Standard I/O Library with the C++ I/O streams library 500
14.2 Make my own classes compatible with cin and cout 503
14.3 Perform complex formatting with cout or another ostream object 504
14.4 Make my own stream manipulators 515

CHAPTER 15
FILE I/O **525**

15.1 Open a file stream 526
15.2 Continually read data until the end of file 529
15.3 Handle stream errors 532
15.4 Read and write binary files 536
15.5 Read from or write to different positions in a file 542

PART VII
Appendixes

APPENDIX A
NAMESPACES **549**

The Rationale Behind Namespaces 550
A Brief Historical Background 550
Large-Scale Projects Are Susceptible to Name Clashes 550
Properties of Namespaces 551
A Fully Qualified Name 551
A using-Declaration and a using-Directive 551
Namespaces Are Open 552
Namespace Aliases 553
Koenig Lookup 554
Namespaces Do Not Incur Additional Overhead 554
The Interaction of Namespaces with Other Language Features 554
:: Operator Should Not Be Used to Designate a Global Function 555
Turning an External Function into a File-Local Function 555
Standard Headers Names 556
Restrictions on Namespaces 557
Namespace std May Not Be Modified 557
User-Defined new and delete Cannot Be Declared in a Namespace 557
Comments 558

APPENDIX B
RUNTIME TYPE INFORMATION **559**

Static Binding 559
Dynamic Binding 560
Historical Background 563
RTTI Constituents 563
Comments 568

INDEX 569

Jan Walter is a freelance computer consultant living around Vancouver, B.C., Canada. He spends most of his time doing network design and implementation, but "would rather be coding." Jan has fulfilled programming contracts with several large companies in the area, mostly using C++. Code optimization and performance tuning are a distinct area of interest, as is compiler technology. The latter came about after spending a lot of time hunting down bugs introduced by parser problems in Borland C++ in one of his projects.

This is his second project with Macmillan Computer Publishing. The first was as contributing author to Que's *Using Linux*, by Bill Ball, 1998.

Jan Walter can be reached at `jwalter@rogers.wave.ca`.

Danny Kalev is a certified system analyst and software engineer with 10 years of experience, specializing in C++ and object-oriented analysis and design. He is now finishing his M.A. degree in applied linguistics at the University of Tel Aviv, Israel. His research focuses on speech recognition algorithms. He is a hi-fi enthusiast and likes all kinds of music. He is also interested in natural languages and philology.

His technical interests involve generic programming, networking, compiler technology, artificial intelligence, and embedded systems. He has contributed several articles to C++ magazines and Web publishers. He is also a member of the ANSI C++ standardization committee. He can be reached at `dannykk@inter.net.il`.

Michael J. Tobler is a senior technical specialist with BSI Consulting in Houston, Texas. He has more than 16 years experience working on software development projects, specializing in architecting, designing, and developing multitier systems using C++ and Java. He is currently the president of the Houston Java Users Group. Michael is an advocate and practitioner of the Unified Modeling process from Rational and a proponent of patterns and pattern languages. He is a contributing author for *C++ Unleashed*. He has discovered that skydiving is a very addicting sport. Michael can be reached at `mtobler@ibm.net`.

Paul Snaith works in the I.T. industry in the UK. He is currently a project leader in software development for a well-known British airline dealing mainly with Web development and electronic commerce. Previously, he spent several years lecturing in modern computer languages such as C++, Java, VB, and Delphi. In the far distant past (only a few years ago but it seems much longer), Paul was involved in the rock music industry as a musician and played with the wonders of electronic computer generation of his work. Paul has just finished another book called *The Complete Idiot's Guide to C++* and is planning other such works in the near future.

Andrei Kossoroukov is a professional developer and a software consultant with 15+ years of business experience. He graduated with a Master of Science in mathematics in 1982 and finished postgraduate studies in relational databases in 1985. Working with computers for the last 25 years, he has developed artificial intelligence systems, financial software, and distributed messaging systems. He is an author of more than 30 scientific and technical articles, papers, and books. Currently he works for I.T. Systems, Inc.(Vancouver, B.C., Canada) as a senior software consultant and specializes in the development of Internet-based systems with distributed data.

Scott Roberts works as a developer support engineer on the Internet Client Development team at Microsoft. He assists developers who are using Visual C++ and COM to create Internet applications. Scott has been a developer for 9 years and has worked at a number of companies on a wide range of products, from back-end communications systems to end-user software applications. Scott has been a frequent contributor to many technical publications, including Microsoft Interactive Developer and Microsoft Systems Journal. In addition, he has spoken at many technical conferences in the United States and Europe. Scott can be reached at `scottrobe@hotmail.com`.

DEDICATION

I dedicate this book to my grandparents. In their time, people went through so much, and many gave their lives to let us have what we have now. It is easy for us today to look back 60 years and say, "Times were tough then," but we have little comprehension of what actually went on.
"Lest we forget" is an apt phrase to take to heart.

—*Jan Walter*

ACKNOWLEDGMENTS

I do also need to thank the staff at Macmillan Computer Publishing for their seemingly infinite patience. Many thanks for encouragement go to Michelle Newcomb, and thanks, Bryan, for your insightful feedback.

—Jan Walter

TELL US WHAT YOU THINK!

As the reader of this book, *you* are our most important critic and commentator. We value your opinion and want to know what we're doing right, what we could do better, what areas you'd like to see us publish in, and any other words of wisdom you're willing to pass our way.

As the executive editor for the Advanced Programming and Distributed Architectures team at Macmillan Computer Publishing, I welcome your comments. You can fax, email, or write me directly to let me know what you did or didn't like about this book—as well as what we can do to make our books stronger.

Please note that I cannot help you with technical problems related to the topic of this book, and that due to the high volume of mail I receive, I might not be able to reply to every message.

When you write, please be sure to include this book's title and author as well as your name and phone or fax number. I will carefully review your comments and share them with the author and editors who worked on the book.

Fax: 317-817-7070

Email: `programming@mcp.com`

Mail: Tracy Dunkelberger
         Executive Editor
         Advanced Programming and Distributed Architectures Team
         Macmillan Computer Publishing
         201 West 103rd Street
         Indianapolis, IN 46290 USA

INTRODUCTION

Despite the development of several new languages over the past five years, C++ has held its own in the development world. Originally developed at AT&T Bell Laboratories by Bjarne Stoustrup, the language has evolved to encompass ever more object-oriented concepts.

With the latest ANSI revision of C++, version 3, the language gets some fine-tuning in memory management, solid exception support, and new typecasting operators. The biggest improvement, however, was the introduction of the *Standard Template Library* (STL), which provides a standard set of container classes and the means to work with them. Before this, most compiler vendors included their own container classes and other objects in their libraries, posing an impediment to porting code from one platform to another where the same vendor's compiler was not supported.

What makes C++ so useful? Some people say that its C language underpinnings are great for getting as close to the hardware as possible without using assembler code. Developers find that the strong typing by the C++ language helps reduce the number of bugs in programs. Some people use C++ as "just a better C," but the point is missed then: The object-oriented programming (OOP) style makes it easier to translate from the problem language and problem world to the solution language.

The great misconception of many people is that object-oriented programming produces slower code. This is not necessarily so. If a problem can be put so that a human mind can understand it better, it is likely that this mind can produce a better solution. Algorithms, and their efficiency, have a much greater impact on program performance than the language does. C++ is only marginally slower than C code overall, and this makes it one of the fastest executing languages for object-oriented programming.

This book is intended to be an eye-opener for C++ programmers. I admit freely that I learn the most from reading other peoples' code, as I learn their approaches to problems. It's easy to get stuck in one way of doing things, and this is dangerous with any creative exercise. Computer programming is no exception. What's written in this book is not gospel, but yet another approach that can be added to your arsenal.

The Waite Group's C++ How-To is divided into 15 chapters, each of which covers a specific feature of the C++ programming language:

- Chapter 1, "A Quick Introduction to the Language"—Before diving into the "deep end" of C++ programming, this chapter provides a gentle introduction into the basic concepts of the language. Loops, calculations, and error handling are all covered here for the beginning C++ programmer.

- Chapter 2, "Object Orientation—Theory and Practice"—To fully make use of the C++ language, object-oriented programming must be understood. Many C, Pascal, and COBOL programmers are assigned to C++ projects and never take the time—or get the opportunity—to fully learn the benefits of OOP. Without focusing on the specific syntax used in C++, this chapter covers the basic object-oriented concepts required to become a great C++ programmer.

- Chapter 3, "Object Orientation—C++ Specifics"—After learning or reviewing the basic concepts of object-oriented programming in Chapter 2, you will learn how these concepts are specifically applied to C++ in this chapter. The basic tenets of OOP—inheritance, polymorphism, and encapsulation—are all covered here as well as the fundamental C++ unit: the class.

- Chapter 4, "Structures Versus Classes"—C++ provides two primary devices that can be used to contain data: structures and classes. Although the two data structures can be identical, classes are much more powerful because they fully support the primary OOP constructs. This chapter compares and contrasts these two data types and provide numerous examples of their use.

- Chapter 5, "Common Mistakes Made with Classes"—Because of the tremendous difference between traditional structured programming and object-oriented programming, many beginning-to-intermediate–level programmers make several common mistakes. This chapter introduces these mistakes, explains why they are mistakes, and offers solutions to them.

- Chapter 6, "Template Classes"—The template class is a mechanism that enables you to write a single solution to a problem that can satisfy all data types. The actual data type required can be specified later, and the template class can then be used for a wide range of data types, all using the same C++ template. This chapter introduces the template class, or templates as they are commonly known.

- Chapter 7, "The Standard Template Library's Container Classes"—In this chapter, you will explore the following containers of the Standard Template Library: vector, string, stack, list, and queue. I also discuss iterators and their role in the STL framework. Finally, you will survey some other containers as well as "almost container" classes of the Standard Library.

- Chapter 8, "The Standard C Library's Included Algorithms"—In this chapter, I survey the algorithms of the Standard C Library. These algorithms enable you to sort an array and find an element in it. In addition, I discuss the random number generation functions of the Standard C Library.

- Chapter 9, "The Standard Template Library's Included Algorithms"—STL algorithms are represented by template functions and provide copying, searching, sorting, and merging functions, as well as other operations on data. Algorithms are not member functions; they are separate from the container classes. You will examine a number of these algorithms in this chapter. I give examples, where possible, showing their use in typical situations.

- Chapter 10, "C-Style Error Handling"—This chapter covers different error-handling methods that work in C and C++ programs and some methods that don't work well in C++ programs. Although this is a C++ book, I discuss C-type error-handling techniques so that you will know what you are dealing with if you run into them in older C and C++ programs.

- Chapter 11, "Exception Handling in C++"—The exception-handling mechanism furnished by the standard provides a common and standard interface for handling program anomalies. Without exception handling, error handling is performed using return values from functions and global status variables. Each developer has his or her own style of handling errors, leading to inconsistency among applications and library packages. In this chapter, you will see various ways to apply the exception-handling mechanisms

- Chapter 12, "new and delete Versus malloc() and free()"—This chapter compares and contrasts the C++ new and delete operators and the C functions malloc() and free(), and it covers their place in C++ memory management. You must understand memory management using C and C++ techniques because of the existence of legacy code and because many existing libraries use the older C language techniques.

- Chapter 13, "Memory Management Techniques Using Classes"—Whereas C-style memory management basically requires the programmer to free variables that have been created, C++-style memory management is much more powerful, although a bit more challenging. This chapter focuses on many advanced memory management techniques that you can use to improve the reliability and performance of your applications.

- Chapter 14, "Understanding the I/O Streams Library"—So many programmers seem to have difficulty with the C++ I/O Streams library that it is quite common to see C++ code still using the old C `stdio` functions to handle program I/O. Although some programmers might consider this approach practical, or even superior, the C `stdio` library does not do much to help good programming practice or catch oversights made by the programmer. This chapter introduces the basic concepts required to use the Streams library and shows why it is a preferred solution to the standard C method.

- Chapter 15, "File I/O"—This chapter covers `IOStreams` with a focus on file streams. Examples are provided that demonstrate how to seek through files, read/write binary files, and manage file I/O errors.

This book also includes two appendixes, one on namespaces and another on runtime type information (RTTI).

WHO IS THIS BOOK INTENDED FOR?

The Waite Group's C++ How-To is designed for C++ programmers of all skill levels, from beginning to advanced. However, I anticipate that readers who pick up this book already have a solid understanding of C++ programming and are looking for "just the answers" to specific programming questions. This is also a great supplemental resource for new C++ programmers searching for information and instruction that goes beyond a typical tutorial.

PART I
LANGUAGE TOPICS

CHAPTER 1

A QUICK INTRODUCTION TO THE LANGUAGE

1

A QUICK INTRODUCTION TO THE LANGUAGE

How do I...

1.1 Write the simplest C++ program without knowing the language?

1.2 Create a program to perform calculations?

1.3 Use the various loop statements that are available in C++?

1.4 Create a program that uses one or more functions?

1.5 Use the derived data types such as arrays and pointers?

1.6 Create data when the program is running?

1.7 Create a program to perform error handling, specifically exception handling?

The C++ programming language is one of the most significant languages to emerge in the past twenty years. The C++ language is also the most popular object-oriented language in use today. I will examine the object-oriented features of C++ beginning with Chapter 3, "Object-Orientation—C++ Specifics." Everything from word processors to spreadsheets, graphics applications, and operating systems is written in the C++ language, and a majority of all custom-written solutions are implemented in C++ as well. Despite this, many programmers have yet to make the switch to C++.

This chapter introduces you to the C++ programming language. The intended audience for this chapter is programmers currently using other languages, such as C and Pascal, among others. If you have experience in the C programming language, much of what you see in the chapter will be familiar, with a few exceptions, of course. This chapter will introduce the basics of the C++ programming language. It is not designed to be an exhaustive tutorial or reference.

Chapter 2, "Object Orientation—Theory and Practice," introduces the three major concepts of object-oriented programming. It also introduces some of the common terms used. Chapter 3 addresses object-oriented programming using C++. You will not find any How-Tos in this chapter addressing object-oriented programming.

1.1 Write the Simplest C++ Program Without Knowing the Language

The quickest way to learn to program in an unfamiliar language is to write a simple program and then analyze it. In this How-To, you will write a very simple program. This program is really a template for a C++ program. The program in this How-To demonstrates the minimum a C++ program must consist of. You are not required to know C or C++ to create this program. You will, although, need a C++ compiler and linker and a text editor.

1.2 Create a Program to Perform Calculations

Most useful programs perform a repetitive task. And almost every program performs calculations of one type or another. In this How-To, a program is presented that will perform some simple calculations. The program will introduce the use of program variables to hold data. It also demonstrates some of the popular mathematical operators. Output operations (displaying text) is presented, as well as acquiring input from the user.

1.3 Use the Various Loop Statements That Are Available in C++

In this How-To, you will write a program that uses the three C++ looping constructs. The three loops discussed are `for`, `do-while`, and `while`. Input and output functionality is also demonstrated. Looping statements are very important for repetitive operations, such as accessing elements of an array, or for visiting some finite or unknown number of objects, or for obtaining continual input from a user.

1.4 Create a Program That Uses One or More Functions

Most programming languages support the use of functions and/or procedures. In this How-To, you will be introduced to functions, including the declaration and definition of functions. Argument passing is also shown; additionally, returning values from functions is presented. You will create a program that uses the facilities of a function to perform a calculation.

1.5 Use the Derived Data Types Such As Arrays and Pointers

Arrays and pointers are considered by many developers as difficult types to work with. This How-To should dispel that myth. A program is presented in this How-To to demonstrate the more common uses of these derived types. You will create a function to perform a calculation and one to display a message and gather input from the user. The C++ `struct` is also introduced.

1.6 Create Data When the Program Is Running

The creation of data at runtime is introduced in this How-To. You will learn how to dynamically allocate memory for various data types. Dynamically creating memory at runtime is an important feature of C++; it allows you to create only the objects that are required by your application. The C++ operators `new` and `delete` are introduced.

1.7 Create a Program to Perform Error Handling, Specifically Exception Handling

Error handling is important to the success of a program. Invalid input, accesses to hardware that is not available, and other program anomalies must be tested for and handled gracefully. This How-To presents the C++ exception handling mechanism. The C++ Standard defines a standardized method for handling exceptions at runtime.

COMPLEXITY
BEGINNING

1.1 How do I...
Write the simplest C++ program without knowing the language?

Problem

I would like to be able to write a C++ program without initially knowing anything about the language. Is there a program I can write without having to know what is required?

Technique

Most programmers investigate a new language by writing a simple program and then go back to understand how it all works. You can do this in C++, too. At a minimum, you will need

- A C++ compiler and linker

- A text editor

You will use the editor to write the source text, referred to as *source code*. Then you will use the compiler and linker to produce the program.

Steps

1. You should create a base source code directory named **SOURCE** and then change to this directory. Next, create a work directory named **FIRST** and change to it.

2. Start your text editor. In a pinch, you could use Notepad if you are running under Windows 95/NT. If you are using UNIX, you could use ed or vi. Refer to your system documentation for details.

3. Type in the following source code, exactly as shown. Pay special attention to symbols, such as brackets and semicolons.

```
// filename: first.cpp - my first C++ program
#include <iostream>
using namespace std ;
int main( ) /* main function */
{
    cout << "My first C++ program!" << endl ;
    return( 0 ) ;
}
```

4. Save the file, naming it **FIRST.CPP**. Then exit the editor and return to the command line.

5. At the command line, type the command required to run the compiler and linker. For example, if you are using Microsoft Visual C++, you would type **cl first.cpp**. The compiler will run and (if you typed all text correctly) return to the command line without any error messages. If the compiler does report an error, refer to the following "Comments" section.

6. At the command prompt, type the name of the executable (called **first**). If you are on a UNIX system and you do not see a file named **first**, look for a file named **a.out**; if you find this filename, execute it. You should see the following message on your screen:

```
My first C++ program!
```

In the next section, "How It Works," I will discuss how this program operates.

How It Works

Now it is time to examine the process in more detail. First, I will review the processes that are required to create a program. Then I will examine the source file itself, line by line.

The procedure to create a program is always the same. First, you create source code and save it in a file so that the compiler can parse it. You can use any text editor to type your source code. If you are using Windows, you can use Notepad or WordPad. If you must use a word processor, be sure to save the file as a pure ASCII text file. If you are using UNIX, you can use vi, emacs, or ed. I recommend that you use a dedicated programmer's editor for serious source editing.

The next step is to type the source code to satisfy the functionality for the program. Visual style for the source layout is important for both you and others who will be maintaining your source code. A number of styles are accepted. See the following "Comments" section for examples.

After you have typed the source code and have saved the file, the compiler must be run against the source file. The compiler reads the source file, performs interpretation, and produces an object file. The object file, in its current form, cannot be executed directly.

Next, the linker must be run to produce the executable. The linker combines the object file(s), plus any required library functions and classes to produce the program. The output of the linker, if everything is successful, is an executable program. This program is now ready to run.

Now shift your attention to the source code itself and discover what each line does.

The first line in the file is identified as a comment. A comment in C++ can be denoted in one of two ways. One way, as is demonstrated in the example, consists of the two-character sequence // (two forward slashes). This style is referred to as the *line comment*. The compiler disregards any text beyond this sequence. The comment in this source text

```
// filename: first.cpp - my first C++ program
```

simply tells any readers that the name of this file is **first.cpp** and that this is your first C++ program. The second form of comment in C++ consists of two individual character sequences /*(slash-star) and */(star-slash) and is commonly referred to as a *block comment*. The sequence /* begins the comment and the sequence */ ends the comment. The difference between the two styles is that block comments can span many lines, whereas the line comment cannot. In addition, program statements can exist after the block comment's end sequence. A block comment is shown in the following example:

```
int main( ) /* main function */
```

The second line of code in the file

```
#include <iostream>
```

is a preprocessor directive. The preprocessor directive is executed before the compiler and is used to perform initial processing of a source file. The **#include** directive instructs the preprocessor to read in the file identified within the brackets (or double quotes, if used). The file is literally inserted into the source file at the point of the directive. After all preprocessing is complete, the compiler is invoked on the resultant file. If your compiler complained about this line of code, please review the following "Comments" section for more information.

The third line in the source file

```
using namespace std ;
```

is a **using** directive and is used in conjunction with the namespace feature. Namespaces are used to partition the global namespace. This eliminates, or at least reduces, name conflicts. Refer to the following "Comments" section for a discussion of the **using** directive if your compiler complains.

The function found on the fourth line of code

```
int main( ) /* main function */
```

is the starting point for a C++ program; the **main** function is a requirement of every C++ program. The **int** is a C++ data type and designates that the return value from **main** is an integer value. In short, the operating system loads a program into memory and then calls the **main** function to start the ball rolling. The body of the **main** function is delineated by the opening and closing braces {}. The "Comments" section that follows discusses an optional declaration of **main**. Functions will be discussed in How-To 1.4.

The statement on the fifth line

```
cout << "My first C++ program!" << endl ;
```

displays a message to standard output (the screen). The insertion operator << is used to put data to the **cout** object. Notice that the insertion operator can be chained. In the example, the first data item sent to the **cout** object is a string of text, followed by the **endl** manipulator. (Note that the last character in **endl** is L, not the numeric value 1.) Finally, a semicolon is used to end the statement.

The last line of code

```
return( 0 ) ;
```

is the **return** statement. The **return** statement directs a function to return to its caller; in this context, **main** returns to the operating system. A **return** expression can optionally return a value to its caller. In this instance, the **return** statement returns a zero to the operating system.

That's all that is required for a C++ program. In this exercise, you have built a very simple, yet straightforward C++ program. All C++ programs must follow this "template." The remainder of a program's functionality is up to you to develop. This book consists of many examples you need to expand on this basic example.

Comments

Source code style is a hotly debated topic. Every programmer develops his or her own style of source code formatting. The sample that follows is the traditional K&R style:

```
if( number < 100 ) {
    // perform some functionality
}
```

The following demonstrates block style:

```
if( number < 100 )
{
    // perform some functionality
}
```

The following sample is a variation of the block style and is known as indented block style:

```
if( number < 100 )
    {
    // perform some functionality
    }
```

The most widely accepted style is the second form, block style. Block style is more visually pleasing and the braces are easier to visually align.

The convention used for the filename identified in the `#include` complies with the Standard C++ convention. No extension is specifically identified for the filename. If your compiler complained that it could not open `iostream`, try replacing the statement:

```
#include <iostream>
```

with the following:

```
#include <iostream.h>
```

If your compiler does not conform to the new convention, it will try to find a file named `iostream`. Changing the name to `iostream.h` should help. If your compiler still complains with `No such file or directory`, you have one of two problems. Either you have a *very* old compiler or your compiler's settings are incorrect. If you are using a very old compiler, I strongly suggest that you upgrade to one of the newer packages. Why? The examples throughout this book assume you are using a current compiler package—older compilers might not understand some of the constructs used. I also mentioned that the compiler's settings might be incorrect. Specifically, check the settings that the compiler uses for file locations, such as path settings or environment variables.

If your compiler complains about the following source code line:

```
using namespace std ;
```

simply remove that line from the source file and recompile. If the compiler no longer complains, it does not support the `namespace` keyword. Alternatively, you can precede the text with the line comment `//` characters, as in the following example:

```
//using namespace std ;
```

Remember that the compiler will ignore any source code beyond the line comment sequence. It is the decision of the compiler vendor whether to implement a language feature or not; the only way to know is to try the feature or check the vendor's documentation.

The optional declaration for `main` is the following:

```
int main( int argc, char *argv[] ) ;
```

The first argument, `int argc`, represents the number of command-line arguments provided to the program. The second argument, `char *argv[]`, is an array of pointers to `char` (specifically, to each of the arguments). Each argument to a C++ program is treated as a string of text. You can pass information to a program using arguments on the command line. For example, the following shows a program that accepts input to multiply two numbers:

```
Prompt> mult 114 23
```

This example will read the two arguments, multiply the two values, and display the result to the standard output.

1.2 How do I...
Create a program to perform calculations?

Problem

I would like to write a program that can perform some calculations. I know that I will have to use data variables, but I am unfamiliar with the various data types and operators in C++.

Technique

Programming languages provide data type variables that can be used to hold values. A value can be stored, accessed, and replaced in a variable. In order to use a variable, you must decide the data type(s) that you need. The C++ language defines a number of variable data types to choose from. The program presented in this How-To will calculate the number of inches for a specified number of feet.

Steps

1. Change to your base source directory and create a new directory named **TOINCH**. Then, start up your text editor.

2. Type in the following source code, exactly as shown:

```cpp
// toinch.cpp - converts feet to inches.
#include <iostream>
using namespace std ;
const int inchesInFoot = 12 ;
int main( )
{
    int numberOfFeet = 0 ;

    cout << "Please enter the number of feet, " ;
    cout << "I will tell you the number of inches" << endl ;
    cin >> numberOfFeet ;

    int numberOfInches = numberOfFeet * inchesInFoot ;
    cout << numberOfInches << " inches are in " ;
    cout << numberOfFeet << " feet" << endl ;
```

```
        return( 0 ) ;
    }
```

3. Save the file, naming it `TOINCH.CPP`. Then, exit out of the editor and return to the command line.

4. Run the compiler and linker, naming `TOINCH.CPP` as the input file.

5. Run the TOINCH program. The following message will be displayed:

```
Please enter the number of feet, I will tell you the number of
inches
```

6. The cursor will be on the next line, awaiting input. Enter the value **2**. The program will perform the calculation and display the following message:

```
24 inches are in 2 feet
```

7. To perform another calculation, simply rerun the program.

How It Works

Let's review the source code and see what is happening. As in How-To 1.1, if your compiler complains about the following two lines of code:

```
include <iostream>
using namespace std ;
```

change them to this one line of code:

```
#include <iostream.h>
```

The third line of code

```
const int inchesInFoot = 12 ;
```

declares a variable of type `int` and is given the name `inchesInFoot`. You must supply a name for every variable in C++. Notice that the modifier `const` is applied to the type name. This modifier says that this variable is a constant; the variable's value cannot be changed.

This source line also introduces the assignment operator =. The assignment operator is used to place the value on the right-hand side of the operator to the variable on the left-hand side. In this example, the value **12** is placed in the variable named `inchesInFoot`. The constant (variable) `inchesInFoot` will hold this value throughout the life of the program (its value cannot be changed). The next line of code is the following:

```
int numberOfFeet = 0 ;
```

This int, named numberOfFeet is declared and initialized to a value of 0. The purpose of this variable is to hold the number of feet that the user specifies at runtime. Note that the const modifier is not applied to this variable definition because numberOfFeet's contents will need to be changed. The next two lines

```
cout << "Please enter the number of feet, " ;
cout << "I will tell you the number of inches" << endl ;
```

are used to output a message (an instruction) to the user. Notice that although the two statements are independent and exist on two separate lines, the message is actually displayed to the user as a single line. The endl manipulator performs two operations. First, it flushes the output buffer and outputs a newline character. Because output is to the screen, the cursor will be placed on the next line, flush with the left margin. Because the first cout statement does not end with an endl, the second message is appended to the first. The next line of code

```
cin >> numberOfFeet ;
```

awaits input from the user. After the user enters a value and presses the Enter key, the cin object will take the value and place it in the variable named numberOfFeet. The cin statement actually performs a conversion behind the scenes. You press the keyboard character 2; cin takes this character and converts it to a C++ integer type and places the value in the variable. This brings you to the next line of code:

```
int numberOfInches = numberOfFeet * inchesInFoot ;
```

This statement introduces the multiplication operator *. This operator is one of many defined by the C++ language. This source line is referred to as a *compound statement*. First, the int variable numberOfInches is declared for use. Next, the value stored in numberOfFeet is multiplied by the value stored in inchesInFoot. The result of this expression is then assigned to the variable numberOfInches. The next two source lines

```
cout << numberOfInches << " inches are in " ;
cout << numberOfFeet << " feet" << endl ;
```

display the result of the conversion to the standard output. Notice that you can stream different data types to the cout object. First, the value stored in numberOfInches is sent to cout, followed by a string. In the next statement, numberOfFeet is sent to cout, followed by another string, and finally the endl manipulator.

The last program statement, the return statement, returns the value 0 returns to the operating system.

Comments

The C++ language defines a number of data types: `bool`, `char`, `int`, `long`, `float`, and `double`. A `bool` is used to represent a Boolean value, either `true` or `false`. The `char` type is used to contain characters, such as 3, #, or m. The types `int` and `long` are integral types and can hold whole numbers only. The types `float` and `double` are used for storing floating-point numbers.

In C++, strings are implemented as an array of `char`. In fact, any data type can be declared as an array. You will look at arrays in a How-To later in this chapter.

The `const` keyword is used to qualify a declaration. You must remember to initialize the `const` variable at the point of declaration; if you don't, you will not be able to assign to it. For example, the compiler will not allow the following:

```
const int inchesInFoot ;
inchesInFoot = 12 ; // error right here!
```

The `const` variable is used as a symbolic constant (or alias) for a value. Using a symbolic name provides a descriptive name for some value. An additional benefit of using `const` is that the value stored in the variable is protected from modification. It also helps with code maintenance. Why? Let's look at a brief example. The following example defines a `char` that is constant. Assume that the `char` is used as a choice within a menu system.

```
const char REPLACE_OPTION = 'S' ; // replace
//...
if( option == REPLACE_OPTION )
//...
```

Using a constant allows you to change the value that the name symbolizes in just one place without having to change all occurrences of that value. In other words, you would have to search for all occurrences of the letter *S* and change them to the new value. Instead, by using a constant, you only have to change the initialization value of the constant declaration. The following line of code shows a decision to change the value of `REPLACE_OPTION` to R:

```
const char REPLACE_OPTION = 'R' ;
```

The change is only required at the declaration. The next step would be to recompile all the code associated with this change. You do not have to worry about searching for every occurrence of R because the compiler will do all the work required.

The `cin` object is used to accept data from the standard input; the default is the keyboard. The extraction operator `>>` directs the input from the `cin` object to the named variable(s). In the previous example, `numberOfFeet` is the recipient of data from `cin`.

1.3 How do I...
Use the various loop statements that are available in C++?

Problem

I have started to sink my teeth into C++ now by writing very simple programs. I need to extend my knowledge of the language and have considered using a loop statement as I've seen in other languages. I need to know the various loops available in C++ and how to use them.

Technique

Looping techniques in C++ are essentially the same as they are in other languages. The loop names might be different, but for the most part, they serve the same purposes. The C++ language serves up three different types of looping statements: for, do-while, and while. The following example will show all three in action.

Steps

1. Change to your base source directory and create a new directory named LOOP. Next, fire up your text editor.

2. Type in the following source code, exactly as shown:

```
// loop.cpp - program to demonstrate C++ loops
#include <iostream>
using namespace std ;
int main()
{
   int value = 0 ;

   cout << "Beginning of while loop" << endl ;
   while( value < 5 )
   {
      cout << "The value of value is: " << value << endl ;
      ++value ;
   }
   cout << "End of while loop" << endl ;

   cout << "\nBeginning of do-while loop" << endl ;
   do {
      cout << "The value of value is: " << value << endl ;
   }while( value < 5 ) ;
   cout << "End of do-while loop" << endl ;
```

```
cout << "\nBeginning of for loop" << endl ;
for( value = 0; value < 5; value++ )
{
    cout << "The value of value is: " << value << endl ;
}
cout << "End of for loop" << endl ;

return 0 ;
}
```

3. Save the file as LOOP.CPP and exit the editor to the command line.

4. Compile and link the LOOP.CPP source file.

5. Run the program; the output should be as follows:

```
Beginning of while loop
The value of value is: 0
The value of value is: 1
The value of value is: 2
The value of value is: 3
The value of value is: 4
End of while loop

Beginning of do-while loop
The value of value is: 5
End of do-while loop

Beginning of for loop
The value of value is: 0
The value of value is: 1
The value of value is: 2
The value of value is: 3
The value of value is: 4
End of for loop
```

How It Works

Starting with the sixth line of code, an int has been declared and initialized with a value of 0. This integer variable will be used by all three loops. In addition to demonstrating loops, this How-To introduces you to the C++ increment (++) and less-than (<) operators.

The next statement sends a message to the screen:

```
cout << "Beginning of while loop" << endl ;
```

It is always a good idea to let the user know what is going on within a program. You can consider these messages as "progress reports."

You begin your investigation of C++ loops with the next line of code:

```
while( value < 5 )
```

The while loop is a precondition (entry condition) loop. First, the test expression within the parentheses is evaluated. If the result of the expression is non-zero (**true**), the statement(s) within the while loop's body are executed. If the result of the expression is **0** (**false**), then the loop exits and control returns to the first statement after the while loop's body. This loop can be verbally expressed as follows: "While the value stored in **value** is less than **5**, execute the statements within the loop's body." It is possible for a loop to never execute if the expression is initially **false**. For example, if the variable **value** is initially set to **20**, the while loop will never execute.

An opening brace begins the body of a while loop and a closing brace ends the body. All statements within the body are executed as long as the loop's expression is **true**. The while loop contains two statements, a message that displays the contents of the variable **value** and an increment (++) expression. You have seen the **cout** statement before; its job is to display data to the standard output. The next statement uses the increment operator ++. This operator simply increments the value of the operand by one. It is shorthand for the following statement:

```
value = value + 1 ;
```

Two versions of the increment operator exist: prefix increment and postfix increment. The version used in the while loop is the prefix increment operator. The prefix increment version increments a variable first and then evaluates the balance of the expression. The postfix increment version does the opposite: The expression is evaluated first, and then the variable is incremented. The following example shows the difference:

```
Line 1: if( ++check < 6 )
Line 2: if( check++ < 6 )
```

Assume the value of check is **5** before the **if** statement. In line 1, the value of **check** is incremented first, and then the expression is evaluated. Because **check** is now **6**, the expression evaluates to **false** (**check** < **6**) and the statements within **if**'s body are not executed. In line 2, the expression within the **if** statement (**check** < **6**) evaluates to **true**, **check** is incremented by 1. Because the expression evaluates to **true**, the statements within the **if**'s body are executed.

After **value** is incremented, program control is returned to the top of the while loop. The while loop's expression is again evaluated and if it is non-zero, the body is again executed; otherwise, the program exits the loop and control jumps to the first statement after the while loop's body. In this example, it is a message to the user that the while loop has ended.

The next statement displays a message announcing the beginning of the **do-while** loop. A **do-while** loop is a postcondition (exit condition) loop. A **do-while** loop is always executed once, even if the test expression evaluates to

false. This behavior is in contrast to the **while** loop. Note that the value contained in **value** is still **5**, yet the **cout** statement is still executed. The test expression within the **while** portion is evaluated as **false** and the loop is terminated. Control resumes at the **cout** statement announcing the end of the **do-while** loop.

Next, you come to the **for** loop. The **for** loop consists of three expressions. The first expression is initialization, followed by a test expression, and finally, the update (or change) expression; each expression is separated by a semicolon. The following is the program's **for** loop:

```
for( value = 0; value < 5; value++ )
```

First, **value** is initialized to **0**. The middle expression (**value < 5**) is the test expression. The test expression is evaluated; if the result is **true**, the loop's body is executed, otherwise, the program exits the loop. After all statements in the body have executed, the third expression is evaluated. After the third expression is evaluated, control returns to the test expression.

Comments

Each of the C++ loops can have either a single statement or multiple statements enclosed within braces. All of the loop examples in this How-To use braces to delineate the loop's body. For example, the **for** loop can be written this way:

```
for( value = 0; value < 5; value++ )
    cout << "The value of value is: " << value << endl ;
```

You can do this because this **for** loop only has one statement associated with it. It is more appropriate to use braces, even if you only have one statement associated with a loop. The reason is that if you come back to add another statement to the single-statement loop, you might forget to add the braces. To demonstrate, assume you want to add a calculation that is performed for every iteration of the loop.

```
for( value = 0; value < 5; value++ )
    cout << "The value of value is: " << value << endl ;
    paycheckAmount = hours * value ;
```

Everything appears fine; the indentation shows that the new statement is part of the loop's body. Don't be fooled by appearances. By visual inspection, it *appears* that the program will execute both statements following the **for** expression. In reality, only the first statement will execute for every iteration of the loop. The second statement will only execute after the loop is finished. To correct the problem, the source code needs to look like the following:

```
for( value = 0; value < 5; value++ )
{
    cout << "The value of value is: " << value << endl ;
    paycheckAmount = hours * value ;
}
```

Now, everything will work as expected.

The third (update) expression in a `for` loop is not restricted to using the increment operator `++`. You might want to use the decrement operator `--`. You can also increment the value by two, three, or more. The expression can also be the result of a multiplication. The following will increment `value` by `20` in the third expression:

```
for( value = 1; value < 100; value = value + 20 )
{
    cout << "The value of value is: " << value << endl ;
}
```

1.4 How do I...
Create a program that uses one or more functions?

Problem

I am ready to move on to the more advanced features of the C++ language, specifically functions. I know that functions are used to accomplish specific tasks. I need to know how to declare and define functions.

Technique

Functions in C++ are the basic building blocks to modularize a program. The technique for creating functions in C++ is the same as it is in any other language. You must decide the specific functionality required for your application. If possible, you should make your functions as general as possible. This allows you to use a function in other programs.

Steps

1. Change to the base source directory and create a directory named FUNC.

2. Start up your text editor and type in the following source code:

```
// func.cpp - program to demonstrate a function in C++
#include <iostream>
using namespace std ;
long multiply( long left, long right ) ;
int main()
{
    long value1 = 0, value2 = 0 ;
```

```
cout << "\nProgram to multiply two integers " ;
cout << "and display the result. " << endl ;

for( long result = 1; result != 0; /*empty expression*/ )
{
    value1 = value2 = result = 0 ;

    cout << "\nTwo zeros will end the program." << endl ;
    cout << "Enter the first integer (and enter key): " ;
    cin >> value1 ;

    cout << "Enter the second integer (and enter key): " ;
    cin >> value2 ;

    if( value1 == 0 && value2 == 0 )
        break ;

    result = multiply( value1, value2 ) ;
    cout << value1 << " multiplied by " ;
    cout << value2 << " = " << result << endl ;
}
return 0 ;
}

// Multiplies the two arguments
// together and returns the results
long multiply( long left, long right )
{
    long result = left * right ;
    return( result ) ;
}
```

3. Save the file as **LOOP.CPP** and exit the editor to the command line.

4. Compile and link the **LOOP.CPP** source file.

5. Run the program; the output should be as follows:

```
Program to multiply two integers and display the result.
Two zeros will end the program.
Enter the first integer: 4
Enter the second integer: 4
4 multiplied by 4 = 16
```

How It Works

If you have been following the previous How-Tos, you will notice a new line of code after the `using namespace std` line:

```
long multiply( long left, long right ) ;
```

This is referred to as a *function declaration*. It is the function's signature. The declaration specifies the number or arguments, if any, and their data type. The declaration also shows the return type (if the function returns a value). In this declaration, `multiply` is the name of the function. The function accepts two arguments; both of them are of type `long`. The first argument has the name `left` and the second argument has the name `right`. The result of the function call, the return value, is of type `long`. The return value does not have a name because a function can only return a single data type.

The program begins with the declaration and initialization of two `long` variables, `value1` and `value2`. These two variables will be used to hold the values that will be passed to the function `multiply`. Next, the program displays an informational message telling the user the intent of the program.

In How-To 1.3, you learned how to use a `for` loop. This `for` loop is used to continually accept new input for subsequent calculations. One difference between this `for` loop and the one demonstrated in the previous How-To is that the third expression is empty.

```
for( long result = 1; result != 0; /*empty expression*/ )
```

This is perfectly legal; an empty expression here makes sense because you do not need to update a counting variable. This `for` loop will check that the value in `result` is not equal to `0`.

The first statement within the `for` loop initializes the variables `value1`, `value2`, and `result` to `0`. Next, the program displays a message to the user how to quit the program.

The next `cout` statement displays a message asking the user to enter the first of two values. The subsequent `cin` statement gathers input from the user and places the value into the variable named `value1`.

Another message is displayed prompting the user to enter the second value required for the calculation. The `cin` statement accepts input from the user and places that value in `value2`.

An `if` statement is introduced. This `if` statement is composed of a compound expression. The equality operator `==` and logical operator `&&` are both used within the `if` statement. The following verbally expresses the statement: "If the contents of `value1` are `0` AND the contents of `value2` are `0`, break out of the `for` loop." If either expression resolves to `0`, the program breaks out of the loop. Otherwise, the program continues executing to the next statement.

The following statement from the program:

```
result = multiply( value1, value2 ) ;
```

is a call to the function named `multiply`. Notice that the two values gathered from the user are passed as arguments to the function. The function uses these two values to perform the multiplication. The order of evaluation for this statement is as follows: the function is called first, and then the result of the function call (the return value) is assigned to the variable named `result`.

The next two statements after the function call display the results of the calculation.

The definition for the function `multiply` is found beyond `main`'s closing brace. A function definition has a body and contains program statements (a declaration does not). The two comments that precede the function name proclaim the intent of the function. As a rule, you should provide more information about a function than is provided in this example. A function definition header might look like this:

```
// name: multiply
// description: this function multiplies the two
//     arguments supplied and returns the result.
// arguments:
//     long left - one of two operands for the calculation
//     long left - second of two operands for the calculation
// return: long - the result of the multiplication
```

The first statement within the `multiply` body is the declaration of a `long` variable named `result`. Notice that the name `result` is declared here and in the `main` function. The `result` variable declared in `main` is not visible to this function, so there is no name clash between the two variables. The variable `result` comes into scope at its declaration and continues to exist until `multiply`'s closing brace. This statement consists of the expression `left * right`; the result of which is assigned to the variable `result`. The last line of code in the function is the `return` statement. The job of the `return` statement is to return the result of the multiplication.

Comments

Error checking is not included in this How-To. The intent of this How-To is to demonstrate the use of functions and function calls. Because of this, the example must be as brief as possible.

It is assumed that the user will enter valid numbers for the inputs requested. Particularly, two statements in the program

```
cin >> value1 ;
//...
cin >> value2 ;
```

are used to gather input from the user. It is hoped that a user will supply a valid integer for each prompt. Unfortunately, as is usually the case, users enter data that you do not expect. Error handling will be addressed in How-To 1.7. Suffice it to say that the results will be unpredictable if you enter anything other than numeric data.

The variables (actually the values) passed to the function `multiply` are copies of those values. This is referred to as *pass-by-value*; the C++ language inherits this trait from the C language. When the compiler sees the following line of code:

```
result = multiply( value1, value2 ) ;
```

it will create a copy of `value1` and `value2` to be passed on to the function `multiply`. The original variables passed as arguments are not operated on. The two arguments `left` and `right` are local to the function `multiply`. Any changes you make to those variables will not be reflected back to the original variables `value1` and `value2` in `main`.

Within the function `multiply`, the variable `result` serves two purposes. It is used to hold the result of the multiplication and is used as the argument to the `return` statement. The compiler makes a temporary copy of `result` and returns it to the calling function.

COMPLEXITY

INTERMEDIATE

1.5 How do I...
Use the derived data types such as arrays and pointers?

Problem

I have written a few C++ programs now and feel very confident. I built programs to take advantage of loops, simple variables, user input and message output, and user defined functions. I need to now explore the use of more advanced data types such as arrays, structures, and pointers.

Technique

If you have an understanding of C++'s basic data types, learning to use the advanced types will come easy. The technique for using derived types is no different from using plain ol' data (POD) types. Most of the derived types are just aggregates of the PODs. This How-To will also demonstrate the use of pointers and references. As usual, you will learn about these advanced types from the source code that follows.

Steps

1. Start at you base source directory and create a new subdirectory named TYPES.

2. As usual, fire up your favorite text editor and type in the following source code:

```cpp
// types.cpp - program to demonstrate the
// advanced types used in C++
#include <iostream>
using namespace std ;
void multiply( long &left, long &right, long &result ) ;
void getValue( const char *message, long *value ) ;

struct values {
    long value1 ;
    long value2 ;
    long result ;
} ;
const int MAX_LEN = 20 ;

int main()
{
    values vals ;

    cout << "\nProgram to multiply two integers " ;
    cout << "and display the result. " << endl ;
    cout << "It will also show the contents of an array" << endl ;

    vals.value1 = vals.value2 = vals.result = 1L ;
    while( vals.result != 0 )
    {
        vals.value1 = vals.value2 = vals.result = 0 ;

        cout << "\nTwo zeros will end the program." << endl ;

        getValue( "Enter the first integer: ", &vals.value1 ) ;
        getValue( "Enter the second integer: ", &vals.value2 ) ;

        if( vals.value1 == 0 && vals.value2 == 0 )
            break ;

        multiply( vals.value1, vals.value2, vals.result ) ;
        cout << vals.value1 << " multiplied by " ;
        cout << vals.value2 << " = " << vals.result" << endl ;
    }

    int iVal ;
    char message[ MAX_LEN +1 ] ;

    for( iVal = 0; iVal < MAX_LEN; iVal++ )
        message[ iVal ] = 'A' + iVal ;
    message[ iVal ] = '\x00' ;

    cout << "\nContents of message[" << message << ']' << endl ;

    char *pc = message ;
    for( iVal = 0; iVal < MAX_LEN; iVal++, pc++ )
        *pc = '\x00' ;

    cout << "\nContents of message[" << message << ']' << endl ;

    return 0 ;
```

```
    }

    // multiply two numbers and put result in third argument
    void multiply( long &left, long &right, long &result )
    {
        result = left * right ;
    }

    // display message, get value
    void getValue( const char *message, long *value )
    {
        cout << message ;

        long result = 0 ;
        cin >> result ;
        *value = result ;
    }
```

3. Save your work in a file named **TYPES.CPP** and exit the editor back to the command line.

4. Run the compiler and linker on the source file.

5. Now, run the program. The output should be similar to the following:

```
Program to multiply two integers and display the result.
It will also show the contents of an array

Two zeros will end the program.
Enter the first integer: 4
Enter the second integer: 4
4 multiplied by 4 = 16

Two zeros will end the program.
Enter the first integer: 0
Enter the second integer: 0

Some letters: ABCDEFGHIJKLMNOPQRST
Contents of message[]
```

How It Works

Your journey begins with lines 5 and 6:

```
void multiply( long &left, long &right, long &result ) ;
void getValue( const char *message, long *value ) ;
```

These function declarations look similar to the declaration in How-To 1.4. The first declaration accepts three arguments, each of which is a reference to a **long**. The second declaration accepts two arguments that are pointers.

The function **multiply** has three arguments that are references to **long**. A reference is exactly what its name implies—it refers to some other object. The reference itself is not the object of interest; the object of interest is accessed using the reference.

The **getValue** function owns two arguments. One is a pointer to a **const char** and the second is a pointer to **long**. A pointer, as its name implies, refers (or points) to some other object. A pointer, as with a reference, is not the object of interest; the object of interest is accessed using the pointer. The argument **value** is a variable, just as you've seen in previous How-Tos; it's just that this variable happens to be pointing to some object (variable) that exists somewhere else in the program. Do not concern yourself with the contents of the pointer itself. You should only be interested in the object to which the pointer points.

You might be asking, "If a reference and a pointer both refer to some other object, what is the difference between the two?" This is a common question and deserves an answer. I mentioned that a pointer is a variable (in the sense that its contents can change), but I did not imply the same for references. Therefore, a difference is that you can change what the pointer points to. With a reference, you cannot do this; a reference must refer to some object. After the reference refers to an object, you cannot change the reference to refer to another object. This implies that a reference always refers to a single object. Do not let me mislead you, however: A pointer can be constant, which means that it can only point to a single object. The following declaration shows this:

```
char theChar = 'B' ;
char * const pconst = &theChar ;
```

This declaration states that **pconst** is a constant pointer to a **char**—namely, **theChar**. Although **pconst** can change the value stored in **theChar**, **pconst** cannot point to anything except **theChar**.

So, what do a reference and a pointer store as their value? Quite simply, they store the address of the object that they refer to. This is how a reference and a pointer gain access to an object. Think of it this way: Every house (or office, and so on) has an address. In your address book, you have the address written down for some friend. The address in your address book is not the actual house, but is simply a reference to the location of the house. You first look up the address and then use it to locate and access the house.

Beginning on line 8, a **struct** declaration is introduced:

```
struct values {
    long value1 ;
    long value2 ;
    long result ;
} ;
```

The keyword **struct** is really shorthand for *structure*. A **struct** is considered a user-defined type. A **struct** is a collection of one or more types. The types (variables) can be PODs, arrays, or other **structs**. Notice the declarations of the variables within the `struct`. The declarations are no different from declaring global or local variables. The difference with a `struct` is that the variable declarations are contained within the `struct`.

The declaration simply defines the layout for the `struct`; it is not a variable declaration. Consider a `struct` declaration as a template only; no memory is set aside for a `struct` declaration. The first statement within the `main` function declares the variable `values` of type `struct`, as shown in the following code:

```
values vals ;
```

This declaration is the same as declaring variables of type `int` or `float`; memory is allocated for the object. You can now access the individual member variables of the `struct`. The dot (membership) operator (`.`) is used to access the member variables of a `struct` through a `struct` variable. For example,

```
vals.value1 = 0 ;
```

assigns the value `0` to the member variable `value1` for the object `vals`.

You can initialize a `struct` variable at the time of declaration also, just as you can with simple (POD) variables. You specify an appropriate initialization value for each member variable, separating each value with a comma. The initializations are enclosed within a pair of braces. The following snippet of code demonstrates this:

```
values someValues = { 10L, 20L, 30L } ;
```

This statement creates a variable of type `struct values` named `someValues`. The three elements of `values` are each initialized to the values `10L`, `20L`, and `30L`, respectively. The postfix `L` on each number says that these constants are `long`.

The next three lines of code send a message to the standard output describing the intent of the program. The next line of code

```
vals.value1 = vals.value2 = vals.result = 1L ;
```

initializes the individual members of the variable `vals` to the value `1L`. You could initialize `vals` using structure initialization as demonstrated above.

The next line of code, a `while` loop, evaluates the variable `vals.result` for a non-zero value. If the value becomes `0`, the loop terminates.

The first line of code inside the loop

```
vals.value1 = vals.value2 = vals.result = 0 ;
```

initializes the member variables of `vals` to `0`. The intent is to put the member variables into a known state.

The next line of code displays a message to the user, giving directions on the use of the program.

The next two lines of code

```
getValue( "Enter the first integer: ", &vals.value1 ) ;
getValue( "Enter the second integer: ", &vals.value2 ) ;
```

call the function **getValue**, with each call passing two arguments to the function. The first argument, a pointer to a **const char**, is a string of text that is displayed to the user. The second argument is a pointer to a **long**. Notice that each argument is separated by a comma.

The second argument's name is prepended with the address-of operator. Because a pointer must contain an address to be useful, the address-of operator is required to represent the address of the variable. Remember that arguments are passed by value, so the expression **&vals.value1** yields the address of the variable. Because the argument is a copy of the actual object, and the object is the address of the variable, the argument is the object expected: a pointer to a **long**.

Let's examine the **getValue** function.

```
// display message, get value
void getValue( const char *message, long *value )
{
    cout << message ;

    long result = 0 ;
    cin >> result ;
    *value = result ;
}
```

The first argument means **message** is a pointer to a **const char**. Effectively, you can change what the pointer points to, but you cannot change the contents to which the pointer points. The second argument is a pointer to a **long**; you can alter the contents (change the value) to which the pointer points. The first line in the function body displays the contents of **message** to the screen. The next line creates a local variable of type **long** named **result**. This variable is used to capture the required input from the user. The last line in the function's body assigns the value contained in **result** to the variable to which **value** points. Notice that the dereference operator (*) is used to perform this magic. The dereference operator is used to access the object through the pointer. Remember that **value** does not contain a **long** value; it merely refers to a **long** variable. Because the pointer **value** points to **vals.value1**, it is **vals.value1** that is the recipient of the value.

Back in the **main** function, the next call to **getValue** performs the same functionality, eventually assigning a **long** value to **vals.value2**.

The **if** statement checks to see whether both **vals.value1** and **vals.value2** are equal to **0**. If so, the **while** loop is terminated. The next line of code within the loop

```
multiply( vals.value1, vals.value2, vals.result ) ;
```

calls the function **multiply**, passing three arguments. In this instance, the target arguments are references to **long**s. Here is the function again, in its entirety:

```
// multiply two numbers and put result in third argument
void multiply( long &left, long &right, long &result )
{
    result = left * right ;
}
```

The only statement within the body of the function is an expression, multiplying the two arguments together to yield the result. The result of the multiplication is assigned to **vals.result** through the reference argument **result**. Notice that the dereference operator is not required with references (to access the object referred to). You do not have to use the dereference operator because dereferencing happens automatically behind the scenes. This allows a more natural notation. For example, this

```
*ptrValue = result ; // assign through pointer
```

is not as intuitive as

```
refValue = result ; // assign through reference
```

The last two lines in the **while** loop display the operands of the multiplication and the result. The loop will continue until **vals.value1** and **vals.value2** equal **0**.

Beyond the **while** loop's body, the next line of code creates a variable of type **int** named **iVal**. On the next line, a second variable is created: an array *of* **char** named **message**. An *array* is an aggregation of a single data type. You could, for example, create an array of 12 **int**s, each individual element representing the number of days in each month. In this program, **message** is a variable that consists of **MAX_LEN (20)** contiguous **char**s. Strings in C++ are represented as an array of **char**, terminated by the **null char** (hex 0x00). A How-To later in the book will introduce the C++ **string** class. The **string** class is an optional and more efficient way to create and use strings in C++.

After the two variable declarations, a **for** loop is used to assign a value to each element of the **char** array. The first offset in an array is **0**, not **1**. This is a source of error for many C++ novices; it is referred to as the "one-off" error. (The problem actually occurs at the end of the array; most developers will access the element one beyond the end of the array.) Take a look at the initialization section of the **for** loop; **iVal** is initialized to **0**.

The **iVal** variable serves three purposes. First, it is used as an incrementing variable; it starts at **0** and counts up to **MAX_LEN**. Second, it is used as a subscripting (or indexing) value to access the individual elements of the array. Brackets are used as a notation for subscripting the individual elements of an array. A variable can be used as the indexing value. This is in contrast to the declaration of an array; the value that specifies the number of elements in an array must be a constant. The third functionality of iVal is to create a unique letter of the alphabet to be stored in each element. The **for** loop's statement

```
message[ iVal ] = 'A' + iVal ;
```

contains the expression

```
'A' + iVal
```

The result of this expression is the character (constant) **A** added to the value of **iVal**. After each pass through the loop, the result of the expression will be the next letter in the alphabet. So, as soon as the loop terminates, the array **message** will contain the first 20 letters of the alphabet.

The statement after the **for** loop assigns the **null** character to the last array element. The next line of code, the **cout** statement, prints out the contents of the array. The output from this statement appears as follows:

```
Contents of message[ABCDEFGHIJKLMNOPQRST]
```

Let's look at the next three lines of code in the program:

```
char *pc = message ;
for( iVal = 0; iVal < MAX_LEN; iVal++, pc++ )
    *pc = '\x00' ;
```

The first line defines a pointer to a character and is initialized to point to the array **message**. Initially, **pc** points to the first element of **message**. This **for** loop is used to set each element of the array to the **null** character. The variable **iVal** is used as the incrementing variable, counting up to **MAX_LEN**. Notice that the update expression of the **for** loop contains two expressions. Both **iVal** and **pc** are incremented by 1. This facilitates the pointer **pc** visiting each element of the array in turn. The **for** loop's statement

```
*pc = '\x00' ;
```

uses the dereference operator to assign the **null** character to the location currently pointed to by **pc**. The line of code after the **for** loop prints out the contents of the array. You should see this:

```
Contents of message[]
```

Notice that no letters are printed between the brackets. This is because **cout**, when printing an array of **char**, stops printing when it sees the **null** character. Because the previous **for** loop set each element of the array to the **null** character, there is nothing to print.

The last line of code in **main**'s body is the **return** statement, effectively ending the program.

Comments

Pointers and references are very powerful mechanisms. They provide you with the ability to access objects that reside somewhere in memory. You can think of pointers and references as *proxy* objects.

Be cautious with pointer use; pointers are the root cause of many headaches. Wild pointers have brought down many good applications. Invalid pointers can be hard to detect because the path through a program is usually never the same for each invocation.

Use references instead of pointers whenever possible. In fact, you should always choose references over pointers.

Arrays are a convenient feature to aggregate like items into one place. Arrays and pointers are usually used together, with pointers being used to access the elements of an array. Accessing an array is much faster using a pointer than using array-offset notation.

COMPLEXITY
INTERMEDIATE

1.6 How do I...
Create data when the program is running?

Problem

I know how to create global and local variables, but at times I don't know exactly how many variables I will need until runtime. Is there a way to dynamically create simple variables and derived types at runtime?

Technique

The technique required to allocate memory is quite easy. The tricky part is the upkeep of allocated memory. When I say upkeep, I mean you are responsible for the creation and deletion of allocated memory. The C++ language is very powerful and offers you a lot of leverage, but you are also accountable for your actions. Keep this in mind when dealing with memory allocation.

The following source code demonstrates how to allocate and deallocate memory for various data types. The source also includes an example of dynamically allocated and deallocated derived types, namely arrays.

Steps

1. Create a new subdirectory named **CREATE** under your base source directory.

2. Start up your editor and type in the following source code:

```cpp
// create.cpp - program to demonstrate the
// allocating and deallocating of memory in C++
#include <iostream>
using namespace std ;

struct values {
    long value1 ;
    long value2 ;
} ;
const int MAX_ELEMENTS = 20 ;

int main()
{
    int *intArray ;
    intArray = new int[ MAX_ELEMENTS ] ;
    int i = 0 ;

    for(i = 0; i < MAX_ELEMENTS; i++ )
        intArray[i] = i ;

    for(i = 0; i < MAX_ELEMENTS; i++ )
        cout << "intArray[i] = " << intArray[i] << endl ;

    delete [] intArray ;

    values *sArray = new values[ MAX_ELEMENTS ] ;

    for(i = 0; i < MAX_ELEMENTS; i++ )
    {
        sArray[i].value1 = i ;
        sArray[i].value2 = i * 10 ;
    }

    for(i = 0; i < MAX_ELEMENTS; i++ )
    {
        cout << "sArray[i].value1 = " << sArray[i].value1 ;
        cout << ", sArray[i].value2 = " << sArray[i].value2 <<
        ↪endl ;
    }
    delete [] sArray ;

    return( 0 ) ;
}
```

3. Save your work in a file named **CREATE.CPP** and return to the command line.

4. Run your compiler and linker on `CREATE.CPP`.

5. The output, when run, should appear as in the following:

```
intArray[i] = 0
intArray[i] = 1
intArray[i] = 2
...
intArray[i] = 19
sArray[i].value1 = 0, sArray[i].value2 = 0
sArray[i].value1 = 1, sArray[i].value2 = 10
sArray[i].value1 = 2, sArray[i].value2 = 20
...
sArray[i].value1 = 19, sArray[i].value2 = 190
```

How It Works

Let's examine the code to see what is happening. Remember, if your compiler gives you an error for either of these two lines

```
#include <iostream>
using namespace std ;
```

simply place block comments (`//`) in front of the second line (or delete it) and change the first line to read `iostream.h`.

Moving through the source file, the next item you see is the declaration of `struct values`. It contains two `int` variables, `value1` and `value2`.

The next line of code declares `MAX_ELEMENTS` to be a constant `int`. This constant is used to declare the maximum number of elements to be allocated.

Look at the first two statements in function `main`:

```
int *intArray ;
intArray = new int[ MAX_ELEMENTS ] ;
```

The first statement declares `intArray` to be a pointer to `int`. The second statement is a new expression. In C++, the result of a new expression is a pointer to the allocated type. This is why `intArray` is declared as a pointer to `int`. The expression on the right side of the assignment operator states "Allocate a block of memory capable of holding `MAX_ELEMENTS` (`20`) `int`s." The memory manager will attempt to locate a contiguous area of memory large enough to hold the 20 `int`s. If operator `new()` obtains the requested memory, it returns a pointer to `int`, otherwise the new expression throws an exception. You will examine exceptions in How-To 1.7.

In C++, a new expression (consisting of operator `new()`) is used to allocate memory from the free store (also referred to as the heap). The free store is an area of memory used for dynamically allocated objects. The free store expands and contracts as objects are allocated and deallocated.

There are three types of **new** expressions. One allocates a single object of some type, the second allocates an array of objects, and the third type is called *placement* **new**. The following example demonstrates all three different types of **new** expressions:

```
int *intArray1,  *intArray2,  *intPlaced ;
intArray1 = new int( 5 ) ;

intArray2 = new int[ MAX_ELEMENTS ] ;

intPlaced = new (memoryBlock) int ;
```

The first statement declares three pointers to **int**. The second statement allocates a single **int** and that **int** contains the value 5. The parenthesized initializer expression is optional. The *initializer expression* is used to initialize an allocated object to some known value.

The second statement is array allocation. The value within the brackets tells operator **new( )** how many objects to allocate. You cannot use the initializer expression when allocating arrays. (The exception to this rule is when allocating user-defined objects.)

The last statement allocates a single **int**; this **int** is placed in an area of memory specified within the parentheses after the keyword **new**. Memory is not actually allocated with placement **new**, but a pointer to the object is returned. The memory block must be a static memory block or allocated with a **new** expression. It is your responsibility to ensure that the memory block is properly deallocated.

The next two lines of code consist of a **for** loop and its statement. The loop is used to assign a value to each individual **int** allocated.

The next two lines consist of a second **for** loop that prints out the value of each individual **int**, thus verifying the contents of each.

The next line of code

```
delete []  intArray ;
```

is the **delete** expression. This particular form is the array **delete** expression; it is identified by the bracket [] notation. This form is used to deallocate an array of objects. To deallocate a single object, use operator **delete** without the bracket notation.

The next statement

```
values *sArray = new values[ MAX_ELEMENTS ] ;
```

allocates MAX_ELEMENTS (20) of type **struct values**. The **for** loop that follows initializes each member of each allocated **struct** to a known value. The subsequent **for** loop then prints out the value of each member of each allocated **struct**.

The statement that follows:

```
delete [] sArray ;
```

deallocates the array of `struct`s sArray. The last line in the `main` function ends the program.

Comments

A thorough understanding of pointers is required when dealing with allocated memory. This is because the `new` expression returns a pointer to the allocated type.

Allocating memory at runtime helps with the efficiency of an application. Massive amounts of data storage do not have to be statically declared at compile time. Memory use can be tailored to the needs of the application.

Dynamically allocating memory can also cause frustration for many development teams. You must always ensure that allocated memory is properly reclaimed (deleted) when it is no longer required. This is the main cause of memory leaks.

COMPLEXITY
INTERMEDIATE

1.7   How do I...
Create a program to perform error handling, specifically exception handling?

Problem

I have heard that exception handling is a way to respond to errors encountered during the execution of a program. I have seen examples of C++ exception handling, but I need to know how to apply the mechanism for use in my programs.

Technique

The C++ language Standard defines a standardized way of handling program anomalies at runtime. Such anomalies occur if your application attempts to acquire memory that is unavailable, tries to open a file that does not exist, or a divide-by-zero error occurs. By using the exception handling mechanism, your application can gracefully recover from errors.

In this How-To, you will create a program that will handle a number of exception conditions. In addition, the program presented here will demonstrate how write functions that throw exceptions.

Steps

1. Change to your base source directory and create a new subdirectory named EXCEPT.

2. Fire up your source code editor and type in the following code into a file named EXCEPT.CPP:

```cpp
// except.cpp - program to demonstrate the
// use of exception handling in C++
#include <iostream>
#include <new>
#include <fstream>
#include <string>
using namespace std ;

static void acquireMemory( int elements ) ;
static void calculate( int value ) throw (int) ;
static void noThrow( void ) throw ( ) ;

const int MAX_ITERATIONS = 20 ;
const int MAX_ELEMENTS = 30000 ;

struct LargeStruct
{
    double bigd1[ MAX_ELEMENTS ] ;
    double bigd2[ MAX_ELEMENTS ] ;
    double bigd3[ MAX_ELEMENTS ] ;
    double bigd4[ MAX_ELEMENTS ] ;
} ;

int errorCode = 0 ;

int main()
{
    int numerator = 10 ;
    int divisor = 0 ;
    int result = 0 ;

    try
    {
        result = numerator / divisor ;
        cout << "\nExpression succeeded!" << endl ;
    }
    catch( ... )
    {
        cout << "\nDivide-by-zero exception!" << endl ;
    }

    try
    {
```

```
            for( divisor = 10; divisor >= 0; divisor-- )
            {
                result = numerator / divisor ;
                cout << numerator << '/' << divisor ;
                cout << " == " << result << endl ;
            }
        }
        catch( ... )
        {
            cout << "for() divide-by-zero exception!" << endl ;
        }

        try
        {
            acquireMemory( 30000 ) ;
        }
        catch( string s )
        {
            cout << s << endl ;
        }
        catch( ... )
        {
            cout << "Exception thrown for " ;
            cout << "acquireMemory()" << endl ;
        }

        try
        {
            for( int i = 1; i >= 0; i-- )
            {
                calculate( i ) ;
                cout << "calculate(" << i ;
                cout << ") succeeded" << endl ;
            }
        }
        catch( int ec )
        {
            cout << "exception for calculate()" << endl ;
        }

        return( 0 ) ;
    }

    void acquireMemory( int elements )
    {
        long cnt = elements * MAX_ELEMENTS ;
        LargeStruct *s = (LargeStruct *)0 ;

        try
        {
            s = new LargeStruct[ cnt ] ;
        }
```

```
        catch( bad_alloc e )
        {
            cout << "Caught bad_alloc" << endl ;
        }
        catch( ... )
        {
            cout << " allocation exception " << endl ;
            throw ;
        }

        if( s == (LargeStruct *)0 )
            throw string( "s is null in acquireMemory" ) ;
        else
            delete [] s ;
    }

    void calculate( int value )
    {
        if( value == 0 )
        {
            errorCode = 1 ;
            throw errorCode ;
        }
    }
```

3. Save the file and return to the command line.

4. Run your compiler and linker on **EXCEPT.CPP**.

5. The output should appear as follows:

```
Divide-by-zero exception!
10/10 == 1
10/9 == 1
10/8 == 1
10/7 == 1
10/6 == 1
10/5 == 2
10/4 == 2
10/3 == 3
10/2 == 5
10/1 == 10
for() divide-by-zero exception!
s is null in acquireMemory
calculate(1) succeeded
exception for calculate()
```

How It Works

You begin your journey with four preprocessor directives at the top of the source file:

```
#include <iostream>
#include <new>
```

```
#include <fstream>
#include <string>
```

The header file **new** contains a declaration for the standard exception class **bad_alloc**. The class **bad_alloc** is derived from the exception handling class **exception**. You must include **new** to use the functionality of **bad_alloc**.

After the namespace **using** directive, three functions are declared. These functions will be called by the **main** function. The second function declaration

```
static void calculate( int value ) throw (int) ;
```

contains an exception specification as part of its declaration. An exception specification is specified using the keyword **throw**, followed by a list of types within enclosing parentheses. An exception specification identifies the types of exceptions that a function will throw. The function declaration for **calculate** specifies that it will throw an **int** and only an **int**.

The last function declaration

```
static void noThrow( void ) throw ( ) ;
```

states that the function **noThrow** is guaranteed not to throw any exceptions; hence the empty specification list. By the way, **noThrow** is not defined in the program; this declaration only serves as an example of an empty exception specification.

Two constants are defined following the function declarations. These are merely used to specify array dimensions.

Next, a **struct** named **LargeStruct** is declared, encapsulating four attributes. Note that this **struct** is rather large (and purposefully so). I want to demonstrate the behavior of an application that fails to allocate memory.

The next definition, **errorCode**, is an integer that will be used as an argument to a **throw** statement.

The first three statements inside the **main** function are integer definitions used for calculations later in the source. Next, you find the first occurrence of exception-handling code. That section of code follows:

```
try
{
    result = numerator / divisor ;
    cout << "\nExpression succeeded!" << endl ;
}
catch( ... )
{
    cout << "\nDivide-by-zero exception!" << endl ;
}
```

In a nutshell, the program attempts to execute the statement within the **try** block; if it is unsuccessful, control is transferred to the **catch** block. Any statements following the statement throwing an exception will be disregarded. If a statement within a **try** block does not throw an exception, control continues on to the next statement, if one exists.

A **try** block consists of the keyword **try**, followed by an opening brace, one or more program statements, and a closing brace. It is assumed that one or more statements within a **try** block will throw an exception; if they don't, there is no need to use the exception mechanism.

A **try** block is the same as any other C++ block. Variables can be declared within the block, but be forewarned that those variables will not be accessible outside the **try** block.

One or more **catch** blocks must follow a **try** block. A **catch** clause is sometimes referred to as an exception handler. The first **catch** block in the program is shown here:

```
catch( ... )
{
    cout << "\nDivide-by-zero exception!" << endl ;
}
```

This is a unique **catch** clause, commonly referred to as the "catch all" clause. The syntax for this **catch** clause consists of an ellipsis (three periods) within the **catch** declaration. The "catch all" **catch** block must be the last one, if more than one **catch** block is defined. If the preceding **try** block throws an exception, the **cout** statement within the **catch** clause will execute, proclaiming a divide-by-zero exception.

The next **try/catch** in the program is

```
try
{
    for( divisor = 10; divisor >= 0; divisor-- )
    {
        result = numerator / divisor ;
        cout << numerator << '/' << divisor ;
        cout << " == " << result << endl ;
    }
}
catch( ... )
{
    cout << "for() divide-by-zero exception!" << endl ;
}
```

This **for** loop is surrounded by a **try** block. The loop will continue to execute until **divisor** is less than **0** or if an exception is thrown. Obviously, the loop will never reach -1 because a divide-by-zero exception occurs when **divisor**'s value becomes **0**.

The next **try/catch** section of code follows:

```
try
{
    acquireMemory( 30000 ) ;
}
catch( string s )
{
    cout << s << endl ;
}
catch( ... )
{
    cout << "Exception thrown for " ;
    cout << "acquireMemory()" << endl ;
}
```

Within this **try** block is a call to a function named **acquireMemory**. Obviously, this function potentially throws an exception of some type. Let's jump ahead and see what is happening within the function **acquireMemory()**. The function's body is shown in the following code:

```
void acquireMemory( int elements )
{
    long cnt = elements * MAX_ELEMENTS ;
    LargeStruct *s = (LargeStruct *)0 ;

    try
    {
        s = new LargeStruct[ cnt ] ;
    }
    catch( bad_alloc e )
    {
        cout << "Caught bad_alloc" << endl ;
    }
    catch( ... )
    {
        cout << "allocation exception" << endl ;
        throw ;
    }

    if( s == (LargeStruct *)0 )
        throw string( "s is null in acquireMemory" ) ;
    else
        delete [] s ;
}
```

The function accepts an integer argument, specifying the number of elements to allocate. The first two statements within the function define a variable that holds the total number of elements to allocate and a declaration of a pointer to **LargeStruct**, respectively. Next, a **try** block is encountered, followed by two **catch** clauses. Within the **try** block, an attempt is made to

allocate an array of LargeStructs. If the allocation fails and **new** throws a
bad_alloc exception, the first **catch** clause processes the exception. If any
other exception is thrown, it will be handled by the "catch all" handler. Notice
the use of **throw** within the "catch all" handler; this instructs the handling
mechanism to throw the same exception up to the next **catch** handler.

The code that follows the "catch all" handler checks to see if the pointer is **0**.
It is possible that your compiler's implementation of **new** does not throw an
exception. The alternative is to check the value of the pointer; a return value of
0 indicates failure, otherwise the pointer will contain a valid memory address.
In the example, if **s** is **0**, the program throws a **string** to the calling function.

Let's reexamine the calling block:

```
try
{
    acquireMemory( 30000 ) ;
}
catch( string s )
{
    cout << s << endl ;
}
catch( ... )
{
    cout << "Exception thrown for " ;
    cout << "acquireMemory()" << endl ;
}
```

The first **catch** clause handles an exception of type **string**. This handler
will process the **throw string** statement in function **acquireMemory**. If any
other exception is thrown, the "catch all" handler will process the exception.
The exception mechanism searches all the **catch** clauses, looking for the clause
that can process the exception.

Moving through the source code, you come to the next **try/catch** section,
shown in the following code:

```
try
{
    for( int i = 1; i >= 0; i++ )
    {
        calculate( i ) ;
        cout << "calculate(" << i ;
        cout << ") succeeded" << endl ;
    }
}
catch( int ec )
{
    cout << "exception for calculate()" << endl ;
}
```

The **try** block surrounds a **for** loop. Within the **for** loop, the function **calculate** is called. Notice that the **catch** clause will handle an exception of type **int**. Now turn your attention to the function **calculate** to see what is happening there. The function's source is as follows:

```
void calculate( int value )
{
    if( value == 0 )
    {
        errorCode = 1 ;
        throw errorCode ;
    }
}
```

The argument's value is compared to 0; if the expression is **true**, the two statements within the **if** block are executed. The first statement assigns the value 1 to **errorCode**; this variable is defined in the global namespace. The next line is a **throw** statement, throwing **errorCode**.

Comments

An optional method for error handling is to return user-defined codes for a function call. This method was commonly accepted before the specification of the exception handling mechanism. In fact, this style is still practiced today. The following example demonstrates this style:

```
bool openFile( const char *name )
{
    bool successfullyOpened = false ;
    ifstream in( name ) ;
    if( in )
    {
        //...
    }
    return( successfullyOpened ) ;
}
//...
if( openFile( "sample.txt") == true )
    //...
```

The return value from a function specifies the success or failure of its operation. Many third-party libraries use the **int** type to specify error codes. For example, a library that manipulates a database might experience different types of errors depending on the access context. As a rule, the value **0** is commonly used to signify success and non-zero values as error codes.

What happens if an exception is thrown, but not caught? The function **std::terminate** will be called.

It is good programming practice to include exception specifications as part of your function declarations. This permits client programmers to know the types of exceptions that your functions will throw. Remember that an empty exception specification guarantees that the function will not throw any exceptions. The lack of an exception specification tells client programmers "This function might throw any number of exceptions."

OBJECT ORIENTATION— THEORY AND PRACTICE

2

OBJECT ORIENTATION— THEORY AND PRACTICE

How do I...

2.1 Understand the object-oriented paradigm?

2.2 Learn the concept of inheritance so that I can apply it programmatically?

2.3 Learn the concept of encapsulation?

2.4 Learn the concept of polymorphism?

Object-oriented programming is a very powerful and important programming paradigm. Object-oriented programs, when properly designed and implemented, provide more flexibility to meet the demands for delivering software in the rapidly changing marketplace. Everything from word processors, to spreadsheets, to graphics applications, to operating systems are written in object-oriented languages, the vast majority in C++.

This chapter introduces you to the concepts of the object-oriented paradigm. The target audience for this chapter is programmers working with procedural languages who are interested in moving to C++. It is suggested that this chapter be read before the chapter that follows. The chapter presents four How-Tos, each designed to provide you with knowledge of basic object-oriented concepts.

This chapter takes a unique approach in the presentation of a How-To. This chapter does not require the use of a special software tool. It does not require the use of any compiler or programming language. You might want to have a notepad or, if you prefer, a word processor. The focus for this chapter is centered on thinking, but thinking in an object-oriented way. The intent is to change your way of thinking about how a program is written. Object-oriented programming is very different from procedural programming. To effectively use an object-oriented language, you must make a paradigm shift.

2.1 Understand the Object-Oriented Paradigm

This How-To presents the common terminology used in object-oriented programming. Brief definitions for the most common terms are given. The How-Tos that follow will go into more detail about each of the terms and concepts.

2.2 Learn the Concept of Inheritance So That I Can Apply It Programmatically

Inheritance is one of three concepts that constitute the object-oriented paradigm. Inheritance implies a parent/child relationship, just as happens in nature. A pseudo programming language is defined in this How-To and is used in the How-Tos that follow.

2.3 Learn the Concept of Encapsulation

Encapsulation encompasses the interface and abstraction of a class. An encapsulated class is said to be cohesive or self-contained. Encapsulation provides a clean separation of interface and implementation of a class.

2.4 Learn the Concept of Polymorphism

Polymorphism literally means *many* (poly) *forms* (morph). An object exhibits polymorphic behavior based on its stance in an inheritance hierarchy. If two (or more) objects have the same interface, but exhibit different behaviors, they are said to be polymorphic. Polymorphism is a very powerful feature for an object-oriented language. It allows the behavior of a member function to vary depending on the type of the object.

2.1 How do I...
Understand the object-oriented paradigm?

Problem

I understand the structured programming paradigm and am eager to move into object-oriented programming. I want to understand the object-oriented paradigm, including terms and fundamental concepts.

Technique

This How-To presents some of the fundamental terms and principles used to describe the concepts of object-oriented programming. Each term is defined in the "Steps" section that follows. You can use this How-To as a reference for the How-To sections that follow. Alternatively, use this How-To as a stepping stone to the How-Tos that follow.

Steps

This section defines common terminology used in object-oriented technology. You can think of this section as a reference, each step providing a definition for some object-oriented term or concept. In each of the How-Tos that follows, these terms will be described in more detail, building upon the basic definitions given here.

- *Attribute*—The data for a class that maintains the current state of an object. The state of an object is determined by the current contents of all the attributes. Attributes should be hidden from users of the object. Access to attributes should be defined through an object's interface.

- *Object*—An object is a something that exists and is identifiable. An object exhibits behavior, maintains state, and has traits. An object can be manipulated. Some examples of objects are telephones, automobiles, buildings, animals, and computers. An object is an instance of a class.

- *Class*—*Class* is synonymous with *type*. A class specifies the traits (data) and behavior that an object can exhibit. A class itself does not exist; it is merely a description of an object. A blueprint for a building is analogous to a class and the building itself is the object. A class can be considered a template for the creation of objects.

- *Inheritance*—This is the relationship of classes. There is an explicit **is-a** relationship between classes. For example, an automobile **is-a** vehicle, a zebra **is-a** mammal, a flower **is-a** plant, and so on. Classes with more specialization inherit from classes with more generalization.

- *Encapsulation*—Encompasses the interface and abstraction of a class. An encapsulated class is said to be cohesive or self-contained.

- *Polymorphism*—Literally means *many* (poly) *forms* (morph). An object exhibits polymorphic behavior based on its stance in an inheritance hierarchy. If two (or more) objects have the same interface, but exhibit different behaviors, they are said to be polymorphic.

- *Interface*—The visible functionality of a class. The interface is the contract an object makes with users of an object. An interface emphasizes a class's abstraction. Users manipulate an object through its interface.

- *Implementation*—The internal functionality and attributes of a class. A class's implementation is hidden from users of the class. Users should manipulate an object through its interface without regard to the object's implementation.

- *Abstraction*—The generalization of a class that distinguishes it from other classes. An abstraction emphasizes the interface of a class, providing a clean separation of its implementation.

How It Works

Each of the object-oriented terms previously defined will be expanded on in the How-Tos that follow.

Comments

This How-To provided brief definitions of commonly used terminology in object-oriented programming.

2.2 How do I...
Learn the concept of inheritance so that I can apply it programmatically?

Problem

I've been learning to write basic C++ programs using a structured methodology and am ready to learn the principles of object-oriented programming. I want to be able to put these principles into practice using the C++ language. I have heard that inheritance is one principle of object-oriented programming. How can I understand the concept?

Technique

The principles of object-oriented programming can be learned with minimal effort. The three basic concepts of object-orientation are inheritance, encapsulation, and polymorphism. Understanding inheritance is a good starting point because it is an easy concept to grasp.

The technique used to apply inheritance is straightforward. Think about your family tree—that is inheritance. The procedure to describe your family tree is the same to describe class inheritance in C++ (or any other object-oriented language, for that matter).

Inheritance is known as an **is-a** relationship. A golden retriever **is-a** dog, a snake **is-a** reptile, and a flower **is-a** plant. Each of these is a specialization of its parent. For example, although a snake and a lizard are both reptiles, they are very different from each other.

To begin applying inheritance, you must decide the base classes that must exist within your application. Those base classes provide basic, default functionality to users of the class. Users, in this context, relate to other objects within your application that create and use instances of the classes you have declared. An instance of a class is also referred to as an object; it is something that "lives and breathes" within your program. An object exists and performs operations upon itself and other collaborating objects. Think of it this way: A blueprint for a building is analogous to a class. The building is the object. The blueprint is just the static representation of the building. The building is the dynamic, living object.

The *interface* of a class is the part that the clients see. An interface is considered a contract the class has with its clients. For example, an automobile has an interface (contract) with its driver. An automobile's interface includes a steering wheel, gas and brake pedals, speedometer, and possibly a clutch and stick shift. This interface provides functionality to you, the driver. Yet, you don't have to know anything about the inner workings of the automobile—you just put the key in, turn it, and drive off. The only functionality you have to worry about is steering, braking, and resuming speed. To you, it does not matter if the car has front-wheel or rear-wheel drive, or if the engine is a four- or eight-cylinder; you just want the car to get you to your destination.

All objects you interact with have the concept of interface. Even the simplest thing, such as a television or room light, has an interface. The television's interface consists of buttons or dials and the interface of a room light is an on/off switch. With the television, all you have to do is to push buttons or turn dials; you do not have to understand electrical circuitry to operate it.

The first step to create a class is to identify the interface that the class must present to its users. Let's proceed through the process using a step-by-step guide to develop a simple hierarchy.

First, for this chapter, I would like to stay away from implementing object-oriented concepts using the C++ language. The next chapter will address how to use the C++ language to implement the object-oriented concepts learned in this chapter.

Second, no special software tool is required for this chapter. The only requirement is that you learn to think in an object-oriented way. You might want to use a text editor (or even longhand) to capture your class descriptions and inheritance hierarchies.

Let's create our own object-oriented declarative language. A simple language is in order. The following is a glossary of our language:

- *thing*—The entity that is described. A thing is analogous to a class (refer to How-To 2.1). A thing can have an interface that users can utilize. A thing will have a name associated with it. A thing can be a superthing, a subthing, or just a thing by itself. A thing will have parts and services, both visible and hidden from users of the thing.

- descendantOf—A keyword that describes that some thing is a descendant of some other thing. For example, you are a descendantOf your mother and father.

- *part*—Used to describe the data to be used by a thing. A part is equivalent to an attribute (refer to How-To 2.1). A thing must have data to represent its current state.

- *service*—An implementation for an operation of a thing. It is defined by functionality provided by a thing to fulfill its interface (contract) to users.

- **exposed**—Available to the outside world (to client objects using this object). Using a thing's name, an object can access a thing's part directly.

- **internal**—The opposite of **exposed**. Only the thing itself can access its part element(s). A thing must provide a service so that client code can either change or get the value of a thing's part.

- *inherit*—This data is accessible by the thing directly and is inherited by its descendants for access. For example, if **child** is a descendant of **parent**, **child** will receive a copy of **parent**'s parts.

- *superthing*—A parent thing. Within a parent-child relationship, the parent is the superthing.

- *subthing*—A child thing. Within a parent-child relationship, the child is the subthing.

You now have a language that describes the entities a program needs to fulfill its tasks. It is also helpful to have a notation to visually describe a class hierarchy. The notation you will use is simple. A box will be used to represent a thing. A line will be used to show the direction of inheritance. The thing (box) pointed to is the parent thing. The thing at the other end of the line is the child. I will also refer to the parent as the superthing and the child as the subthing. Figure 2.1 demonstrates a parent-child relationship.

Figure 2.1 The parent-child relationship.

For this How-To, let's use a hierarchy for vehicles. You first have to decide the base thing and then determine the other subthings that are descendants of the base thing.

Steps

1. First, you have to give a name to the base thing. Notice that the name of the thing is capitalized. You do it like this:

thing Vehicle

2. Then you have to describe the interface. This is a list of services that clients can use:

```
thing Vehicle
    exposed service powerSwitch
    exposed service accelerate
    exposed service decelerate
```

3. The next step is to extend the functionality of `Vehicle` by declaring a descendent of `Vehicle`, say, `MotorVehicle`:

```
thing MotorVehicle descendantOf  Vehicle
```

4. Next, you have to describe the interface that a `MotorVehicle` will provide to users of this thing:

```
thing MotorVehicle descendantOf  Vehicle
    exposed service powerSwitch
    exposed service accelerate
    exposed service decelerate
    exposed service steering
```

5. It is decided that you have to further specialize `MotorVehicle` by creating a new thing named `Truck`:

```
thing Truck descendantOf MotorVehicle
    exposed service fourWheelDrive
```

6. The last step is to draw the inheritance using the notation defined, as shown in Figure 2.2.

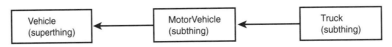

Figure 2.2   The inheritance diagram for `Vehicle`.

How It Works

You must first identify the base things that will make up your application. In this How-To, you create a base thing named `Vehicle`. The declaration looks like this:

```
thing Vehicle
    exposed service powerSwitch
    exposed service accelerate
    exposed service decelerate
```

`Vehicle` is a generic classification that can be extended through inheritance. The interface (or services) that all `Vehicle`s must exhibit is `powerSwitch`, `accelerate`, and `decelerate`. Think about it: All `Vehicle`s must start up somehow; the `powerSwitch` provides that functionality. The keyword `exposed` designates that these services are accessible to users of a `Vehicle` object. For each thing that inherits from a *Vehicle*, you have to specify the functionality for powerSwitch. For example, a powerSwitch for an F-14 fighter aircraft will operate differently than a powerSwitch for a MotorVehicle. The intent is the same, but the actual implementation of each is different.

A Vehicle must also accelerate and decelerate. Notice that the terms *accelerate* and *decelerate* are used instead of "gas pedal" and "brake." Why? Not all Vehicles have a brake; a boat is a good example. Now that you have defined what a basic Vehicle must do, you will specialize, or inherit from, Vehicle.

The thing Vehicle is hardly useful considering its current definition, so the next step is to define a new thing by inheriting from Vehicle. This is specified by the line

thing MotorVehicle *descendantOf* Vehicle

This definition is very straightforward. This statement declares that MotorVehicle is a descendant (child) of Vehicle (the parent). A MotorVehicle is a specialization of a Vehicle; the MotorVehicle will require a steering wheel, brake pedal, and gas pedal (among other obvious things). You could continue the definition of a MotorVehicle by specifying tires, an engine, a transmission, and so on. The intent in this How-To is to explain the concept of inheritance without making the things overly complicated. Notice that the names of things are capitalized. In the case of MotorVehicle, each word of the compound word is capitalized. This is accepted naming practice in object-oriented programming.

If some thing is a descendant of a Vehicle, it inherits the services defined in Vehicle. You then extend the functionality of Vehicle (otherwise, why inherit from it?). If you don't need to specialize Vehicle, simply create an instance of Vehicle in your application.

Next, you have to inherit from MotorVehicle, namely a Truck. That is reflected in the following declaration:

thing Truck *descendantOf* MotorVehicle
    exposed service fourWheelDrive

A Truck inherits all the functionality of a MotorVehicle, specifically powerSwitch, accelerate, decelerate, and steering. This Truck extends the functionality of a MotorVehicle by providing four-wheel drive capability. This is reflected in the declaration of a new service named fourWheelDrive.

Last, you draw the hierarchy to provide a visual representation of the inheritance tree.

Comments

In step 1, you declared a Vehicle thing to serve as a base thing. This base thing functions as a template for all subsequent descendents of Vehicle; you do not intend to create objects of type Vehicle. This is not always the case when defining classes for an application. You might find that defining a lone thing suffices to represent some entity. Do not use inheritance just for the sake of using inheritance. No requirement of the object-oriented paradigm states you must always create an inheritance tree.

It is important to remember that you should only provide a minimal interface for a thing. An overabundant interface is as bad a design as an inadequate interface.

2.3 How do I...
Learn the concept of encapsulation?

Problem

I want to extend my knowledge of object-oriented concepts. I am familiar with inheritance and am ready to learn about encapsulation. I hear encapsulation is an important principle of object-oriented programming and I want to take advantage of its traits.

Technique

As with any programming concept (especially object orientation), the technique required is quite easy. The technique is to begin with something simple and build upon that. You will continue the use of the definitive language outlined in How-To 2.2.

In the following "Steps" section, you will use the `Vehicle` thing from How-To 2.2. Vehicles have various (physical) parts, so those parts will be described by the `parts` keyword.

Steps

1. Declare parts for the `Vehicle` thing. Those parts represent the state of an object at some point in time.

```
thing Vehicle
    exposed service powerSwitch
    exposed service accelerate
    exposed service decelerate
    inherit part speed
    inherit part isMoving
    inherit part available
```

2. Now provide services for the Vehicle, so users can obtain the values of Vehicle parts.

```
thing Vehicle
    exposed service powerSwitch
    exposed service accelerate
    exposed service decelerate
    inherit part speed
    inherit part isMoving
    inherit part available
    exposed service getSpeed
    exposed service isMoving
    exposed service getAvailable
```

3. Now specify services for Vehicle, so that users can change the values of this Vehicle parts.

```
thing Vehicle
    exposed service powerSwitch
    exposed service accelerate
    exposed service decelerate
    inherit part speed
    inherit part isMoving
    inherit part available
    exposed service getSpeed
    exposed service isMoving
    exposed service getAvailable
    exposed service setSpeed
    exposed service setAvailable
```

How It Works

Encapsulation specifies the containment of functionality (services) and parts within a thing. The concept specifies that you should hide parts within a thing. Only the thing should know about its internal parts.

Another aspect of encapsulation is maintaining responsibility for a thing's parts and services. Each thing has a contract stating a responsibility to its clients. A thing should be able to maintain its own existence—that is, to stand on its own. A thing is considered cohesive if it can fully encapsulate itself.

You must remember to protect the internal state of your objects; if you don't, those objects will become unstable or corrupt. An unstable object is untrustworthy; you can never count on the state of a corrupt object.

Comments

Inheritance and encapsulation are very important with respect to object-oriented principles. However, they are but two important concepts. A third concept, namely polymorphism, is addressed in the next How-To.

2.4 How do I...
Learn the concept of polymorphism?

Problem

I have a good understanding of inheritance and encapsulation and feel I have to grasp the concept of polymorphism to round out my knowledge of object-oriented technology.

Technique

Of the three object-oriented principles, polymorphism is probably the most difficult to comprehend. Effective polymorphic behavior relies on proper implementation of inheritance and encapsulation. The technique for ensuring effective polymorphic behavior is to fully understand its intent and when polymorphism should and should not be used.

Returning to the `Vehicle` example from previous How-Tos, let's apply polymorphism to the picture.

Steps

1. The declaration of Vehicle is reproduced here:

```
thing Vehicle
    exposed service powerSwitch
    exposed service accelerate
    exposed service decelerate
    inherit part speed
    inherit part isMoving
    inherit part available
    exposed service getSpeed
    exposed service isMoving
    exposed service getAvailable
    exposed service setSpeed
    exposed service setAvailable
```

2. Next, the declaration of MotorVehicle:

```
thing MotorVehicle descendantOf Vehicle
    exposed service powerSwitch
    exposed service accelerate
    exposed service decelerate
    inherit part speed
    inherit part isMoving
```

```
inherit part available
exposed service getSpeed
exposed service isMoving
exposed service getAvailable
exposed service setSpeed
exposed service setAvailable
exposed service steering
```

3. The following is the declaration for Truck:

```
thing Truck descendantOf MotorVehicle
    exposed service powerSwitch
    exposed service accelerate
    exposed service decelerate
    inherit part speed
    inherit part isMoving
    inherit part available
    exposed service getSpeed
    exposed service isMoving
    exposed service getAvailable
    exposed service setSpeed
    exposed service setAvailable
    exposed service steering
    exposed service fourWheelDrive
```

4. The following is a snippet of code using the pseudo-language:

```
Truck aTruck := create Truck.
aTruck->setSpeed(55).
Vehicle baseVehicle := aTruck.
integer speed := baseVehicle->getSpeed.
Print(speed).
Print(aTruck->getSpeed).
MotorVehicle anotherVehicle := create MotorVehicle.
anotherVehicle->setSpeed(40).
baseVehicle := anotherVehicle.
Print(baseVehicle->getSpeed).
baseVehicle->setSpeed(85).
Print(anotherVehicle->getSpeed).
```

5. The output from this program is

```
55
55
40
85
```

How It Works

In the first three steps, the declarations for **Vehicle**, **MotorVehicle**, and **Truck** are reproduced from previous How-Tos. This is done merely for the convenience of the reader.

Although each derived thing inherits a service from its parent thing, you expect that each derived thing will re-implement each service it inherits. This is considered specialization. Each derived thing will specialize the functionality defined by its parent thing. The following is an example to provide some clarification:

```
thing RaceCar descendantOf MotorVehicle
//...
```

Considering the previous declaration of `RaceCar`, it can be assumed that the service `accelerate` will function differently than the `accelerate` service for `Truck`. I hope that a `RaceCar` object accelerates at a much faster rate than a `Truck` object. Let's look at what is happening in step 4.

The first line of code

```
Truck aTruck := create Truck.
```

creates an instance of a `Truck`. The object (instance) will be known by the declared name `aTruck`. Using the object, you can call upon the various services defined for a `Truck` thing. The next line of code demonstrates this:

```
aTruck->setSpeed(55).
```

This call to `setSpeed` is made for the `setSpeed` service implemented by the `Truck` thing. The implementation explicitly sets the value of the `speed` part to `55`.

The next line of code

```
Vehicle baseVehicle := aTruck.
```

creates an reference variable of type `Vehicle` and is named `baseVehicle`. This is only a reference; `baseVehicle` is not actually an object of type `Vehicle`. The assignment expression `baseVehicle := aTruck` binds the reference (`baseVehicle`) to refer to the object `aTruck`. Although `baseVehicle` is a `Vehicle` reference, it is referring to a type `Truck` object. It is important to understand this. Figure 2.3 expresses the relationship.

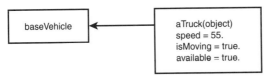

Figure 2.3   Base reference relationship to derived object.

The line of code that follows

```
integer speed := baseVehicle->getSpeed.
```

creates a program variable of type `integer`; the service `getSpeed` is called using the reference `baseVehicle`. Which `getSpeed` is called: the one implemented in `Vehicle`, the one defined in `MotorVehicle`, or the one implemented in `Truck`? The `getSpeed` called is the one implemented in `Truck`. This is the expected behavior, considering the definition of polymorphism. The service called depends on the actual object referred to, not the reference to the object. Because `baseVehicle` actually refers to a `Truck` object, it is `Truck->getSpeed` that is called. The next two lines of code verify that fact by printing the value of `aTruck->speed`. First, the value stored in the local variable `speed` is printed. Next, the value stored in `aTruck->speed` is printed. The next two lines of code in the program fragment

```
MotorVehicle anotherVehicle := create MotorVehicle.
anotherVehicle->setSpeed(40).
```

create an object named `anotherVehicle` of type `MotorVehicle`. The second line then sets the `speed` part of this object to `40`. The line of code that follows

```
baseVehicle := anotherVehicle.
```

sets the reference `baseVehicle` to refer to the object `anotherVehicle`.

The last three lines of code from the program follow:

```
Print(baseVehicle->getSpeed).
baseVehicle->setSpeed(85).
Print(anotherVehicle->getSpeed).
```

The first line prints the contents of `anotherVehicle->speed`, which is `40`. The next line sets the contents of `anotherVehicle->speed` to `85` through the reference `baseVehicle`. Finally, the value of `anotherVehicle->speed`, which is now `85`, is printed out, thus verifying the call to `setSpeed` through `baseVehicle`.

Comments

This How-To provided a definition for polymorphism and demonstrated its mechanism using a sample program. In the next chapter, polymorphism is demonstrated using the C++ programming language.

The descriptions and definitions in this chapter are a good introduction to thinking in "object mode" rather than structure mode.

CHAPTER 3

OBJECT ORIENTATION—C++ SPECIFICS

OBJECT ORIENTATION—C++ SPECIFICS

How do I...

3.1 Create a simple class in C++?

3.2 Implement the use of inheritance in C++?

3.3 Apply the use of encapsulation in a C++ program?

3.4 Implement polymorphism in C++?

3.5 Implement static members of a class?

In this chapter, you will explore the world of object-oriented programming using the C++ language. In Chapter 1, "A Quick Introduction to the Language," the fundamentals of the language are introduced. In Chapter 2, "Object Orientation—Theory and Practice," the three basic concepts of object-oriented programming are introduced: inheritance, encapsulation, and polymorphism.

The first four How-Tos in this chapter will mirror the first four How-Tos in Chapter 2. This will provide you with a basic understanding of implementing inheritance, encapsulation, and polymorphism. The last How-To demonstrates the use of static members of a class.

3.1 Create a Simple Class in C++

This How-To shows how to create a user-defined type, known specifically as a class. You will also learn how to separate the declaration and definition of a class.

3.2 Implement the Use of Inheritance in C++

This How-To explores the concept of inheritance by providing a concrete example. Inheritance is a powerful concept and is easily implemented in the C++ language. The example given in the How-To will guide you through the process of creating an inheritance hierarchy.

3.3 Apply the Use of Encapsulation in a C++ Program

Encapsulation is one of three basic concepts of object-oriented programming. Encapsulation is the grouping of a class interface and its implementation, and providing a clean separation of the two. This How-To will introduce the concept, providing an example to illustrate the concept.

3.4 Implement Polymorphism in C++

Inheritance and encapsulation are two (of three) important features of object-oriented programming. The third important feature, polymorphism, is demonstrated in this How-To.

3.5 Implement Static Members of a Class

The use of static data members and static member functions can be useful in certain programming situations. The decision to use this feature should be dealt with during the design of your classes. In this How-To, you will see how to exploit the use of static members of a class.

COMPLEXITY
BEGINNING

3.1 How do I...
Create a simple class in C++?

Problem

I have a good understanding of the C++ language in general, and am ready to explore the use its object-oriented features. I understand that the class is the basic building block for implementing all the concepts of object-oriented programming in C++. Is there some class I can define that will demonstrate the basic organization of a class?

Technique

Every class in C++ implies the use of object-oriented functionality. You should follow some basic rules when defining your classes. This How-To demonstrates those rules by creating a class and showing how to create an object of that class at runtime. This technique will demonstrate the principles of class declaration and definition.

This How-To will also show how to separate a class declaration from its implementation by using separate files. You will use a header file to contain the class declaration and define the functionality of the class in an implementation file.

Steps

1. Change to your base source directory and create a new subdirectory named VEHICLE.

2. Fire up your source code editor and type the following code into a file named VEHICLE.H:

```
// vehicle.h - this file contains a class
// declaration for the vehicle type.
class Vehicle
{
public:
    enum Switch { SWITCH_ON, SWITCH_OFF } ;
    Vehicle( ) ;
    ~Vehicle( ) ;

    bool powerSwitch( Switch onOrOff ) ;
    unsigned int accelerate( unsigned int amount ) ;
    unsigned int decelerate( unsigned int amount ) ;
    bool isMoving( void ) const ;
    unsigned int getSpeed( void ) const ;
    unsigned int setSpeed( unsigned int speedIn ) ;
protected:
    bool moving ;
private:
    unsigned int speed ;
} ;
```

Please note that if your compiler does not support the **bool** data type, you can add the following line of code at the top of this header file:

```
enum bool { false = 0, true } ;
```

3. Create a new file named VEHICLE.CPP and type the following code into that file:

```
// declaration of Vehicle
#include "vehicle.h"
```

```cpp
Vehicle::Vehicle( ) :
    speed( 0 ), moving( false )
{
}

Vehicle::~Vehicle( )
{
    speed = 0;
    moving = false ;
}

bool Vehicle::powerSwitch( Switch onOrOff )
{
    bool on = false ;

    if( onOrOff == SWITCH_OFF )
    {
        speed = 0 ;
        moving = false ;
    }

    return( on ) ;
}

unsigned int Vehicle::accelerate( unsigned int amount )
{
    speed += amount ;
    moving = true ;

    return( speed ) ;
}

unsigned int Vehicle::decelerate( unsigned int amount )
{
    if( amount > speed )
        speed = 0 ;
    else
        speed -= amount ;

    moving = (speed == 0) ? false : true ;

    return( speed ) ;
}

bool Vehicle::isMoving( ) const
{
    return( moving ) ;
}

unsigned int Vehicle::getSpeed( ) const
{
    return( speed ) ;
}
```

```
unsigned int Vehicle::setSpeed( unsigned int speedIn )
{
    speed = speedIn ;
    moving = true ;

    return( speed ) ;
}
```

4. Save this file and create a new file named MAIN.CPP. This file should contain the following:

```
#include <iostream>
#include "vehicle.h"

int main( )
{
    Vehicle  vehicle ;
    Vehicle *pv = new Vehicle() ;

    vehicle.setSpeed( 10 ) ;
    pv->setSpeed( 20 ) ;

    cout << "vehicle's speed: " << vehicle.getSpeed() << endl ;
    cout << "pv's speed      : " << pv->getSpeed() << endl ;

    delete pv ;

    return 0 ;
}
```

5. Save MAIN.CPP and return to the command line. Next, compile and link MAIN.CPP and VEHICLE.CPP as in the following example:

```
gcc -c main.cpp vehicle.cpp
```

If your compiler complains about the statement

```
#include <iostream>
```

comment out (or remove) the **using** directive following it and change the #include line to

```
#include <iostream.h>
```

6. Run the program; the output should be as follows:

```
vehicle's speed: 10
pv's speed      : 20
```

If you are using the DJGPP compiler, you might have to rename the executable from A.OUT to MAIN.EXE to execute the program.

How It Works

Let's begin by examining the header file **VEHICLE.H**. A class declaration in C++ begins with the keyword **class**, followed by an opening brace, one or more declarations, and ends with a closing brace and semicolon. Declaring a class is declaring a new type (user-defined type), just as an **int** or **double**. A class bundles together data and functionality into a self-contained package.

The first source line within the class declaration is the access specifier **public**. The three access specifiers available are **public**, **protected**, and **private**. A class member that has **private** visibility can only be accessed by member functions of the class and **friend**s of the class. A How-To in this chapter discusses the **friend** keyword and its use. Any class member declared with **protected** visibility is accessible by the member functions of the class and the class's descendents. Any member of a class with **public** visibility is accessible outside of the class. The default access for a class is **private**. You can also declare a user-defined type using the **struct** (versus **class**) keyword. The only difference between **struct** and **class** is that the default access for **struct** is **public**.

The next declaration within the class:

```
enum Switch { SWITCH_ON, SWITCH_OFF } ;
```

defines an enumeration type and offers two values for the **Vehicle** class. This trick permits you to define constants that are only visible to the class; the definitions are not accessible outside the class. The advantage is that the global namespace is not polluted with excess constants.

The next line

```
Vehicle( ) ;
```

is a declaration of a constructor for the class. The constructor is a special member function that is used to initialize an instance of a class. Whenever an object is created at runtime, the appropriate constructor for the class will be called to initialize the object. Notice I use the word *appropriate* because constructors can be overloaded. Operators, such as =, can also be overloaded for a class. To overload a member function is to use the same name for multiple versions of the function; each overloaded function must differ by its argument signature. For example, the following class declaration specifies three different constructors for a user-defined **Date** class:

```
class Date {
    Date( ) ;
    Date( int year ) ;
    Date( int year, int month ) ;
    Date( int year, int month, int day ) ;
    //...
} ;
```

At the point of instantiation, you could call one of the constructors as appropriate. The following instantiation creates an object of type **Date** specifying the year and month:

```
Date today( 1999, 1 ) ;
```

The next declaration

```
~Vehicle( ) ;
```

is the destructor for the class. The destructor is the compliment to the constructor; it is called when an object is destroyed. The name of the destructor is the name of the class with a tilde ~ character prepended to the name. A constructor and destructor for a class should be declared with **public** access. A constructor or destructor can be declared with **protected** or **private** access; demonstrating this and the reasons why you would do it are beyond the scope of this How-To.

The next six declarations

```
bool powerSwitch( Switch onOrOff ) ;
unsigned int accelerate( unsigned int amount ) ;
unsigned int decelerate( unsigned int amount ) ;
bool isMoving( void ) const ;
unsigned int getSpeed( void ) const ;
unsigned int setSpeed( unsigned int speedIn ) ;
```

declare member functions for the class. A member function has scope within the declaring class. This means that a member function cannot be accessed outside of the context of a class instance. The dot or arrow member access operator is used to access a member of a class. This will be demonstrated later in this How-To.

The member functions of a class that have **public** visibility define the interface of the class. The *interface* of a class is the contract that a class makes with users of the class. The users of a class alter and retrieve an instance state through the interface. Users of a class should never have access to a class's data members. Each one of the member functions of **Vehicle** is used by users to get or set the instance data. For example, the declaration

```
unsigned int getSpeed( void ) const ;
```

returns the speed of the **Vehicle** instance. Notice that the function is declared with the **const** modifier. This modifier states that this function will not modify any data member of the class. This makes sense because this function simply returns the value of the **speed** data member. This type of member function is normally referred to as an *accessor*. A *mutator* function is used to alter one or more data members of a class. For example, the member function

```
unsigned int setSpeed( unsigned int speedIn ) ;
```

modifies the **speed** data member.

Just after the member function declarations, you find the following two lines of code:

```
protected:
bool moving ;
```

Again, any members declared after this access specifier are hidden from users of the class. Only member functions of the class and derived classes can access the members declared with **protected** visibility.

Examine the next two lines of code:

```
private:
unsigned int speed ;
```

Again, any members declared after this access specifier are hidden from users of the class. Only member functions of the class can access any members declared with **private** visibility.

Next, examine the implementation for class **Vehicle**. The implementation is found within **VEHICLE.CPP**. The first member function definition is that of the class's constructor. The definition begins with the name of the class, followed by the scope resolution operator, the constructor's name (again, the name of the class), and any arguments that might be declared. The definition of the constructor for the **Vehicle** class follows:

```
Vehicle::Vehicle( ) :
    speed( 0 ), moving( false )
{ }
```

The member initializer list follows the colon operator and precedes the constructor's opening brace. The initializer list can only be used with constructors and is the preferred method of initializing class data members. Notice that you do not use the assignment operator to assign a value to a data member; only constructor notation is allowed within the initializer list. Any number of program statements can appear within the constructor's body; in this example, no further functionality is required.

The next function definition in the implementation file is that of the destructor. Remember that the destructor is called for any instance of a class that is about to be destroyed. Within the body of a destructor is any logic required to properly de-initialize an instance of a class. For example, if your class allocates memory within the constructor, you should deallocate the memory in the destructor. The rule of thumb is to release any resources used by the class within the destructor. If an instance of a class is dynamically allocated and subsequently deallocated with **delete**, the destructor of the object is first called, and then the memory for the object is reclaimed.

The definition of `powerSwitch` follows the definition of the destructor. Notice that, besides constructors and destructors, the name of a member function is preceded by the name of the class and the scope resolution operator. Be sure that the return type is specified along with any arguments to the member function.

After the definition for `powerSwitch` are definitions for the functions `accelerate`, `decelerate`, `isMoving`, `getSpeed`, and `setSpeed`. A brief description of each function follows.

The member functions `accelerate` and `decelerate` are used to increase and decrease the speed of a `Vehicle` instance, respectively. The `isMoving` member function merely returns the value contained in the instance variable `moving`. The `getSpeed` member function does the same for the variable `speed`. Users of the class utilize the `setSpeed` member function to change the value of the variable `speed`.

Let's turn our attention to the third source file: `MAIN.CPP`. This file contains the function `main`. The first two statements within `main`'s body follow:

```
Vehicle  vehicle ;
Vehicle *pv = new Vehicle() ;
```

The first statement instantiates an object of type `Vehicle` on the stack. The second statement uses the `new` expression to create a `Vehicle` object from the free store. The result of the allocation is a pointer of type `Vehicle`; this pointer points to the newly created object. There is a fundamental difference between the two. The lifetime of the object `Vehicle` will expire when it leaves the block from which it is created. The object created with the `new` expression continues to exist until `delete` is called for the pointer to the object.

The next two statements

```
vehicle.setSpeed( 10 ) ;
pv->setSpeed( 20 ) ;
```

are a call to the `setSpeed` member function for each object. The first method uses the member dot operator and the second uses the arrow member access operator. The dot operator is used to access a member of a class instantiated on the stack. The arrow member access operator is used to access a member of a class (through a pointer) that is dynamically allocated.

The two source statements that follow:

```
cout << "vehicle's speed: " << vehicle.getSpeed() << endl ;
cout << "pv's speed    : " << pv->getSpeed() << endl ;
```

simply print out the value of the `speed` instance variable for each object. The value is returned by the member function `getSpeed`.

The next-to-last statement in `main` is

```
delete pv ;
```

and is called to delete the dynamically allocated object that is pointed to by `pv`. Remember that if `delete` is called for a dynamically created object, the destructor is called first, and then the memory for the object is reclaimed.

It is not explicitly shown, but the `vehicle` object will be destroyed at the end of the `main` function; the sequence of events will result in a call being made to the destructor. Following that, the object will be destroyed.

Comments

Although this class is not very interesting with respect to functionality, the class does serve to demonstrate the basics of a C++ user-defined type.

A user-defined declaration begins with the keyword `class` (or `struct`), followed by a name for the class and an opening and closing brace, and ends with a semicolon. Declarations within the class body default to `private` access for `class` declarations and `public` for `struct` declarations. Any members declared with `protected` access are directly accessible to members of derived classes, yet are inaccessible to users of the class.

Place your data members in the `private` section and provide accessor and mutator member functions so clients of the class can access those data members. Be cautious because some data members should be completely shielded from client access. Only provide accessors and mutators where absolutely required.

Remember that you should place your class declaration in a header file and the implementation in a separate file, normally with a `.cpp` extension. Common practice is to put each class declaration in its own header file and each class definition in its own `.cpp` file.

COMPLEXITY

INTERMEDIATE

3.2 How do I...
Implement the use of inheritance in C++?

Problem

I know how to declare and implement a class in C++ and am now ready to implement a class hierarchy using inheritance. Is there a simple example that will demonstrate inheritance in C++?

Technique

Declaring and implementing user-defined types (classes) is a powerful feature of C++. This power is extended using class inheritance. Many abstractions are best represented in an inheritance hierarchy. For example, circles, squares, and polygons are all shapes. This suggests the use of a base class (possibly) named **Shape**. This base class will declare functionality and attributes that is common to all shapes. Then each specific type, such as **Square**, will derive from **Shape** and modify or extend the functionality for its specific purpose.

In this How-To, you will create an application that uses inheritance. You will be using the **Vehicle** class from the previous How-To as a base class. You will create a new class that derives basic functionality from **Vehicle**.

Steps

1. Create a new subdirectory named **CAR**, change to that subdirectory, and start your source code editor.

2. Copy the files named **VEHICLE.H** and **VEHICLE.CPP** from the **VEHICLE** subdirectory (used in the last How-To). The file **VEHICLE.H** follows:

```
// vehicle.h - this file contains a class
// declaration for the vehicle type.

class Vehicle
{
public:
    enum Switch { SWITCH_ON, SWITCH_OFF } ;
    Vehicle( ) ;
    ~Vehicle( ) ;

    bool powerSwitch( Switch onOrOff ) ;
    unsigned int accelerate( unsigned int amount ) ;
    unsigned int decelerate( unsigned int amount ) ;
    bool isMoving( void ) const ;
    unsigned int getSpeed( void ) const ;
    unsigned int setSpeed( unsigned int speedIn ) ;
protected:
    bool moving ;
private:
    unsigned int speed ;
} ;
```

Please note that if your compiler does not support the **bool** data type, you can add the following line of code at the top of this header file:

```
enum bool { false = 0, true } ;
```

3. Create a new file called **CAR.H** and type the following class declaration:

```
// car.h - this file contains a class declaration
// for the Car type, derived from Vehicle
#include "vehicle.h"

class Car : public Vehicle
{
public:
    enum { MAX_SPEED = 80 } ;
    Car( ) ;
    ~Car( ) ;

    unsigned int setSpeed( unsigned int speedIn ) ;
    void steer( int degrees ) ;
    void headLights( Switch onOrOff ) ;
private:
    int degrees ;
    Switch drivingLights ;
} ;
```

4. Create a file named **CAR.CPP** and type the following code:

```
// car.cpp implementation file
// for a Car; derived from Vehicle
#include "car.h"

Car::Car( ) : Vehicle(),
    degrees( 0 ), drivingLights( SWITCH_OFF )
{
}

Car::~Car( )
{
    degrees = 0 ;
    drivingLights = SWITCH_OFF ;
}

unsigned int Car::setSpeed( unsigned int speedIn )
{
    if( speedIn > MAX_SPEED )
        speedIn = MAX_SPEED ;

    Vehicle::setSpeed( speedIn ) ;
    moving = true ;

    return( Vehicle::getSpeed() ) ;
}

void Car::steer( int degrees )
{
    if( moving )
```

```
    {
        if( degrees == 0 )
            this->degrees = 0 ;
        else
            this->degrees += degrees ;
    }
}

void Car::headLights( Switch onOrOff )
{
    drivingLights = onOrOff ;
}
```

5. Save **CAR.CPP** and create a file named **MAIN.CPP**. This file should contain the following:

```
#include <iostream>
using namespace std ;
#include "car.h"

int main( )
{
    Car *sporty = new Car() ;
    Car *luxury = new Car() ;

    sporty->setSpeed( 120 ) ;
    luxury->setSpeed( 35 ) ;

    luxury->steer( 20 ) ; // turn to right

    luxury->headLights( Vehicle::SWITCH_ON ) ;
    luxury->accelerate( 15 ) ;

    cout << "sporty's speed : " << sporty->getSpeed() << endl ;
    cout << "pLuxury's speed: " << luxury->getSpeed() << endl ;

    if( sporty->isMoving( ) )
        cout << "sporty is moving" << endl ;
    else
        cout << "sporty isn't moving" << endl ;

    delete luxury ;
    delete sporty ;

    return 0 ;
}
```

6. Save **MAIN.CPP** and return to the command line. Next, compile and link **MAIN.CPP**, **VEHICLE.CPP**, and **CAR.CPP** as shown in the following:

```
gcc -c main.cpp vehicle.cpp car.cpp
```

If your compiler complains about the statement

```
#include <iostream>
```

comment out (or remove) the **using** directive following it and change the
#include line to

```
#include <iostream.h>
```

7. Run the program; the output should be as follows:

```
sporty's speed : 80
pLuxury's speed: 50
sporty is moving
```

If you are using the DJGPP compiler, you might have to rename the
executable from **A.OUT** to **MAIN.EXE** to execute the program.

How It Works

Let's start by examining the file **CAR.H**. In this file, you find the declaration of
the user-defined type **Car**. After the **#include** directive, you come to the
declaration for **Car**, as shown following:

```
class Car : public Vehicle
```

The keyword **class** introduces a user-defined type, followed by the name.
Next is the colon operator, followed by the **public** keyword and a class name.
The colon operator introduces one or more base classes from which this class
derives. The derived class is **Car** and the base class is **Vehicle**. This is known as
an **is-a** relationship; in other words, **Car is-a Vehicle**. This is the same as any
other inheritance relationship you find in the world around you. A dog **is-a**
mammal. A house **is-a** building, and so on. So, **Car** inherits from **Vehicle**.

Next you find the **public** access specifier, followed by a class scope constant
named **MAX_SPEED**. Then come the constructor, destructor, and three member
functions.

The first member function, **setSpeed**, is also found in the base class
Vehicle. The member function **setSpeed** is overridden in **Car** because the
signatures in **Vehicle** and **Car** match exactly. In other words, the function in
Car is redefined because **Car** specializes the functionality.

The next function declaration

```
void steer( int degrees ) ;
```

is a new member function introduced for **Car**. Obviously, you have to steer a
Car, so this member function provides that functionality. You are probably
asking, "All vehicles must be steerable, so why not provide that function in
Vehicle?" Think about a train. The engineer does not actually steer the train
because the act of steering a train is controlled by the train tracks. When
deciding on your abstractions, you have to think about minimal functionality in

the base class. This style of thinking will remove any restrictions that might be passed on to derived classes. For example, if you had declared the function steer in the base class, and decided to create a derived train class, you would end up with an invalid interface. A client developer will take a look at the available interface and wonder what the steer function will provide for a train.

Next, you find the declaration

```
void headLights( Switch onOrOff ) ;
```

This member function is required so that the headlights for a Car object can turn on and off. This also provides additional functionality not provided by the base class Vehicle.

Following the declaration for headlight, you come upon the access specifier private. Within the private section, you find two attributes declared: degrees and drivingLights. The attribute degrees is used to hold the amount of degrees that the steering wheel is moved and the drivingLights attribute is used to hold the state of an object's headlights. Access to these attributes is controlled by the two member functions previously discussed.

Let's now look at the implementation file for Car. The first definition, the constructor, is as follows:

```
Car::Car( ) : Vehicle(),
    degrees( 0 ), drivingLights( SWITCH_OFF )
{ }
```

After the colon operator, you find a constructor call to the base class Vehicle within the initializer list. Whenever a derived class object is instantiated at runtime, the base class object is first constructed. Here, you are explicitly calling the base class constructor. After the constructor call, a comma-separated list of class data members is initialized. No additional functionality of the class is required, so the constructor's body is empty.

Following the definition of the constructor, you come upon the function definition for setSpeed. Remember that this definition overrides the definition found in Vehicle. The reason you override the member function is that you have to control the upper limit of the object's speed. Take a look at the following two statements within this member function:

```
Vehicle::setSpeed( speedIn ) ;
moving = true ;
```

In the member function, you first include some logic to verify the object's speed. Next comes the call to the member function setSpeed found in the base class; this is done by specifying the name of the base class followed by the scope resolution operator. This call will set the speed attribute found in Vehicle. How about the assignment to the moving variable, you ask? No attribute named `moving` is in the declaration of `Car`. It turns out that this data member is declared in the base class `Vehicle`. Because you have inherited this data member and it has `protected` visibility, the member functions of this derived class can access the variable directly. Also notice the `return` statement; a call is made to `Vehicle`'s `getspeed` member function. This call must happen because the `speed` data member is inaccessible to `Car`.

Next, you find the definitions for the member functions `Car::steer` and `Car::headLights`. These two functions provide an implementation to steer the object and turn the driving lights on and off.

Now examine the file named `MAIN.CPP`. This file contains the `main` function for the program. The first two statement within `main` follow:

```
Car *sporty = new Car() ;
Car *luxury = new Car() ;
```

Each of these statements dynamically creates an object of type `Car` using the `new` expression.

The next two lines of code

```
sporty->setSpeed( 120 ) ;
luxury->setSpeed( 35 ) ;
```

call the member function `setSpeed` for each object. Remember that you provided functionality to limit the speed of an object; in a moment, you will see if this functionality works properly.

The following three lines

```
luxury->steer( 20 ) ; // turn to right
luxury->headLights( Vehicle::SWITCH_ON ) ;
luxury->accelerate( 15 ) ;
```

alter the state of the object `luxury`. The first statement steers the object to the right 20 degrees. The next statement turns the headlights on for the object. Note that you cannot use the constant `SWITCH_ON` directly; the class name and scope resolution operator must be used to access the value.

The next two statements use `cout` to print the speed of each vehicle. The output from `sporty` confirms the logic of the `setSpeed` member function. The best you can do is 80, even though you really want to go 120.

Next, you find an `if-else` statement pair, checking to see if the `sporty` object is moving. A call is made to the member function `isMoving`, yet this member function is not declared or defined in `Car`. This member function is found in the base class; because this member function is not overridden in `Car`, a call is made to the base class function.

Finally, the two `delete` expressions in the `main` function destroy the two `Car` objects.

Comments

You have seen a concrete example of inheritance in this How-To. The amount of code required to implement a `Car` has been minimized because the base class provides some default functionality. You did not have to reapply the functionality found in `Vehicle` to the `Car` class. This is the power of inheritance.

Object-oriented programming dictates more forethought concerning program design. You must think of the problem domain and flush out the abstractions. The first task is always to identify the classes that must support the application. Do you find that some classes exhibit common functionality between them? If so, you should abstract that common functionality into a base class and then inherit for specialization.

COMPLEXITY

INTERMEDIATE

3.3 How do I...
Apply the use of encapsulation in a C++ program?

Problem

I have read the term *encapsulation* and understand its meaning to some degree. I would like to see how this concept is implemented in C++.

Technique

You will examine the practice of encapsulation in this How-To. There are no hard-and-fast rules for encapsulation. This is the responsibility of the class designer. Ask six different class architects to provide a class declaration for a radio and you will get six different class declarations!

Encapsulation involves the collection of a class's interface, its data members, and its implementation. A class that is properly encapsulated is said to be cohesive, or self-sufficient. The term *data hiding* is sometimes used as a synonym for encapsulation. The two terms are not the same, yet data hiding is an aggregate of encapsulation. Data hiding is one of the goals of encapsulation; it is the shielding of data from users of a class.

You will make use of the `Vehicle` class declared in How-To 3.1. If you did the example in How-To 3.1, change to the **VEHICLE** subdirectory and skip to step 3 in the "Steps" section that follows; otherwise, proceed to the "How It Works" section that follows.

Steps

1. If you did not do How-To 3.1, change to your base source directory and create a new subdirectory named **VEHICLE**. Start your source editor and type the following code into a file named **VEHICLE.H**:

```
// vehicle.h - this file contains a class
// declaration for the vehicle type.
class Vehicle
{
public:
    enum Switch { SWITCH_ON, SWITCH_OFF } ;
    Vehicle( ) ;
    ~Vehicle( ) ;

    bool powerSwitch( Switch onOrOff ) ;
    unsigned int accelerate( unsigned int amount ) ;
    unsigned int decelerate( unsigned int amount ) ;
    bool isMoving( void ) const ;
    unsigned int getSpeed( void ) const ;
    unsigned int setSpeed( unsigned int speedIn ) ;
protected:
    bool moving ;
private:
    unsigned int speed ;
} ;
```

Please note that if your compiler does not support the **bool** data type, you can add the following line of code at the top of this header file:

```
enum bool { false = 0, true } ;
```

2. If you did not do How-To 3.1, create a new file named **VEHICLE.CPP** and type the following code into that file:

```
// declaration of Vehicle
#include "vehicle.h"

Vehicle::Vehicle( ) :
    speed( 0 ), moving( false )
{
}

Vehicle::~Vehicle( )
{
    speed = 0;
    moving = false ;
}

bool Vehicle::powerSwitch( Switch onOrOff )
{
    bool on = false ;
```

```
            if( onOrOff == SWITCH_OFF )
            {
                speed = 0 ;
                moving = false ;
            }

            return( on ) ;
        }

        unsigned int Vehicle::accelerate( unsigned int amount )
        {
            speed += amount ;
            moving = true ;

            return( speed ) ;
        }

        unsigned int Vehicle::decelerate( unsigned int amount )
        {
            if( amount > speed )
                speed = 0 ;
            else
                speed -= amount ;

            moving = (speed == 0) ? false : true ;

            return( speed ) ;
        }

        bool Vehicle::isMoving( ) const
        {
            return( moving ) ;
        }

        unsigned int Vehicle::getSpeed( ) const
        {
            return( speed ) ;
        }

        unsigned int Vehicle::setSpeed( unsigned int speedIn )
        {
            speed = speedIn ;
            moving = true ;

            return( speed ) ;
        }
```

How It Works

There are two views of a class. One view is the public interface and the second is the private implementation. The interface is the contract that a class makes available to users of the class. It is the means by which a user of a class controls the state of an object. The implementation of a class is of no concern to users of a class. How an object actually alters its state should be shielded from the users of an object. There should be a clean separation of interface and implementation. This allows you to change the implementation without disturbing the interface to the users of the class.

The interface of the `Vehicle` class includes a constructor, destructor, and six member functions. Users of the class can only change the state of an instance of `Vehicle` through these six member functions. The user can not access the `protected` and `private` class members.

Each member function provides program logic to maintain the integrity of each instance of the class. This is the cornerstone of implementation—to maintain the integrity and state of each class instance. If the data members are exposed to users of the class, any instance of a class is in jeopardy. Moreover, if an instance of a class is in jeopardy, your application is in jeopardy.

The member functions `accelerate`, `decelerate`, and `setSpeed` are used by clients of the class to alter the state of the `speed` attribute. The implementation of each of these member functions should provide checks to ensure that the `speed` attribute is not corrupted or assigned a meaningless value. One safeguard is that the attribute is declared as an `unsigned int`. You have to ask yourself: "Does it make sense to have a speed of –23?" The `powerSwitch` member function is provided so that users of the class can start up or turn off an object. These member functions are commonly referred to as mutator functions because they alter the internal state of an object.

The remaining member functions, `isMoving` and `getSpeed`, are known as accessor member functions. These functions are provided so that users of the class can examine specified attributes of a class. You should only provide accessor functions that make sense as it might not be desirable for clients to examine every instance variable of a class. You should only return a copy of the instance variable; never return a pointer or reference to an internal variable. Otherwise, why make it `private`? If you return a pointer (or reference) to an internal variable, users of the class can manipulate the attribute directly. You might want to refer to How-To 1.5 concerning pointers.

As you can expect, the attributes of the class are hidden within the `protected` and `private` sections of the class declaration. The `moving` data member has `protected` visibility; this allows the class declaring it and any derived classes to access the object directly. Users of the class cannot access the data member directly; users can only access the variable through the class's interface, if so provided. The data member `speed` is declared with `private` visibility.

Although the `Vehicle` class does not demonstrate it, member functions can also be declared with `protected` or `private` visibility. Your classes might require member functions that implement internal functionality to support the class's interface. For example, you might have a **private** member function named meterGasoline or adjustAirMeter to support the **public** member function accelerate.

3.4 How do I...
Implement polymorphism in C++?

Problem

I am familiar with the term *polymorphism* and understand its concept. I have not implemented this feature in C++ and would like to know how.

Technique

This How-To demonstrates polymorphism by providing a simple program. Polymorphism is a powerful feature that is synonymous with dynamic function binding. Polymorphism is derived from Latin and means "many (poly) forms (morph)." It is a facility whereby a member function having the same signature in a hierarchy of classes, each having a different implementation, is dynamically bound (called) at runtime based on the type of the object.

Steps

1. Create a new subdirectory named **PCAR** and change to that subdirectory. Copy the files named **VEHICLE.H** and **VEHICLE.CPP** from the **VEHICLE** subdirectory (used in How-To 3.2).

2. Open up the header file **VEHICLE.H** in your editor and add the **virtual** keyword as shown in the following (the changes are bolded):

```
// vehicle.h - this file contains a class
// declaration for the vehicle type.

class Vehicle
{
public:
    enum Switch { SWITCH_ON, SWITCH_OFF } ;
    Vehicle( ) ;
    virtual ~Vehicle( ) ;

    virtual bool powerSwitch( Switch onOrOff ) ;
    virtual unsigned int accelerate( unsigned int amount ) ;
    virtual unsigned int decelerate( unsigned int amount ) ;
    virtual bool isMoving( void ) const ;
```

```
    virtual unsigned int getSpeed( void ) const ;
    virtual unsigned int setSpeed( unsigned int speedIn ) ;
protected:
    bool moving ;
private:
    unsigned int speed ;
} ;
```

Please note that if your compiler does not support the **bool** data type, you can add the following line of code at the top of this header file:

```
enum bool { false = 0, true } ;
```

3. Create a new file called **CAR.H** and type the following class declaration:

```
// car.h - this file contains a class declaration
// for the Car type, derived from Vehicle
#include "vehicle.h"

class Car : public Vehicle
{
public:
    enum { MAX_SPEED = 80 } ;
    Car( ) ;
    ~Car( ) ;

    unsigned int setSpeed( unsigned int speedIn ) ;
    virtual void steer( int degrees ) ;
    virtual void headLights( Switch onOrOff ) ;
private:
    int degrees ;
    Switch drivingLights ;
} ;
```

4. Create a file named **CAR.CPP** and type the following code:

```
// car.cpp implementation file
// for a Car; derived from Vehicle
#include "car.h"

Car::Car( ) : Vehicle(),
    degrees( 0 ), drivingLights( SWITCH_OFF )
{
}

Car::~Car( )
{
    degrees = 0 ;
    drivingLights = SWITCH_OFF ;
}

unsigned int Car::setSpeed( unsigned int speedIn )
{
    if( speedIn > MAX_SPEED )
        speedIn = MAX_SPEED ;
```

```
        Vehicle::setSpeed( speedIn ) ;
        moving = true ;

        return( Vehicle::getSpeed() ) ;
}

void Car::steer( int degrees )
{
    if( moving )
    {
        if( degrees == 0 )
            this->degrees = 0 ;
        else
            this->degrees += degrees ;
    }
}

void Car::headLights( Switch onOrOff )
{
    drivingLights = onOrOff ;
}
```

5. Save **CAR.CPP** and create a file named **MAIN.CPP**. This file should contain the following:

```
#include <iostream>
using namespace std ;
#include "car.h"

int main( )
{
    Vehicle *sporty = new Car() ;
    Car *luxury = new Car() ;

    sporty->setSpeed( 120 ) ;
    sporty->decelerate( 20 ) ;
    luxury->setSpeed( 35 ) ;
    luxury->steer( 20 ) ;
    luxury->headLights( Vehicle::SWITCH_ON ) ;
    luxury->accelerate( 15 ) ;

    cout << "sporty's speed : " << sporty->getSpeed() << endl ;
    cout << "pLuxury's speed: " << luxury->getSpeed() << endl ;

    if( sporty->isMoving( ) )
        cout << "sporty is moving" << endl ;
    else
        cout << "sporty isn't moving" << endl ;

    delete luxury ;
    delete sporty ;

    return 0 ;
}
```

6. Save MAIN.CPP and return to the command line. Next, compile and link MAIN.CPP, VEHICLE.CPP, and CAR.CPP as shown in the following:

```
gcc -c main.cpp vehicle.cpp car.cpp
```

If your compiler complains about the statement

```
#include <iostream>
```

comment out the **using** declaration following it and change the **#include** line to

```
#include <iostream.h>
```

7. Run the program; the output should be as follows:

```
sporty's speed : 60
pLuxury's speed: 50
sporty is moving
```

If you are using the DJGPP compiler, you might have to rename the executable from A.OUT to MAIN.EXE to execute the program.

How It Works

In the file VEHICLE.CPP, you prefixed the **virtual** keyword to Vehicle's destructor and six member functions. Only member functions and class destructor can be virtual; class data members can not be virtual. The C++ language uses the **virtual** keyword to specify a member function that is dynamically bound at runtime. Non-virtual member functions are statically bound; this means that the compiler knows the proper function to call at compile time. The call is made depending on the type of the reference. Conversely, a virtual member function call is determined at runtime. The member function that is called depends on the actual type of the object. Even if a pointer to the object is a base pointer of the object, the proper function will be called.

The virtual behavior of a member function is inherited by derived classes. If a member function is redeclared in a derived class, and that member function is declared **virtual** in the base class, the derived class member function is also **virtual**. Some class designers insist that the **virtual** keyword be applied to virtual member functions in derived classes. This is a visual reminder to developers that the member functions are indeed virtual.

Notice that in VEHICLE.H the **virtual** keyword is prefixed to each of the **public** member functions and the destructor. It is especially important that you apply the **virtual** keyword to the destructor of a class that will be inherited from. This guarantees the proper chain of destruction for the derived class object and for each base class object.

Now turn your attention to the declaration of the Car class found in CAR.H. The Car class is inherited from the Vehicle class. In the public section, you will find declarations for the constructor and destructor of the class.

The next declaration in the class

```
unsigned int setSpeed( unsigned int speedIn ) ;
```

redeclares the member function setSpeed found in the base class Vehicle. Remember that setSpeed is declared with the virtual keyword in Vehicle, so Car's setSpeed function is also virtual.

The next two member function declarations

```
virtual void steer( int degrees ) ;
virtual void headLights( Switch onOrOff ) ;
```

introduce two new member functions for class Car. Neither of these two member functions is declared in Vehicle. You do, however, declare them virtual so that any derived class of Car can use the dynamic binding mechanism.

The class declaration is finished with the declaration of two private data members named degrees and drivingLights. The degrees variable will maintain the state of degrees of steering and drivingLights will hold the state of the headlights (on or off).

You should familiarize yourself with the implementation of the Car class found in the CAR.CPP file. I will not detail the functionality of the Car class here, but will concentrate on the functionality of the main function found in MAIN.CPP.

Each of the first two statements in function main creates an instance of type Car as shown here:

```
Vehicle *sporty = new Car() ;
   Car *luxury = new Car() ;
```

Notice that the first statement declares sporty to be a pointer to a Vehicle object, whereas luxury is declared to be a pointer to a Car object. It is important to remember this as you move through the code. The new expression in each statement both creates an object of type Car and returns a pointer. The pointer returned to luxury is of type Car, but for sporty, the pointer returned is of type Vehicle.

Look at the next two lines of code:

```
sporty->setSpeed( 120 ) ;
sporty->decelerate( 20 ) ;
```

The first statement is a call to the member function `setSpeed` through the pointer `sporty`. Is the call made to the `setSpeed` member function defined in `Vehicle` or `Car`? You might think that because the pointer is of type `Vehicle` that `Vehicle`'s `setSpeed` function is called. However, in actuality, it is `Car`'s `setSpeed` function that is invoked. Remember that the `setSpeed` member function is declared `virtual` in the base class. The rule is this: A function is invoked based on the type of the object, not the reference (or pointer) to the object. This behavior is confirmed with the output of `sporty`'s speed, which is `60`. If `setSpeed` were called for the `Vehicle` class, the speed reported for `sporty` would be `100`.

Each of the next four lines of code that follow

```
luxury->setSpeed( 35 ) ;
luxury->steer( 20 ) ;
luxury->headLights( Vehicle::SWITCH_ON ) ;
luxury->accelerate( 15 ) ;
```

calls the specified member function of the `Car` class, with the exception of `accelerate`. The member function `accelerate` is not redeclared for the `Car` class, so it is `Vehicle::accelerate` that is invoked.

The two `cout` statements print out the speed value for each object. The `if-else` statement that follows reports whether the `sporty` object is moving.

Finally, the `delete` expression is called for each dynamically allocated object.

Comments

The power of polymorphism offers you the opportunity to manipulate more than one derived type object with just a base class pointer (or reference). Because you can refer to a derived type object using a base class pointer, you can write programs without regard to the actual object.

The following example should help to clarify the power of polymorphism. Suppose you create two new classes, `SportsCar` and `StationWagon`, both derived from `Car`. Obviously, an object of type `SportsCar` accelerates and decelerates differently than an object of type `StationWagon`. Without the use of polymorphism, a possible implementation would be as follows:

```
//...
if( typeid(StationWagon) == typeid(*pType) )
{
    StationWagon *p = (StationWagon *)pType ;
    p->steer( 14 ) ;
    p->accelerate( 5 ) ;
}
else if( typeid(SportsCar) == typeid(*pType) )
```

```
{
    SportsCar *p = (SportsCar *)pType ;
    p->steer( 25 ) ;
    p->accelerate( 20 ) ;
}
else if( typeid(Car) == typeid(*pType) )
{
    Car *p = (Car *)pType ;
    p->steer( 16 ) ;
    p->accelerate( 10 ) ;
}
```

The **typeid** operator is used to return a **const** reference to a **type_info** object. The argument to **typeid** is either a type name or expression. An expression can be a reference or pointer of some type. If the expression is a reference or pointer, the **type_info** reference reveals the actual type referred to, not the type of the reference (or pointer). You can use the **operator==** and **operator!=** member functions to determine the equality, or inequality, of two **type_info** objects.

Consider what would be required if you added another type derived from **Car** to your hierarchy. You would have to visit all runtime type information (RTTI) logic, make appropriate enhancements, and recompile the whole affair. As the name suggests, RTTI is used to retrieve information about an object at runtime. The runtime identification mechanism is implemented with respect to polymorphic types. This implies that a class must contain at least one virtual function. The performance and readability penalty will also be high with all the **if-else**s to step through. Virtual functions are a more elegant solution to this type of runtime logic, as you have seen in this How-To.

COMPLEXITY
INTERMEDIATE

3.5 How do I...
Implement static members of a class?

Problem

I have heard that class members can be declared with the **static** keyword. I would like to know when to use a static member for a class and the syntax required for declaring one.

Technique

In this How-To, a program will be used to demonstrate the use of a static data member of a class. Static data members can be quite useful for certain programming situations. In this How-To, you will discover one such use with the program provided.

Steps

1. Change to the base directory and create a new subdirectory named STATIC.

2. Start your code editor and type the following code into a file named STATIC.CPP:

```cpp
// static.cpp - this file contains a class
// that utilizes a static member.
#include <iostream>
using namespace std ;

class Base
{
public:
    Base( )  { ++instanceCnt ; }
    ~Base( ) { --instanceCnt ; }
    int count( ) const { return( instanceCnt ) ; }
private:
    static int instanceCnt ;
} ;

int Base::instanceCnt = 0 ;

int main( )
{
    Base *b[ 10 ] ;
    int i = 0 ;

    for( i = 0; i < 10; i++ )
        b[ i ] = new Base ;

    cout << "Instance count #1: " << b[ 0 ]->count( ) << endl ;

    for( i = 0; i < 9; i++ )
        delete b[ i ] ;

    cout << "Instance count #2: " << b[ 0 ]->count( ) << endl ;
    delete b[ 0 ] ;

    return 0 ;
}
```

3. Save STATIC.CPP and return to the command line. Next, compile and link STATIC.CPP as in the following example:

```
gcc -c static.cpp
```

If your compiler complains about the statement

```
#include <iostream>
```

comment out (or remove) the **using** directive following it and change the #include line to

```
#include <iostream.h>
```

4. Run the program; the output should be as follows:

```
Instance count #1: 10
Instance count #2: 1
```

If you are using the DJGPP compiler, you might have to rename the executable from A.OUT to STATIC.EXE in order to execute the program.

How It Works

Let's begin by examining the declaration of **Base** in **STATIC.CPP**. The first declaration in the class is the default constructor, as shown here:

```
Base( ) { ++instanceCnt ; }
```

The constructor is defined as an inline member function because its definition occurs inside the class's declaration. The constructor contains only a single statement, incrementing the static member variable **instanceCnt**.

The next declaration, which is also an inline member function, is the destructor. The logic found in the destructor is the inverse of the constructor: to decrement the static data member **instanceCnt**.

The third declaration

```
int count( ) const { return( instanceCnt ) ; }
```

is also the definition of a **const** member function that returns the value contained in **instanceCnt**. This member function is also considered for inlining because its definition occurs inside the class declaration.

Rounding out the class declaration, in the **private** section, you find the declaration of a static member, as shown here:

```
static int instanceCnt ;
```

This declaration is no different from any other data member declaration, except for the **static** keyword prefix. What is the difference between a static and non-static data member? Only a single instance will exist for a static data member at runtime, no matter how many objects are created for the class. For non-static data members, a copy will exist for every object instance. Data members that are non-static are also referred to as instance variables. This suggests that each instance of a class will get its own unique set of non-static data members. The opposite occurs with static data members—no matter if there is one class object or thirty objects at runtime, a single copy of each static data member will exist for all objects instantiated. All instances of a class share any static data members declared.

The next line of code in the file

```
int Base::instanceCnt = 0 ;
```

defines and initializes the static data member. All static data members of a class must be defined outside of the class declaration. Notice that the name of the class followed by the scope resolution operator is given, in addition to the name of the static data member.

The first statement within the **main** function declares an array of 10 pointers of type **Base**. The second statement within **main** defines **i** as an integer variable.

Next, a **for** loop is introduced. Ten objects of type **Base** are created in the free store. A pointer to each of those objects is accumulated in the array named **b**.

The next line of code

```
cout << "Instance count #1: " << b[ 0 ]->count( ) << endl ;
```

prints out the contents of the static data member. Moving through the code, you find a second **for** loop. This loop is used to deallocate the objects that were allocated in the previous loop. The difference is that the loop only counts up to ten because you want to leave one object around for the next program statement:

```
cout << "Instance count #2: " << b[ 0 ]->count( ) << endl ;
```

The value 1 is printed, as expected. The line that follows this **cout** statement deletes the last remaining object.

Comments

Class member functions can also be declared **static**. A static member function can be invoked, even if there are no instances of the class where it is declared. The only data members that a static member function can access are static data members because a static member function is not associated with any particular instance of a class. The following class declaration contains a declaration and the definition of a static member function:

```
class Base
{
public:
    static int count(void) ;
} ;
int Base::count( )
{
//...
}
```

Notice that the **static** keyword is not used at the definition of the member function. Because **count** is declared with **public** visibility, it can be invoked as shown in the following code snippet:

```
int main()
{
    Base::count() ;
//...
}
```

Because it belongs to a class, a static data member does not pollute the global namespace. This helps to reduce name clashes that might otherwise occur. You should not define a static data member inside the header file containing the class declaration; define it in the implementation file.

PART II
DATA STRUCTURES

STRUCTURE OF
CLASSES

STRUCTURES VERSUS CLASSES

How do I...

4.1 Create my own data type?

4.2 Hide my data from external programs?

4.3 Use encapsulation? What steps are required to encapsulate data?

4.4 Create my own operators?

4.5 Overload relational and equality operators?

4.6 Provide access to encapsulated data to certain classes?

4.7 Maintain global data in my program?

4.8 Know when I should use structures and when I should use classes?

One of the most important things to understand in C++ programming is the usage of classes. Classes can be thought of as the fundamental building blocks of object-oriented programming. The notion of classes is a new one for C programmers. Even if they know the language syntax it is sometimes hard to get a proper understanding of the new programming paradigm. Data encapsulation and private and public members can confuse even an experienced programmer.

Structures in C (and C++) provide a powerful ability to create new data types. Using standard data types and other programming constructs, one can combine them in a very sophisticated structure. Programmer's skills can be proven by an appropriate structural description of data. Combining logically connected data in one set makes programs more readable and easier to maintain. This is very important because it leads to decreased maintenance costs.

A very confusing feature of C++ is that there is no technical difference between classes and structures. They differ only in default access rights to their members. Therefore, the question "What should I use: classes or structures?" becomes very important.

This chapter is intended to answer that question and describe the process of encapsulation by showing it step by step. Encapsulation is one of the main features of object-oriented programming languages, and it is discussed in detail in order to show how you can use it to create your own data types or maintain global variables.

Other class features closely related to encapsulation are discussed. This chapter shows how you can overload operators to make the code more readable and create friend functions for related classes.

4.1 Create My Own Data Type

Standard C++ data types such as `int`, `char`, `float`, and `double` never satisfied programmers. Maintaining date and time as a variable of one `DateTime` type instead of using 5 or 6 different integers was always a very convenient approach. This How-To is an introduction to C++ structures, and it shows how to create, copy, and pass structures as function parameters, as well as return them as function results.

4.2 Hide My Data from External Programs

Classes are one of the most important features of C++ programming. In fact, C++ was originally called "C with classes." This How-To explains how to create classes using the idea of encapsulation. The process of the `stack` class creation is described in detail. The example also shows that changing a member function's definition does not result in changes of the calling program.

4.3 Use Encapsulation? What Steps Are Required to Encapsulate Data

A common mistake some programmers make is thinking that encapsulation can provide security for class data. The main idea of encapsulation is to improve the code by making it simpler and more readable. This How-To uses the `employee` class to show step by step how to implement encapsulation.

4.4 Create My Own Operators

Creating new data types is a process of describing objects to store data as well as methods to operate on that data. When a class is implemented as a new data type, you create member functions to support data operations. However sometimes modifying the + operator (via operator overloading) instead of creating an Add function can dramatically improve the code. This How-To describes how and when a user can use operator overloading.

4.5 Overload Relational and Equality Operators

Operator overloading is one of the very attractive features of C++. Almost all C++ operators can be overloaded and significantly increase the language capabilities. This How-To describes the basic concept of operator overloading using the example of relational and equality operators.

4.6 Provide Access to Encapsulated Data to Certain Classes

Encapsulation is a powerful methodology that makes objects independent and less vulnerable. In the ideal-world model, you could make all objects talk to each other by means of public methods. However, in real life you often have to allow certain classes access to private data of another class. To help do this, C++ supports the concept of friend functions and friend classes. This How-To describes how to use them.

4.7 Maintain Global Data in My Program

Old-style programmers often ask: "Should I use global data in my programs?" The question is very important because even in a well-structured program that follows a modular approach, data can be shared by many modules. Making the data global was a standard technique of procedural programming for years. This How-To shows how to create global data using classes and encapsulation.

4.8 Know When I Should Use Structures and When I Should Use Classes

The only difference between classes and structures in C++ is the default access to their members. It can be confusing for C programmers who used structures very extensively. This How-To creates an example of a linked list implementation. This example illustrates a common approach for using structures to store a new data type and for using classes as programming units.

4.1 How do I...
Create my own data type?

Problem

Every time I need to use dates in my program I experience a problem working with three different entities: days, months and years. It works fine if I use them separately such as when I want to present numeric values based on month names. However, it is too boring to write three statements if I need to copy one date to another date or if I need to pass dates as parameters to a function. Can I use the date variables both as three separate entities and as one entity depending on my needs?

Technique

To combine different variables into one data type in order to maintain them together as a unit, you can use structures. Data combined into a structure can be utilized as separate variables, too. By using structures in C and C++, you can create your own data types. C programmers already know how to use structures and the **struct** keyword in their programs. In C++, the syntax of structures is a little different than in the C programming language.

Steps

1. Determine the variables

When designing a program, you have to analyze the data that you are going to use in that program. Any data type is described by the data range it can handle and by the operations that can be performed on the data. Assume in this example that you are creating a big program that will calculate date difference, display the dates and the number of days from the beginning of the year, construct the dates in future based on the current date, and do a lot of other data manipulation. The program is going to work with days, months, and years, and that means it needs these three variables at a minimum.

2. Determine the variable data types

Days in a month range from 1 to 31, months range from 1 to 12, and the years range depends on the application. Assume you are writing a business application that handles dates from 1900 to 2100. Note that you can define the variables as integers, floats, char arrays, or use other data types as well. The decision about the data type is often based on the operations you are going to perform. The very first thing you are going to do is to display the dates; then you definitely want to calculate the dates by adding or subtracting a certain number of days to the dates.

Because we don't want to confuse ourselves with decimal points and because there is no need to use them, we are not going to use **floats**. We won't use strings because of the addition and subtraction that we want to perform. It's much simpler to add integers than strings, isn't it? Therefore, the logic forces us to select an **integer** data type for all variables.

Now we can specify the variables:

```
int ddate;
int mmonth;
int yyear;
```

3. Using the variables separately

Let's assume that our first task is to calculate the date next to the given date and to display it. We assume that a user does not make mistakes in entering the data, so we don't have to trap the mistakes.

```
// incdate.cpp
// The program increments a given date
// and displays the result

#include <iostream.h>

int main()
{

    int DaysInMonth[12] = {31, 28, 31, 30, 31, 30,
                           31, 31, 30, 31, 30, 31};
    int LeapYear;

    int dday1, dday2;
    int mmonth1, mmonth2;
    int yyear1, yyear2;

// Enter a base date
    cout << "Enter day (integer): ";
    cin >> dday1;
    cout << "Enter month (integer): ";
    cin >> mmonth1;
    cout << "Enter year (integer): ";
    cin >> yyear1;

// Calculate the next date
    if ((yyear1 % 4) == 0) LeapYear = true;
    dday2 = dday1+ 1;

    if ((LeapYear) && (dday1 == 29) && (mmonth1 == 2))
        { dday2 = 1; mmonth2= 3; yyear1 = yyear1;}
    else if (dday2 > DaysInMonth[mmonth1 - 1])
```

```
        {
        mmonth2 = mmonth1+ 1;
        dday2 = 1;
        }
    else
        mmonth2 = mmonth1;

    if (mmonth2 == 13 )
        {
        mmonth2 = 1;
        yyear2 = yyear1 + 1;
        }
    else
        yyear2 = yyear1;

// Display the result
    cout << "The next date after " << dday1 << "/" << mmonth1;
    cout << "/" << yyear1 << " is " << dday2 << "/" << mmonth2;
    cout << "/" << yyear2 << endl;

    return 0;
```

4. First step is to combine the data

The previous program works just fine if we don't have to do anything else. In an actual application, every step increases the complexity of the program and makes it less readable. The first reasonable step in practicing better coding is to combine the variables into the structures so we don't have to consider them as separate entities.

Let's rewrite the program using structures.

```
// incdate1.cpp
// The program increments a given date
// and displays the result

#include <iostream.h>

int main()
{

    int DaysInMonth[12] = {31, 28, 31, 30, 31, 30,
                           31, 31, 30, 31, 30, 31};
    int LeapYear;

    struct DDate{
        int dday;
        int mmonth;
        int yyear;
        };

    DDate ddate1, ddate2;

// Enter a base date
    cout << "Enter day (integer): ";
```

```
        cin >> ddate1.dday;
        cout << "Enter month (integer): ";
        cin >> ddate1.mmonth;
        cout << "Enter year (integer): ";
        cin >> ddate1.yyear;

// Calculate the next date
        if ((ddate1.yyear % 4) == 0) LeapYear = true;
        ddate2.dday = ddate1.dday+ 1;

        if ((LeapYear) && (ddate1.dday == 29) && (ddate1.mmonth == 2))
            { ddate2.dday = 1; ddate2.mmonth= 3; ddate2.yyear =
            ➥ddate1.yyear;}
    else if ((LeapYear) && (ddate1.dday == 28) &&
➥(ddate1.mmonth == 2))
            { ddate2.dday = 29; ddate2.mmonth= 2; ddate2.yyear =
            ➥ddate1.yyear;}
        else if (ddate2.dday > DaysInMonth[ddate1.mmonth - 1])
            {
            ddate2.mmonth = ddate1.mmonth+ 1;
            ddate2.dday = 1;
            }
        else
            ddate2.mmonth = ddate1.mmonth;

        if (ddate2.mmonth == 13 )
            {
            ddate2.mmonth = 1;
            ddate2.yyear = ddate1.yyear + 1;
            }
        else
            ddate2.yyear = ddate1.yyear;

// Display the result
        cout << "The next date after " << ddate1.dday << "/" <<
        ➥ddate1.mmonth;
        cout << "/" << ddate1.yyear << " is " << ddate2.dday << "/" <<
        ➥ddate2.mmonth;
        cout << "/" << ddate2.yyear << endl;

        return 0;
}
```

Please note that you don't have to use word **struct** in the **DDate** type declaration as you did in C.

In the preceding example the structure is defined by

```
struct DDate{
    int dday;
    int mmonth;
    int yyear;
    };
```

Please note the semicolon at the end of the **struct** definition. This is one of the very few places in C++ where a semicolon is used after curly braces.

5. Create functions

Did we make the program more readable? Did we save a few lines in the code? I doubt it. What's the advantage of using structures?

The advantage will appear when we start to extend our program. Therefore, the next thing we are going to do is create functions in our program. The first function will enable the entering data, the second function will display dates, and the third function will calculate the next date based on a given date.

```cpp
// incdate2.cpp
// The program increments a given date
// and displays the result

#include <iostream.h>

struct DDate{
  int dday;
  int mmonth;
  int yyear;
};

DDate GetDate(void);
void DisplayDate(DDate);
DDate GetNextDate(DDate);

int main()
{

    DDate ddate1, ddate2;

// Enter a base date
    ddate1= GetDate();
// Calculate the next date
    ddate2= GetNextDate(ddate1);
// Display the result
    cout << "The next date after ";
    DisplayDate(ddate1);
    cout << " is ";
    DisplayDate(ddate2);
    cout << endl;

    return 0;
}

// GetDate function gets the date into
// a DDate variable
DDate GetDate(void)
{
    DDate ddate;

    cout << "Enter day (integer): ";
    cin >> ddate.dday;
    cout << "Enter month (integer): ";
```

```
        cin >> ddate.mmonth;
        cout << "Enter year (integer): ";
        cin >> ddate.yyear;

        return ddate;
    }

    // Displays a variable of DDate type
    void DisplayDate(DDate ddate)
    {
        cout << ddate.dday << "/" << ddate.mmonth << "/" <<
        ➥ddate.yyear;

    }

    // Calculates the next date
    DDate GetNextDate(DDate ddate)
    {
        DDate ddateNext;

        int DaysInMonth[12] = {31, 28, 31, 30, 31, 30,
                               31, 31, 30, 31, 30, 31};
        int LeapYear;


        if ((ddate.yyear % 4) == 0) LeapYear = true;
        ddateNext.dday = ddate.dday+ 1;

        if ((LeapYear) && (ddate.dday == 29) && (ddate.mmonth == 2))
            { ddateNext.dday = 1; ddateNext.mmonth= 3;
            ➥ddateNext.yyear = ddate.yyear;}
    else if ((LeapYear) && (ddate1.dday == 28) &&
    ➥(ddate1.mmonth == 2))
            { ddate2.dday = 29; ddate2.mmonth= 2; ddate2.yyear =
            ➥ddate1.yyear;}
        else if (ddateNext.dday > DaysInMonth[ddate.mmonth - 1])
            {
            ddateNext.mmonth = ddate.mmonth+ 1;
            ddateNext.dday = 1;
            }
        else
            ddateNext.mmonth = ddate.mmonth;

        if (ddateNext.mmonth == 13 )
            {
            ddateNext.mmonth = 1;
            ddateNext.yyear = ddate.yyear + 1;
            }
        else
            ddateNext.yyear = ddate.yyear;

        return ddateNext;
    }
```

Now we can say that we created our own data type: **DDate**. We can define
variables of this data type, use this data type in function definitions, and
we can pass parameters of this data type to the functions.

In fact, as long as we work with the main program we even don't need to know what is included in this data type.

6. Using the assignment (=) operator

A big advantage of using structures is that we can assign one variable of a new type to another variable of the same type just by writing

```
a = b;
```

where **a** and **b** are variables of the same structure. For example, let's write a program that takes a **DDate** variable, copies it to another variable, and displays both variables. We are going to use **GetDate** and **DisplayDate** functions from the previous example.

```cpp
// assignd.cpp
// The program increments a given date
// and displays the result

#include <iostream.h>

struct DDate{
  int dday;
  int mmonth;
  int yyear;
};

DDate GetDate(void);
void DisplayDate(DDate);

int main()
{

    DDate ddate1, ddate2;

// Enter a base date

    ddate1= GetDate();
// copy ddate1 to ddate2
    ddate2= ddate1;
// Display the result
    cout << "The first date is ";
    DisplayDate(ddate1);
    cout << endl;
    cout << "The second date is ";
    DisplayDate(ddate2);
    cout << endl;

    return 0;
```

```
    }

    // GetDate function gets the date into
    // a DDate variable
    DDate GetDate(void)
    {
        DDate ddate;

        cout << "Enter day (integer): ";
        cin >> ddate.dday;
        cout << "Enter month (integer): ";
        cin >> ddate.mmonth;
        cout << "Enter year (integer): ";
        cin >> ddate.yyear;

        return ddate;
    }

    // Dispalys a variable of DDate type
    void DisplayDate(DDate ddate)
    {
        cout << ddate.dday << "/" << ddate.mmonth << "/" <<
        ➥ddate.yyear;

    }
```

Comments

Creating a C++ structure creates a new data type that can be accessed by its own name, such as **DDate** in the previous example. When declaring a new structure, you don't have to use the **struct** keyword as in C. The individual elements of a structure are called *structure members* and can be accessed by the structure member (.) operator (dot operator).

Structures are very helpful if you want to logically combine different variables to use them as a set. They are similar to arrays in the sense that both arrays and structures are sets of variables stored under the same name. However, arrays are aggregates of the elements of the same nature and therefore the same data type. Structure members usually represent data of a different nature and can have different types.

You can create many instances of the same structure just as you can create many variables of the same type. You can assign objects of structure types to other objects of the same type, you can pass them as function parameters, or return them as a function result.

4.2 How do I...
Hide my data from external programs?

Problem

I want to create functions that use my own data types. For example, I often use stacks and I want other modules working with my module not to have the ability to change my implementation of stacks. In other words, I want my implementation to be hidden from external modules.

Technique

In C++, you can create your own data type (such as a stack or a queue) and specify operations on this data type. To make the specification of the data type complete, you can hide all internal information in a class.

Steps

1. Define data

The purpose of this example is to create a new data type to maintain stacks. As you might know, a stack is a data structure with a very simple access rule: last in, first out. Data elements stored in a stack should be of the same type (however, the elements can be of a simple standard data type like integer, or they can have a complex data type like pointer to structures). Data elements are stored in a stack in a linear fashion, one by one, and the stack capacity is predefined. Figure 4.1 shows the stack operations.

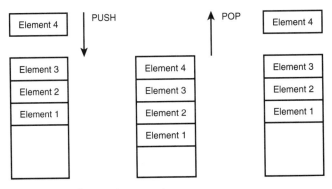

Figure 4.1 The stack operations.

We are going to start with a stack that handles characters. The stack length will be 256, and will be implemented as an array. This means that our data will be described as an array of characters:

```
char SStackBuffer[256];
```

2. Specify functions according to the operations

The next step will describe the operations that we can perform on the stack and the functions that we are going to implement.

Traditionally we consider a stack to be a data storage structure where we can push the data in or pop the data out. Usually, when we think of pushing the data into the stack, we assume that the other elements are moving to the stack bottom. When we imagine popping an element from the stack, we assume that the other elements are moving to the top. However, this is not a necessary behavior. The only thing we care of when implementing the stack is to follow the last in, first out (LIFO) rule.

To push and pop elements we are going to create two functions, **Push** and **Pop**. These functions' declarations are as follows:

```
// The Push method pushes the c character into the stack.
// It returns 1 if success.
// It returns 0 if failure (the stack is full).
   int Push (char c);
```

```
// The Pop method moves the top character from the stack
// to the c character.
// It returns 1 if success.
// It returns 0 if failure (the stack is empty).
   int Pop (char& c);
```

We constructed the stack as an array and declared two functions to support the stack operations. However, the two functions bring up two problems: What should the program do if we try to push an element into the stack and there is no space for it? Also, what should the program do if we try to move the top element out of the empty stack?

These questions result in two more functions, **IsEmpty** and **IsFull**:

```
// The IsEmpty method determines if the stack is empty.
// If yes, it returns 1 (true).
// If no, it returns 0 (false).
   int IsEmpty(void);
```

```
// The IsFull method determines if the stack is full.
// If yes, it returns 1 (true).
// If no, it returns 0 (false).
   int IsFull(void);
```

3. Create a class

Classes are the core of C++ programming. In the very beginning of C++ history, Bjarne Stroustrup, the author of the language, called C++ "C with classes." We can consider classes as new data types at least at this stage. Let's create a class declaration for our stack and learn a little about class components.

```cpp
// This is a stack class
//

class SStack
{

private:

char SStackBuffer[256];
int CurrentElement;

public:

    SStack(void);              // Constructor
    ~SStack(void);             // Destructor

// The Push method pushes the c character into the stack.
// It returns 1 if success.
// It returns 0 if failure (the stack is full).
    int Push (char c);

// The Pop method moves the top character from the stack
// to the c character.
// It returns 1 if success.
// It returns 0 if failure (the stack is empty).
    int Pop (char& c);

// The IsEmpty method determines if the stack is empty.
// If yes, it returns 1 (true).
// If no, it returns 0 (false).
    int IsEmpty(void);

// The IsFull method determines if the stack is full.
// If yes, it returns 1 (true).
// If no, it returns 0 (false).
    int IsFull(void);

};
```

The preceding code represents a class declaration. This is very similar to structure declarations (and, in C++, classes and structures differ only in default access rights to the data). Let's see how the class is constructed.

The **SStack** class specifies data members

```cpp
char SStackBuffer[256];
int CurrentElement;
```

and member functions

```
int Push (char c);
int Pop (char& c);
int IsEmpty(void);
int IsFull(void);
```

The main concept behind classes is the combination into one single entity of data and algorithms that process the data. The data items are called *data members* and the algorithms are called *member functions*. In other books you can find names such as methods and function members for member functions.

There are two new functions in the class:

```
SStack(void);            // Constructor
~SStack(void);           // Destructor
```

SStack() and ~SStack() are the constructor and destructor of the class. The name of the constructor is the same as the name of the class itself. The name of the destructor is the name of the class starting with a tilde (~). The functions play a special role. After an instance of the class is created, the constructor is executed. When a class object finishes its life cycle, the destructor is called. At this point, we are not going to define the functions, we just declared them for future use.

In this class declaration we use two access control keywords: `private` and `public`. By default, all data members and member functions are private. However, including the `private` keyword in the code makes it more readable and structured. Figure 4.2 specifies these important features of classes.

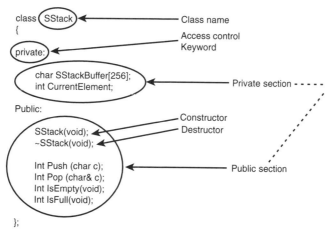

Figure 4.2 Important features of classes.

Now we are ready to answer the question of this section: "How do I hide my data?" The answer is to make the data private and create public functions to access the data. Other programs should know nothing about the implementation of the **SStack** data type and consider the data type as data storage with a few possible operations on it.

The methodology of hiding data inside classes is called *encapsulation*. One of the main components of encapsulation is to allow objects direct access only to their own data. The objects' communication is shown in Figure 4.3.

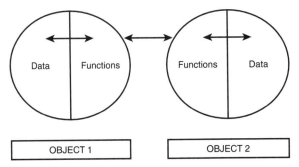

Figure 4.3 Encapsulation.

4. Class implementation

To code actual class functions, we have to design the logic of maintaining the stack. Because we decided to use an array for the stack implementation, we are going to change the strategy of actual elements moving inside the stack. Figure 4.4 shows the implementation of the stack.

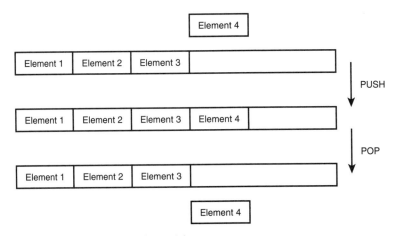

Figure 4.4 Implementation with arrays.

The following code defines the stack class:

```
// Class declaration
// file stack.h

class SStack
{

private:

char SStackBuffer[256];
int CurrentElement;

public:

    SStack(void);              // Constructor
    ~SStack(void);             // Destructor

    int Push (char c);
    int Pop (char& c);
    int IsEmpty(void);
    int IsFull(void);

};
```

The preceding code is the class declaration. It is a well-known practice to separate class declarations in header files. In this example the code is located in the file stack.h.

```
// Class definition
// file stack.cpp

#include "stack.h"

// Constructor

SStack::SStack(void)
{
    CurrentElement = -1;
}
// Destructor
// is empty yet

SStack::~SStack(void)
{

}

// The IsEmpty method determines if the stack is empty.
// If yes, it returns 1 (true).
// If no, it returns 0 (false).

int SStack::IsEmpty(void)
{
if (CurrentElement < 0) return 1;
else return 0;
```

```
}

// The IsFull method determines if the stack is full.
// If yes, it returns 1 (true).
// If no, it returns 0 (false).

int SStack::IsFull(void)
{
    if (CurrentElement >= 256) return 1;
    else return 0;
}

// The Push method pushes the c character into the stack.
// It returns 1 if success.
// It returns 0 if failure (the stack is full).

int SStack::Push (char c)
{
    if (IsFull()) return 0;
    SStackBuffer[++CurrentElement]= c;
    return 1;
}

// The Pop method moves the top character from the stack
// to the c character.
// It returns 1 if success.
// It returns 0 if failure (the stack is empty).
int SStack::Pop (char& c)
{
    if (IsEmpty()) return 0;
    c= SStackBuffer[CurrentElement--];
    return 1;
}
```

The preceding code is the class implementation (or class definition). Note that we used the scope resolution operator (::) to define the member functions in our class.

The **SStack** constructor initializes the **CurrentElement** variable. The variable is intended to handle the number of the element most recently pushed into the stack. The variable is initialized with **–1** to show that at the very beginning there is no current element in the stack.

The **IsFull** and **IsEmpty** functions check whether the **CurrentElement** is within the limits from 0 to 255. They are executed in **Push** and **Pop** functions, respectively.

5. Test the class

To test that our class works correctly, we are going to write a small program that displays **Hello, world!** in the reverse order. Please note that we are creating the program in a separate file. Therefore, we included **stack.h** in the program.

```
// Test program for the stack class
// the program displays "Hello, world!"
// in the reverse order

#include <iostream.h>
#include <string.h>

#include "stack.h"

int main()
{
    unsigned int i;

    SStack TestStack;
    char buffer[80];
    memset (buffer, 0x00, 80);
    strcpy (buffer, "Hello, world!");

    for (i= 0; i <strlen (buffer); i++)
        TestStack.Push(buffer[i]);

    i= 0;
    while (!TestStack.IsEmpty())
        TestStack.Pop(buffer[i++]);

    cout << buffer << endl;

    return 0;
}
```

The program simply takes the string **Hello, world!**, pushes it into the stack, and then moves the stack elements into the buffer in the reverse order. If you run this program the line

```
!dlrow ,olleH
```

will appear on the screen.

The **main** program shows the result of the encapsulation. The program doesn't know anything about the array implementation of the stack. Because the data is hidden in the class using the **private** keyword, the **main** program can't see the data. Also, because the member functions **Pop** and **Push** are the only tools to access the stack (and we took care of the **IsFull** and **IsEmpty** situations), no external program can change or destroy the data in the class.

6. More advantages of encapsulation

I personally don't like the implementation of the stack that we've created. The array that we defined in the class is a good approach if we don't want to extend the stack. Currently we are limited to 256 elements of our stack. What would we do if we needed a bigger stack? In that case, we would have to change this number and recompile the class. This is too much of a hassle when working with a big project.

Let's create a more flexible class and change the array to a string with nonfixed length. The actual length will be passed from the main program as a parameter to the class constructor.

```
// Class declaration
// file stack.h

class SStack
{

private:

int SStackLength;
char* SStackBuffer;
int CurrentElement;

public:

    SStack(int IniLength=256);          // Constructor
    ~SStack(void);                      // Destructor

    int Push (char c);
    int Pop (char& c);
    int IsEmpty(void);
    int IsFull(void);

};
```

In the class declaration we changed the data section. We added one more variable that will represent the length of the stack and changed the array to the pointer to a string of characters.

In the function section we changed the constructor function. It will accept the length of the stack defaulting to 256.

To support the new stack implementation, we have to change the class definition.

```
// Class definition
// file stack1.cpp

#include "stack1.h"

// Constructor

SStack::SStack(int IniLength)
{

    CurrentElement = -1;
    if (IniLength < 256) SStackLength = 256;
    else SStackLength = IniLength;
```

```
    SStackBuffer = new char [SStackLength];
}
// Destructor
// is empty yet

SStack::~SStack(void)
{
    delete [] SStackBuffer;
}

// The IsEmpty method determines if the stack is empty.
// If yes, it returns 1 (true).
// If no, it returns 0 (false).

int SStack::IsEmpty(void)
{
if (CurrentElement < 0) return 1;
else return 0;

}

// The IsFull method determines if the stack is full.
// If yes, it returns 1 (true).
// If no, it returns 0 (false).

int SStack::IsFull(void)
{
    if (CurrentElement >= SStackLength) return 1;
    else return 0;
}

// The Push method pushes the c character into the stack.
// It returns 1 if success.
// It returns 0 if failure (the stack is full).

int SStack::Push (char c)
{
    if (IsFull()) return 0;
    *SStackBuffer++= c;
    CurrentElement++;
    return 1;
}

// The Pop method moves the top character from the stack
// to the c character.
// It returns 1 if success.
// It returns 0 if failure (the stack is empty).
int SStack::Pop (char& c)
{
    if (IsEmpty()) return 0;
    c= *--SStackBuffer;
    CurrentElement--;
    return 1;
}
```

The most important changes in the class were made to create the buffer dynamically in the constructor using the **new** operator and destroy the buffer in the destructor using the **delete** operator.

7. Should we change the **main** function?

No, we will not have to change the **main** function in our example.

The changes that we have made to the class implementation are internal changes. A user of the class usually doesn't know how the class is implemented. Because the data is hidden, and the function declarations haven't been changed, an external program remains the same.

The changes that we made to the class constructor don't change the **main** program because we allow a default initialization value for the stack length. However, because the class provides us now with a more powerful constructor, we can select the length of the class ourselves in the external program. For example

```
SStack TestStack(800);
```

would initialize a stack 800 characters long.

Comments

Classes provide us with a lot of powerful features to do object-oriented programming. We can encapsulate data and create member functions for the data access. This produces modular code and allows parts of the code to be changed without redesigning the whole program.

Interestingly, that C++ syntax allows us to use structures exactly as we use classes. The only difference between classes and structures is that the default access is **private** in classes and **public** in structures. Basically, the question "When do I use structures and when do I use classes?" is a question of programming style. The most common programming style is to use structures only for pure data handling and for creating new data types without specifying operations on them. If you create a program that uses member functions in structures, it will work but other programmers will have a tougher time maintaining it.

Encapsulation is a methodology that hides data in classes, allowing access to that data only by functions defined in the class. The functions also provide necessary operations on the data, thereby increasing the power of classes as new data types. Classes can be distributed as class libraries in an object form with the interface defined by the member functions.

4.3 How do I...
Use encapsulation? What steps are required to encapsulate data?

Problem

I want to hide data in my class library in a way that nobody has access to it. How can I use encapsulation to make sure that nobody will be able to change or destroy my data?

Technique

A very important thing to understand is that hiding data from other programmers working on the same project is not always a wise choice. This can result in making the code more complicated and therefore less maintainable. Encapsulation does not put vulnerable data in restricted memory areas; it just hides the data at compilation time.

Another very important thing to understand is that the intention to hide the data from other people is wrong. There is no technique on the language level for securing the data, and encapsulation was invented to make the code more readable and object-oriented. The process of data encapsulation has a few steps.

We are going to give an example of encapsulation by creating an `employee` data type for a business application.

Steps

1. Determine the data

Creating a new data type involves describing components of the data in the application. If we decide to create a new `employee` data type, we have to specify the information about employees that our application needs.

First of all, we need `FirstName` and `LastName` fields. The fields can be character strings and be defined later in the code or they can be character arrays with fixed lengths. In our example, we'll use arrays to make the code a little simpler. Another group of fields that we definitely need is a `BirthDate` (didn't I say that we would create an application for Human Resources?) For the date of birth, we are going to use the `DDate` structure we defined in How-To 4.1. We will also add a last piece of data named `Salary` that we can declare as `int`.

The data can be declared as shown in the following:

```
struct DDate{
    int dday;
    int mmonth;
    int yyear;
    };
char FirstName[35];
char LastName[35];
DDate BirthDate;
int Salary;
```

2. Structures or classes?

Now we have to decide what we are going to use. If we were not going to encapsulate the data, or if we just needed the data for keeping the employee information, or if we were not going to create functions for handling the data, it would be reasonable to use structures:

```
struct DDate{
    int dday;
    int mmonth;
    int yyear;
    };
struct Employee{
char FirstName[35];
    char LastName[35];
DDate BirthDate;
    int Salary;
    };
```

However, we want to hide the data using encapsulation and create functions to access the data. Therefore, we are going to create a class for supporting the new data type. This is a common practice and following it makes your code more understandable for other programmers.

3. Create access functions

Because we are going to hide the employee data from other program modules, it is important to provide functions to access the data. Assuming that the only operation we want to make the data visible is displaying the data, we declare the appropriate function:

```
void Display(void);
```

The function will be a member of the class that handles the employee data, so it does not need parameters.

Another function should enable the addition of the employee data; for example, by typing it on the keyboard. We declare the **SetEmployee** function for this purpose:

```
void SetEmployee(void);
```

When we hide data by encapsulation, we often provide functions to access the data: a function for reading the data and/or a function for setting the data.

4. Declaring a class

To write a class declaration we have to specify the following: a class name (which is going to be `Employee`), a private section, and a public section. Because we want to hide the data, we are going to write an appropriate declaration in the private section. The functions are indented to provide data access for external modules, so they will be located in the public section.

```
// employee class declaration
// file employee.h
class Employee{

private:
    struct DDate{
        int dday;
        int mmonth;
        int yyear;
        };
char FirstName[35];
    char LastName[35];
DDate BirthDate;
    int Salary;

public:
    Employee(void);         // constructor
    ~Employee(void);        // destructor
    void DisplayEmployee(void);
    void SetEmployee(void);
};
```

5. Implementing a class

Writing a class implementation consists of creating constructor and destructor functions and of defining other member functions to access the class data.

```
// class definition
// file employee.cpp

#include <iostream.h>
#include <string.h>
#include "employee.h"

Employee::Employee(void)
{
    memset(LastName, 0x00, strlen(FirstName));
    memset(LastName, 0x00, strlen(LastName));
}
```

```
Employee::~Employee(void)
{
}

void Employee::DisplayEmployee(void)
{
    cout <<    FirstName << " " << LastName << endl;
    cout << "Date of birth: " << BirthDate.dday;
    cout << "/" << BirthDate.mmonth << "/" << BirthDate.yyear;
    cout << endl;

}

void Employee::SetEmployee(void)
{
    char bdString[80];

    cout << "Enter First Name: ";
    cin >> FirstName;
    cout << "Enter Last Name: ";
    cin >> LastName;
    cout << "Enter Salary: ";
    cin >> Salary;

    while (true)
    {
        cout << "Enter Birthdate (mm/dd/yy)";
        cin >> bdString;
        BirthDate.dday =    (bdString[3] - '0')*10 +
                            bdString[4] - '0';
        BirthDate.mmonth = (bdString[0] - '0')*10 +
                            bdString[1] - '0';
        BirthDate.yyear = (bdString[6] - '0')*10 +
                            bdString[7] - '0';

        if ((BirthDate.dday >= 1) && (BirthDate.dday <= 31))
        if ((BirthDate.mmonth >= 1) && (BirthDate.mmonth <= 12))
            break;
    }

}
```

The constructor and destructor functions are quite obvious. The most interesting part of the code is access functions.

The **SetEmployee** function enables reading the data that the user enters via a keyboard. The function fills the private data members with the entered data. Because we hide the data (we cannot access the data directly), this function becomes very important. Actually, this function provides the only way to set an employee's data.

A very common approach is to add validation procedures to this type of function. In our case, the validation routine checks the correctness of the entered date (not very intelligently, however). If the date is incorrect, the function repeats the question to enter the date of birth. Adding a validation code is very important because this is the way to control the class data.

The `DisplayEmployee` function provides another window to the external world. This function shows the data in the class. Assuming that the `Salary` field might be confidential, we don't display it.

6. Testing the class

To make sure that our class works, we are going to run a simple program that defines an `Employee` object, gets the data, and then displays the data on the screen.

```cpp
// file empltest.cpp

#include "employee.h"

int main()
{

    Employee EmplTest;
    EmplTest.SetEmployee();
    EmplTest.DisplayEmployee();

    return 0;
}
```

If you try to access the data members directly, the compiler will generate error messages. For example, if you try to display the employee's last name with the following statement:

```cpp
cout << EmplTest.LastName;
```

the compiler will complain.

7. Amending the class

The two access functions provide a minimum set of operations on the class data. This pair of operations (sometimes it is `Get` and `Set`, or `Read` and `Write`) is usually needed for a new data type.

Other operations are usually very specific. In our example, the operations can be `GetSalary` (for getting the `Salary` member) and `CompareEmployees` (for comparing two `Employee` objects).

```cpp
int Employee::GetSalary(void)
{
    return Salary;
}

int Employee::CompareEmployees(Employee E1, Employee E2)
```

```
    {
        return strcmp(E1.LastName, E2.LastName);
    }
```

Comments

Encapsulation provides a methodology for creating true object-oriented programs. By hiding the data from other objects and specifying access functions, you can create a new data type with complete operational support.

Encapsulation does not provide security for the data. It only prevents programming mistakes and can't prevent the destruction of data if someone really wants to destroy it. Using encapsulation allows for more understandable programs and produces a better programming style.

COMPLEXITY
INTERMEDIATE

4.4   How do I...
Create my own operators?

Problem

When I create new data types and specify functions, sometimes I don't like to use functions when I could be using operators. For example, when creating a class for complex numbers, I prefer to use the (+) operator rather than the **Add** member function and the (-) operator rather than the **Subtract** member function. In other words, I prefer

```
Complex1 = Complex2 + Complex3;
Complex1 = Complex2 - Complex3;
```

to

```
Complex1 = Complex2.Add(Complex3);
Complex1 = Complex2.Subtract(Complex3);
```

where **Complex1**, **Complex2**, and **Complex3** are objects of the complex numbers class.

Technique

To perform this kind of addition of class objects, you have to create special member functions that overload the binary addition operator (+) and subtraction operator (-) when they appear between two objects of the complex numbers class.

The technique, known as *operator overloading*, allows you to overload almost all C++ operators except (.), (.*), (::), (?:), and **sizeof**. In this section we cover in detail the technique for overloading binary operators.

Steps

1. Create a complex number class

The class we define in this example will have only add and subtract operations. Creating multiplication and division operations is a good exercise that will be left to the reader.

```cpp
// CComplex class declaration
// file ccomplex.h

class CComplex
{
private:
    float rreal;        // real part
    float iimage;        // imaginary part

public:

    CComplex(void);        // constructor
    ~CComplex(void);    // destructor

// access functions
    void GetComplex(void);
    void DisplayComplex(void);

// arithmetic operations
    CComplex Add(CComplex);
    CComplex Subtract(CComplex);

};

// CComplex class definition
// file complex.cpp

#include <iostream.h>
#include "ccomplex.h"

CComplex::CComplex()
{
    rreal = 0.0;
    iimage = 0.0;
}

CComplex::~CComplex()
{
}

// gets real and imaginary parts of the complex number
void CComplex::GetComplex()
{
    cout << "Enter Real Part: ";
    cin >> rreal;
    cout << "Enter Imaginary Part: ";
    cin >> iimage;
}
```

```
// displays the object of class CComplex
void CComplex::DisplayComplex()
{
    cout << rreal;
    if (iimage >= 0)
        cout << " + " << iimage;
    else
        cout << " - " << -iimage;
    cout << "i" << endl;
}

// adds two objects of class CComplex
CComplex CComplex::Add(CComplex Complex1)
{

    CComplex NewComplex;
    NewComplex.rreal = rreal + Complex1.rreal;
    NewComplex.iimage = iimage + Complex1.iimage;

    return NewComplex;
}

// subtracts CComplex object form another CComplex object
CComplex CComplex::Subtract(CComplex Complex1)
{

    CComplex NewComplex;
    NewComplex.rreal = rreal - Complex1.rreal;
    NewComplex.iimage = iimage - Complex1.iimage;

    return NewComplex;
}
```

The class we created consists of **rreal** and **iimage** data members that are used for the real and imaginary parts of a complex number. We specified **float** data types for both parts.

The class supports access functions such as **GetComplex** and **DisplayComplex** for inputting the real and imaginary parts and displaying the complex number on the user's monitor screen.

2. Testing the class

To test the class we created a small program that accepts two complex numbers (**Complex1** and **Complex2**), adds them together, and stores the result in the **Complex3** object of type **CComplex**. The program then subtracts **Complex2** from **Complex1** and stores the result in the **Complex4** object. Finally, the program shows **Complex3** and **Complex4** on the user screen.

```
// file comptest.cpp

#include "ccomplex.h"
```

```
int main()
{
    // define complex numbers
    CComplex TestComplex1, TestComplex2;
    CComplex TestComplex3, TestComplex4;
    // perform keyboard input of Complex1 and Complex2
    TestComplex1.GetComplex();
    TestComplex2.GetComplex();

    // add and subtract Complex1 and Complex2
    TestComplex3 = TestComplex1.Add(TestComplex2);
    TestComplex4 = TestComplex1.Subtract(TestComplex2);

    // display the result
    TestComplex3.DisplayComplex();
    TestComplex4.DisplayComplex();

    return 0;
}
```

3. Replacing **Add** and **Subtract** member functions with overloaded operators

To use convenient notations for add and subtract operations, we have to replace the **Add** and **Subtract** member functions with overloaded operators.

In the class declaration section (file **ccomplex.h**), we replace the lines

```
CComplex Add(CComplex);
CComplex Subtract(CComplex);
```

with the lines

```
CComplex operator+(CComplex);
CComplex operator-(CComplex);
```

In the class definition section (file **ccomplex.cpp**), we replace the **Add** and **Subtract** functions with the following code:

```
CComplex CComplex::operator+(CComplex Complex1)
{

    CComplex NewComplex;
    NewComplex.rreal = rreal + Complex1.rreal;
    NewComplex.iimage = iimage + Complex1.iimage;

    return NewComplex;
}
CComplex CComplex::operator-(CComplex Complex1)
{
```

```
          CComplex NewComplex;
          NewComplex.rreal = rreal - Complex1.rreal;
          NewComplex.iimage = iimage - Complex1.iimage;

          return NewComplex;
}
```

Interestingly, the function bodies remain the same. We didn't change the actual code. We just changed the function names from **Add** to **operator+** and from **Subtract** to **operator-**.

4. Testing the new operators

To test the + and - operators, we just replace the lines

```
TestComplex3 = TestComplex1.Add(TestComplex2);
TestComplex4 = TestComplex1.Subtract(TestComplex2);
```

with the following lines:

```
TestComplex3 = TestComplex1 + TestComplex2;
TestComplex4 = TestComplex1 - TestComplex2;
```

Would you believe it? The program displays the same results.

Comments

Operator overloading is a very powerful feature of C++. Good programming style assures code readability is dramatically increased with operator overloading. Creating new data types and implementing standard operations would be incomplete without this feature.

To understand and remember the syntax of the overloading operator definition, you can start creating a member function to support the operation. In our example we use the following syntax for the **Add** function declaration, definition, and call:

```
CComplex Add(CComplex);
CComplex CComplex::Add(CComplex Complex1)
TestComplex3 = TestComplex1.Add(TestComplex2);
```

To change the **Add** function to the + operator, we have to just replace **Add** with **operator+** in the function declaration and definition:

```
CComplex operator+(CComplex);
CComplex CComplex::operator+(CComplex Complex1)
```

Function calls will be naturally replaced with

```
TestComplex3 = TestComplex1 + TestComplex2;
```

Similarly you can overload unary operators such as ++ or --. The only problem is in distinguishing between prefix and postfix notation. C++ convention defines the difference in operator declarations. For prefix notation, you can use an approach similar to binary operator overloading. For example, the prefix ++ operator can be declared as

```
CComplex operator++();
```

For postfix notation you should use the **int** keyword (surprise!) in the operator declaration. For example, postfix - - operator can be declared as

```
CComplex operator--(int);
```

COMPLEXITY
INTERMEDIATE

4.5 How do I...
Overload relational and equality operators?

Problem

For many classes that describe new data types, I want to specify an order for the elements of a class. For example, I am always able to say whether a date is greater than or less than another date. I want to use this order in my applications and I want to overload relational and equality operators (<, <=, >, >=, ==, =!) to specify that order.

Technique

Operator overloading is a powerful feature of C++. If it is consistently applied to a class, it can make the code much simpler and therefore more reliable. To overload the operators, the appropriate functions have to be added to the class. Every function will overload one operator, and together they will create the complete set of relational and equality operators.

Steps

1. Creating a class

For this example, the **DDate** structure that was created in the beginning of this chapter will be transferred into the **DDate** class. To keep the example simple, the code creates only one member function that sets up the date. As usual, create the two files: the class declaration file (**ddate.h**) and the class definition file (**ddate.cpp**).

```
// ddate.h

class DDate{

private:
  int dday;
  int mmonth;
  int yyear;
```

```
public:
  // constructor
  DDate(void);
  // destructor
  ~DDate(void);
  // creates a new DDate object
  // for the specified day, month, and year
  void SetDate(int, int, int);

};
// ddate.cpp

#include "ddate.h"

// constructor
DDate::DDate()
{
}

// destructor
DDate::~DDate()
{
}

// creates a new DDate object
// for the specified day, month, and year
void DDate::SetDate(int InDay, int InMonth, int InYear)
{
    dday = InDay;
    mmonth = InMonth;
    yyear = InYear;
}
```

The class declaration has a private section with the **dday**, the **mmonth**, and the **yyear** integer variables. This section is similar to the structure of How-To 4.1. The public section contains the constructor, the destructor, and the **SetDate** member function. The **SetDate** function sets up the date based on the day, month, and year arguments.

2. Overloading the relational and equality operators

The syntax of the declaration of overloaded operators declaration is similar to the syntax of declaration of the overloaded operators in How-To 4.4. The syntax of the declaration is similar to the syntax of the declaration of a function. The difference is that instead of a function name, the keyword **operator** and the actual operator are used. For example, to declare the overloaded > operator for the **DDate** class use

```
bool operator>(DDate);
```

You must specify the return value of the functions, which is **bool**, because the overloaded operators must have the same behavior as the regular relational and equality operators. The code will need to use the operators in logical expressions and in statements such as

```
if (Date1 > Date2) Destroy_All();
```

Therefore, the class declaration will be the following:

```
// ddate.h

class DDate{

private:
  int dday;
  int mmonth;
  int yyear;

public:
  // constructor
  DDate(void);
  // destructor
  ~DDate(void);
  // creates a new DDate object
  // for the specified day, month, and year
  void SetDate(int, int, int);
  // overloaded operator >
  bool operator>(DDate);
  // overloaded operator >=
  bool operator>=(DDate);
  // overloaded operator <
  bool operator<(DDate);
  // overloaded operator <=
  bool operator<=(DDate);
  // overloaded operator ==
  bool operator==(DDate);
  // overloaded operator !=
  bool operator!=(DDate);

};
```

The class definition will need quite trivial functions. The following code covers three of the six operators (<, >, and ==). You can add the rest to prove your knowledge of operator overloading.

```
// constructor and destructor
DDate::DDate()
{}
DDate::~DDate()
{}

// overloaded operator >
bool DDate::operator>(DDate InDDate)
{
    if (yyear > InDDate.yyear) return true;
```

```
    if (yyear < InDDate.yyear) return false;

    // years are equal
    if (mmonth > InDDate.mmonth) return true;
    if (mmonth < InDDate.mmonth) return false;

    // months are equal
    if (dday > InDDate.dday) return true;
    return false;

}

// overloaded operator <
bool DDate::operator<(DDate InDDate)
{
    if (yyear < InDDate.yyear) return true;
    if (yyear > InDDate.yyear) return false;

    // years are equal
    if (mmonth < InDDate.mmonth) return true;
    if (mmonth > InDDate.mmonth) return false;

    // months are equal
    if (dday < InDDate.dday) return true;
    return false;
}

// overloaded operator ==
bool DDate::operator==(DDate InDDate)
{
    if (yyear != InDDate.yyear) return false;

    // years are equal
    if (mmonth != InDDate.mmonth) return false;

    // months are equal
    if (dday == InDDate.dday) return true;
    return false;
}
// Readers can add the code to the functions below
bool DDate::operator<=(DDate InDDate)
{}
bool DDate::operator>=(DDate InDDate)
{}
bool DDate::operator!=(DDate InDDate)
{}
```

All functions defined in the preceding are similar to the other binary functions. The major question to be answered is "What is the order of the parameters in these functions?" For example, when the > (greater than) operator is defined, is **InDDate** the first or the second parameter? If you write

```
DDate Date1, Date2;
if (Date1 > Date2) do_something;
```

will the **InDDate** parameter be replaced with the **Date1** argument or the **Date2** argument?

The rule is simple: The parameter in any function that represents an overloaded binary operator is replaced with the second argument. The first argument is considered to be an object of the defined class itself. Therefore, in this example the **InDDate** parameter in the functions

```
bool DDate::operator>(DDate InDDate)
bool DDate::operator<(DDate InDDate)
bool DDate::operator==(DDate InDDate)
```

will be replaced with the **Date2** argument for the statements

```
if (Date1 > Date2) do_something;
if (Date1 < Date2) do_something;
if (Date1 == Date2) do_something;
```

To prove it we have to create a simple test example.

3. Testing the overloaded operators

Create the following example to test the operator:

```
#include <iostream>
using namespace std;

#include "ddate.h"

int main()
{
    DDate Date1, Date2, Date3;
    Date1.SetDate (19, 05, 1998);
    Date2.SetDate (19, 05, 1998);
    Date3.SetDate (19, 01, 1998);

    cout << "The first date ";
    if (Date1 > Date2)
        cout << "is ";
    else
        cout << "is not ";
    cout << "greater than the second date" << endl;

    cout << "The first date ";
    if (Date1 == Date2)
        cout << "is ";
    else
        cout << "is not ";
    cout << "equal to the second date" << endl;

    cout << "The first date ";
    if (Date1 < Date3)
        cout << "is ";
    else
        cout << "is not ";
```

```
    cout << "less than the third date" << endl;

    return 0;
}
```

First of all, the code defines the **Date1**, **Date2**, and **Date3** objects and initializes them with the dates May 19, 1998, May 19, 1998, and January 19, 1998. Then the dates are compared using the overloaded operators. The result should be

```
The first date in not greater than the second date
The first date is equal to the second date
The first date is not less than the third date
```

Comments

Operator overloading is a very powerful feature of C++. The idea behind it is to make code more readable and intuitive. If overloaded operators don't serve this idea, the results can be terrible. Let's consider the following code:

```
int operator== (int InValue)
{
    if (InValue > 5 ) then return 5;
    else return InValue;
}
```

In this example, the equality operator (==) was overloaded with a function that returns the lesser of 5 and the function argument. If another programmer wants to use this function to compare two variables, just imagine what the result could be.

COMPLEXITY

INTERMEDIATE

4.6   How do I...
Provide access to encapsulated data to certain classes?

Problem

In How-To 4.4, we created an overloaded operator for adding two complex numbers. I understand that if I want to use the + operator in the expressions like

```
Complex1 + 2.3;
```

or

```
Complex1 + FloatNumber;
```

where **FloatNumber** is a variable of a type **float**, I could define the overloaded operator. I simply have to change the declaration to

```
CComplex operator+(float);
```

and the definition to

```
CComplex CComplex::operator+(float float1)
{

    CComplex NewComplex;
    NewComplex.rreal = rreal + float1;
    NewComplex.iimage = iimage;

    return NewComplex;
}
```

What should I do if I want to use expressions like

```
2.3 + Complex1;?
```

I can't overload this operator because I would have to simulate the function

```
CComplex CComplex::Add(float, CComplex)
```

and I have no idea how to do it. I would use

```
CComplex operator+(float, CComplex)
```

as a normal function but I need to have direct access to the private data of **CComplex** class. How do I use the private data without breaching the encapsulation?

Technique

C++ introduced the notion of friend functions and friend classes. A *friend* function can access private data of a class without being a member function of the class. In the following example, the **FFriend** function can access the private data of the **TestClass** class.

```
Class TestClass
{
private:
public:
    friend int FFriend(int);
};

int FFriend(int data)
{

}
```

We are going to create friend functions for our **CComplex** class that will support + and - operators in expressions like

```
2.3 + Complex1
4.76 - Complex1;
```

Steps

1. Analyze the class and specify operations that cannot be represented by member functions

This step is very important. The idea of friend functions has been discussed a lot, and it has both good points and bad points. The biggest problem pointed out by many writers is that the friend functions break the wall that encapsulation creates. However, we can follow this rule: Don't use friend functions if you don't have to. A limited usage of friend functions increases the power of C++ and can significantly improve the readability of the code.

In our example that created the **CComplex** class, we figured out a way of supporting + and - operators for a few types of expressions. The only type of arithmetic expression in which + and - can't be represented by member functions is with a **float** variable as the first argument.

Therefore, we start creating functions to support expressions such as

```
2.3 + Complex1;
```

2. Declaring a friend function

We already know that the function declarations should be

```
friend CComplex operator+(float, CComplex);
```

and

```
friend CComplex operator-(float, CComplex);
```

A friend function declaration can be placed in either the private or public part of a class declaration. We prefer to put it in the public section to show the accessibility of the function.

Even when declared within the class declaration, a friend function is not a member function of this class.

3. Writing the function definition

The function definition is no different from the other functions. For our + and - operations, the functions could be

```
// + operator support for the cases
```

```
// 2.3 + Complex1
//
CComplex operator+(float float1, CComplex Complex1)
{

    CComplex NewComplex;
    NewComplex.rreal = float1 + Complex1.rreal;
    NewComplex.iimage = Complex1.iimage;

    return NewComplex;
}

// - operator support for the cases
// 2.3 - Complex1
//
CComplex operator+(float float1, CComplex Complex1)
{

    CComplex NewComplex;
    NewComplex.rreal = float1 - Complex1.rreal;
    NewComplex.iimage = Complex1.iimage;

    return NewComplex;
}
```

A similar approach could be used if we wanted to add support for other data types.

4. Creating a friend class

The two created functions just return CComplex values because they are friend functions, not member functions of the class. In actuality, they are not yet added to any class, which means the functions are accessible from everywhere in the code. However, we are not going to use these functions with all classes that we can create in the program. Therefore, it is a good idea to combine them into one class.

```
class COperators
{
CComplex operator+(float float1, CComplex Complex1)
CComplex operator-(float float1, CComplex Complex1)

};
```

Also, you have to change the declarations to

```
friend CComplex COperators::operator+(float, CComplex);
friend CComplex COperators::operator-(float, CComplex);
```

specifying the scope of the functions. You can simply write

```
friend class COperators;
```

and all functions in the **COperators** class will be declared as friends of **CComplex** class.

Comments

Using friend functions in a program contradicts the idea of encapsulation. The feature breaks the wall around the data encapsulated in a class. Therefore, don't use friend functions unless they are absolutely necessary. One possible required usage of friend functions is described in this How-To. Another very common reason to use friend functions is to improve the syntax of a class and increase the readability of the code.

COMPLEXITY
INTERMEDIATE

4.7 How do I...
Maintain global data in my program?

Problem

When creating a large application, I need to have global data in the program. For example, I often need to maintain the application parameters such as application filename or application title. When creating business applications, I need to create global data such as a company registration number or a company address. How do I create global data using encapsulation?

Technique

The traditional approach in procedural programming assumes that many program modules can share certain data. The data that can be accessed from any module of a program used to be called global data. If we tried to combine global data and object-oriented programming, we would have a program with the structure shown in Figure 4.5.

To avoid this ugly implementation and make the program look more beautiful, we can create classes that work as global data but in which the data is encapsulated.

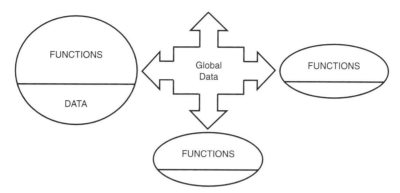

Figure 4.5 Encapsulation and global data.

Steps

1. Determining the global data

The first step is to specify classes, encapsulate data, and specify member functions. The data should be combined into logical groups according to the objects that the program will need to operate.

In most cases you will find that no data is left. If the design was good, the classes should cover all data. However, what do we do if there is data that can't be a member of any class? For example, where should we store the application title and application program filename? No class handles this information, but a lot of classes need it. The application title works very well as a caption for all message boxes or dialog boxes. The application filename can be used to check whether the necessary files exist. Therefore, this data can be considered global (belonging to the whole program).

2. If the class doesn't exist, create it!

We said that we could not figure out the class that would handle the application title and filename. Therefore, let's create it.

```
class Application
{
private:
char* AppTitle;
char* AppFilename;
public:
Application(void);
~Application(void);
char* GetAppTitle();
char* GetAppFilename;
};
```

We declare `AppTitle` and `AppFilename` variables as `char*`. Therefore, we have to reserve memory space and initialize them. The best place to do this is within the class constructor. The destructor will free the space.

Because no module can change the application title and filename, we are not providing functions to change the data. The only place that changes the data is the constructor. However, we supply an ability to get the data using `GetAppTitle` and `GetAppFilename` member functions.

3. Making one copy of the data

The implementation of the class is quite obvious, and we are not going to concentrate on it. What is more interesting is the behavior of the class instances. Suppose we've created two instances of the class:

```
Application App1;
Application App2;
```

This looks strange but just imagine that the two instances belong to two different parts of the program. Whatever we do, the two copies of the class in the memory will be created. It is not a big deal in our case but creates a problem if the class allows the data to be changed.

To make the data behave like global data (one shared copy), we have to change the data member declarations:

```
class Application
{
private:
static char* AppTitle;
static char* AppFilename;
public:
Application(void);
~Application(void);
char* GetAppTitle();
char* GetAppFilename;
};
```

Now the data is declared as **static char***. The **static** keyword makes the data exist in only one copy, no matter how many instances of the class exist. No instance of the class needs to be declared in order for the static data to exist.

Comments

Using global data in object-oriented programming requires that a class be created to handle this data. In this case, the data remains encapsulated. Usually we can create a few classes that handle groups of global data. For example, we can create an `Application` class to store the application filename and application title, or a `Company` class to keep company information such as registration number and address.

If we can't define sets of global data, we can create one class named `Environment` (or any other name) and encapsulate all global data in it.

4.8   How do I...
Know when I should use structures and when I should use classes?

Problem

I want to work with a linked list. When creating the linked list implementation in C, I normally use structures. Should I use the same technique in C++ or do I have to change all structures to classes?

Technique

To show the technique of using classes rather than structures, we are going to create the implementation of linked lists in C++.

Steps

1. Determining the linked list class

A linked list is an aggregated data type. Elements of a linked list can be of any type. In this example, we'll consider only **integer** elements. A linked list starts with a pointer to the first element. If the linked list is empty, the first element is **NULL** as shown in Figure 4.6.

First:	NULL

Figure 4.6   An empty linked list.

Elements of a linked list consist of data and a pointer to the next element in the list. The last element consists of its data and NULL pointer. An example of a linked list is shown in Figure 4.7.

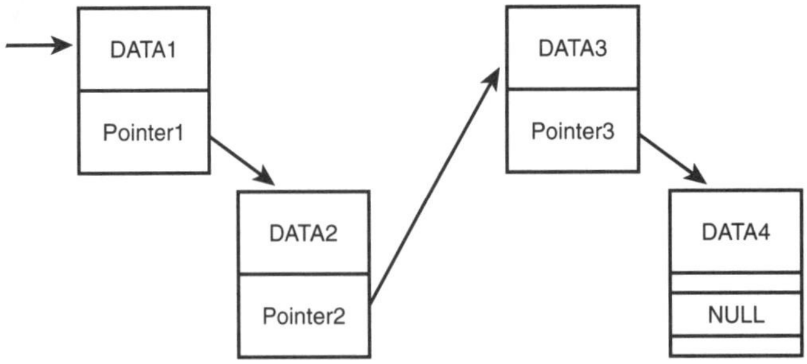

Figure 4.7 A linked list.

A linked list as a data type needs the following operations: add, remove, and insert. In this example, we are going to implement only the add operation. The operation allows you to add a new element to the beginning of the list.

The following is the class declaration:

```
// file linkedli.h

#include <iostream.h>

// list elements
struct llink
{
    int elem;
    llink* nextelem;

};

// linked list
class linkedlist
{
private:
    llink* firstelem;
public:
    linkedlist(void);
    ~linkedlist(void);
    void AddElement (int elem1);
    void DisplayList(void);

};
```

2. Defining and testing the class

The implementation of the class needs a constructor, an operation to add new elements, and an operation to display the list.

```
// file linkedli.cpp

#include "linkedli.h"
```

```cpp
// constructor
linkedlist::linkedlist()
{
    firstelem=NULL;
}

// destructor
linkedlist::~linkedlist(void)
{
    // here should be a code
    // to free memory
}

// add new element
void linkedlist::AddElement(int elem1)

{
    llink* newlink= new llink;
    newlink->elem= elem1;
    newlink->nextelem= firstelem;
    firstelem= newlink;
}

// Display list elements one by one
void linkedlist::DisplayList()
{
    llink* currentelem= firstelem;
    while (currentelem!= NULL)
    {
        cout << currentelem->elem << " - ";
        currentelem= currentelem->nextelem;
    }
    cout << "END" << endl;
}
```

To test the implementation, let's write a program that adds a few elements to the list and then displays the list on the screen:

```cpp
// file listtest.cpp

#include "linkedli.h"

int main()
{
    linkedlist TestList;

    TestList.AddElement(5);
    TestList.AddElement(54);
    TestList.AddElement(3);
    TestList.AddElement(25);

    TestList.DisplayList();

    return 0;
}
```

The program will display

25 · 3 · 54 · 5 · END

Comments

Now we can discuss details of the linked list implementation and the difference in using classes and structures.

We used a C++ structure to create a single element:

```
struct llink
{
    int elem;
    llink* nextelem;

};
```

The linked list element consists of two parts of different data types. Therefore, it was very convenient to combine them using the **struct** keyword. Remember that we can't use arrays for creating a data aggregate of pieces of different data types. The first structure member handles the data (sometimes called *satellite data*). In our example, the data has an **integer** value but linked lists can maintain any type of data, for instance, pointer to image structures.

The second structure member provides a pointer to the next list element. Note that we use a kind of recursion because the pointer points to an element of the **llink** type that is defined by the structure. This is an important feature that makes C++ structures really powerful.

So far we have dealt with data and the data describes a linked list element. Do we need to extend it to a class? The answer is no; there is no need to add operations. Elements don't need operations on themselves. There is no such thing as incrementing a list element or the addition of two elements. Even display functions should display the whole list rather than a separate element.

Because we want to use a common approach, we will leave the structure without moving it to a class. This is mostly a question of programming style. For historical reasons, we deal with structures if we deal with pure data and if there is no need of operations on this data.

Now we can consider the linked list itself. No doubt, it should be a class for several reasons.

First, we can encapsulate all data members. Fortunately we don't need many of those. The important thing is that we have to define operations with this linked list. There are list elements involved in the operations; however, the elements are hidden from external objects.

Creating a linked list involves quite a bit of logic. In our design we decided that an empty list was just a **NULL**. It means that we reserve the space for the list on-the-fly while adding the elements. Therefore (if we were writing a real program), we have to destroy the memory items when we don't need the elements.

These operations need a constructor and a destructor that are class member functions.

The last class elements we have to specify are the functions `AddElement` and `DisplayList`. The functions provide a necessary interface for the encapsulated data. We definitely need more functions and their creation is left as a good assignment for the reader.

CHAPTER 5
COMMON MISTAKES MADE WITH CLASSES

COMMON MISTAKES MADE WITH CLASSES

How do I...

5.1 Know when to take an object-oriented approach or a procedural approach?

5.2 Use and access a class's data members?

5.3 Use the scope resolution operator?

5.4 Use dot notation to access the member functions of an object?

5.5 Know which constructor to use when there are several to choose from?

5.6 Implement function overloading?

5.7 Correctly make use of inheritance?

5.8 Pass parameters back through the C++ inheritance mechanism to parent classes?

5.9 Distinguish between virtual classes and nonvirtual classes? How do I know when to use virtual classes and what does the word *virtual* mean in C++?

After a programmer progresses to the levels of object-oriented programming (OOP), whether new to programming or coming from a non-OOP language, she immediately discovers common mistakes made over and over again by many programmers. Often, it is because C++ is such a large language to learn that the underlying basics of OOP are left out. It is these basic ideas that trap beginning OOP programmers in the early stages and leave them scratching their heads. Often, they are left wondering what the error message actually means and also whether there is anyone around who understands it. This chapter is designed to help you understand the basic ideas of OOP and covers some of the more common mistakes made by beginning C++ programmers.

5.1 Know When to Take an Object-Oriented Approach or a Procedural Approach

When writing a program using an object-oriented language, many new programmers don't know whether to write the program using objects or in a procedural fashion. Often, many think that because C++ is object-oriented, all programs should be written using objects. That is not true and often programs don't need to be written in an object style. It is important to learn when to use objects and when not to.

5.2 Use and Access a Class's Data Members

A class can have data members (variables). It is these members that store the data internally to their class. This method encapsulates the data inside the class in a tightly bound, single entity. When an instance of a class is created, these data members are also created with it and given their own space in memory. For each instance of the class, a new set of data members is created. However, because they are stored within a class, they only exist inside of an object at runtime and can only be accessed via that object. How are values assigned to them?

5.3 Use the Scope Resolution Operator

The scope resolution operator has two main functions. First, it can be used in a program to access a global variable that has the same name as a local variable. By placing the scope resolution operator in front of the variable, you can directly control which variable the compiler uses. The second use is within object-oriented programs. The scope resolution operator is used to identify which class a particular function is a member of. This allows classes to share function names but keep each one separate in the program.

5.4 Use Dot Notation to Access the Member Functions of an Object

In object-oriented programs, the use of the dot operator is vital to access member functions. Often new C++ programmers either forget or don't know where or how to use the operator. The use of the dot is often confused when calling standard functions mixed with member functions. It is the member functions that require the dot and not the standard functions.

5.5 Know Which Constructor to Use When There Are Several to Choose From

Classes often use more than one constructor to gather data. Because each constructor has a different signature, it is important to know how to access each one. To understand this, function overloading should be addressed as the constructors each have the same name but will have different parameters. By using multiple constructors, the programmer can increase the usefulness of the class because he can control the amount of data passed to the class.

5.6 Implement Function Overloading

In programs, you quite often need a function that can perform several different tasks but use the same interface. Overloaded functions are the simple solution. For example, you might have several functions using the same name but handling different data types. The programmer would then have one common interface but be able to use mixed data types.

5.7 Correctly Make Use of Inheritance

Inheritance is a very useful and powerful tool in any object-oriented programming language. It gives the programmer access to pre-written classes that perform specific jobs. By utilizing inheritance, the programmer can rapidly create programs knowing there will be minimal debugging time. This is because any classes inherited by the program will (in theory) be pre-tested. The main problem people find when working with inheritance is simply how to use it in the first place.

5.8 Pass Parameters Back Through the C++ Inheritance Mechanism to Parent Classes

Beginning C++ programmers find writing inherited constructors very difficult. It can be very confusing to know which parameters are used in the derived class and which ones to pass on to the base class. For a hierarchical structure to work, there must be a coherent structure wherein all parameters have a destination.

5.9 Distinguish Between Virtual Classes and Nonvirtual Classes? How Do I Know When to Use Virtual Classes and What Does the Word *Virtual* Mean in C++?

When building up a hierarchical inheritance network, it is difficult to know when to use virtual and nonvirtual classes. The difference is in the way the classes are inherited. Nonvirtual inheritance means the derived class makes a copy of the base class. Inheriting a virtual class means that only a reference to the base class is used. There is no actual copy, only an "image."

5.1 How do I...
Know when to take an object-oriented approach or a procedural approach?

Problem

Both OOP- and procedural-style programs seem to achieve the same results as far as input and output are concerned. In addition, to the beginning OOP programmer, object-oriented programming might seem long-winded and confusing whereas procedural programming might seem direct and concise.

Technique

To point out the differences, you will attempt to solve the following problem:

Write a program that will accept two letters as input, compare these two letters, and then determine whether these two letters are the same or not. A message stating the result must be displayed to the screen.

Steps

First of all, you will take a look at a "normal" procedural solution to the problem. More than one way to lay out such a program exists, but the first issue is that the main program contains the variables `first`, `second`, and `tested`. These variables are passed by value to and from the functions in which their copies are manipulated. The variables belong to the main program and not the functions. Control of the entire program is orchestrated from the main program and control is maintained there at all times.

1. The main program asks the function `GetLetter()` to return a letter. That letter is then placed into the variable `first`, which exists only within `main` (see Figure 5.1):

```
first = GetLetter();
```

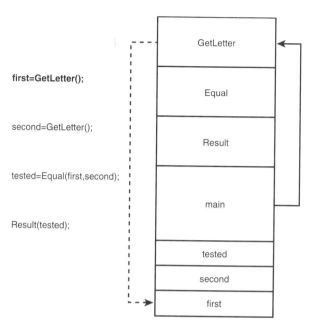

first=GetLetter();

second=GetLetter();

tested=Equal(first,second);

Result(tested);

Figure 5.1 main calls GetLetter, which returns a value to first.

2. The same thing happens to obtain a value for **second** (see Figure 5.2):

```
second = GetLetter();
```

3. In order to determine the relationship between **first** and **second**, they are handed to the function **Equal()** and the outcome of that comparison is returned to the main program where it is stored in the variable **tested** (see Figure 5.3):

```
tested = Equal(first,second);
```

4. Finally, the value contained in **tested** is handed to the function **Result()** where it is displayed to the screen (see Figure 5.4):

```
Result(tested);
```

Now compare the "normal" solution with the object-oriented approach. The difference is subtle but very important.

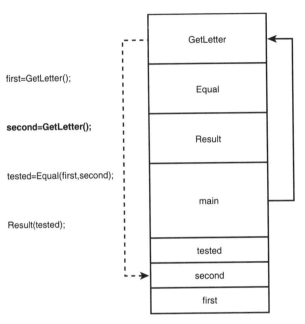

Figure 5.2 main calls GetLetter again, which returns a value to second.

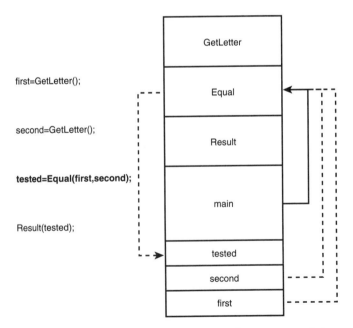

Figure 5.3 The function Equal is called from main and the variables first and second are copied into the function.

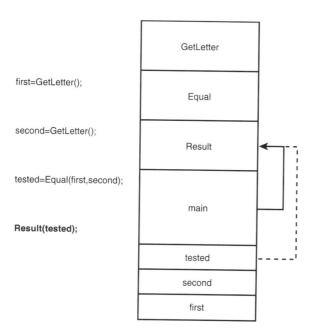

Figure 5.4 The function `Result` is called from `main` and the variable `tested` is copied into the function.

1. No variables are stored in the main program. From within the main program, control is given to the **pilot** object and its `GetLetter` member function is called into life. The user input of two letters is stored internally within the **pilot** object. After the **pilot** object has done its work, it returns control back to the main program. No variables are exchanged as in "normal" programming (see Figure 5.5):

```
pilot.GetLetter();
```

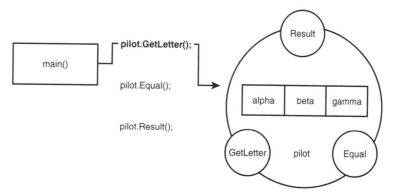

Figure 5.5 Control is given to the **pilot** object by `main`, and the `GetLetter` member function is activated.

2. Control is then passed again to the `pilot` object where the `Equal` member function acts upon the variables stored within itself. After the actions of `Equal` are completed, control is passed back to `main` (see Figure 5.6):

```
pilot.Equal();
```

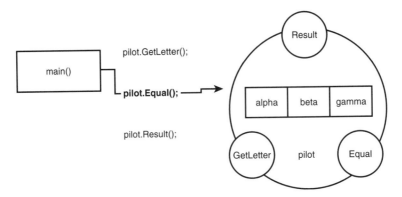

Figure 5.6 Control is given to the `pilot` object by `main`, and the `Equal` member function is activated.

3. Again, control is passed to the `pilot` object where the `Result` member function acts upon the variables stored within the object. When the actions of `Result` are completed, control is passed back to `main` (see Figure 5.7):

```
pilot.Result();
```

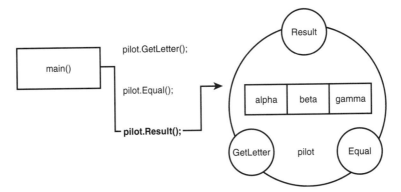

Figure 5.7 Control is given to the `pilot` object by `main`, and the `Result` member function is activated.

How It Works

In the procedural model, variables are stored within the main body of the program and passed to the functions. The functions are tools that are called to act upon the data. Control always remains with the main program and the data and member functions are distinctly separate items. Here is the procedural program in full:

```cpp
// None OOP version
#include <iostream.h>

bool Equal(char alpha, char beta);
char GetLetter(void);
void Result(bool b);

main()
{
    char first;
    char second;
    bool tested;

    first = GetLetter();
    second = GetLetter();
    tested = Equal(first,second);
    Result(tested);
    return(0);
}

bool Equal(char alpha, char beta)
{
    if (alpha == beta)
        return(true);
    else
        return(false);
}

char GetLetter(void)
{
    char letter;

    cout << "Enter the letter : ";
    cin >> letter;
    return(letter);
}

void Result(bool b)
{
    if (b == true)
        cout << "Letters are the same";
    else
        cout << "Letters are not the same";
    cout << endl << endl;
}
```

In the object-oriented model, no variables are stored within the main program. Objects have their own variables and member functions that act upon those variables specifically. An object is a mini-program in its own right and the main program passes control to it. After control is given to the object, it acts upon its own internal variables using its own member functions. Here is the program:

```cpp
// OOP version
#include <iostream.h>


class LetterTest {
                private:
                    char alpha;
                    char beta;
                    bool gamma;

                public:
                    void Equal(void);
                    void GetLetter(void);
                    void Result(void);
                };

void LetterTest::Equal(void)
{
    if (alpha == beta)
        gamma = true;
    else
        gamma = false;
}

void LetterTest::GetLetter(void)
{
    cout << "Enter the first letter : ";
    cin >> alpha;
    cout << "Enter the second letter : ";
    cin >> beta;
}

void LetterTest::Result(void)
{
    if (gamma == true)
        cout << "Letters are the same";
    else
        cout << "Letters are not the same";
    cout << endl << endl;
}

main()
{
    LetterTest pilot;

    pilot.GetLetter();
    pilot.Equal();
    pilot.Result();
    return(0);
}
```

Comments

There are no hard and fast rules about when you should use OOP and "normal" programming styles. You can achieve the same user interaction with either. However, OOP is by far the more powerful of the two styles, especially in larger, more complicated programs. For example, writing GUI programs is a major undertaking in traditional linear programming, but is much simpler with OOP. The OOP feature of inheritance makes the life of the programmer far easier and rapid application development (RAD) is achievable. Object-oriented programming is as much a way of thinking as a programming style. After you get into that mindset, you might wonder how you ever lived without OOP.

COMPLEXITY
BEGINNING

5.2 How do I...
Use and access a class's data members?

Problem

Many beginning C++ programmers are confused by the issue of public and private variables. A common question is "How do I access a data member within a class?" Quite often, a beginner simply defines a global (global to the whole program) variable that she can then use anywhere. Obviously, this is not the optimal solution because after you start using global variables, they are not then tied to any particular class. In the end, your program ends up redeclaring several variables that exist both in the class and the main program. In essence, this misses the point of encapsulation (and therefore object-oriented programming) altogether.

Technique

Data members are used within a class to hold internal data that is needed by that class's member functions. It is a basic principle of object-oriented programming that data members can be accessed only by an object's own member functions. For this reason, a class's data members are often declared as private.

The idea of keeping the data members private to the class is the standard method of programming because it takes away the need of the programmer to know how things inside of the class are stored. All the user has to know is how to correctly create an instance of the class to use the class to perform its required job. A *class* is an abstract notion that states the relationship between member variables that hold data and are hidden within the class and the member functions that manipulate that hidden data. The specification of this relationship needs to be written only once. When a programmer creates an instance of a class, computer memory is allocated to house the member variables and the member functions. This physical presence of the class is called an object; it is said to be concrete. The act of creating an instance of a class can be repeated many times; therefore, many concrete objects can be created from a single class.

Steps

During the design of a class, the programmer should plan what internal data needs to be stored. The programmer then needs to decide whether the data is to be private to the class or public to the program by remembering that the data members should be invisible to the user. As an example, you will design a program that creates a class that makes use of global variables. You will then modify the class to use private data members. Hopefully, you will see the difference.

1. Open up your C++ development environment (or a text editor) and create a new C++ source file called `list5.21.cpp`.

2. Add the following class to the editor.

```
// Usage of Global Variables.

#include <iostream.h>

float Area=0;
int Height=0;
int Length=0;

class Test
        {
            public:
                void CalcArea();
                void ShowArea();
        };
```

Immediately, you can see that the variables (data members) are not where they are supposed to be. In fact, they are declared as global variables.

3. Add the member function definitions:

```
void Test::CalcArea()
{
    Area += Height*Length;      //Find Area
}

void Test::ShowArea()
{
    cout << "The Area is " << Area << endl;
}
```

Here the member functions are manipulating the variables `Area`, `Height`, and `Length`, but these variables are not declared anywhere in the class. This will cause problems later.

4. Finally, add the main section of the program.

```
void main(void)
{
    cout << "Enter a Height ";        //Gather input
    cin >> Height;
    cout << "Enter a Length ";
    cin >> Length;

    Test Square;               //Create instance
    Square.CalcArea();         //Call Member Functions
    Square.ShowArea();

    cout << "Enter a Height ";        //Gather input
    cin >> Height;
    cout << "Enter a Length ";
    cin >> Length;

    Test Box;                  //Create Another Instance
    Height++;                  //Main has altered a value!!
    Box.CalcArea();
    Box.ShowArea();
}
```

Both **main** and the class can see and use those variables. The key is that *both* can alter them. Because two instances of the class are using the same variables, the data might not be up-to-date. In fact, the program has been designed to show this exact thing. In the calculation for **Area**, you are using +=, which adds to a value. Because **Area** is being used elsewhere, it might not be initialized to **0**. Therefore, the resulting answer will be incorrect.

Figure 5.8 shows what's going on...

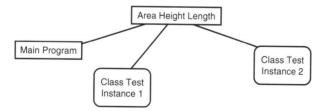

Figure 5.8 Using global variables.

The figure shows that all parts of the program can see and use the variables. If Instance 1 alters them, they are altered for Instance 2. Therefore, the result for Instance 2 will be incorrect.

5. To correct the problem, you must store the data as member variables of the **Test** class and pass values to them via a constructor.

Figure 5.9 shows the required design.

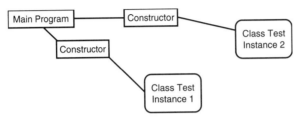

Figure 5.9 Correct scope of variables.

In this example, the class has three member variables. All the user needs to do is use a constructor to pass in values to **Length** and **Height**. The member functions then perform their duties and calculate a resulting area. By using private data members, the user only needs to know that the class requires two inputs. From there, the class performs the calculation internally. Because the data members are private to their own instance, they are totally separate. This means the data has not been altered before the member functions use it; therefore, every instance will produce the correct answer.

6. This sample program fragment uses the correct object-oriented method. First of all, look at the class declaration.

```
#include <iostream.h>

class Test
        {
        private:
            float Area;
            int Height;      //Private DataMembers
            int Length;

        public:
            void CalcArea();
            void ShowArea();
                Test(int H, int L);     //Constructor
        };
```

Include the member variables in the private section of the class. By doing this, only the member functions can utilize them.

7. Next, add the member function definitions as shown in the next program fragment.

```
void Test::CalcArea()
{
```

```
            Area = Height*Length;      //Find Area
      }
      void Test::ShowArea()
      {
            cout << "The Area is " << Area << endl;
      }

      Test::Test(int H, int L)
      {
            Height = H;        //Pass parameters
            Length = L;
      }
```

The constructor is used to pass information from the main program across the class boundary to the internal private data members.

8. Finally, add the main program section that creates two instances of the class and utilizes the two member functions each time.

How It Works

One of the most common problems encountered by beginning C++ programmers is that they end up using far too many variables. This problem is transferred to object-oriented programs, and the beginner immediately finds that he has variables in the main program and the same variables in the class. Obviously, the two sets of variables are totally different because they have different scope. The programmer finds the only solution is to create public or global variables that can be accessed from anywhere within the program. The whole idea of individual, separate class modules is thrown out the window and the user is virtually back to a linear style of programming.

The correct way to encapsulate data is to use private data members in the class and utilize a constructor to pass by value local variables from **main** into the class. The member functions can then see and use the data as it is now in scope. In addition to passing data to an object at instantiation, it is also possible to read data into an object using the **iostream** member function **get()** and to write data out using the member function **set()**.

The following is a full program listing of the correct method.

```
// Correct use of Private Data Members

#include <iostream.h>

class Test    {
      private:
          float Area;
          int Height;      //Private DataMembers
          int Length;
public:
          void CalcArea();
          void ShowArea();
```

```
                    Test(int H, int L);      //Constructor
        };

void Test::CalcArea()
{
    Area = Height*Length;     //Find Area
}

void Test::ShowArea()
{
    cout << "The Area is " << Area << endl;
}

Test::Test(int H, int L)
{
    Height = H;         //Pass parameters
    Length = L;
}


void main(void)
{
    int Height,Length;

    cout << "Enter a Height ";        //Gather input
    cin >> Height;
    cout << "Enter a Length ";
    cin >> Length;

    Test Square(Height,Length);       //Create instance
    Square.CalcArea();        //Call Member Functions
    Square.ShowArea();

    cout << "Enter a Height ";     //Gather input
    cin >> Height;
    cout << "Enter a Length ";
    cin >> Length;

    Test Box(Height,Length);     //Create Another Instance
    Box.CalcArea();
    Box.ShowArea();
```

Comments

If you are using global variables, the class becomes useless. The idea of good class design is that each instance of a class is its own single unique entity. Each instance has its own data and member functions to manipulate that data. By using global variables, each instance of the class will be overwritten and use only one piece of data. Therefore, the information used is not necessarily the correct data because another instance of the class might have altered it.

5.3 How do I...
Use the scope resolution operator?

Problem

Object-oriented programming is very different from standard linear programming. The use of objects requires the programmer to use member functions. Each class will have its own member functions. In standard C++ programs, the programmer uses a prototype to declare a function and then writes a function definition to accompany it. That function is public to the whole program. However, member functions are different. They are functions that belong to a class, making them separate from the rest of the program. In order to use these functions, the programmer must use the scope resolution operator to tell the compiler that this function definition belongs to a particular class. A major problem for programmers new to OOP is knowing where and when to use the scope resolution operator.

Technique

The scope resolution operator (::) can be used in two distinct ways. Both techniques relate to using global members or variables. For example, you might have a program that uses a global variable named **Length**. However, if you declare a new variable also named **Length** in a local fashion, you have to use the scope resolution operator to access the global variable.

In relation to classes, the scope resolution operator is used to tie a function to a certain class. For example, you might have two functions called **Area** with each existing within a different class. You use the scope resolution operator during the definition of each function to specify which class it belongs to. Therefore, **Alpha::Area()** and **Beta::Area()** are two different functions located in two different classes.

Steps

1. You will first examine the use of the scope resolution operator with global variables.

You can tell the compiler to use a global variable rather than a local variable by using the scope resolution operator.

The following example has two variables called **Length**. One is global and the second is local to function **main**.

```
// The Scope Resolution Operator

#include <iostream.h>

int Length  = 789; //Global Variable

void main()
{
    int Length = 123; //Local Variable

    cout << ::Length; //Output Global using ::
    cout << endl;
    cout << Length;    //Output Local;
}
```

When you run the program both values are output to the screen. For the first value, you have told the compiler to output the global variable by prefixing the variable name with the scope resolution operator. For the second value, you have simply used the variable name. Therefore, the compiler refers back to the local variable **Length** within the main program.

2. This example focuses on the use of the scope resolution operator with member functions.

During the construction of a member function definition, you have to specify in the header which class this function belongs to. To achieve this, you must use the scope resolution operator. This tells the compiler the name of the class associated with the function. By doing this, you can have several functions with the same name but attached to different classes.

The following program shows how you can have multiple functions with the same signature. However, they are actually methods of unique classes.

This program has two classes: **Alpha** and **Beta**. **Alpha** takes two integers, adds them together, and then shows the result.

Beta is similar to **Alpha** except that **Beta** multiplies the two integers together.

3. Create the following class named **Alpha**.

```
//The Scope Resolution Operator

#include <iostream.h>
```

```
class Alpha{
    private:
        int Val1,Val2;
        int total;
    public:
        void Calc();
        void Show();
        Alpha(int x,int y);
    };
```

4. Now add another class named **Beta**.

```
class Beta{
    private:
        int Val1,Val2;
        int total;
    public:
        void Calc();
        void Show();
        Beta(int x,int y);
    };
```

The classes are similar in that both have private member variables named **Val1**, **Val2**, and **total**. They also have the same member functions (**Calc** and **Show**). The constructors accept two integer values as input.

5. Now add the function definitions for **Alpha**'s member functions. At this point, the scope resolution operator is used.

```
void Alpha::Calc()
{
    total = 0;
    total = Val1 + Val2;
}

void Alpha::Show()
{
    cout << "The total is " << total << endl;
}

Alpha::Alpha(int x, int y)
{
    Val1 = x;
    Val2 = y;
}
```

Note how the scope resolution operator works. You specify the name of the class to which the member function belongs. Next, insert the scope resolution operator, and then insert the name of the function (see Figure 5.10).

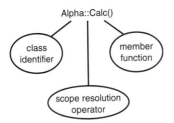

Figure 5.10 The scope resolution
operator.

6. Now, insert the definitions for the **Beta** member functions.

```
void Beta::Calc()
{
    total = 0;
    total = Val1 * Val2;
}

void Beta::Show()
{
    cout << "The Product is " << total << endl;
}

Beta::Beta(int x, int y)
{
    Val1 = x;
    Val2 = y;
}
```

As you can see, the definitions are virtually identical but are differentiated
by the use of the scope resolution operator to relate them to a unique
class.

7. Finally, you must add a main function that will call instances of the two
classes using the member functions.

```
void main()
{
    int Num1,Num2;

    cout << "Enter Number 1 ";
    cin >> Num1;
    cout << "Enter Number 2 ";
    cin >> Num2;

    Alpha First(Num1,Num2);
    First.Calc();
    First.Show();

    Beta Second(Num1,Num2);
    Second.Calc();
    Second.Show();
}
```

This function has two local variables named Num1 and Num2. They are passed to the constructors of the two classes when the instance is created. The member functions are then used to manipulate the data.

How It Works

The private member variables and public member functions are declared in the class declarations. The member functions become methods of the class they belong to.

In the definitions of the member functions, you use the scope resolution operator to specify the class to which the member function belongs. By doing this, you can have member functions that have the same names but are, in fact, individual methods of their class.

In the preceding program, you created an instance of Alpha named First. You then used dot notation to invoke the member functions of Alpha. Note that only the member functions of class Alpha are being used at this point. In reality, the member functions for Beta don't exist yet; they are not created until the class is instantiated.

Finally, an instance of class Beta is created and its member functions are used to perform another calculation using the same two pieces of data.

```
//The Scope Resolution Operator

#include <iostream.h>

class Alpha{
          private:
              int Val1,Val2;
              int total;
          public:
              void Calc();
              void Show();
              Alpha(int x,int y);
};
class Beta{
          private:
              int Val1,Val2;
              int total;
          public:
              void Calc();
              void Show();
              Beta(int x,int y);
        };

void Alpha::Calc()
{
    total = 0;
    total = Val1 + Val2;
}

void Alpha::Show()
```

```
{
    cout << "The total is " << total << endl;
}

Alpha::Alpha(int x, int y)
{
    Val1 = x;
    Val2 = y;
}

void Beta::Calc()
{
    total = 0;
    total = Val1 * Val2;
}

void Beta::Show()
{
    cout << "The product is " << total << endl;
QQ again, change sum to "product".  9/28 DM
}

Beta::Beta(int x, int y)
{
    Val1 = x;
    Val2 = y;
}
void main()
{
    int Num1,Num2;

    cout << "Enter Number 1 ";
    cin >> Num1;
    cout << "Enter Number 2 ";
    cin >> Num2;

    Alpha First(Num1,Num2);
    First.Calc();
    First.Show();

    Beta Second(Num1,Num2);
    Second.Calc();
    Second.Show();
}
```

Comments

In this example, you created two classes with member functions using the same name. This is the easiest way to show how to use the scope resolution operator in order to distinguish the member functions from each other. In reality, you wouldn't create two classes like this (one to add two numbers together and another to multiply them). The easiest way would be to create one member function for each different calculation.

5.4 How do I...
Use dot notation to access the member functions of an object?

Problem

Anyone used to working with traditional-style programs, whether those programs are linear or procedural, finds it potentially confusing to work with objects. An object is a mini-program in its own right and carries its own member variables and functions. Member functions are accessed with dot notation, whereas no dot is used when constructing the object. Why is this so?

Technique

The constructor is used to create an instance of the class and give that instance a unique name. Dot notation is not used to achieve this action. This has the effect of allocating enough computer memory to hold all the member variables and the code for the member functions of the class. After it has been created, or instantiated, that memory block is known as an *object*. Figure 5.11 shows the constructor in action.

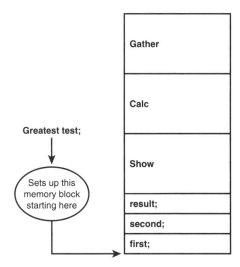

Figure 5.11 The constructor allocates memory and attaches a unique name to an object.

After an object is created, you need to access individual member functions within it. This is done using what is known as dot notation. Dot notation tells the compiler which member function is being called. At machine level, the member function name is a symbolic reference that specifies how far the member function code is removed from the start of the object memory block. This is shown in Figures 5.12 and 5.13.

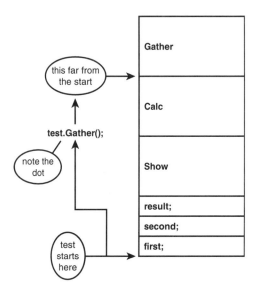

Figure 5.12   The member function Gather is removed by this number of bytes from the starting base address of the object test.

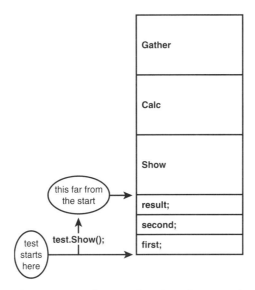

Figure 5.13 The member function Show is removed by this number of bytes from the starting base address of the object test.

Steps

In this example, the actions of constructing an object and invoking its member functions are done in the main body of the program.

1. The first step is to create the object with this line of code. *Do not* use dot notation to create an object. This line is used to allocate computer memory.

```
Greatest test;
```

2. Then invoke the Gather() member function using dot notation.

3. Invoke the Calc() member function, again using dot notation to perform an action.

```
test.Calc();
```

4. The Show() member function is invoked to display the data member result to the screen. Like all member functions, it is invoked using dot notation to separate the object name and the required member function.

```
test.Show();
```

How It Works

To get information into an object, you must state the name of the object and the member function within that object that you are referring to.

```
test.Gather();
```

First, set up the class definition. The class is called `Greatest` and has the following capabilities:

1. Gathering two integer values and storing these values in the private data members `first` and `second`.

2. Calculating which of these two integer values is greater and storing the greater value in the private data member `result`.

3. Showing `result` to the screen.

4. The constructor initializes `result` to `0` as an object is created and issues the comfort message `New test object created` just to prove that the constructor has done its job.

5. The destructor issues the comfort message `Test object destroyed` to prove that the object no longer exists.

The `main()` function contains a `while` loop that continually creates a new object called `test` using the class constructor. The user is invited to enter two integer values using the member function `Gather()`. Those two values are compared using the member function `Calc()` and the greater value is stored in the data member `result`. The member function `Show()` simply displays the result to the screen.

There is an valid point to be made here. Note that you have a definition of the destructor `~Greatest`. That destructor is never called into action, but you will see its message on the screen every time the `while` loop does its job. Destructors are automatically invoked every time an object goes out of scope, and your `test` object goes out of scope at the end of the `while` loop.

Here is the full program listing.

```
// Accessing member functions using dot notation.

#include <iostream.h>

class Greatest {
            private:
                int first;
                int second;
                int result;
            public:
                Greatest();
                ~Greatest();
                void Gather(void);
```

```cpp
                void Calc(void);
                void Show(void);
        };

Greatest::Greatest()
{
    result = 0;
    cout << "New test object created" << endl << endl;
}

Greatest::~Greatest()
{
    cout << "Test object destroyed" << endl << endl;
}


void Greatest::Gather(void)
{
    cout << "Enter the first number : ";
    cin >> first;
    cout << "Enter the second number : ";
    cin >> second;
}

void Greatest::Calc(void)
{
    if (first > second)
        result = first;
    else
        result = second;
}

void Greatest::Show(void)
{
    cout << "The greatest number is : " << result
<< endl << endl;
}

main()
{
    char again;

    while(1)
    {
        Greatest test;
        test.Gather();
        test.Calc();
        test.Show();
        cout << "Again : ";
        cin >> again;
        if (again != 'y')
            break;
    }
    return(0);
}
```

Comments

The jargon used in object-oriented programming is difficult to pick up and doesn't help the novice.

The terms *instance* and *object* are used interchangeably. When an object is constructed, it is said to be an instance of the class. In other words, you instantiate a class to create an object. This process can be repeated many times to create many objects from the same class. Don't forget that a class is the specification, whereas an object is the physical memory within the computer used to create an instance of the class.

In the early days of OOP, the code that manipulated the member variables was called either member functions or methods. Depending upon which camp you came from, only one naming methodology was correct. To laymen, methods and member functions are exactly the same thing. They are computer code used to manipulate data members. Don't be confused: Member functions and methods are the same thing.

COMPLEXITY
BEGINNING

5.5 How do I...
Know which constructor to use when there are several to choose from?

Problem

In this How-To, you will develop and study a class named **Shape**. The **Shape** class finds the area or volume of the following geometric shapes: circle, rectangle, and cube. To do this, you can use the same class but build the object with a different constructor. Depending upon how the constructor definitions are written, you can impose actions upon the class as it instantiates the object.

Technique

A constructor always has the same name as its class. However, you can have as many constructors as you want within the same class as long as they have different signatures. The word *signature* simply means the constructors have different numbers or data types of input parameters. The technique of using constructors with different signatures is known as *overloading*. Because of the different signatures, the C++ compiler can differentiate between the constructors and select the one most appropriate for the task of building the object.

Steps

1. When following constructor is invoked

```
Shape circle(5);
```

the compiler spots that only one input parameter is of type **integer**. The only signature that fits this call is the constructor that has only one input parameter of type **integer**. Therefore, that constructor is the one used to instantiate the object.

```
Shape::Shape(int a)
{
    result = 3.143 * a * a;
}
```

2. The object is built and given the unique (within this program) variable name of **circle** (see Figure 5.14).

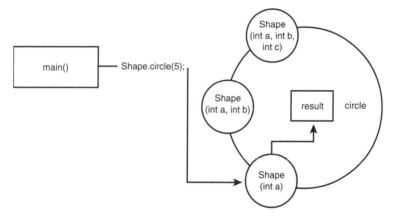

Figure 5.14 The Shape constructor called with a single integer input leads to this object.

3. When the following alternative constructor is invoked

```
Shape square(3,4);
```

the compiler spots that two input parameters are of type **integer**. The only signature that fits this call is the constructor that has two input parameters of type **integer**. Therefore, that constructor is the one used to instantiate the object.

```
Shape::Shape(int a, int b)
{
    result = a*b;
}
```

4. The second object is built and given the unique name of **square** (see Figure 5.15).

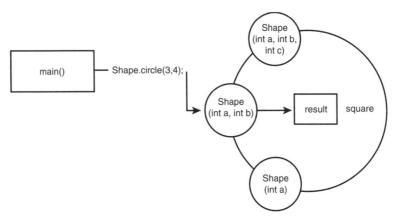

Figure 5.15 The Shape constructor called with two integer input leads to this object.

5. Finally, when the following constructor is invoked

```
Shape box(3,4,5);
```

the compiler spots that three input parameters are of type **integer**. The only signature that fits this call is the constructor that has three input parameters of type **integer**. Therefore, that constructor is the one used to instantiate the object.

```
Shape::Shape(int a, int b, int c)
{
    result = a*b*c;
}
```

6. The third object is built and given the name **box** (see Figure 5.16).

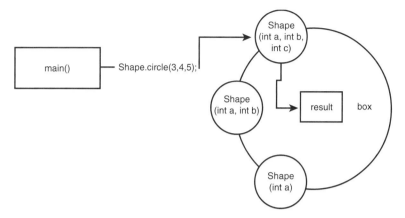

Figure 5.16 The Shape constructor called with three integer inputs leads to this object

How It Works

In the following program, the class **Shape** has a private member variable named **result** of type **double**. This variable is used to hold the answer calculated by the object. The program uses three overloaded constructors, each of which has its own signature. The difference in signatures leads to the use of one of three possible definitions when an object is created from the class. A final member function called **Show** is used to access the private member variable **result** and show it to the screen. The complete program is as follows:

```
// A class with three constructors
// This is overloading

#include <iostream.h>

class Shape     {
            private:
                double result;
            public:
                Shape(int a);
                Shape(int a, int b);
                Shape(int a, int b, int c);
                void Show(void);
            };

// This constructor is for circles
Shape::Shape(int a)
{
    result = 3.143 * a * a;
}

// This constructor is for rectangles
Shape::Shape(int a, int b)
{
```

```
        result = a*b;
}

// This constructor is for boxes
Shape::Shape(int a, int b, int c)
{
    result = a*b*c;
}

void Shape::Show(void)
{
    cout << "The result is : " << result << endl;
}

main()
{
    Shape circle(5);
    Shape square(3,4);
    Shape box(3,4,5);
    circle.Show();
    square.Show();
    box.Show();
    return(0);
}
```

Comments

In the preceding program, three objects were created from the **Shape** class. It is worth noting that each one is completely separate and unique. Each one has its own data member **result** and its own **Show** member function. They all exist at the same time and are objects that can be called into life by the main program. This is shown in Figure 5.17.

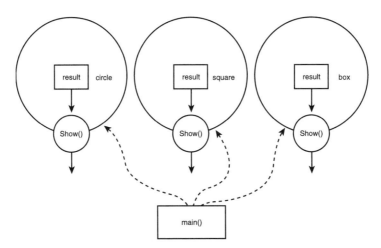

Figure 5.17 The relationship to main after three objects have been constructed from the Shape class.

5.6 How do I...
Implement function overloading?

Problem

Often a specific task must be performed on inputs to functions. It might be that different data types or different numbers of parameters are required for such operations. Traditionally, in languages such as C, you could define a function including the parameters to that function by a name only once. If a variety of flavors of the function were required, each flavor had to have a different name so that essentially it was a different function. In OOP languages such as C++, both the name and the input parameters differentiate functions. The function name and its parameters are known as the signature of the function. This allows for groups of related functions that perform similar tasks and have the same name, but that can be distinguished from one another by their input parameters. This is called function overloading.

The following example creates and makes use of overloaded functions.

Technique

Some simple rules must be followed to implement function overloading. Basically, overloading means one function name will have many definitions. Note that this allows a common interface to deal with different situations.

Steps

1. The first step is to create a program that deals with one situation. You can then build on that as needs occur.

The following listing deals with integers. The function **Alpha** accepts two integers as input, multiplies them together, and returns the result. The result is fed to the function **Show**, which takes an integer as input. This value is shown onscreen.

```
// Overloaded Functions

#include <iostream.h>

int Alpha(int x,int y);
void Show(int Result);

void main()
{
    int x,y;
```

```
    cout << "Enter an Integer : ";
    cin >> x;
    cout << endl << "Enter another Integer : ";
    cin >> y;

    Show(Alpha(x,y));
}

int Alpha(int x,int y)
{
    return x*y;
}

void Show(int Result)
{
    cout << endl << "The Result is " << Result;
}
```

2. The problem in the preceding example lies in the fact that you should only enter integers. What if you wanted to enter a floating-point number or a character? As the program stands, you can't enter anything other than an integer because it gives weird results. In a real-life situation, the programmer should add extra code to check that the input is of the correct data type and reject any incorrect input. This error checking can be used to force the user to enter the correct form of input. However, in the example this is where function overloading comes in. The next step is to design two new functions, also called **Alpha**, that can deal with the different data types. Also, you must design two more function definitions for the **Show** function to deal with the other data types.

```
// Overloaded Functions

#include <iostream.h>

int Alpha(int x,int y);             //Integers
float Alpha(float x,float y);       //Floats
char Alpha(char x,char y);          //Characters
void Show(int Result);
void Show(float Result);
void Show(char Result);

void main()
{
    int x,y;
    float s,t;
    char a,b;

    cout << "Enter an Integer : ";
    cin >> x;
    cout << endl << "Enter another Integer : ";
    cin >> y;

    Show(Alpha(x,y));
```

```
        cout << endl << "Enter a Float : ";
        cin >> s;
        cout << endl << "Enter another Float : ";
        cin >> t;

        Show(Alpha(s,t));

        cout << endl << "Enter a Character : ";
        cin >> a;
        cout << endl << "Enter another Character : ";
        cin >> b;

        Show(Alpha(a,b));

}

int Alpha(int x,int y)
{
        return x*y;
}

void Show(int Result)
{
        cout << endl << "The Result is " << Result << endl;
}

float Alpha(float x,float y)
{
        return x*y;
}

void Show(float Result)
{
        cout << endl << "The Result is " << Result << endl;
}

char Alpha(char x,char y)
{
        if (x<y)
                return x;
        else
                return y;
}

void Show(char Result)
{
        cout << endl << "The First Character is " << Result  << endl;
}
```

How It Works

In the preceding sample program, there are two integer variables, two float variables, and two character variables within the main body of the program. First, the code in the main program establishes that the user will be invited to enter two integer values at runtime. These two variables are offered to the overloaded function **Alpha** as its two input parameters. At compile time, the correct version of **Alpha**—the one with an input of two integers—is established and that version is used. The other two versions of **Alpha** are different functions and are ignored at this point in time. The next section of code in **main** performs the same operation for two float inputs. Again, overloaded function **Alpha** is offered two inputs, but this time they are floats. At compile time, the correct version of **Alpha** is established and the correct version is used. The same process occurs for the next two inputs. These two inputs are characters, but due to overloading the compiler can parse the code and determine the correct version of the function to use. The process of determining the correct version of the overloaded function that will be used is established at compile time. This is known as early binding.

Comments

The example shown deals with only three combinations of data types. You could quite easily create other overloaded functions that use mixed data types. You could create as many as you like covering all possibilities of input. A more advanced way around selecting differing data types is covered within the topic of template classes in Chapter 6, "Template Classes."

COMPLEXITY
INTERMEDIATE

5.7 How do I...
Correctly make use of inheritance?

Problem

Beginning C++ programmers often run into several problems when trying to use inherited classes. The most common mistake is forgetting to declare the inheritance from a base class. The programmer must also be aware that in order for member variables to be inherited, they must be declared as protected and not private. These errors might cause other developers using your base class to try to re-declare the member variables in the derived class because they cannot gain access to the private base class member variables. By making this error, you are including a class that is not being used.

Technique

When designing a class, it is very important to decide whether the class will be used in the future via inheritance. If it will be, you must make sure that the data members are protected and not private. Also, if you are going to allow the member functions to be used and altered, you must declare them as virtual functions.

To declare the inheritance of a class, you must use the syntax shown in Figure 5.18.

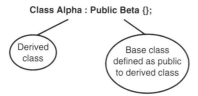

Class Alpha : Public Beta {};

Derived class

Base class defined as public to derived class

Figure 5.18 Alpha class inheriting from Beta base class.

You will be creating a new class called **Alpha** that inherits all the member variables and functions found in class **Beta**, and makes them public to the new derived class.

Also, the way you use the constructor is slightly different. Because you are inheriting from another class (the base class), **Beta** needs to have some information passed to it. As you know, you use a constructor to pass information into a class. The following syntax is used to call a derived class's constructor.

```
Alpha::Alpha(x,y,z):Beta(x,y)
```

Here, you use the standard syntax of a constructor but you add a colon to the end and add a call to the base class constructor. Also, you can pass on some of the data (in this case, x and y).

Steps

1. In this example, you are going to create a derived class called **Alpha**, which inherits from class **Beta**. Remember that **Beta** is the base class, so it will be designed first.

```
#include <iostream.h>

class Beta    {
       protected:
           int Val1,Val2;
           int total;
       public:
           void Calc(void);
           void Show(void);
           Beta(int x, int y);
       };
```

Note that the data members are protected not private. This allows them to be accessed by derived classes.

2. The next step is to create the member function definitions for the class.

```
void Beta::Calc(void)
{
t    otal = Val1 * Val2;
}

void Beta::Show(void)
{
    cout << "The total is " << total << endl;
}

Beta::Beta(int x, int y)
{
    Val1 = x;
    Val2 = y;
}
```

These are straightforward definitions. The constructor accepts two integer inputs. The **Calc** function multiplies the two values together and stores the result in **total**.

3. To test the class, create a main function to invoke the class.

```
void main(void)
{
    int x,y;
    cout << "Enter a Number ";
    cin >> x;
    cout << endl << "Enter another Number ";
    cin >>y;

    Beta First(x,y);
    First.Calc();
    First.Show();
}
```

4. Now, you must design the derived class that will inherit from class **Beta**.

```
class Alpha : public Beta{
              protected:
                  int Val3;
                  int Newtotal;

              public:
                  void CalcII(void);
                  void ShowII(void);
                  Alpha(int z,int x,int y);
              };
```

You can see in the header line of the class declaration that you specify that the class inherits from class **Beta**. This makes **Beta**'s member functions and member variables public to it.

5. Next, you must add member function definitions for the new derived class. Remember that you need to design only the new functions required for this new class because the functions for the base class are already written and tested. At no time should you alter the base class.

```
void Alpha::CalcII(void)
{
    Newtotal = Val1 * Val2 * Val3;
}

void Alpha::ShowII(void)
{
    cout << "The newtotal is " << Newtotal << endl;
}
Alpha::Alpha(int z, int x, int y):Beta(x,y)
{
    Val3 = z;
}
```

Take special note of the constructor design. The derived class **Alpha** requires three inputs, but it passes on two of them to the base class Beta. Also, note that the **CalcII** function is using member variables **Val1** and **Val2**, which actually belong to class **Beta** not class **Alpha**. This is allowed because the class is designed to have protected member variables. Therefore, all member variables are public within the classes.

6. The final stage is to alter the main program to make use of the new derived class **Alpha**. Remember, it is the **Alpha** class that you will use. **Alpha** will be able to call member functions from the base class if required.

```
void main(void)
{
    int x,y,z;
    cout << "Enter a Number ";
    cin >> x;
    cout << endl << "Enter another Number ";
    cin >>y;
        cout << endl << "Enter a third Number ";
        cin >> z;

    Alpha First(z,x,y);
    First.Calc();      //Base Class
        First.CalcII();   //Derived Class
    First.Show();      //Base Class
        First.ShowII();   //Derived Class
}
```

In this example, the user enters three integers. An instance of derived class **Alpha** is created and passed the three values. **Alpha**'s constructor passes on two of the values to base class **Beta**. After the data is in the correct member variable, the calculations can be performed. To prove that all member functions are available to the derived class, a call is made to each one.

How It Works

When a class is designed, the programmer must decide whether the class is to be used via inheritance. If so, the data members must be declared to be protected. After the class is designed and tested, the programmer can forget about it because she knows that the class does its job.

Because the class has been tested, if it is to be used as a base class the programmer should simply be able to use it and not worry whether it will work.

When designing a derived class, it is very important to remember to specify the name of the base class in the header of the derived class. Also, specify that the base class is public to the new derived class.

During the design of the derived class constructor, the programmer must pass on the correct number of inputs to the base class constructor. This is the correct way to pass parameters to the base class.

After this is done, the programmer has access to all member variables and functions of both classes.

If required, the programmer can call functions from both the base and derived class, thus extending the capability of the program.

```
// Inheritance
#include <iostream.h>

class Beta     {
                protected:
                    int Val1,Val2;
                    int total;
                public:
                    void Calc(void);
                    void Show(void);
                    Beta(int x, int y);
             };

class Alpha : public Beta{
                protected:
                    int Val3;
                    int Newtotal;

                public:
                    void CalcII(void);
                    void ShowII(void);
                    Alpha(int z,int x,int y);
                };

void Beta::Calc(void)
{
    total = Val1 * Val2;
```

```
}

void Beta::Show(void)
{
    cout << "The total is " << total << endl;
}

Beta::Beta(int x, int y)
{
    Val1 = x;
    Val2 = y;
}

void Alpha::CalcII(void)
{
    Newtotal = Val1 * Val2 * Val3;
}

void Alpha::ShowII(void)
{
cout << "The newtotal is " << Newtotal << endl;
}
Alpha::Alpha(int z, int x, int y):Beta(x,y)
{
    Val3 = z;
}

void main(void)
{
    int x,y,z;
    cout << "Enter a Number ";
    cin >> x;
    cout << endl << "Enter another Number ";
    cin >>y;
        cout << endl << "Enter a third Number ";
        cin >> z;

    Alpha First(z,x,y);
    First.Calc();      //Base Class
        First.CalcII();    //Derived Class
    First.Show();      //Base Class
        First.ShowII();    //Derived Class
}
```

Comments

The most common problem beginning developers encounter is forgetting to set the data members of a base class as protected. If this is not done, developers have difficulty later when trying to inherit from the class. Another common mistake is forgetting to add the extra call to the base constructor at the end of the header for the derived constructor. Because of these mistakes, many C++ programmers end up redefining data members and member functions in a derived class that already exists in the base class. By doing so, they miss the whole point of being able to inherit something that already exists.

5.8 How do I...
Pass parameters back through the C++ inheritance mechanism to parent classes?

Problem

One of the most difficult things encountered by C++ programmers is the construction of a coherent inheritance model. They find constructors an especially difficult practical exercise and become terribly confused by parameters and where they are eventually stored.

Technique

The sample program later in this How-To creates a simple OOP program that creates a base class named **Triangle** and a child class named **Prism**. Triangles are two-dimensional objects with three sides. Prisms have three dimensions and have triangular side profiles; thus a prism is a triangle with depth (see Figure 5.19). The basic characteristics of a triangle apply to a prism, so those properties can be inherited and extended to create a prism. The ability to extend existing characteristics is the fundamental feature of inheritance.

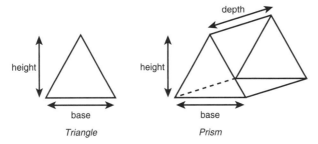

Figure 5.19 The relationship between a triangle and a prism.

Steps

1. The **Triangle** class contains three protected member variables named **base**, **height**, and **area,** respectively. As their names imply, these member variables will store the base and height dimensions of a triangle. **base** and **height** can be used to calculate the area of the triangle.

```
protected:
    double base;
    double height;
    double area;
```

2. The constructor is used to initialize the **base** and **height** data members when a triangle object is created.

```
Triangle(double b, double h)
{
    base = b;
    height = h;
}
```

This is shown in Figure 5.20.

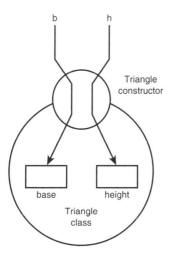

Figure 5.20 The constructor passes data to the protected member variables within the Triangle class.

3. As a side issue, if you are writing classes that will be inherited, declare your data members as protected if you want them to be used by the derived classes.

4. The **Triangle** class contains two public member functions. The first is **CalcArea**, which is used to calculate the area of the triangle. It also stores the result in the protected member variable **area**.

```
void CalcArea(void)
{
    area = (base * height) / 2;
}
```

5. The second method, **ShowArea**, is used to print the area to the screen.

```
void ShowArea(void)
{
    cout << "The area is : " << area << endl;
}
```

6. There is nothing too dramatic about those two member functions. The **Triangle** class could be used on its own to calculate the areas of triangles by simply instantiating an object and using the **CalcArea()** and **ShowArea()** member functions. The apparent confusion comes when you inherit those basic characteristics and write the **Prism** class. Many beginners find it difficult to grasp the concept that although the member variables **base**, **height**, and **area**, and the member function **ShowArea** are declared within the **Triangle** class, they are freely available to use in any **Prism** object.

7. The class has only one protected member variable named **depth**. However, because of inheritance, it also has copies of the member variables **base** and **height** available to it. The constructor for **Prism** has to deal with the instantiation of these member variable when it creates a **Prism** object. It is done with the following code fragment:

```
Prism(double d, double b, double h):Triangle(b,h)
{
    depth = d;
}
```

8. The **Prism** constructor accepts three data items. It knows what to do with the first one **d**, but has no instructions about the second two, **b** and **h**. Because the **Prism** constructor doesn't know what to do with them, it passes them to the **Triangle** constructor, which is attached to the end of the **Prism** constructor definition (see Figure 5.21). The **Prism** constructor is satisfied and couldn't care less what the **Triangle** constructor does with the two spare values. If the **Triangle** constructor can deal with the two values, it will do so (and in fact does in our case). If not, it will flag a compilation error.

9. Here is an alternative way of looking at the construction of an inherited object (see Figure 5.22).

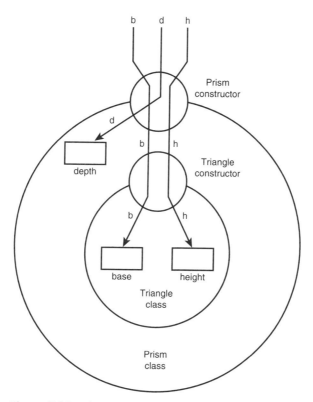

Figure 5.21 The Prism constructor passes data its own member variable depth, but passes the remaining data to the protected data members within the Triangle class.

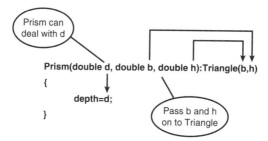

Figure 5.22 An alternative view of the Prism constructor passing its own member variable depth, but passing the remaining data to the protected member variables within the Triangle class.

How It Works

The basic functionality of `Triangle` is defined in the `Triangle` class. Inline definitions are used for the member functions because they are very short and simple. The `Prism` class inherits the characteristics of the `Triangle` base class and adds its own enhancements to it. These enhancements consist of a third member variable named `depth` and a member function named `CalcArea`. This new version of `CalcArea` is used to calculate the area of a prism rather than a triangle and is said to override the definition of `CalcArea` in the `Triangle` base class. When an instance of `Prism` is created, it uses the `CalcArea` associated with the `Prism` class. If an instance of `Triangle` is created, it uses the `CalcArea` associated with the `Triangle` class.

The main section of the following program creates an instance of `Prism` named `test` and gives it three values. Invisible to the programmer, the first parameter is acted on by the `Prism` constructor and the other two parameters are passed on to the `Triangle` constructor. Had a suitable `Triangle` constructor not been available a compilation error would have been flagged.

The rest of the program simply calculates the volume of the prism and displays the result to the screen. Here is the full listing.

```
// Inheritance

#include <iostream.h>

class Triangle    {
            protected:
                double base;
                double height;
                double area;
            public:
                Triangle(double b, double h)
                {
                    base = b;
                    height = h;
                }
                void CalcArea(void)
                {
                    area = (base * height) / 2;
                }
                void ShowArea(void)
                {
                    cout << "The area is : "
<< area << endl;
}
};

class Prism:public Triangle
{
    protected:
        double depth;
    public:
    Prism(double d, double b, double h):Triangle(b,h)
```

```
    {
        depth = d;
    }
    void CalcArea(void)
    {
        area = (base * height * depth) / 2;
    }
};

main()
{
    Prism test(3,5,10);
    test.CalcArea();
    test.ShowArea();
    return(0);
}
```

Comments

Confusion can arise when an appropriate constructor buried deep in the inheritance model cannot be found, and therefore all of the parameters cannot be dealt with. The example I have given you will always work because the correct number of parameters and the appropriate constructors are in the inheritance chain. But modify your main program as follows and see the result. As shown in the following code, I have only supplied two parameters to the constructor instead of three.

```
main()
{
    Prism test(3,5);
    test.CalcArea();
    test.ShowArea();
    return(0);
}
```

My compiler simply says:

```
-----------------Configuration: Listing 5.8b - Win32 Debug-----------------
Compiling...
Listing5.8b.cpp
F:\How To\Chapter 05\Listing5.8b\Listing5.8b.cpp(44) : error C2661:
   'Prism::Prism' : no overloaded function takes 2 parameters
Error executing cl.exe.

Listing5.8b.obj - 1 error(s), 0 warning(s)
```

Unless you really are experienced in C++ programming this message means very little and it simply scares the beginner.

Now try the following amendment to the **main** program. This time I have given it four parameters instead of three.

```
main()
{
    Prism test(3,5,10,4);
    test.CalcArea();
```

```
    test.ShowArea();
    return(0);
}
```

My compiler simply says:

```
-----------------Configuration: Listing5.8b - Win32 Debug------------------
Compiling...
Listing5.8b.cpp
F:\How To\Chapter 05\Listing5.8b\Listing5.8b.cpp(44) : error C2661:
    'Prism::Prism' : no overloaded function takes 4 parameters
Error executing cl.exe.

Listing5.8b.obj - 1 error(s), 0 warning(s)
```

I was using Microsoft Visual C++ version 5 at the time of writing. If you are using a different compiler, the error message and format will be different. The actual error will, of course, be the same.

The error message tells you that the compiler could not find an appropriate constructor, or chain of constructors, to deal with the given number of parameters in the creation of the object.

COMPLEXITY

INTERMEDIATE

5.9 How do I...
Distinguish between virtual classes and nonvirtual classes? How do I know when to use virtual classes and what does the word *virtual* mean in C++?

Problem

When building up a hierarchical inheritance network, it is difficult to know when and when not to use the word *virtual*. Often it seems to make no difference whether classes are declared as virtual or not.

Technique

Some simple rules can be applied to verify whether functions should be declared as virtual. It depends upon whether multiple inheritance is to be used. The key is an understanding of the meaning of the term virtual. When a function is declared as virtual, the derived class contains only a reference back to the original base class, and so uses the single occurrence of the original (see Figure 5.23). You can declare any member function as virtual and in most cases there is (to the end user) no apparent difference. However, in order to avoid redefinition of functions in a multiple inheritance model you should always declare functions to be virtual.

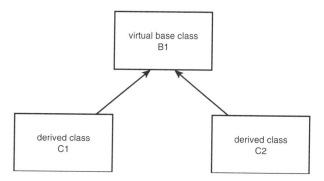

Figure 5.23 Two derived classes sharing a virtual base class.

When a function is declared as nonvirtual, the derived class contains a copy of the original base class; therefore, multiple occurrences of the original exist within the inheritance hierarchy (see Figure 5.24).

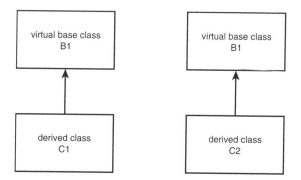

Figure 5.24 Two derived classes containing copies of the base class.

To demonstrate the art of virtual functions you will build up a sequence of programs that inherit from a simple base class and add ever more functionality to the derived classes. You will use a model based upon Ohm's Law. Ohm's Law is the underlying principle of all DC electric circuits and it concerns the relationship between resistance, voltage, and current (see Figure 5.25). Do not be concerned if you aren't into electronics, it is only the three simple equations that you are interested in.

$$V = I * R$$

$$I = \frac{V}{R}$$

$$R = \frac{V}{I}$$

where   V=voltage

           I=current

           R=resistance

Figure 5.25 The three Ohm's Law equations used in this section.

Steps

1. Start by writing a simple class that holds the value of a resistor (in ohms) and displays the value to the screen. The following code declares the member function **Rout** to be virtual, but you will find that if you remove the word **virtual** it makes no difference to the program. The word **virtual** only has an effect on derived classes of which, as yet, there are none.

```
// Inheritance

#include <iostream.h>

class Resistance
    {
    protected:
        int R;
    public:
        Resistance(int r) { R = r ;}
        virtual void Rout(void) { cout << R << endl;}
    };

main()
{
    Resistance R1(47000);
    R1.Rout();
    return(0);
}
```

2. Using the functionality of the **Resistance** class, you can take advantage of inheritance in C++ to create two new classes. The **Voltage** class accepts the voltage (**V**) and resistance (**R**) and then uses them to calculate the current (**I**). Note the first line definitions of the **Voltage** class and the **Current** class. They both refer to **Resistance** as **virtual**.

```
class Voltage : virtual public Resistance
```

```
class Current : virtual public Resistance
```

This gives rise to the inheritance model shown in Figure 5.26.

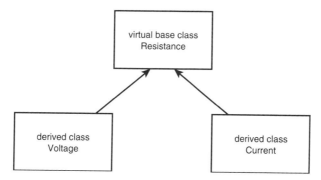

Figure 5.26 The virtual inheritance model used by Voltage and Current.

3. Here is the program; give it a try.

```
// Inheritance

#include <iostream.h>

class Resistance
    {
    protected:
        int R;
    public:
        Resistance(int r) {R = r;}
        virtual void Rout(void) {cout << R << endl;}
    };

class Voltage : virtual public Resistance
    {
    protected:
        double V;
        double I;
    public:
        Voltage(double v, int r):Resistance(r)
            {V = v;}
        virtual void CalcI(void)
            {I = V/R;}
        virtual void Iout(void)
            {cout << I << endl;}
    };

class Current : virtual public Resistance
    {
    protected:
        double V;
        double I;
    public:
        Current(double i, int r):Resistance(r)
```

```
                    {I = i;}
            virtual void Vout(void)
                {cout << V << endl;}
            virtual void CalcV(void)
                {V = I*R;}
    };

main()
{
    // Given the voltage and resistance
    // We can calculate the current
    Voltage V1(10,27000);
    V1.CalcI();
    V1.Rout();
    V1.Iout();
    cout << endl;

    // Given the current and the resistance
    // We can calculate the voltage
    Current I1(0.2,68000);
    I1.CalcV();
    I1.Rout();
    I1.Vout();
    cout << endl;

    return(0);
}
```

4. You can modify the preceding program to produce a nonvirtual inheritance model by simply removing the keyword **virtual** from the declarations of **Voltage** and **Current**.

```
class Voltage : public Resistance
```

```
class Current : public Resistance
```

This modification gives rise to the nonvirtual inheritance model shown in Figure 5.27.

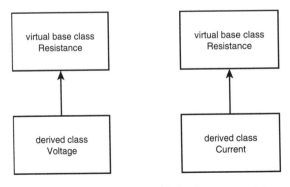

Figure 5.27 The nonvirtual inheritance model used by Voltage and Current.

5. Here is the nonvirtual version of the program. Again, at this level it works and appears to be identical to its virtual counterpart.

```
// Nonvirtual Inheritance

#include <iostream.h>

class Resistance
        {
        protected:
            int R;
        public:
            Resistance(int r)
                {R = r;}
            virtual void Rout(void)
                {cout << R << endl;}
        };

class Voltage : public Resistance
        {
        protected:
            double V;
            double I;
        public:
            Voltage(double v, int r):Resistance(r)
                {V = v;}
            virtual void CalcI(void)
                {I = V/R;}
            virtual void Iout(void)
                {cout << I << endl;}
        };

class Current : public Resistance
        {
        protected:
            double V;
            double I;
        public:
            Current(double i, int r):Resistance(r)
                {I = i;}
            virtual void Vout(void)
                {cout << V << endl;}
            virtual void CalcV(void)
                {V = I*R;}
        };

main()
{
    // Given the voltage and resistance
    // We can calculate the current
    Voltage V1(10,27000);
    V1.CalcI();
    V1.Rout();
    V1.Iout();
    cout << endl;
```

```
// Given the current and the resistance
// We can calculate the voltage
Current I1(0.2,68000);
I1.CalcV();
I1.Rout();
I1.Vout();
cout << endl;

    return(0);
}
```

6. Having created classes to deal with resistance, voltage, and current, it makes sense to unite them into a single OhmsLaw class because that is their common root. You will do this using a multiple inheritance model that draws together all the functionality developed so far. Figure 5.28 shows that model.

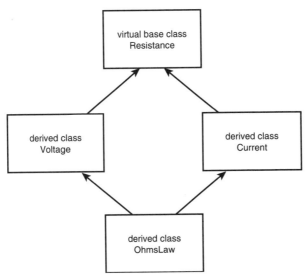

Figure 5.28 The virtual multiple inheritance model of the OhmsLaw class.

7. The following program pulls together all the operations for Ohm's Law in order to calculate and display any combination of voltage, resistance, and current. The important point is that you have used multiple inheritance and virtual classes to collect those actions.

```
// Multiple Inheritance

#include <iostream.h>

class Resistance
    {
```

```
                    protected:
                        int R;
                    public:
                        Resistance(int r)                    {R = r;}
                        virtual void Rout(void)
                                {cout << R << endl;}
                    };

        class Voltage :  virtual public Resistance
                    {
                    protected:
                        double V;
                        double I;
                    public:
                        Voltage(double v, int r):Resistance(r)
                                {V = v;}
                        virtual void CalcI(void)
                                {I = V/R;}
                        virtual void Iout(void)
                                {cout << I << endl;}
                    };

        class Current : virtual public Resistance
                    {
                    protected:
                        double V;
                        double I;
                    public:
                        Current(double i, int r):Resistance(r)
                                {I = i;}
                        virtual void Vout(void)
                                {cout << V << endl;}
                        virtual void CalcV(void)
                                {V = I*R;}
                    };

        class OhmsLaw : public Voltage, public Current
                {
                public:
                    OhmsLaw(double i, double v, int r)
                            :Current(i,r),Voltage(v,r),Resistance(r){ }
                };

        main()
        {
            OhmsLaw L1(0.02,10,1000);
            L1.CalcV();
            L1.CalcI();
            L1.Rout();
            L1.Vout();
            L1.Iout();
            cout << endl;

            return(0);
        }
```

How It Works

I now invite you to convert the virtual class model in the previous program into a nonvirtual inheritance model by simply removing the keyword `virtual` from the declarations of `Voltage` and `Current` just as before.

```
class Voltage : public Resistance
```

```
class Current : public Resistance
```

This modification gives rise to the nonvirtual inheritance model shown in Figure 5.29 and this is where the problems arise. Because the derived classes `Voltage` and `Current` inherit from a nonvirtual `Resistance` class, each makes a physical copy of `Resistance`. At the `Voltage` and `Current` class level this does not present a problem because they are separate classes. However, when they are combined into the `OhmsLaw` class using multiple inheritance, the compiler sees two identical versions of the `Resistance` class and flags an error.

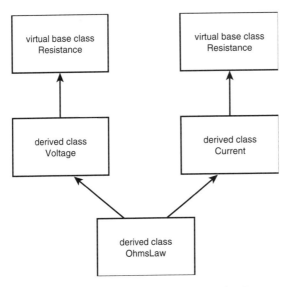

Figure 5.29 The nonvirtual multiple inheritance model of the `OhmsLaw` class.

Figure 5.29 shows two references to the `Resistance` class and they come together in the `OhmsLaw` class. This is illegal in C++. Two items with exactly the same name cannot exist because the program will refuse to compile. Here is the complete program listing; it is just the code listing from step 7 with the virtual class directives removed. Try out the modification and experience the compilation errors.

```
// Nonvirtual Multiple Inheritance
// WARNING THIS PROGRAM DOES NOT WORK
```

```cpp
// IT IS DESIGNED TO SHOW AN ERROR

#include <iostream.h>

class Resistance
      {
      protected:
          int R;
      public:
          Resistance(int r)
              {R = r;}
          virtual void Rout(void)
              {cout << R << endl;}
      };

class Voltage :  public Resistance
      {
      protected:
          double V;
          double I;
      public:
          Voltage(double v, int r):Resistance(r)
              {V = v;}
          virtual void CalcI(void)
              {I = V/R;}
          virtual void Iout(void)
              {cout << I << endl;}
      };

class Current :  public Resistance
      {
      protected:
          double V;
          double I;
      public:
          Current(double i, int r):Resistance(r)
              {I = i;}
          virtual void Vout(void)
              {cout << V << endl;}
          virtual void CalcV(void)
              {V = I*R;}
      };

class OhmsLaw : public Voltage, public Current
    {
    public:
        OhmsLaw(double i, double v, int r)
            :Current(i,r),Voltage(v,r),Resistance(r){ }
    };

main()
{
    OhmsLaw L1(0.02,10,1000);
    L1.CalcV();
    L1.CalcI();
    L1.Rout();
```

```
    L1.Vout();
    L1.Iout();
    cout << endl;

    return(0);
}
```

My compiler gave the following set of error messages. When you see this for the first time it's quite frightening, but the secret is to make sure that an inherited base class that is later recombined through multiple inheritance is defined as virtual.

```
Compiling...
Listing5.10e.cpp
F:\How To\Chapter 05\Listing5.10e\Listing5.10e.cpp(47) : error C2614:
    'OhmsLaw' : illegal member initialization: 'Resistance' is not a base
    or member
F:\How To\Chapter 05\Listing5.10e\Listing5.10e.cpp(56) : error C2385:
    'OhmsLaw::Rout' is ambiguous
F:\How To\Chapter 05\Listing5.10e\Listing5.10e.cpp(56) : warning C4385: could
    be the 'Rout' in base 'Resistance' of base 'Voltage' of class 'OhmsLaw'
F:\How To\Chapter 05\Listing5.10e\Listing5.10e.cpp(56) : warning C4385: or the
    'Rout' in base 'Resistance' of base 'Current' of class 'OhmsLaw'
Error executing cl.exe.

Listing5.10e.obj - 2 error(s), 2 warning(s)
```

Comments

Virtual classes can be very confusing and difficult to use. As long as you understand the inheritance model, you can predict where duplication will occur and avoid the problem.

An added bonus is that virtual classes use less memory. Recall that they do not copy the class and make several versions of it; they only refer to the original. Therefore, there is only one copy: the original. In a large application, this memory savings can be quite significant.

6

TEMPLATE CLASSES

How do I...

6.1 **Create a template class to represent any simple data type and understand how to use the template in a working C++ program?**

6.2 **Create a template class to represent any simple data type and extend it to read in data to a variable of any data type?**

6.3 **Create a template class to represent a compound data type and understand how to use the template in a working C++ program?**

6.4 **Write a template class that has two undefined data types that can be resolved at a later time?**

6.5 **Use a template class to handle a structure?**

C++ is a strongly typed language. This means the compiler checks to see whether an integer variable is being assigned an integer value, a float variable is being assigned a float value, and so on. This is good, safe programming practice because it imposes discipline on the programmer. However, this same imposed discipline also imposes the need to write unique solutions for every data type even if the problem is the same.

This problem was realized way back in the early days of C++; therefore, a concept known as template classes was incorporated into the language. A *template class* is a mechanism that allows a single solution to a problem to be written that can satisfy all data types. The actual data type required can be specified later and the template class can then be used for a wide range of data types, all using the same C++ template.

6.1 Create a Template Class to Represent Any Simple Data Type and Understand How to Use the Template in a Working C++ Program

The processes performed on simple data are often fairly standard. However, using conventional programming, those processes would have to be written for every conceivable data type likely to be encountered. This means any class that operates in such a way potentially requires many definitions. Writing and maintaining this code can be a lengthy and costly business. Using a template class, you can overcome this problem and write a single solution that meets all your needs for the desired process.

6.2 Create a Template Class to Represent Any Simple Data Type and Extend It to Read in Data to a Variable of Any Data Type

The process of using a data constant embedded within a program presents no real problem. However, rather than storing and displaying a data constant, data from the keyboard often needs to be read in. A template class that can be customized to handle any simple C++ data type is initially set up and then customized in the main program to handle a specific simple data type.

6.3 Create a Template Class to Represent a Compound Data Type and Understand How to Use the Template in a Working C++ Program

Much of computing is about the storage of large quantities of data. A data structure used to store this data is called an array and is referred to as a compound data type. As with simple data types, many class definitions are needed to store every conceivable compound data type, and again the problem is overcome with the use of templates.

6.4 Write a Template Class That Has Two Undefined Data Types That Can Be Resolved at a Later Time

In practice, most, if not all, computer programs deal with multiple variables of varying data types. If several data types are involved and similar processes are applied to them, many definitions of those processes would be required. The definition of a process to deal with several variables can also be captured in a template.

6.5   Use a Template Class to Handle a Structure

The problem with structures is that they are a user-defined data type, and therefore have an infinite number of possible definitions. The problem appears to be that a template cannot be written for a problem that has an infinite number of solutions. However, this is not the case, and structures can actually be dealt with by the same solution as a simple variable. Thus, templates can be used to solve this problem.

COMPLEXITY
INTERMEDIATE

6.1   How do I...

Create a template class to represent any simple data type and understand how to use the template in a working C++ program?

Problem

Often when designing a program, it is required to perform a specific operation on different simple data types. This means any class that has such a requirement potentially requires many definitions of that class to deal with all conceivable data types likely to be encountered. This can be a lengthy and costly process.

Technique

By using a template, you can design a single class that operates on data of many types instead of creating a separate class for each individual type you are likely to use. This means you can reduce this duplication to a single class definition. In turn, this significantly reduces source code size and increases code flexibility without compromising type safety.

Templates are used to create a class that can operate on data of any type. The advantages are that templates are easy to write, and you create only one generic version of your class instead of writing many specialized but similar variations of the same thing. In addition, template classes are said to be type-safe because the types the template acts upon are known at compile time. At compile time, type checking is performed and errors are picked up before they occur at runtime.

Steps

1. Before diving in, I will introduce you to the "data type" that the entire process hinges on. In C++, the letter *T* is used to specify an unknown data type. The use of the letter *T* is a convention so other letters will be recognized by the compiler. You will see the use of other letters later in this chapter. *T* is used whenever I want to specify a data type that will be defined later. This will be used when the template is applied to a specific application of the class after the actual data type is known.

2. In the first example given in Listing 6.1, you will learn how to set up a template class that contains a single variable whose data type will be defined in the main program.

3. The first step is to define the class. Figure 6.1 shows a very simple example that holds a single member variable and a single member function to display the contents of that member variable.

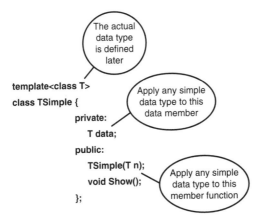

Figure 6.1 A simple template class definition.

4. Defining the constructor is just like defining a normal member function except that you prefix the definition with the line **template <class T>** and specify the input data type as **T** (see Figure 6.2).

5. The member function is even easier. Just prefix the definition with the instruction **template <class T>** as shown in Figure 6.3.

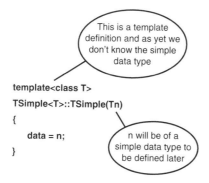

```
template<class T>
TSimple<T>::TSimple(Tn)
{
    data = n;
}
```

Figure 6.2 A simple template class constructor definition.

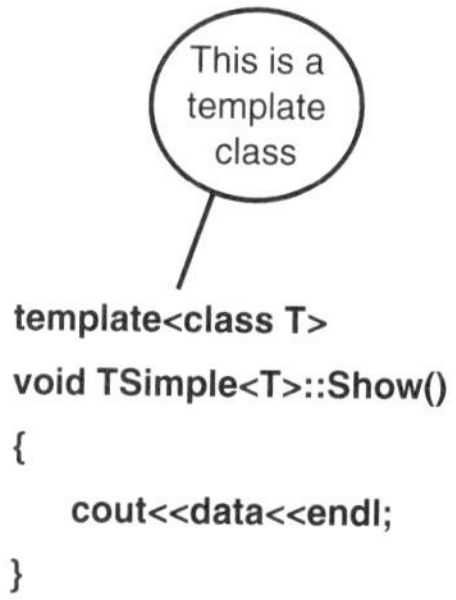

```
template<class T>
void TSimple<T>::Show()
{
    cout<<data<<endl;
}
```

Figure 6.3 A simple template member function definition.

6. So far, you have set up the class definitions and created a template class that can be of any data type. When you move into the main program you tell the class what the actual data type is to be. In this example, choose the `integer` data type (see Figure 6.4).

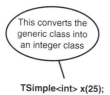

```
TSimple<int> x(25);
```

Figure 6.4 Customizing the template class to `integer`.

7. The action is virtually identical when the template class is converted into a `character` class (see Figure 6.5).

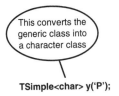

This converts the generic class into a character class

TSimple<char> y('P');

Figure 6.5 Customizing the template class to character.

8. When the template class is defined to `double` the process is identical (see Figure 6.6).

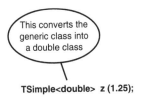

This converts the generic class into a double class

TSimple<double> z (1.25);

Figure 6.6 Customizing the template class to double.

How It Works

Listing 6.1 shows how the class is defined to accept any simple data type. The constructor and single member function are also type independent. In the main body of the program, three instances of the generic template class are created. The first object, x, has its member variable data created as type `integer`. The second object, y, is created using type `char` and the third object, z, is created using type `double`. The program simply shows how the single template class can be configured to deal with any simple data type.

Listing 6.1 A Single Class Template with a Simple Member Variable; Three Objects Are Created, Each Using a Different Data Type

```
// Template using simple data types.
// T is used to specify unknown data type.

#include <iostream.h>

template <class T>
class TSimple {
        private:
                T data;
            public:
                TSimple(T n);
                    void Show();
        };
```

```
template <class T>
TSimple<T>::TSimple(T n)
{
    data = n;
}

template <class T>
void TSimple<T>::Show()
{
    cout << data << endl;
}

main()
{
    TSimple<int> x(25);
        x.Show();
    TSimple<char> y('P');
        y.Show();
    TSimple<double> z(1.25);
        z.Show();
    return(0);
}
```

The screen output should look something like this:

```
25
P
1.25
```

Comments

Try changing the code to use other simple data types such as `float` and see
how flexible the template class can be.

COMPLEXITY
INTERMEDIATE

6.2 How do I...

Create a template class to represent any simple data type and extend it to read in data to a variable of any data type?

Problem

The problem here is very similar to that described in the previous How-To. This
time however, rather than storing and displaying static data, you are reading in
some data from the keyboard. You do not know what that data type is initially,
but you can set up a template class that can be customized to handle any
simple C++ data type.

Technique

The technique is virtually identical to the technique introduced in the previous How-To. All you need to do is add a member function to your template class that asks the user to enter some data. This new member function is set up to handle any simple data type. Within the main program when you create an object based upon the class, instruct the class to handle a simple data type such as an `integer` or `character`. After that has been done, all data types represented by `T` become an integer or character.

Steps

1. All you need to do is add a new member function, which I have called `Gather()`. Notice that I have changed the signature of the constructor. In the previous How-To, the constructor was used to initialize a data constant in your object. In this example, you are using `Gather()` to collect data at runtime.

```
template <class T>
class TSimple    {
             private:
                   T data;
             public:
                   TSimple();
                void Gather();
                void Show();
             };
```

2. Next, you must give a definition of your new `Gather()` member function. Other than the first line describing the template, it is exactly the same as a normal OOP definition of a member function.

```
template <class T>
void TSimple<T>::Gather()
{
    cout << "Enter the data : ";
    cin >> data;
}
```

3. In the main body of the program, create an instance of `TSimple` and stamp the data type as `integer`. From then on, simply invoke the member function in normal OOP fashion and it behaves in an integer manner.

```
main()
{
    TSimple<int> x;
    x.Gather();
    x.Show();
    return(0);
}
```

How It Works

Listing 6.2 is a full program that shows how to set up the TSimple class for any simple data type. The first call deals with integers, the second call with characters, and the third call with doubles. After all the data is read in using the new Gather() member function, the data is shown to the screen.

Listing 6.2   Listing 6.2 Is an Extension of Listing 6.1 and Has an Additional Member Function That Allows Runtime Input

```
// Template reads in a simple data type.
// T is used to specify an unknown data type.

#include <iostream.h>

template <class T>
class TSimple    {
              private:
                      T data;
              public:
                      TSimple();
                  void Gather();
                  void Show();
              };

template <class T>
TSimple<T>::TSimple()
{
    cout << "Template class constructed" << endl;
}

template <class T>
void TSimple<T>::Gather()
{
    cout << "Enter the data : ";
    cin >> data;
}

template <class T>
void TSimple<T>::Show()
{
    cout << data << endl;
}

main()
{
    TSimple<int> x;
    x.Gather();

    TSimple<char> y;
    y.Gather();

    TSimple<double> z;
    z.Gather();
```

```
    x.Show();
    y.Show();
    z.Show();

    return(0);
}
```

My screen looked like this:

```
Template class constructed
Enter the data : 77
Template class constructed
Enter the data : P
Template class constructed
Enter the data : 1.2345
77
P
1.2345
Press any key to continue
```

Try out the program and see how yours compares.

Comments

Again the simple data type can be made to be any legal C++ simple data type. I have used `integer`, `character`, and `double`, but there is no reason why you couldn't use `float` or even `bool` if you wanted to. Try modifying the preceding program to accept other simple data types and observing the results.

COMPLEXITY
INTERMEDIATE

6.3 How do I...
Create a template class to represent a compound data type and understand how to use the template in a working C++ program?

Problem

Much of computing is about the storage of large quantities of data items. One storage structure that can store multiple data items is an array. As in the problem with simple data types, lots of class definitions would be needed to store every conceivable data type. The problem is overcome with the use of templates.

Technique

The technique is virtually identical to the example in the previous How-To. The main difference is you specify that the member variable holding the data of unknown data type is a pointer to a block of memory. You should recall that any array variable is in fact a pointer to an area of memory (see Figure 6.7).

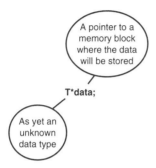

Figure 6.7 The pointer to the array of as yet unknown underlying data type.

Steps

1. The first step (as in the examples in the previous How-Tos) is to define the class. I will again give a very simple example that holds a single member variable that is a pointer to an area of memory. The size of the memory block will be defined later when the object is constructed. Member functions are used to collect the data to be stored in the array and to display the contents of the array to the screen.

```
template <class T>
class TArray    {
                private:
                        T *data;
                    int size;
                public:
                        TArray(int n);
                    void Gather();
                    void Show();
                };
```

2. The definition of the constructor is relatively simple. A single integer input parameter specifies the size of the array. The actual underlying data type of the array is defined in the main body of the program each time you create an instance of the class. Hence, the use of the letter T.

```
template <class T>
TArray<T>::TArray(int n)
```

```
{
    data = new T[n];
    size = n;
}
```

3. The member function that collects the data to be stored in the array is called Gather(), and other than the template directive as its first line, it is normal C++ code. It uses a **for** loop to read in data of an as-yet-unknown data type to be stored in the array.

```
template <class T>
void TArray<T>::Gather()
{
    int i;

    for (i = 0; i < size; i++)
    {
        cout << "Enter a number : ";
        cin >> data[i];
    }
}
```

4. The Show() function is used to display the contents of the array to the screen. Apart from the template directive, it is just like a normal C++ member function. Note that a **for** loop is used to display each item in the array to the screen.

```
template <class T>
void TArray<T>::Show()
{
    int i;

    for (i = 0; i < size; i++)
        cout << data[i] << endl;
}
```

5. The main program creates as object named x and defines the underlying data type to be **integer**. The array contains five elements; therefore, an array that can contain five integer values is created.

```
main()
{
    TArray<int> x(5);
    x.Gather();
    x.Show();
    return(0);
}
```

How It Works

When this program is run, the underlying data type is defined to be of type integer and the array to contain five elements. This information is used to construct an object named x. Next, the member function Gather() is invoked, which prompts the user to enter five integer values. Then the member function Show() is invoked, which displays the five integer values stored in the array to the screen. This is shown in the following screen display:

```
Enter a number : 44
Enter a number : 23
Enter a number : 87
Enter a number : 12
Enter a number : 29
44
23
87
12
29
Press any key to continue
```

Try out the program in Listing 6.3. Try entering your own values and verify the program operation.

Listing 6.3 A Template Class Designed to Display an Array of Any Simple Underlying Data Type

```cpp
// Template using array data types.
// T is used to specify unknown data type.

#include <iostream.h>

template <class T>
class TArray    {
                private:
                    T *data;
                  int size;
                public:
                    TArray(int n);
                  void Gather();
                  void Show();
                };

template <class T>
TArray<T>::TArray(int n)
{
    data = new T[n];
    size = n;
}
```

```
template <class T>
void TArray<T>::Gather()
{
    int i;

    for (i = 0; i < size; i++)
    {
            cout << "Enter a number : ";
        cin >> data[i];
    }
}

template <class T>
void TArray<T>::Show()
{
    int i;

    for (i = 0; i < size; i++)
        cout << data[i] << endl;
}

main()
{
    TArray<int> x(5);
    x.Gather();
    x.Show();
    return(0);
}
```

Comments

If you want to create an array to hold **double** values, it's just a question of changing **int** to **double** in the construction of **x**. This is shown in the next program fragment. All you need to do is change that single line in Listing 6.3.

```
main()
{
    TArray<double> x(5);
    x.Gather();
    x.Show();
    return(0);
}
```

If you want to increase the number of items stored in the array, simply change the **5** to whatever value you require, say **12**. Don't get too adventurous and use huge numbers here; it will take you ages to type in lots of values.

```
main()
{
    TArray<double> x(12);
    x.Gather();
    x.Show();
    return(0);
}
```

6.4 How do I...
Write a template class that has two undefined data types that can be resolved at a later time?

Problem

So far, you have dealt with templates that have a single undefined data type that is resolved in the main program. In practice, it is common to have more than one unknown in the template because several data types are often involved in any single program.

Technique

The way around the problem is straightforward. The previous three How-Tos dealt with templates that described a single simple data type and a single array data type. The example in this How-To deals with how two simple variables can be incorporated into a class template. Previously, the symbol T was used to describe the unknown; now the symbols T1 and T2 are used to describe the two unknowns.

Steps

1. First of all, create a template that can hold two simple data types. Define them as T1 and T2 (see Figure 6.8).

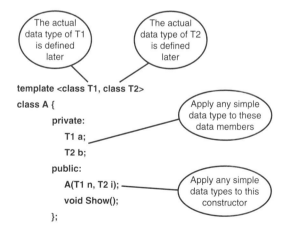

Figure 6.8 The template class definition for two simple variables.

2. The next step is to define the constructor that can be configured to translate into any two simple data types (see Figure 6.9).

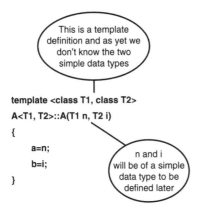

```
template <class T1, class T2>
A<T1, T2>::A(T1 n, T2 i)
{
        a=n;
        b=i;

}
```

Figure 6.9 The template constructor definition for two simple variables.

3. The definition of the member function `Show()` is just like a normal C++ member function, except for the distinguishing feature of the template directive for two undefined data types at its start (see Figure 6.10).

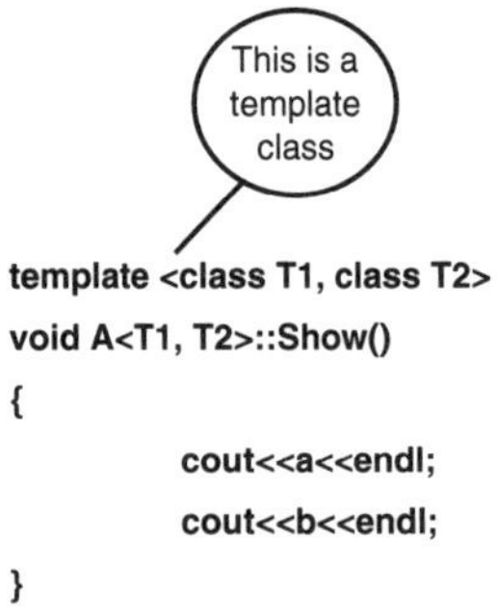

```
template <class T1, class T2>
void A<T1, T2>::Show()
{
        cout<<a<<endl;
        cout<<b<<endl;

}
```

Figure 6.10 The template member function definition for two simple variables.

4. When the template class is called into action, you specify the two simple data types to be used. This example uses **integer** and **double**, but any combination is legal as long as the actual values used match the declaration (see Figure 6.11).

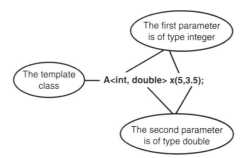

Figure 6.11   Template class A configured to hold an `integer` and a `double`.

How It Works

This is a basic example of how to get two items of data not necessarily of the same data type into a template class. The program does nothing else except that task. The template is set up as described earlier in this How-To. The data type of two member variables, **a** and **b**, is designated in the main program. Here the constructor collects the data, creates an object called **x**, and defines the two member variables to be of type **integer** and **double**, respectively. The **Show()** member function displays the values to the screen to prove that everything worked. When I ran the program in Listing 6.4a I got the following output:

```
5
3.5
Press any key to continue
```

Listing 6.4a   How to Define Two Variables in a Template Class and Define Their Actual Data Type in the Main Program

```cpp
// Template using two simple data types.

#include <iostream.h>

template <class T1, class T2>
class A    {
      private:
          T1 a;
          T2 b;

      public:
          A(T1 n, T2 i);
          void Show();
      };
```

```
template <class T1, class T2>
A<T1, T2>::A(T1 n, T2 i)
{
    a = n;
    b = i;
}

template <class T1, class T2>
void A<T1, T2>::Show()
{
    cout << a << endl;
    cout << b << endl;
}

main()
{
    A<int, double> x(5,3.5);
    x.Show();
    return(0);
}
```

As an additional example, take a look at a program that finds the result of a number raised to a power. The full code is given in Listing 6.4b. It is very similar to Listing 6.4a with the addition of a member function called Calc(). In the main program, the template data types are configured to be **double** and **double**; then the values **5** and **3.5** are applied to the constructor. The member function Calc() does the calculation and stores the result in the member variable result. The Show() member function displays the member variable result to the screen.

When I ran my program with the stated inputs I got the following output:

```
279.508
Press any key to continue
```

Listing 6.4b A Template Class That Raises a Number of Any Simple Data Type to a Power of Any Simple Data Type

```
// Template using two simple data types.

#include <iostream.h>
#include <math.h>

template <class T1, class T2>
class A    {
        private:
            T1 a;
            T2 b;
            double result;
```

```
        public:
            A(T1 n, T2 i);
            void Calc();
            void Show();
    };

template <class T1, class T2>
A<T1, T2>::A(T1 n, T2 i)
{
    a = n;
    b = i;
}

template <class T1, class T2>
void A<T1, T2>::Calc()
{
    result = pow(a,b);
}

template <class T1, class T2>
void A<T1, T2>::Show()
{
    cout << result << endl;
}

main()
{
    A<double, double> x(5,3.5);
    x.Calc();
    x.Show();
    return(0);
}
```

Comments

You can have as many undefined data types as you want in a class template; however, if you use too many, the code begins to get unwieldy and difficult to use. Try to keep it simple. As a further example, the following is a template class with four unknowns:

```
template <class T1, class T2, class T3, class T4>
class B    {
        private:
            T1 a;
            T2 b;
            T3 c;
            T4 d;
            double result;
        public:
            A(T1 n, T2 i, T3 x, T4 y);
            void Calc();
            void Show();
    };
```

A typical constructor would look like this:

```
template <class T1, class T2, class T3, class T4>
A<T1, T2, T3, T4>::A(T1 n, T2 i, T3 x, T4 y)
{
    a = n;
    b = i;
c = x;
d = y;
}
```

And so the pattern continues.

COMPLEXITY
INTERMEDIATE

6.5   How do I...
Use a template class to handle a structure?

Problem

The problem with structures is that they are a user-defined data type and therefore have an infinite number of possible definitions. At first glance, it seems impossible to account for every possible combination in a template.

Technique

The solution is incredibly easy. You have already seen how to create a template to handle any simple data type. The template to handle a structure is the same as the one that handles a simple data type. The trick lies outside the template. The insertion operator is overloaded to handle the user-defined structure and the template is used to send the data held in the structure to **cout**.

Steps

1. Writing the template class is straightforward; in fact, it's the same as the one described in How-To 6.1 apart from some altered identifier names to make it look original. The single member variable **d** is of a yet undefined data type, so there are no problems there. The constructor **TNotSimple** accepts a single input whose data type will be defined in the main program. The member function **Show()** is used to send the contents of the member variable **d** to the screen.

```
template <class T>
class TNotSimple    {
            private:
```

```
                T d;
public:
        TNotSimple(T n);
    void Show();
};
```

2. The tricky part here actually has very little to do with templates and can be used in any program. The difficulty lies in overloading the insertion operator to output a structure to the screen.

3. Before the insertion operator is overloaded, a specific structure must be set up. It is called **data** and holds a string, an integer, and a double as its three fields. Here is the code fragment:

```
struct data{
        char name[20];
        int  age;
        double height;
        };
```

4. Now that a structure exists, an insertion overload can be defined to deal with that specific data type. This is shown in Figure 6.12.

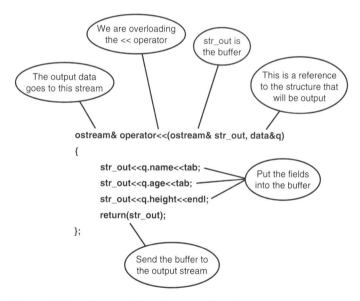

Figure 6.12 How the insertion overload works.

5. In the main program, a variable named **man** is set up and initialized.

```
struct data man = {"BOBBY",45,1.98};
```

6. The `TNotSimple` constructor is invoked and its data type defined to that of your user-defined structure. The single input parameter is the variable `man`, hence the three fields of the structure are passed into the template class.

```
TNotSimple<data> x(man);
```

How It Works

The program in Listing 6.5a defines a structure named **data**. This code overloads the insertion operator to deal with that structure. The template class **TNotSimple** is very simple and is the same as the one shown in How-To 6.1. A constructor and a member function are declared to allow manipulation of the data. In the main program, you stamp the data type **struct data** on the template class and offer the fields contained in the internal variable **man** as input to the object **x**. To prove things have really worked, the **Show()** function displays the contents of the class to the screen. My output looks like this:

```
Structures, Template Classes And Constant Data.

BOBBY
45
1.98
Press any key to continue.
```

Listing 6.5a   This Template Class Can Also Handle Structures Through the Process of Overloading

```
// Template using single data item.

#include <iostream.h>

#define tab '\t'

struct data{
            char name[20];
            int  age;
            double height;
          };

ostream& operator << (ostream& str_out, data& q)
{
    str_out << q.name << tab;
    str_out << q.age << tab;
    str_out << q.height << endl;
    return(str_out);
};
```

```
template <class T>
class TNotSimple    {
              private:
                   T d;
              public:
                   TNotSimple(T n);
                 void Show();
              };

template <class T>
TNotSimple<T>::TNotSimple(T n)
{
    d = n;
}

template <class T>
void TNotSimple<T>::Show()
{
    cout << d << endl;
}

main()
{
    struct data man = {"BOBBY",45,1.98};

    TNotSimple<data> x(man);
    x.Show();
    return(0);
}
```

Having seen how to output a structure containing constant data from a template class, it's only a small step to read data into a structure at runtime. Again, you do not need to take special provisions in the template, it's just a question of overloading the extraction operator to handle a specific user-defined structure. Here is the code fragment that performs the required action:

```
istream& operator >> (istream& str_in, data& q)
{
    cout << "Enter name : ";
    str_in >> q.name;
    cout << "Enter age : ";
    str_in >> q.age;
    cout << "Enter height : ";
    str_in >> q.height;
    return(str_in);
};
```

With this overload defined, it's just a question of adding a member function that I have called Gather(). Gather() reads in data to the member variable d, which has been set up as the data type of the structure. When I ran my program, I got the following output:

```
Template class constructed
Enter name : MAGGIE
Enter age : 21
Enter height : 1.64
MAGGIE   21       1.64

Press any key to continue
```

Listing 6.5b shows the program in full.

Listing 6.5b   Overloading Both the Insertion and Extraction Operator Allows a Template to Handle Runtime Data Entry

```cpp
// Template using single data item.

#include <iostream.h>

#define tab '\t'

struct data{
            char name[20];
            int  age;
            double height;
          };

ostream& operator << (ostream& str_out, data& q)
{
    str_out << q.name << tab;
    str_out << q.age << tab;
    str_out << q.height << endl;
    return(str_out);
};

istream& operator >> (istream& str_in, data& q)
{
    cout << "Enter name : ";
    str_in >> q.name;
    cout << "Enter age : ";
    str_in >> q.age;
    cout << "Enter height : ";
    str_in >> q.height;
    return(str_in);
};

template <class T>
class TNotSimple    {
                private:
                        T d;
                public:
                        TNotSimple();
                    void Gather();
                    void Show();
                };
```

```
template <class T>
TNotSimple<T>::TNotSimple()
{
    cout << "Template class constructed" << endl;
}

template <class T>
void TNotSimple<T>::Gather()
{
    cin >> d;
}

template <class T>
void TNotSimple<T>::Show()
{
    cout << d << endl;
}

main()
{
    TNotSimple<data> x;
    x.Gather();
    x.Show();
    return(0);
}
```

Comments

You are at liberty to set up a user-defined structure and pass it to a template class as if it were a simple data type. In that respect, you can treat structures and simple data types as the same thing.

CHAPTER 7

THE STANDARD TEMPLATE LIBRARY'S CONTAINER CLASSES

7

THE STANDARD TEMPLATE LIBRARY'S CONTAINER CLASSES

How do I...

7.1 **Create a container object that automatically grows or shrinks as needed?**

7.2 **Read a single element of a container?**

7.3 **Modify a single element of a container?**

7.4 **Use a generic LIFO data model?**

7.5 **Prevent automatic reallocation of a container?**

7.6 **Traverse through a container's elements?**

7.7 **Implement a queue data model?**

A container is essentially an object that can hold other objects as its elements. Generally, you can add an element to a container and remove an existing element from it. A container is not confined to a specific type—it can store objects of any kind. Such a container is said to be *generic*. C supports one container type in the form of built-in arrays (more information on arrays can be found in Chapter 1, "A Quick Introduction to the Language"). Other languages support other data models. Pascal, for example, has a **set** type, and Lisp supports lists (hence its name).

C++ inherited its support for arrays from C. Arrays have several properties that, more or less, correspond to the mathematical notion of a vector:

- Arrays can store any data type.

- Arrays provide random access, meaning the time needed to access any element is identical, regardless of the element's position (this is not the case in lists, for example).

Still, under some circumstances, arrays are less convenient than other data models—for example, it is impossible to insert a new element in the middle of an array. Furthermore, you cannot append new elements to the end of an array. Other containers enable these operations. Conversely, a list enables you to append new elements at its end. A special type of a list, a heterogenic list, can hold elements of different types at the same time.

For years, programmers were implementing their own lists, queues, sets and other container types to make up for the lack of language support. Yet homemade containers incur significant drawbacks. They are not portable; they are sometimes less than 100 percent bug free; their interfaces vary from one implementer to another; they can be less than optimal in terms of runtime performance and memory usage.

In the latest phase of the standardization of C++, Alex Stepanov, a professor and a mathematician, suggested adding a generic library of containers and algorithms to C++. He based his proposal on a similar generic library that he designed for Ada a decade earlier. At that time (November 1993), the committee was under pressure to complete the ongoing standardization process as quickly as possible. Consequently, suggestions for language extensions were rejected, one after another. Yet Stepanov's proposal was too good to be forsaken. The committee adopted it unanimously.

In essence, the proposed generic library was a collection of containers based on mathematical data models such as vectors, queues, lists, and stacks. It also contained a set of generic algorithms such as sort, merge, find, replace, and so on. Because both constituents of the library, namely containers and algorithms, were designed to be completely generic, they were implemented with templates. To create a uniform interface, operator overloading was also used extensively.

In this chapter, you will explore the following containers of the Standard Template Library (STL): vectors, strings, stacks, lists, and queues. Iterators and their role in the STL framework will also be discussed. Finally, some other containers, as well as "almost container" classes of the Standard Library, will be discussed.

Please note that several compilers will generate warnings from some of the sample code listings used throughout the chapter. You can be safely ignore warnings regarding mixed unsigned/signed integers in relational expressions, and warnings that method names are too long and have to be truncated by the debugger. These warnings result from the specific implementation of the Standard Template Library your compiler is using. The code will run if the warnings are ignored.

7.1 Create a Container Object That Automatically Grows or Shrinks as Needed

This How-To shows how to create an instance of a container object. The demonstration starts with the most widely used container, the vector.

7.2 Read a Single Element of a Container

Two ways to read a single element are from a `vector` and a `string`. The first is by using the overloaded subscript operator. The second is by using the member function `at()`. The benefits and drawbacks of each access method will be explained, and rules of thumb provided for choosing the appropriate one.

7.3 Modify a Single Element of a Container

The two methods for reading an element of a vector also enable the user to modify the element's value. This How-To will demonstrate how it is done.

7.4 Use a Generic LIFO Data Model

For some applications, a last-in-first-out (LIFO) data model is very convenient. This How-To demonstrates how to use the `stack` container to simulate a simplified exception handling mechanism.

7.5 Prevent Automatic Reallocation of a Container

The best thing about STL containers is that they free the programmer from worrying about manual reallocation of memory after a container has consumed its initial storage. When the container has consumed its free storage and additional elements have to be inserted, the container reallocates itself. The reallocation process consists of four steps. First, a new memory buffer is allocated large enough to store the container plus additional headroom. Second, existing elements are copied to the new location. Third, the destructors of the elements in their previous location are invoked. Finally, the previous memory buffer is released. Reallocation is therefore costly in terms of performance. Moreover, it invalidates existing iterators. This How-To will demonstrate how one can avert reallocation.

7.6 Traverse Through a Container's Elements

This How-To will explore the issue of iterators in STL. This How-To will explain what iterators are, how they differ from built-in pointers, and how they are used. In addition, `const` iterators are differentiated from plain iterators.

7.7 Implement a Queue Data Model

This How-To will demonstrate how to implement a queue using STL's generic queue container. The properties of a queue data model and some of its real-world applications are discussed.

COMPLEXITY

INTERMEDIATE

7.1 How do I...

Create a container object that automatically grows or shrinks as needed?

Problem

My program has to read an unknown number of data items into a buffer. However, the size of the buffer has to vary at runtime to accommodate every new item read. Because the number of items can only be known after all the items have been read, it is impossible to allocate in advance a buffer of the appropriate size. What I really need is a buffer that adjusts its size automatically at runtime. It should take care of increasing its storage as required, avoid memory leaks and overruns, and optimize memory usage.

Technique

The Standard Template Library provides several class templates that automatically manage their memory. This How-To will show how to use STL containers for efficient, reliable, portable, and robust applications.

Steps

1. Change to your base source directory and create a new subdirectory named `DYNAMIC_VECTOR`.

2. Start your source code editor and type the following code into a file named `MAIN.CPP`.

```
// main.cpp this program demonstrates
// how to use STL vector class
// as a dynamic buffer

#include <vector>
#include <iostream>
using namespace std;
void main()
{
  vector <int> vi; //create a vector of ints
  for (;;) //read numbers from a user's console until 0 is input
  {
    int temp;
    cout<<"enter a number; press 0 to terminate" <<endl;
    cin>>temp;
    if (temp == 0 ) break; //exit from loop?
    vi.push_back(temp); //insert int into the buffer
  }
  cout<< "you entered "<< vi.size() <<
➥" elements into a dynamic vector" << endl;
}//end main
```

3. Save MAIN.CPP and return to the command line. Next, compile and link MAIN.CPP.

If your compiler complains about the following #include statements:

```
#include <vector>
#include <iostream>
```

comment out (or remove) the **using** directive just below these #include statements and change them to

```
#include <iostream.h>
#include <vector.h>
```

4. Compile and link the program.

5. Run the program; the output should be as follows:

```
enter a number; press 0 to terminate
```

6. Press 1 and then Enter. The output should be as follows:

```
enter a number; press 0 to terminate
```

7. Press 10 and Enter. Again, the output should be as follows:

```
enter a number; press 0 to terminate
```

8. Now press 0 and Enter. The output should be as follows:

```
you entered 2 elements into a dynamic vector
```

How It Works

Let us begin by examining the first `#include` statement in `MAIN.CPP`:

```
#include <vector>
```

`vector` is a class template defined in the standard `<vector>` header file. Because all STL containers are declared in namespace `std`, a `using` directive is required to instruct the compiler to resolve all subsequent references to `vector` to namespace `std`.

The first source line in `main()` defines an instance of `vector`:

```
vector <int> vi;
```

The angle brackets after a template's name declare the particular type for which the template is defined. The sequence of a template name and angle brackets containing a type is termed *specialization*. In this case, `vi` is a vector object of the specialization `vector<int>`. Remember that a template's name alone is not a type; a specialization is.

Please note the size of the vector is not specified, nor is the size of an element in it. The object, `vi`, takes care of all the necessary bookkeeping automatically.

The following `for` statement is an infinite loop that reads a number from the standard input, tests whether it's not zero, and inserts it into the vector. The loop exits when the user inputs `0`.

```
for (;;) //read numbers from a user's console until 0 is input
```

The first source line inside the `for` statement body declares an `int` serving as a temporary storage. After instructing the user to input a number and press Enter, read the number into the temporary `int`, and test its value.

```
cin>>temp;
    if (temp == 0 ) break; //exit from loop?
```

Because our loop is infinite, a zero value is the signal to exit from the loop. As you can see, the number of the loop iterations is unlimited, as long as the user does not enter zero.

The real action begins at the following statement:

```
vi.push_back(temp); //insert int into the buffer
```

It inserts the value of the temporary `int` into the vector. The member function `push_back()` adds its argument at the end of its vector object. In other words, a vector is a dynamic array that adjusts its size as needed.

The `for` loop could, in fact, insert as many numbers as you like into `vi`. However, you didn't see any explicit operations associated with memory management at all—the operators `new` and `delete` are never called. The secret lies inside the vector object.

Every STL container has an embedded allocator, which is basically a memory manager. After a vector object is instantiated, it starts its life with a default size of a pre-allocated memory buffer. The actual initial size is implementation dependent, but on most platforms, it is equivalent to the size of a memory page. The vector object stores its elements in the pre-allocated buffer. When no available room exists for additional elements, vector first tries to reallocate a contiguous chunk of memory. However, the neighboring memory might not be available (it can be too small, or it is already used to store other variables in the program). In that case, a full reallocation takes place—raw memory from the heap is allocated with a size large enough to store all the current elements plus additional headroom. The existing vector elements are copied to the new memory location, and the original storage is freed. Of course, the programmer is free from that bother—those operations are automatic. Still, when reallocation occurs frequently, the incurred performance penalty might become unacceptable. Remember that copying elements implies construction of every element object in its new memory location, and destruction of every element object in the previous memory location.

Comments

This example used the specialization `vector<int>`. However, STL containers and algorithms are entirely generic; that is, they are applicable to every data type. This example could have used, for instance, a `vector<string>` specialization. Furthermore, `vector < vector <char> >` could have been used to represent a two-dimensional dynamic array.

To see the real strength of generic programming, let's look at a slightly changed version of the example. This time, use `vector<string>` specialization. Thus, the vector now stores string objects instead of integers. As you can see, the interface remains the same, regardless of the specialization used.

```cpp
#include <vector>
#include <iostream>
#include <string>

using namespace std;
void main()
{
  vector <string> vs; //create a vector of strings
  for (;;) //read numbers from a user's console until "stop" is input
  {
    string temp;
    cout<<"enter a string and press enter; press \"stop\" to terminate" <<endl;
    cin>>temp;
    if (temp == "stop" ) break; //exit from loop?
    vs.push_back(temp); //insert int into the buffer
  }
  cout<< "you entered "<< vs.size() <<" elements into a dynamic vector" << endl;
}//end main
```

7.2 How do I...
Read a single element of a container?

Problem

In How-To 7.1, I learned how to insert a new element into a vector. However, I would like to read the value of an existing element from a vector.

Technique

An element in a built-in array can be accessed directly using *operator* [].
Vector overloads the subscript operator, [], enabling by that random access to an element of a vector, as if it were an element of a built-in array. However, vector has an additional method for accessing an element, in the form of the member function at(). at() takes a subscript as an argument, and returns the corresponding element by reference. As you are about to see, the methods differ from one another in two crucial aspects.

Steps

1. Change to your base source directory and create a new subdirectory named VECTOR_SUBSCRIPT.

2. Start your source code editor and type the following code into a file named MAIN.CPP.

```
// this program demonstrates
// two methods of accessing
// a vector element

#include <vector>
#include <iostream>
using namespace std;
void main()
{
  vector <char> vc; //create a vector of chars
  for (int i = 0; i < 10; i++) //fill vc with 10 elements
  {
    char temp = 'a' + i; //'a' 'b' 'c' etc.
    vc.push_back(temp);
    cout<<"element "<<"["<< i<<"]" << " is: "<< vc[i] <<endl;
                                //using subscript operator
    cout<<"element "<<"at"<<" "<< i << " is: "<< vc.at(i) <<endl;
                                //using at() member function
  }
}//end main
```

3. Save MAIN.CPP; next, compile and link MAIN.CPP.

If your compiler complains about the following #include statements:

```
#include <vector>
#include <iostream>
```

comment out (or remove) the using directive just below them and change them to read:

```
#include <iostream.h>
#include <vector.h>
```

4. Compile and link the program.

5. Run the program; the output should be as follows:

```
element [0] is: a
element at 0 is: a
element [1] is: b
element at 1 is: b
...
```

and so forth. The final line displays element [9], the letter j.

How It Works

Let us begin by examining the first source line inside main().

```
vector <char> vc; //create a vector of chars
```

In this line, an object named vc is declared as a vector of chars.

Next, a for loop is reiterated ten times. First, temp is initialized with the value equivalent to the sum of 'a' + i.

```
for (int i = 0; i < 10; i++) //fill vc with 10 elements
{
  char temp = 'a' + i;
```

Then use the push_back() member function to store the value of temp in vc.

```
vc.push_back(temp);
```

Finally, display the element just inserted into vc using the overloaded subscript operator in the first statement, and the at() member function in the second one:

```
cout<<"element "<<"["<< i<<"]" << " is: "<< vc[i] <<endl; //using subscript
                                                    //operator
cout<<"element "<<"at"<<" "<< i << " is: "<< vc.at(i) <<endl; //using at()
                                                    //member function
```

Comments

Both function templates and class templates are not truly reused. Rather, the boilerplate code is reduplicated for every specialization used. Using large templates such as STL's containers and algorithms can lead to a significant increase in the size of the executable, a phenomenon sometimes termed "code bloat."

Templates behave differently than ordinary inheritance. A member function defined in a base class is not copied to its subclasses. Rather, it is shared. Therefore, only a single copy exists, which is accessible to every object instance of this class, as well as any object instance of its subclasses. The following example demonstrates that:

```
class Base { public: void f();};
void Base::f()
{ cout<<"f"<<endl; } } //1
class Derived : public Base {};
Base b;
Derived d;
b.f(); //executes the code defined in //1 above
d.f();//also executes the code defined in //1 above
```

Another important aspect of templates is their strongly typed nature. Every distinct type also entails a distinct specialization. Thus, if you instantiate a vector<int> and a vector<long> on a machine that represents int and long types as a four-byte unit, you still get two distinct specializations. The same rule applies to the use of signed and unsigned specifiers—vector<unsigned int>, vector<signed int>, and vector<int> are completely different types, so the compiler will expand the template code for each one of these.

The same problem arises with pointers. Stack<char *> and stack<unsigned char *> are two distinct entities. Similarly, derived classes and base classes are considered distinct types for template specializations. You can imagine how easy it is to bloat your code inadvertently.

To avert—or at least minimize—unnecessary reduplication of template code, you should try to use a common denominator type. A single vector specialization is sufficient for short, unsigned short, int, and so on. When you pass arguments of different integral types to a function template, try to cast the arguments to a uniform type first. This will ensure that only a single specialization is instantiated.

COMPLEXITY
INTERMEDIATE

7.3 How do I...
Modify a single element of a container?

Problem

I know now how to insert elements into a vector and how to read their values. However, I need to modify the value of an existing element in a vector.

Technique

As mentioned before, a vector's element can be accessed using *operator* [] or the **at**() member function. Both return a non-**const** reference to an element of a vector. Also, they can be used to modify the element's value.

Steps

1. Change to your base source directory and create a new subdirectory named VECTOR_MODIFICATION.

2. Start your source code editor and type the following code into a file named MAIN.CPP.

```cpp
// demonstrating how to modify the
// value of a vector's element

#include <vector>
#include <iostream>
#include <string>
using namespace std;
void main()
{
  vector <string> vs; //instantiate a vector of string objects
  string temp = "hello world"; //instantiate a string object and
                               //initialize it
  vs.push_back(temp); //insert first element to vs
  cout<<"first element using []: "<< vs[0] <<endl; //using
                      //subscript operator
  cout<<"first element using at(): "<< vs.at(0) <<endl; //using
                      //at() member function
  temp = "hello STL";  //assign a new value
  vs[0] = temp; //modify the value of the first element of vs
  cout<<"first element modified using []:  "<< vs[0] <<endl;
  temp = "hello vector";
  vs.at(0) = temp; //assign a new value to the first element of vs
  cout<<"first element modified using at(): "<< vs.at(0) <<endl;
}//end main
```

3. Save MAIN.CPP. Next, compile and link MAIN.CPP.

If your compiler complains about the following #include statements:

```
#include <vector>
#include <iostream>
#include <string>
```

comment out (or remove) the using directive just below these #include statements and change them to read:

```
#include <vector.h>
#include <iostream.h>
#include <string.h>
```

4. Compile and link the program.

5. Run the program; the output should be as follows:

```
first element using []: hello world
first element using at(): hello world
first element modified using []: hello STL
first element modified using at(): hello vector
```

How It Works

Let us begin by examining the three #include statements in the beginning of the source file:

```
#include <vector>
#include <iostream>
#include <string>
```

The first statement includes the definition of class **vector**. The second includes the definitions of **iostream** class library and the third includes the definition of the **string** class.

Now let's look at the first source line inside main(). In this line, an object of type **vector<string>** named **vs** is instantiated:

```
vector <string> vs;
```

The following line declares and initializes a string object. The initial value stored in the string is the immortal "hello world".

```
string temp = "hello world";
```

Then, the first element is inserted into **vs** using the member function push_back(). The element inserted is the string object temp that you instantiated in the previous source line.

```
vs.push_back(temp); //insert first element
```

The following two lines display the value of the first element of **vs**. The subscript operator is used first, and then the at() member function:

```
cout<<"first element using []: "<< vs[0] <<endl; //using subscript operator
cout<<"first element using at(): "<< vs.at(0) <<endl; //using at()
                                              //member function
```

Having examined the first element, now change its value. The following statement modifies the value of the **temp** string:

```
temp = "hello STL";
```

Next, assign a new value to the first element of **vs** using the overloaded subscript and assignment operator, exactly as a new value is assigned to an element in a built-in array:

```
vs[0] = temp; //modify the value of the first element of vs
```

To see the effect of the assignment, reexamine the value of the first element:

```
cout<<"first element modified using []:  "<< vs[0] <<endl;
```

Now modify the value of the first element again, but this time use the member function at() instead of the overloaded subscript operator. As in the previous modification, first assign a new value to **temp**:

```
temp = "hello vector";
```

The actual modification of the first member of **vs** takes place in the following statement:

```
vs.at(0) = temp;
```

Again, to see the effect of the assignment, reexamine the value of the first element. This time, use the member function at():

```
cout<<"first element modified using at(): "<< vs.at(0) <<endl;
```

Comments

You're probably asking yourself, "Why have two different access methods, namely *operator* [] and the at() member function, to perform the same operation?" Seemingly, this duality is redundant. However, it isn't. In real-world situations, two additional factors not addressed so far will influence your design: performance and safety. This is where these accessing methods differ.

The overloaded [] operator was designed by the C++ Standardization Committee to be as efficient as the subscript operator of a built-in array was. Therefore, it does not check whether its argument actually refers to a valid member. Using an illegal subscript yields undefined behavior. However, the lack of runtime checks also ensures the fastest access time (the overloaded operator [] is usually inline, so the overhead of a function call is avoided). When performance is paramount, and when the code is written carefully so that only legal subscripts are accessed, you should use the subscript operator. It is also more readable and intuitive.

Nonetheless, runtime checks are unavoidable under some circumstances. at() is less efficient than *operator* [], but it is safer because it performs range checking. In an attempt to access an out-of-range member, it throws an exception of type **std::out_of_range**. Indeed, the samples did not have any **try** blocks or **catch** statements surrounding every invocation of **at()**. This is because the samples were carefully crafted and tested not to access an out-of-range subscript. In large-scale projects, that cannot always guaranteed. Sometimes the subscript argument is received from an external source: a function, a database record, a network message, or a human operator. Keeping track of every vector object and its current valid number of members is impractical in large applications. In these cases, it is advisable to let the underlying mechanism handle access violations in an automated and well-behaved manner; for example, throw an exception rather than let the program corrupt its memory, or crash.

When **at()** is used, your code has to handle a **std::out_of_range** exception, as in the following example:

```
#include <vector>
#include <iostream>
#include <string>
using namespace std;
void main()
{
  try
  {
     vector<string> vs; // vs has no elements currently
     cout<< vs.at(0) <<endl; //oops! no elements exist in vs; exception thrown
  }
  catch(std::out_of_range & except)
  {
    // diagnostics and remedies for an out-of-range subscript
  }
  catch(...) //handle all other exception, e.g., memory exhausted
  {
    // do something
  }
}//end main
```

Note that exception handling incurs runtime overhead and larger executable size. C++ leaves you the choice.

7.4 How do I...
Use a generic LIFO data model?

Problem

I need a data model that simulates a function call chain. The first function calls another one and so on, until the lowermost function has been called. When the lowermost function exits, control is returned to its caller, and so forth.

Technique

A stack, also termed last-in-first-out (LIFO), is an ideal data model to implement a function call chain. This How-To will use the STL's stack container.

A comprehensive explanation of how to implement a full-blown function call mechanism or how to simulate an exception handling mechanism is well beyond the scope of this book. This How-To only focuses on the data model aspects of the implementation.

Exception handling (EH) in C++, as you will read in the following chapters, works in a LIFO model. When an exception is thrown by a function, the EH mechanism tries to locate a corresponding handler (a **catch** statement) for this particular exception in the current function. If such a handler does not exist, the exception is propagated to the function one level higher in the calling chain—that is, the function from which the current one was called and the current function is exited. This process is repeated until a handler is reached or the program is aborted.

The highest function in the calling chain, **main()**, is the first element pushed into the stack. Next is a function called from **main()** that is pushed into the call stack, and so on. When an exception is thrown and no appropriate handler can be found, the stack is popped, meaning the lowermost function in the calling chain is removed from the stack and control is returned to the caller. This process is reiterated until the stack has been emptied, which in our case means program abortion.

Steps

1. Change to your base source directory and create a new project named STACK_DEMO.

2. Start your source code editor and type the following code into a file named CALLCHAIN.H:

```cpp
#include <string>
#include <stack>
using namespace std;

enum status { success, failure }; // return codes

class CallChain {

private:
  stack <string> st;

protected:
  bool CallChain::HandlerExists(const string& excep);
  void ExitCurrentScope();

public:
  CallChain();
  ~CallChain();
  status Call(const string& function);
  void Throw(const string& excep);
};
```

3. Save CALLCHAIN.H. Create a new file named CALLCHAIN.CPP under the same project and type the following code into that file:

```cpp
#include <iostream>
#include "callchain.h"
using namespace std;

CallChain::CallChain()
{
  st.push("main");  // first we push main onto the stack
  cout<<"pushed main; total "<<st.size()<<endl;
}

CallChain::~CallChain()
{
  if (!st.empty() )  //pop main if it hasn't been popped before
    st.pop();
}

status CallChain::Call(const string& function)
{
  st.push(function); //call another function
  cout<<"pushed " <<function<< "; total: "<< st.size() <<endl;
  if (function == "bad_func")  //is it the offending one?
    return failure;
  return success;
}
```

```
void CallChain::Throw(const string& excep)
{
  while (!st.empty()) //unwind the stack
  {
    if (! HandlerExists(excep))
      ExitCurrentScope(); //terminate current function
    else
      break; // a handler for the current exception was found
  }
}

bool CallChain::HandlerExists(const string& excep)
{
  return false; //in this simulation, no handlers exist
}

void CallChain::ExitCurrentScope()
{
 string func = st.top(); // display the last function called
 st.pop(); //  remove it
 cout<<"popped " << func <<"; total "<< st.size() <<endl;
}
```

4. Save CALLCHAIN.CPP. Create a new file named MAIN.CPP under the same project of CALLCHAIN.H and type the following code into that file:

```
#include "callchain.h"

void main()
{
 status stat = success;
 CallChain chain;

 stat = chain.Call("func1"); //push first function after main
 if (stat != failure) //then call another one
 {
  stat = chain.Call("bad_func"); // call the offending function,
                                 // which throws an exception
 }
 if (stat != success)
 {
  chain.Throw("disaster!"); //unwind stack
 }

}//end main
```

5. Save MAIN.CPP and compile your project.

If your compiler complains about the following #include statements in CALLCHAIN.H or CALLCHAIN.CPP:

```
#include <stack>
#include <string>
#include <iostream>
```

comment out (or remove) the `using` directive just below these `#include` statements and change them to read:

```
#include <stack.h>
#include <string.h>
#include <iostream.h>
```

6. Compile and link the project.

7. Run `main.exe`; the output should be as follows:

```
pushed main; total: 1
pushed func1; total: 2
pushed bad_func; total 3
popped bad_func; total 2
popped func1; total 1
popped main; total 0
```

How It Works

Let us begin by examining the header file `CALLCHAIN.H`.

The first source line includes the definition of the class `string`. The second line includes the definition of the STL `stack` container. The following `using` directive instructs the compiler to resolve all references to namespace `std`.

In the following source line

```
enum status { success, failure };
```

an `enum` type named `status` is defined. It is used to return a success or failure code from the member functions defined in `CallChain` class. Class `CallChain` itself is declared in the following source line. This class is used to simulate a simplified mechanism of a function call chain.

```
class CallChain {
```

Next, declare the first class member named `st` as a `private` member:

```
stack <string> st;
```

`st` is an object of type `stack <string>`. `st` holds `string` elements. A `string` object is sued to denote a function. That is, the entities are the *names* of the functions. You could have chosen a different method to represent a function, say a pointer, or a class. However, `string` is a simple and clear representation for the purposes of this How-To.

Next, declare two `protected` member functions:

```
protected:
  bool CallChain::HandlerExists(const string& excep);
  void ExitCurrentScope();
```

The first member function is used to examine whether a handler for the current exception exists in the current scope. In this case, the member function is a stub, which always returns **false**. The second member function performs a forced exit from the current scope. In other words, it *pops* the current function from the stack. These member functions are declared **protected** because they are more of helper functions used by other members of the class; they are not supposed to be invoked directly.

The interface of a class consists of its public members. **CallChain**'s interface is specified in the following source lines.

First, declare a constructor:

```
CallChain();
```

A destructor comes next:

```
~CallChain();
```

The **Call** member function simulates a function call, which is in fact a push operation performed on the stack.

```
status Call(const string& function);
```

Finally, the member function **Throw** performs a complete stack unwinding; it performs iterative push operations until the stack is empty. This is equivalent to throwing an exception that has no handler—the program is aborted.

```
void Throw(const string& excep);
```

Now you have a basic idea of how the exception handling mechanism works, and how it relates to the stack data model. Let's take a look at **CALLCHAIN.CPP**. This file contains the implementation of the **CallChain** class. First, include the **<iostream>** header. The next header file is **callchain.h**, which contains the declaration of the class **CallChain**, as you just saw. A **using** directive is necessary for the compiler to resolve accurately the names of **<iostream>**.

Let's examine the constructor of **CallChain**:

```
CallChain::CallChain()
{
  st.push("main");
  cout<<"pushed main; total "<<st.size()<<endl;
}
```

The first statement in the constructor performs a push operation. That is, it pushes an element onto our stack. It pushes an argument of type **string**, which is the expected type for the specialization **stack<string>** you used. As in a vector, every push operation applied to a stack inserts a new member into a position higher than the previous one. In this case, the constructor pushes the first element onto the **st**. Thus, a **CallChain** object begins its life with a stack that has one element—main.

The destructor performs the opposite action; that is, it pops the stack, unless it is already empty. Remember that popping an empty stack is an error, so `stack::empty()` is called first to check whether the stack is empty.

```
CallChain::~CallChain()
{
  if (!st.empty() )
    st.pop();
}
```

The member function `Call` calls a function. It receives the function name as its argument, and pushes it on the stack.

```
status CallChain::Call(const string& function)
{
  st.push(function);
  cout<<"pushed " <<function<< "; total: "<< st.size() <<endl;
  if (function == "bad_func")
    return failure;
  return success;
}
```

However, one of the functions called is an offender—it throws an exception for which no handler exists. This function is identified by its name: `bad_func`. The `Call` member function checks whether the function it has just pushed is the offending function by comparing the function's name. If this function throws an exception, `Call` returns a failure value, which indicates that an exception has occurred.

The `Throw` member function, as said before, performs stack unwinding; that is, it empties the stack by recurrent pop operations, each of these removing the last element from the stack until the stack is empty:

```
 void CallChain::Throw(const string& excep)
{
  while (!st.empty())
  {
    if (! HandlerExists(excep))
      ExitCurrentScope();
    else
      break; // a handler for the current exception was found
  }
}
```

The `HandlerExists` member function looks for an appropriate handler for the thrown exception. Because a full-blown exception handling mechanism is not implemented, the member function always returns `false`. (If it returned `true`, it would mean that the current exception was caught and handled, so there was no need to unwind the stack.)

```
 bool CallChain::HandlerExists(const string& excep)
{
  return false;
}
```

ExitCurrentScope performs a forced function exit. It terminates the current function by pooping it from the stack. But before a function is popped from the stack, take its name by calling the **stack::top** member function. **Top()** returns a reference to the element at the highest position in the stack (that is, the one pushed latest). **size()** is another member function that returns the number of elements currently stored in a stack. **size()** is used to display the increasing number of functions pushed on the stack, and during stack unwinding, it is used to display the decreasing number of elements.

```
void CallChain::ExitCurrentScope()
{
 string func = st.top();
 st.pop();
 cout<<"popped " << func <<"; total "<< st.size() <<endl;
}
```

Now let's look at MAIN.CPP. First, include the header file **callchain.h** that contains the declaration of class **CallChain**, as shown earlier.

```
#include "callchain.h"
```

The first statement in **main** declares a variable of type **status** and initializes it to **success**.

```
status stat = success;
```

An object of type **CallChain** is instantiated with a name **chain**.

```
CallChain chain;
```

chain simulates function calls. As you remember, one function was already called by the constructor, **main**. Now call another function named **func1** from **main** and check the returned status.

```
stat = chain.Call("func1"); // call another function from main
if (stat != failure)
```

Because **func1** did not throw an exception, as the status returned from **Call** indicates, you can now call another function from **func1**

```
{
 stat = chain.Call("bad_func"); //now call thrower
}
```

As you might guess from its name, **bad_func** threw an exception, as the returned status indicates. Because you have no handler for the thrown exception, you have to perform stack unwinding. This is done by calling the member function **Throw**:

```
chain.Throw("disaster!"); //unwind stack
```

Comments

The STL stack container is generic. That is, it applies to any data type. This example used it with `string` for the sake of brevity; however, you can use it to model a LIFO with built-in types, objects, pointers, and so on.

COMPLEXITY

INTERMEDIATE

7.5 How do I...
Prevent automatic reallocation of a container?

Problem

I'm using a container that has to meet strict performance demands. In peak times, it can store as many as thousands of objects within minutes. However, the default reallocation scheme is unsatisfactory because my container has to reallocate itself frequently. The reallocation process imposes significant runtime overhead: the existing elements have to be copied to a new memory location. Copying implies an invocation of every element's destructor as well as a reconstruction every element in its new location. Is there a way to optimize my container's performance?

Technique

The memory allocation scheme of STL containers has to address two conflicting demands. On the one hand, a container should not pre-allocate large amounts of memory—it might impair system performance. On the other hand, it is inefficient to let a container reallocate memory whenever it stores a few more elements. The allocation strategy has to walk a thin line. However, in cases in which you can estimate in advance how many elements the container will have to store, you can force it to pre-allocate sufficient amount of memory and the recurrent reallocation process will be avoided.

Imagine a mail server of some Internet service provider. The server is almost idle at 4:00 AM in the morning. However, at 9:00 AM it has to transfer thousands of emails every minute. The incoming emails are first stored in a `vector` before they are routed to other mail servers across the Web. Letting our vector reallocate itself, little by little, with every few dozen emails is a recipe for a traffic bottleneck. Fortunately, you know in advance that 9:00–17:00 are peak hours, so you can avoid reallocation by calling the member function `vector::reserve()`. `Reserve(n)` ensures that its container reserves sufficient free memory for at least at least `n` more elements.

Steps

1. Change to your base source directory and create a new subdirectory named PRE_ALLOC.

2. Start your source code editor and type the following code into a file named MAILSERVER.H.

```
#include <vector>
using namespace std;

struct message { char text[1000];}; //a simplified representation
                                     //of an email message

class MailServer {

public:

   bool RushHour() const;
   bool MoreMessages() const;
   message& GetNewMsg() const;
};
```

3. Save MAILSERVER.H. Create a new file with the name MAILSERVER.CPP and type the following code into it:

```
#include <iostream>
#include "mailserver.h"
using namespace std;

bool MailServer::RushHour() const // is the current time
                                  // considered peak-time?
{
 bool rush = true;
 return rush;
}

bool MailServer::MoreMessages() const //are there more incoming
                                      //messages?
{
  bool more = true;
  return more;
}

message& MailServer::GetNewMsg() const // store an incoming
                                       // message
{
  static message msg; //static object is instantiated only once
  return msg;
}
```

4. Save `MAILSERVER.CPP`. Create a new file with the name `MAIN.CPP` and type the following code into it:

```cpp
// demonstarting how to
// avoid recurrent memory
// reallocations of vector

#include <iostream>
#include "mailserver.h"

using namespace std;

void main()
{
 MailServer server;
 vector <message> vm;   //emails transmitted from the server are
                        //stored here

 if (server.RushHour())
  vm.reserve(5000); //make room for at least 5000 more messages
                    //without reallocation
 while (server.MoreMessages())
 {

    static int count =0;    // control how many times this loop
                            // executes
    vm.push_back( server.GetNewMsg() ); //insert a new email into
                                        //vm
    count++;
    if (count > 5000)
      break; //loop exited after 5000 iterations
 }//while

}// end main
```

5. Save `MAIN.CPP` and compile your project.

If your compiler complains about the following `#include` statement in `CALLCHAIN.H` or `CALLCHAIN.CPP`:

```cpp
#include <vector>
```

comment out (or remove) the **using** directive just below the `#include` statement and change them to read:

```cpp
#include <vector.h>
```

6. Compile and link the project.

7. Run `main.exe`.

How It Works

Let's look at `MAILSERVER.H`. The first source line includes STL `<vector>` definitions. Next, a `struct` named `message` is declared that represents a typical email message. The class `MailServer` is also declared. This class represents a rudimentary mail server. It has four public member functions and no data members, constructors, or destructors.

For a more detailed description of each member function, let's look at `MAILSERVER.CPP`. The first source line includes the declaration of class `MailServer`.

```
#include "mailserver.h"
```

The following lines define `MailServer`'s member functions. The member function `RushHour` returns `true` if the current time falls between 9:00 and 17:00. To simplify things, use a stub that always returns `true` to avoid time calculations that are impertinent to this discussion. The reason a local variable is used and initialized (rather than simply returning a literal `true`) is to enable you to change its value from a debugger and test the resulting effect. `RushHour` is declared `const` because it does not change its object's state.

```
bool MailServer::RushHour() const
{
 bool rush = true;
 return rush;
}
```

`MoreMessages` is the second member function of `MailServer`. Again, a stub is used here that always returns `true`. `MoreMessages` checks whether new messages are coming. In real-world conditions, it would probe the shared memory or a communication port.

```
bool MailServer::MoreMessages() const
{
  bool more = true;
  return more;
}
```

In case more messages are on the way, the member function `GetNewMessage` is invoked. In this case, hold a static instance of a message `struct`, and return it by reference. Static variables are instantiated and initialized only once during a program's execution, so they are more efficient than local variables that are instantiated anew every time. The returned message is stored in the container, as you will immediately see in `MAIN.CPP`.

```
message& MailServer::GetNewMsg() const
{
  static message msg;
  return msg;
}
```

Let's look at MAIN.CPP. The first source line inside main() instantiates server, an object of type MailServer.

```
MailServer server;
```

In the following line, a vector object named vm is instantiated, whose type is vector<message>. The container vm will store the email messages coming from the server object.

```
vector <message> vm;
```

The next if statement queries server whether the current time is considered rush hour. If it is, vm must be prepared to handle the traffic load by reserving enough room for at least 5000 more messages.

```
if (server.RushHour())
   vm.reserve(5000);
```

Remember that vector::reserve takes the number of objects as an argument, not the number of bytes. Thus, vm has to reserve memory in the size of 5000 * sizeof(message) bytes, which is nearly 5MB.

The while condition is, in fact, an infinite loop because it tests a condition that is always true (as you might recall, MoreMessages always returns true). Exit from the loop by using a static int, which is incremented with every iteration, until the loop has executed 5000 times.

```
while (server.MoreMessages())
{
  static int count =0;
```

The message is retrieved from the server, and stored in vm. For that purpose, invoke push_back with the message returned from GetNewMsg() as an argument. Next, increment count, the loop counter, and test whether the loop has already executed 5000 times. If it has, break from the loop. Otherwise, the loop executes once more.

```
  vm.push_back( server.GetNewMsg() );
  count++;
  if (count > 5000)
    break;
}//while
}// end main
```

Comments

In this example, you have to adjust a vector's memory according to need. When you have to use a vector that is always required to hold large amounts of memory—for example, a vector that holds all of the records of a large database table—you can use a different technique.

Up until now, you have instantiated vectors with their default constructor. However, vector has another constructor that takes as an argument the initial number of elements for which storage has to be reserved. In other words, you could have instantiated vm like this:

```
vector <message> vm(5000);  // prepare enough room for 5000 messages initially
```

But that would be a waste of the system's resources if it wasn't working during rush hours.

You are probably wondering why you should bother so much about avoiding reallocations when a vector can do the necessary bookkeeping automatically. The motive in this How-To was to optimize performance and to ensure the highest responsiveness. Nevertheless, there is another reason for avoiding reallocations, which is discussed in length in How-To 7.6.

COMPLEXITY

INTERMEDIATE

7.6 How do I...
Traverse through a container's elements?

Problem

Up until now, I have accessed a single element at a time. However, I need a convenient method for accessing all the elements in a container so I can display them on the screen.

Technique

Pointers are used when traversing built-in arrays. For example, the standard C routines, `strcpy` and `strcmp`, use a pointer to `char` that points to the first element of the `char` array. This pointer is incremented to move to the next `char` in the array.

STL by its nature is a generic framework. Genericity means type independence. Built-in pointers, on the other hand, narrow the choice of supported types. For example, a pointer on most platforms is represented as a 32-bit integer. This size is insufficient for traversing a container larger than 2GB. STL, therefore, uses iterators rather than bare pointers.

Iterators can be thought of as generic pointers. They behave much like pointers. You can dereference an iterator to examine the element it points to. You can use the operators ++ and -- with an iterator to move one position ahead or back in a container, and so on. Yet, the underlying representation of an iterator needn't be a pointer.

The following example demonstrates how to use iterators to access a container's elements. This example will use `string` as its container. `string` resembles a `vector<char>`. It shares many common features with `vector`. However, `vector` is generic, whereas `string` is only applicable to `char`. `string` and `vector` are probably the most widely used STL containers. The sample program will show how to create a `string` object, initialize it, and iterate through its elements with iterators.

Steps

1. Change to your base source directory and create a new subdirectory named `STL_STRING`.

2. Start your source code editor and type the following code into a file named `MAIN.CPP`:

```
#include <string>
using namespace std;

// demonstrating iterators
#include <iostream>
#include <string>
using namespace std;
void main()
{
  string str = "hello world";
  string::const_iterator p = str.begin(); //create and initialize
                                           //a const iterator

  while ( p != str.end())
  {
    cout<< *p <<endl;
    p++;  //prpceed to the next element
  }
}
```

3. Save `MAIN.CPP` and compile your project.

If your compiler complains about the following `#include` statements in `MAIN.CPP`:

```
#include <vector>
#include <string>
```

comment out (or remove) the **using** directive just below these `#include` statements and change them to read:

```
#include <vector.h>
#include <string.h>
```

4. Compile and link `main`.

5. Run `main.exe`. The output should look like this:

```
h
e
l
l
o

w
o
r
l
d
```

How It Works

The first source line in `MAIN.CPP` includes the definition of the `iostream` class library. Next, the definition of `string` class is included. `string` is declared in namespace `std`, therefore, the third source line contains a `using` directive to instruct the compiler to look up all references to `string` in `std`:

```
#include <iostream>
#include <string>
using namespace std;
```

The first source line inside `main()` instantiates an object, `str`, of type `string`, and initializes it with a most original value, `"hello world"`.

```
string str = "hello world";
```

The following source line introduces us to the notion of STL iterators. Let's analyze it in detail:

```
string::const_iterator p = str.begin();
```

The sequence `string::const_iterator` is a type name. Class `string`, like every container in STL, contains several types of iterators that are used to traverse its elements. Note that when you define an ordinary pointer, you have to specify to which type of object the pointer points; for example, `char *` is a pointer to `char`. In STL, you use a specialization followed by the scope resolution operator, `::`, to indicate the specialization to which the iterator can be applied. Please note that `string` is a specialization; `string` is a shorthand for the following unwieldy specialization:

```
basic_string<char, char_traits<char>, allocator<char> >
```

Whew! Fortunately, this arcane syntax is well hidden by a friendlier `typedef` named `string`. In other words, `string` is a char-specialized version of the `basic_string` container.

An ordinary pointer can be used to modify the object to which it points. When a pointer is not supposed to modify its object, declare it as pointing to a const object. For example:

```
int strcmp (const char *, const char *); //the arguments of strcmp
                                         //may not be modified
```

The const specifier guarantees the pointer is not used to modify the pointed object. The pointer itself, however, can be modified—it can be assigned a new value, incremented, and so on. Likewise, there are two basic types of iterators: const_iterator and plain iterator. The rule of thumb is to use a const_iterator unless you have a good reason to use a plain iterator. This example displays the contents of a string without modifying its elements. Therefore, a const_iterator is used.

The string::const_iterator is named p. It is initialized to point to the first element of str. The member function begin(), which is a member of other STL containers, as you will see next. returns the address of the first element in its object. Remember that the value returned from begin() is not the first element itself, but its address. To make this distinction clearer, compare it to built-in arrays:

```
char car[10];
const char * p =  &car[0]; //p gets the address of the first array
                           //element, not the element itself
```

Now that you have created a const_iterator pointing at the first element of str, you can use it to access all the other elements thereof. For that purpose, use a while loop. The loop checks in each iteration whether you have reached the last element of the container by invoking the member function string::end():

```
while ( p != str.end())
```

The loop body consists of two operations. First, the current element is displayed. As you can see, in order to access the element the iterator must be dereferenced, as you would dereference an ordinary pointer. The trick here is that all STL iterators overload *operator* *, which enables you to use pointer syntax. Nifty, isn't it?

```
cout<< *p <<endl;
```

The following statement in the loop body increments p using the overloaded ++ operator. The effect of which, you can guess, is to move p to the next element of str.

```
p++;
```

Of course, you could have combined these separate operations in a single statement, like this:

```
cout<< *p++ <<endl;
```

but it's less readable.

Comments

When you want to modify elements of a container, you need to use non-const iterators. The following example demonstrates how it is actually done.

In the following program, use list as your container. The STL list class template is defined in the header <list>. The specialization list<double> is used to instantiate an object named salaries. Next, three elements of type double are inserted to salaries.

Imagine salaries represents a payroll. Now suppose you want to raise by 15% the salaries of all employees. In order to do that, you need to traverse through the elements currently stored in salaries and modify each one. For that purpose, use a plain iterator.

```
#include <iostream>
#include <list>
using namespace std;

void main()
{
 list <double> salaries; // a payroll
 salaries.push_back(5000.00);
 salaries.push_back(4500.00);
 salaries.push_back(1333.33);
 list<double>::iterator p = salaries.begin(); //point to the first element

 while ( p != salaries.end())
 {
   cout<<"salary before a raise: "<< *p <<endl;
   *p = *p * 1.15; //add 15 percent to the existing rate
   cout<<"salary after a 15% raise: "<< *p <<endl;
   p++; //proceed to the next salary
 }
}// main
```

Our first step is to create a suitable iterator. This iterator is intended to modify the elements; therefore, you have to use an ordinary iterator rather than a const iterator. Our iterator is defined in the following line:

```
list<double>::iterator p = salaries.begin();
```

p is initialized with the address of the first element in the list, which is the value returned from begin(). Next, define a while loop that traverses through the elements of salaries.

```
while ( p != salaries.end())
{
  cout<<"salary before a raise: "<< *p <<endl;
```

```
*p = *p * 1.15;
cout<<"salary after a 15% raise: "<< *p <<endl;
p++;
```

The first statement inside the loop displays the element to which **p** currently points. Next, change the element just displayed. Increase the element by 15%. Remember that you have to dereference the iterator to obtain the element. After changing the element, display it once more. Finally, increment the iterator to point to the next element in **salaries**. The loop is reiterated as long as **p** does not reach the last element of **salaries**.

You might have noticed something suspicious here: The loop is reiterated as long as the final element hasn't been reached. Still, when this program is run you will notice that *all* of the elements in **salaries** have been modified—including the last one. How can it be? Here is the secret. The member function **end()** does not really return the position of the last element, but one position *past* the last element. Surprising as it might seem, you can find similar behavior in C strings. A **null** character is always appended one position past the last position of the char array. The **null** character marks the boundary of the string. A similar trick is applied in STL containers. Every container automatically appends another element one position after the last one. This special element is equivalent to the **null** character in C strings, or the EOF marker at the end of a file. Thus, our iterator **p** does reach the final element in the loop.

As noted before, besides the incurred performance penalty, reallocation has another undesirable side effect. When a container reallocates its elements, their addresses change correspondingly, invalidating existing iterators. Therefore, you have to reassign the iterators' values by invoking the appropriate member function once more. Using an invalid iterator yields undefined behavior—exactly as if you were using a pointer with the address of a deleted object. Because the reallocation process is automatic, the programmer has no way of knowing when it takes place, and when an iterator becomes invalid. By forestalling reallocation, not only do you get enhanced performance, but you also eliminate the chance of dangling iterators.

COMPLEXITY
INTERMEDIATE

7.7 How do I...
Implement a queue data model?

Problem

I need a container that implements the first-in-first-out (FIFO) data model. FIFO is a queue of elements. As opposed to a stack, the first element inserted into a queue is located at the topmost position, whereas the last element inserted is located at the bottom. When a pop operation is performed, the element at the topmost position (which was the first to be inserted) is removed from the queue, and the element located one position lower is now at the top. Remember that the terms *queue* and *FIFO* mean the same thing, so they are used here interchangeably.

Technique

In this example, you will see how to use STL's **queue** container to implement a FIFO data model.

Steps

1. Change to your base source directory and create a new subdirectory named QUEUE.

2. Start your source code editor and type the following code into a file named MAIN.CPP.

```
// demonstrating STL's queue
#include <iostream>
#include <queue>
using namespace std;

void main()
{
 queue <int> iq; //instantiate a queue of ints

 iq.push(93); //insert the first element, it is the top-most one
 iq.push(250);
 iq.push(25);
 iq.push(10); //last element inserted is located at the bottom

 cout<<"currently there are "<< iq.size() << " elements" << endl;

 while (!iq.empty() )
 {
   cout <<"the last element is: "<< iq.front() << endl;
             //front returns the top-most element
   iq.pop(); //remove the top-most element
 }
}
```

3. Save MAIN.CPP and compile your project.

If your compiler complains about the following #include statements in MAIN.CPP:

```
#include <queue>
#include <iostream>
```

comment out (or remove) the using directive just below these #include statements and change them to read:

```
#include <queue.h>
#include <iostream.h>
```

4. Compile and link main.

5. Run main.exe. The output should look like this:

```
currently there are 4 elements
the last element is: 93
the last element is: 250
the last element is: 25
the last element is: 10
```

How It Works

Let's examine the program carefully. The first source line in MAIN.CPP includes the definition of the iostream class library. Next, the definition of STL's queue class template is included. Both iostream and queue are declared in namespace std. The following using directive instructs the compiler where it should look for the definitions of iostream and queue.

```
#include <iostream>
#include <queue>
using namespace std;
```

The first statement inside main() declares iq as a queue of ints.

```
void main()
{
 queue <int> iq;
```

The following statement inserts the first element into iq. Recall that the first element always remains at the top of the queue until it is popped.

```
iq.push(93);
```

The next three statements insert additional elements into iq. Each element occupies one position below the previously inserted one.

```
iq.push(250);
iq.push(25);
iq.push(10); //last element inserted is located at the bottom
```

The following statement displays how many elements currently exist in iq. Again, use the member function size() for that purpose.

```
cout<<"currently there are "<< iq.size() << " elements" << endl;
```

Now define a loop that displays the topmost element in `iq`, and then removes it until `iq` has been emptied. The following `while` statement checks whether `iq` contains more elements first. Recall that popping an empty queue is an error.

```
while (!iq.empty() )
{
   cout <<"the last element is: "<< iq.front() << endl; //front returns
                                                        //the top-most element
   iq.pop(); //remove the top-most element
}
}
```

Comments

The FIFO, or queue, data model is heavily used in task-oriented programming, such as a print manager. Usually, a single printer serves several users. Because the printer can handle only a single job at a time, the other print jobs have to wait their turn. This is the role of a print manager—it stores incoming print jobs, sends them one-by-one to the printer, and waits for a notification that the printer has completed the current job. Only when the printer is free will the print manager send a new job to it. Every print job has a unique ID assigned to it by the print manager. The waiting jobs are stored in a queue. When the print manager receives a completion notification from the printer, it deletes this job from the queue. A print manager uses a queue to hold the pending jobs. The first job inserted to the queue is also the first to be printed and removed from it.

Implementing a print manager requires knowledge of event-driven programming and serial port communication. Therefore, it is left as an exercise for readers who are experienced in such programming tasks.

Summary

In this chapter, you have learned how to use STL containers. First, the theoretical aspects of generic programming were discussed. Next, you implemented various data models: vector, string, stack, list, and queue. As you might have noticed, they share some common features such as automatic memory management, the notion of iterators that behave like pointers, `begin()` and `end()` member functions, and more. Still, every container is an abstraction of a distinct data model. The rich collection of STL containers enables you to pick up the most suitable container that fits your programming tasks. STL containers have several advantages over homemade ones:

1. Portability. All standard conforming C++ implementations supply them.

2. Performance. STL containers were designed and implemented to meet strict efficiency demands.

3. Reliability. These containers are already debugged and tested.

4. Uniformity. STL ensures standard names and conventions.

5. Genericity. STL containers can be used with every data type and object.

The Standard Library has a few more "almost containers." These template classes behave in many ways like ordinary containers: they have automatic memory management, they have iterators, and they have member functions such as `begin()` and `end()`. Still, they are not considered "first class citizens" in the STL catalog because they are not generic. You saw an example of that in the shape of `string`, which is similar to `vector` but is confined to the `char` data type. `Valarray` is another "almost container" that was not discussed. It also resembles `vector`, albeit with a strong bias toward numerical and mathematical computations. The third class in this category is `bitset`. `Bitset` is a container designed to store and manipulate bits in an efficient way. These "almost containers" have a limited use for general purposes, except for `string`.

STL has a few more containers that were not discussed here. These containers include associative arrays, sets, and multisets.

An associative array is an array whose indexes needn't be integers. The `map<>` container is an example of this. It can take any data type as a subscript for its elements. A map element is a pair consisting of a key and a value. For example, a URL serving as a key and a corresponding HTML page as its value. However, associative array elements have to meet other requirements so that they can be sorted and compared to one another. This is usually achieved by defining a *functor*, or a function object.

`Multimap<>` is a map that can hold nonunique keys. Likewise, `multiset<>` is a set that can hold nonunique elements. Readers who wish to learn more about these advanced data models are referred to the following titles:

STL Tutorial and Reference Guide: C++ Programming with the Standard Template Library, David R. Musser and Atul Saini. Reading, MA: Addison Wesley Longman (1996). (ISBN: 0201633981)

The C++ Programming Language, 3rd ed., Bjarne Stroustrup. Reading, MA: Addison Wesley Longman (1997). (ISBN: 0201889544)

PART III
ALGORITHMS

LIBRARY INCLUDED ALGORITHMS

8

THE STANDARD C
LIBRARY'S INCLUDED
ALGORITHMS

How do I...

8.1   Sort an array?

8.2   Find an element in an array?

8.3   Locate an element in a nonsorted array?

8.4   Choose between _lfind and _lsearch?

8.5   Generate a sequence of random numbers?

This chapter surveys the algorithms of the Standard C Library. These algorithms enable you to sort an array and find an element in it. In addition, the random number generation functions of the Standard C Library are discussed.

C++ provides its own set of generic algorithms. However, there are at least three reasons why a C++ programmer should be familiar with C algorithms.

- Legacy code. Familiarity with these algorithms is needed to maintain legacy C code.

- Efficiency. You cannot apply STL algorithms to data items that are not stored in a container. Rather, you have to store these elements in an STL container first, and only then can you sort these elements. This is a costly process in terms of runtime overhead.

- Applicability to non-OO data types. The default == and < operations are either not defined or meaningless when applied to aggregates (plain structs or built-in arrays). In order to apply an STL algorithm to aggregates, you have to wrap every data member by an object that defines meaningful operations for == and < operators. It's tedious and incurs a considerable performance overhead, which might be unacceptable, or at least unnecessary, under some circumstances.

This chapter adheres to pure C. The source files used here contain pure C code, so they can be compiled and linked with either a C or C++ compiler. The aim is to enable the source files to compile in C as well as in C++ without having to modify them. Some of the writing conventions in this chapter include

- All comments are C-style comments, such as /* comment */.

- All variables are declared at the beginning of a function.

- The C-style cast operator is used exclusively, as in **(long) var**. The new cast operators of C++, **static_cast<>**, **reinterpret_cast<>**, **const_cast<>**, and **dynamic_cast<>** are not supported in C.

- Classes and objects are not used.

- The **<stdio.h>** family of functions, such as **printf**, is used to perform I/O operations.

A final remark about standard header files—the new convention of C++ for standard header files, such as **<cstdio>** and **<iostream>**, is not supported in C. Therefore, this chapter uses the traditional header file notation, **#include <stdio.h>**.

8.1 Sort an Array

This How-To shows how to sort an array of any data type. The How-To starts with an example of an array of integers, showing how to use the function **qsort** to sort an array. Following that is a detailed explanation of how the callback routine of **qsort** has to be defined. This topic leads to a thorough grounding in pointers to functions and their properties. The How-To shows how pointers to functions differ from data pointers, and demonstrates how to define, assign, and use them. Next is a demonstration of how to use **qsort** with a different data type, **char ***. The aim is to show the generic nature of **qsort** and C generic functions in general.

8.2 Find an Element in an Array

This How-To explains how to locate an element in an array by using the algorithm bsearch. It demonstrates the generic nature of bsearch and explains how to use it. Finally, the How-To discusses the restrictions on bsearch usage.

8.3 Locate an Element in a Nonsorted Array

bsearch is applicable only to sorted arrays. However, it is not always desirable or even possible to sort an array before you try to find an element in it. Instead of bsearch, you can use the functions _lsearch and _lfind to locate an element in a nonsorted array. This part shows how to use _lfind to locate an element in an array that has not been sorted.

8.4 Choose Between _lfind and _lsearch

This part explains the differences between these functions. The How-To also discusses their efficiency.

8.5 Generate a Sequence of Random Numbers

This How-To shows how to generate a sequence of random numbers using the Standard C Library's functions. The How-To starts with the function rand and demonstrates how to use it. Then it shows how to use rand's counterpart, srand, to ensure a unique random sequence on every run.

COMPLEXITY
INTERMEDIATE

8.1 How do I...
Sort an array?

Problem

I have an array of integers that I need to sort. How do I sort it in plain C?

Technique

Standard C has a generic algorithm, qsort, for this purpose. Because C does not have built-in constructs for generic programming such as templates and polymorphism, generic functions like qsort make extensive use of void pointers and function callbacks. The following demonstrates several examples and analyzes them systematically.

Steps

1. Change to your base source directory and create a new subdirectory named C_SORT.

2. Start your source code editor and type the following code into a file named COMPARE.H:

```
#ifndef COMPARE_H
#define COMPARE_H

int __cdecl compare (const void* pfirst, const void * psecond);

#endif
```

3. Save COMPARE.H. Type the following code into a new file named COMPARE.CPP:

```
int __cdecl compare (const void* pfirst, const void * psecond)
{
  const int first = * ( (const int *)  pfirst);
                      /* dereference first arg */
  const int second = *( (const int*) psecond);
                      /* dereference second arg */

  return (first - second);
}
```

4. Save COMPARE.CPP. Type the following code into a new file named MAIN.CPP:

```
#include <stdlib.h>
#include <stdio.h>
#include "compare.h"

void main()
{
  int iarr[10] = {9, 83, 100, 1, 645, -7645, 4, 23, 543, 9};
  int j = 0; /* loop counter */

  for(; j < 10; j++) /* display array before sorting */
    printf ("element %d of iarr is: %d\n", j, iarr[j]);

    /* sort iarr using qsort function */
  qsort( iarr,                /* address of array's beginning */
            10,               /* number of elements in array */
            sizeof (int),  /* sizeof each element */
            compare);
               /* pointer to user-defined comparison function */

            printf ("sorted\n\n");
            j = 0;  /* reset loop counter */

  for(; j < 10; j++) /* display sorted array */
    printf ("element %d of iarr is: %d\n", j, iarr[j]);
}
```

5. Save MAIN.CPP. Compile MAIN.CPP and COMPARE.CPP, and link MAIN.CPP.

If you are not working in a Windows environment, your compiler might complain about the __cdecl specifier in the prototype and the definition of the function compare. In that case, comment out or remove the specifier __cdecl from COMPARE.H and COMPARE.CPP.

6. Run the program; the output should be as follows:

```
element 0 of iarr is: 9
element 1 of iarr is: 83
element 2 of iarr is: 100
element 3 of iarr is: 1
element 4 of iarr is: 645
element 5 of iarr is: -7545
element 6 of iarr is: 4
element 7 of iarr is: 23
element 8 of iarr is: 543
element 9 of iarr is: 9
sorted

element 0 of iarr is: -7545
element 1 of iarr is: 1
element 2 of iarr is: 4
element 3 of iarr is: 9
element 4 of iarr is: 9
element 5 of iarr is: 23
element 6 of iarr is: 83
element 7 of iarr is: 100
element 8 of iarr is: 543
element 9 of iarr is: 645
```

How It Works

Let's look at MAIN.CPP first. The first source line includes the declarations and definitions of the C Standard Library. The function qsort is also declared in it. The second source line includes the prototype of the function printf() that is used in this program. The third line includes the prototype of compare, which is discussed in detail soon.

```
#include <stdlib.h>
#include <stdio.h>
#include "compare.h"
```

The first source line inside the body of main() defines an array of 10 integers. The array is initialized with 10 random values. The value **9** appears twice, and a negative value appears to test the robustness of qsort.

```
int iarr[10] = {9, 83, 100, 1, 645, -7645, 4, 23, 543, 9};
```

Next, a loop control variable is defined and initialized to **0**.

```
int j = 0; /* loop counter */
```

The following for statement displays the elements of iarr before sorting.

```
for(; j < 10; j++) /* display array before sorting */
  printf ("element %d of iarr is: %d\n", j, iarr[j]);
```

After the elements of iarr are displayed, they are sorted using qsort:

```
qsort( iarr,
       10,
       sizeof (int),
       compare);
```

qsort takes four arguments. Let's examine the role of each one of them. The first argument is the address of the array to be sorted. As you probably know, the name of an array in C/C++ is equivalent to its address. In other words, the argument iarr is equivalent to the expression &iarr[0]. The second argument is the number of elements in the array. The third argument is the size of a single element in the array. Because the size of an int is implementation dependent, an expression that returns the correct size of an int is always used. The fourth argument is the most interesting one. It will be discussed when the two other source files are analyzed. For now, suffice it to say the fourth argument is the address of a comparison function called by qsort.

Having sorted iarr, the program displays the sorted array. But before that is done, it resets the loop counter j.

```
j = 0;  /* reset loop counter */
```

Now the sorted array can display. Again, use a for loop to traverse the elements of iarr and display each one of them.

```
for(; j < 10; j++) /* display sorted array */
  printf ("element %d of iarr is: %d\n", j, iarr[j]);
```

In this example, qsort is applied to a built-in data type. However, qsort is a generic function. It can be applied to any data type. What makes this genericity work? The short answer—a callback function.

Callback Functions

A callback function is one not invoked explicitly by the programmer; rather, the responsibility for its invocation is delegated to another function that receives the address of the callback function. Before a demonstration of how it is done in this particular example, some basic facts are necessary about the way functions are stored in memory.

Data Pointers Versus Code Pointers

C and C++ make a clear-cut distinction between two types of pointers—data pointers and code pointers. The memory layout of a function is very different from the memory layout of a variable. Without delving too deeply into low-level machine architecture, a function consists of several components such as a list of arguments, a return-to address, and machine instructions. A data pointer, on the other hand, only holds the address of the first byte of a variable. The substantial difference between data pointers and code pointers led the C standardization committee to prohibit the use of data pointers to represent function pointers and vice versa. In C++ this restriction was relaxed, yet the results of coercing a function pointer to a void pointer are implementation dependent. Conversion of data pointers to function pointers is, of course, a recipe for a core dump. Recall also that unlike a data pointer, a function pointer cannot be dereferenced, and that you cannot pass a function by value.

Platforms have a different underlying representation for code pointers and data pointers. In some architectures, a 16-bit address can be used to hold the address of a data variable, whereas a larger unit will hold a function address.

A data pointer declaration contains a specific data type to which the pointer can point. Thus, a pointer to **char** can only point to a variable of type **char**. Similarly, a function pointer declaration contains a specific signature to which the pointer can be assigned. For example, a pointer to a function that takes no arguments and returns an **int** can only be assigned to a function that has the same signature. It is illegal to assign an address of a function with a different signature to such a pointer.

As you saw earlier, the fourth argument of **qsort** is a pointer to a callback function. However, you are free to pass an argument with the address of any function you want to, as long as that function conforms to an agreed-upon signature. The expected signature is specified in the prototype of **qsort**. Let's have a look at it:

```
void  qsort(void *, size_t, size_t, int (cmp*)(const void *, const void *));
```

The highlighted part in the prototype is the signature of the expected function pointer. Unfortunately, function pointers have a most intricate syntax, for both humans and compilers. Still, they are a very capable feature in C/C++—they are the basis for dynamic binding. *Dynamic binding*, also termed *late binding*, is a delayed resolution of which function is invoked. The resolution is delayed until runtime, as opposed to compile-time resolution. The most prominent manifestation of dynamic binding is virtual member functions in C++.

The syntax of a function pointer is very similar to the prototype of a function. To see that, let's examine the following statement:

```
void f ();
```

This statement declares a function named **f** that takes no arguments and does not return a value. A pointer to such a function has the following type:

```
void (*) ();
```

The asterisk in parentheses is the nucleus of a function pointer. Two additional components are required—the return type, which is **void** in this example, and a parameter list enclosed in parentheses on the right. In this case, the parameter list is empty. Please note that you did not define a pointer in the declaration **void** (*) (), only a *type* of a pointer. A pointer variable, of course, has to have a name. Here is an example of a pointer variable with the same signature:

```
void (*p) ();   //p is a pointer to a function that does not
                //return a value and takes no arguments
```

The name of a pointer variable appears on the right of the asterisk, within the parentheses. After a pointer variable is declared, a value can be assigned to it. A value is simply the name of a function that has an identical signature, for instance:

```
void func() {}
p = func;
```

A different value can be assigned to **p** as long as the value assigned to it is an address of a function with an identical signature. Please note that the name of a function is not a part of its type.

Let's get back to **qsort**. The fourth argument of **qsort** is a pointer to a function of the type:

```
int (*) (const void *, const void *)
```

Now you can parse this expression. The leftmost token is the return value, **int** in this case. The asterisk enclosed in two parentheses denotes a function pointer. The parameter list appears next. It declares the type of the function's arguments—a **void** pointer to a **const** object and another **void** pointer to a **const** object. Thus, any function that takes two **void** pointers to **const** objects (no additional arguments are allowed) and returns an **int** is suitable for **qsort**. **qsort** is responsible for invoking this callback function through its address. That is, the callback function "registers" itself in **qsort**, and lets **qsort** call it as needed.

What is the role of **qsort**'s callback function? A sorting operation consists of two independent stages. First, the elements have to be compared to one another. In the second stage, the result of the comparison is used to relocate elements to their relative positions in the array. As you can see, the first stage is type dependent; in order to compare two elements, their types and values are needed. However, the second phase, that is, the elements' relocation process, is type independent. All it needs is the size of an element, its address, and the total number of elements in order to reposition them in memory. This information is contained in the first three arguments of qsort. The fourth argument is a pointer to the callback function. The callback function compares the elements and therefore, it has to know their type.

To summarize, the sorting algorithms can be divided into two tasks: one responsible for memory relocations, and a second task, which is responsible for performing comparisons. The memory relocation task is implemented in a generic function; the comparison task is implemented in a callback function.

Let's look at MAIN.CPP again to see the invocation of qsort.

```
qsort( iarr,          /* address of array's beginning */
       10,            /* number of elements in array */
       sizeof (int),  /* sizeof each element */
       compare);      /* pointer to user-defined comparison function */
```

The address of compare, the callback function, is passed in the fourth argument. compare itself is declared in COMPARE.H like this:

```
int __cdecl compare (const void* pfirst, const void  * psecond);
```

As you can see, compare has a signature that complies with the signature expected by qsort. compare returns an int and takes two void pointers that point to const data. (The __cdecl specifier is a Microsoft-specific flag that instructs the compiler to use the C calling convention.) The return value has to be in one of three ranges: 0 indicates the arguments are equivalent. A negative value indicates the first argument is smaller than the second one, and a positive value indicates the first argument is greater than the second one.

Now that you know what compare basically does, let's look at COMPARE.CPP to see how it does it.

compare takes two arguments, pfirst and psecond. As you already know, the comparison is aware of the type of the array elements. Therefore, compare first casts pfirst and psecond into pointers to const int, and dereferences the resulting pointers. Two local const ints, first and second, hold the values recovered from the dereferenced pointers.

```
int __cdecl compare (const void* pfirst, const void  * psecond)
{
  const int first = * ( (const int *)  pfirst);  /* dereference first arg */
  const int second = *( (const int*) psecond);  /* dereference second arg */
```

The rest is simple. Subtract second from first and return the result:

```
return (first - second);
```

compare is invoked by qsort, which in turn examines the value returned from compare to relocate the elements of the array in an ascending order.

Comments

qsort, as noted earlier, is a generic function. To see how it sorts an array of C strings, use a revised version of the preceding example.

Steps

1. Erase the contents of the COMPARE.CPP file entirely and type the following code into it:

```
#include <string.h>

int __cdecl compare (const void * pfirst, const void  * psecond)
{
  return strcmp(*(const char**) pfirst, *(const char **) psecond);
}
```

2. Save COMPARE.CPP. Erase the contents of the MAIN.CPP entirely and then type the following code into it:

```
#include <stdlib.h>
#include <stdio.h>
#include "compare.h"

void main()
{
  /* define an array of pointers to char and initialize */
  /* its elements */
  char * sarr[] = {"Stroustrup", "Koenig", "Ritchie",
➥"Kernighan"};
  int j = 0; /* loop counter */

  for(; j < 4; j++) /* display array before sorting */
    printf ("element %d of sarr is: %s\n", j, sarr[j]);
    /* sort sarr using qsort function */
  qsort( sarr,              /* address of array's beginning */
         4,                 /* number of elements in array */
         sizeof (char *), /* sizeof each element */
         compare);          /* pointer to user-defined */
                            /* comparison function */

  printf ("sorted\n\n");
  j = 0;  /* reset loop counter */

  for(; j < 4; j++) /* display sorted array */
    printf ("element %d of carr is: %s\n", j, sarr[j]);
}
```

3. Save MAIN.CPP. Compile MAIN.CPP and COMPARE.CPP, and link MAIN.CPP.

If you are not working in a Windows environment, your compiler might complain about the __cdecl specifier in the prototype and the definition of the function compare. In that case, comment out or remove the specifier __cdecl from COMPARE.H and COMPARE.CPP.

4. Run the program; the output should be as follows:

```
element 0 of sarr is: Stroustrup
element 1 of sarr is: Koenig
element 2 of sarr is: Ritchie
element 3 of sarr is: Kernighan
sorted

element 0 of sarr is: Kernighan
element 1 of sarr is: Koenig
element 2 of sarr is: Ritchie
element 3 of sarr is: Stroustrup
```

How It Works

Let's look at MAIN.CPP. This program sorts an array of char *. The array contains four elements—the names of C and C++ creators. No changes are added to the flow of the program. The only changes are those deriving from the different type of the array elements and the size of the array.

Let's look at COMPARE.CPP to see the changes. The first source lines includes the header file <string.h>, which contains the declaration of strcmp.

```
#include <string.h>
```

The prototype of compare, as expected, is the same. However, the function body has changed. strcmp is used to compare the arguments, which you know are C strings. Luckily, strcmp does not return a Boolean value indicating whether the strings are identical; it would be useless for our purpose. Rather, it performs a lexicographical comparison. A *lexicographical comparison* compares two strings in a method similar to the way two words are compared to decide which comes first in a dictionary. A lexicographic comparison treats every character of the compared strings as an integer. The value of the character of the second string is subtracted from the corresponding value of the first string. The result can be 0, which means that the two strings are identical. A positive value indicates the first string ranks lexicographically higher than the second one. A negative value indicates the first string ranks lexicographically lower than the second one. This is exactly what qsort expects to get from its callback function, so compare has only to invoke strcmp and return the result. In order to call strcmp, you have to cast the void pointers to their real types.

```
int __cdecl compare (const void * pfirst, const void * psecond)
{
  return strcmp(*(const char**) pfirst, *(const char **) psecond);
}
```

Comments

qsort, as you have seen, is a powerful algorithm. It is efficient, generic, and standardized. However, you have to bear in mind that it does not support C++ objects. Unlike STL containers, qsort will not reconstruct a relocated object, nor will it invoke the destructor of that object in its previous location. In other words, qsort and STL's sort are not interchangeable, but are complementary. You should use qsort with arrays (and arrays only) of plain data types such as char, int, pointers of all kind, and structs.

COMPLEXITY

INTERMEDIATE

8.2 How do I...
Find an element in an array?

Problem

I know how to sort an array but I need to find an element in it. How do I do it in C?

Technique

Standard C has a generic function for searching an element in an array—bsearch. bsearch performs a binary search on a sorted array of elements. If your array is not sorted, you should sort it before using bsearch. Later you will see how it is possible to locate an element in a nonsorted array.

bsearch tries to locate an element in an array. If the element exists, bsearch returns a pointer to it. Otherwise, it returns null. bsearch and qsort are similar both in the way they are used and in the principles of their implementation. Therefore, it is advisable for you to read this How-To after reading How-To 8.1. Remember also that this How-To uses two source files from the "Comments" section of How-To 8.1—COMPARE.H and COMPARE.CPP. The text states whether a source file is identical to any of the source files used in previous examples.

Steps

1. Change to your base source directory and create a new subdirectory named C_BSEARCH.

2. Start your source code editor and type the following code into a file named COMPARE.H. (Note: The following source file is identical to the source file COMPARE.H from the "Comments" section in How-To 8.1.)

```
#ifndef COMPARE_H
#define COMPARE_H

int __cdecl compare (const void* pfirst, const void  * psecond);

#endif
```

3. Save COMPARE.H. Type the following code into a new file named
COMPARE.CPP (Note: The following source code is identical to the source
code file COMPARE.CPP from the "Comments" section in How-To 8.1.)

```
#include <string.h>

int __cdecl compare (const void * pfirst, const void  * psecond)
{
  return strcmp(*(const char**) pfirst, *(const char **) psecond);
}
```

4. Save COMPARE.CPP. Type the following code into a new file named
MAIN.CPP:

```
#include <stdlib.h>
#include <stdio.h>
#include "compare.h"

void main()
{
  /* define an array of pointers to char and initialize it */
  char * sarr[] = {"Kernighan", "Koenig", "Ritchie",
  ➡"Stroustrup"};
  char *pkey  = "Stroustrup";
  char *pkey2 = "Stepanov";
  void *p - NULL;

  printf ("\nlooking for %s...\n", pkey);

  p = bsearch( &pkey,     /* address of key */
               sarr,      /* address of array's beginning */
               4,         /* number of elements in array */
               sizeof (char *), /* sizeof each element */
               compare); /* pointer to user-defined */
                         /* comparison function */
  if (p)
    printf("%s was found!\n", *(const char **) p);
  else
    printf("requested item was NOT found\n");

  printf ("\nlooking for %s...\n", pkey2);

  p = bsearch( &pkey2,    /*address of key */
               sarr,      /* address of array's beginning */
               4,         /* number of elements in array */
```

```
                    sizeof (char *), /* sizeof each element */
                    compare); /* pointer to user-defined */
                               /* comparison function */
        if (p)
          printf("%s was found!\n", *(const char **) p);
        else
          printf("requested item was NOT found\n");
      }
```

5. Save MAIN.CPP. Compile MAIN.CPP and COMPARE.CPP, and link MAIN.CPP.

If you are not working in a Windows environment, your compiler might complain about the __cdecl specifier in the prototype and the definition of the function compare. In that case, comment out or remove the specifier __cdecl from COMPARE.H and COMPARE.CPP.

6. Run the program; the output should be as follows:

```
looking for Stroustrup...
Stroustrup was found!

looking for Stepanov...
Requested item was NOT found
```

How It Works

Let's look at MAIN.CPP. The first source line includes <stdlib.h>, which contains the prototype of bsearch. The second source line includes <stdio.h>, which contains the prototype of printf(). The third line includes the prototype of compare, the callback function used by bsearch:

```
#include <stdlib.h>
#include <stdio.h>
#include "compare.h"
```

An array of C strings is defined and initialized inside main(). The array has four elements, and it is initialized in a sorted order.

```
void main()
{
  /* define an array of pointers to char and initialize it */
  char * sarr[] = { "Kernighan", "Koenig", "Ritchie", "Stroustrup"};
```

The following keys hold values that bsearch will look up in the array. The first key exists in the array; the other one does not.

```
char *pkey  = "Stroustrup"; //exists in array
char *pkey2 = "Stepanov";   //does not exist in array
```

A void pointer, p, stores the result of bsearch.

```
void *p = NULL;
```

bsearch is invoked twice. Here is the first invocation:

```
printf ("\nlooking for %s...\n", pkey);

p = bsearch( &pkey,      /* address of key */
             sarr,       /* address of array's beginning */
             4,          /* number of elements in array */
             sizeof (char *), /* sizeof each element */
             compare); /* pointer to user-defined comparison function */
```

The arguments passed to bsearch are the same as the arguments of qsort, except for the first one. Let's examine the role of each argument. The first one is the address of a key that bsearch has to look up. That is, the address of a value to be located in the array. In this case, the array in question holds elements of type char *; therefore, a pointer to char * is passed as the first argument.

The rest should look familiar. The second argument is the address of the array. The third argument is the total number of elements in the array. The fourth argument is the size of an element in the array. Finally, pass the address of the callback function. It is the same function compare used in the previous How-To.

The result returned from bsearch is stored in p. bsearch returns the address of the element that holds the value of the key, or null when the key does not exist in the array. You test the returned value and print a message accordingly:

```
if (p)
  printf("%s was found!\n", *(const char **) p);
else
  printf("requested item was NOT found\n");

printf ("\nlooking for %s...\n", pkey2);
```

bsearch looked for an element with the value "Stroustrup". Such an element exists in the array. In the second invocation of bsearch, a key is used with the value "Stepanov". No element in the array holds this value, so you can expect to get null.

```
p = bsearch( &pkey2,     /*address of key */
             sarr,       /* address of array's beginning */
             4,          /* number of elements in array */
             sizeof (char *), /* sizeof each element */
             compare); /* pointer to user-defined comparison function */
if (p)
  printf("%s was found!\n", *(const char **) p);
else
  printf("requested item was NOT found\n");
}
```

And null is what you get.

8.3 How do I...
Locate an element in a nonsorted array?

Problem

I have to look up a value in an array. I cannot use **bsearch** for this purpose because the array is not sorted. How can I locate an element in the array without having to sort it first?

Technique

Standard C does not offer a solution to this problem. However, many vendors ship with their compiler libraries two additional lookup functions—**_lsearch** and **_lfind**. Both can locate an element in any array, sorted and nonsorted alike.

Steps

1. Change to your base source directory and create a new subdirectory named FIND_AND_SEARCH.

2. Start your source code editor and type the following code into a file named COMPARE.H. (Note: The following source file is identical to the source file COMPARE.H from the "Comments" section in How-To 8.1.)

```
#ifndef COMPARE_H
#define COMPARE_H

int __cdecl compare (const void* pfirst, const void  * psecond);

#endif
```

3. Save COMPARE.H. Type the following code into a new file named COMPARE.CPP (Note: The following source code is identical to the source code file COMPARE.CPP from the "Comments" section in How-To 8.1.)

```
#include <string.h>

int __cdecl compare (const void * pfirst, const void  * psecond)
{
   return strcmp(*(const char**) pfirst, *(const char **) psecond);
}
```

4. Save COMPARE.CPP. Type the following code into a new file named MAIN.CPP:

```c
#include <stdlib.h>
#include <stdio.h>
#include <search.h>
#include "compare.h"

void main()
{
  /* define an array of pointers to char and initialize it */
  char * sarr[] = {"Kernighan", "Ritchie", "Koenig","Stroustrup"};
  char *pkey  = "Stroustrup";
  char *pkey2 = "Stepanov";
  void *p = NULL;
  unsigned int num = 4; /* number of array elements */

  printf ("\nlooking for %s...\n", pkey);

  p = _lfind( &pkey,       /* address of key */
              sarr,        /* address of array's beginning */
              &num,        /* number of elements in array */
              sizeof (char *), /* sizeof each element */
              compare);  /* pointer to user-defined */
                           /* comparison function */
  if (p)
    printf("%s was found!\n", *(const char **) p);
  else
    printf("requested item was NOT found\n");

  printf ("\nlooking for %s...\n", pkey2);

  p = _lfind( &pkey2,    /* address of key */
              sarr,      /* address of array's beginning */
              &num,      /* number of elements in array */
              sizeof (char *), /* sizeof each element */
              compare);/* pointer to user-defined */
                         /* comparison function */
  if (p)
    printf("%s was found!\n", *(const char **) p);
  else
    printf("requested item was NOT found\n");
}
```

5. Save MAIN.CPP. Compile MAIN.CPP and COMPARE.CPP, and link MAIN.CPP.

If you are not working in a Windows environment, your compiler might complain about the __cdecl specifier in the prototype and the definition of the function compare. In that case, comment out or remove the specifier __cdecl from COMPARE.H and COMPARE.CPP.

6. Run the program; the output should be as follows:

```
looking for Stroustrup...
Stroustrup was found!
```

```
looking for Stepanov...
Requested item was NOT found
```

How It Works

Let's look at MAIN.CPP. The first source line includes <stdlib.h>, which contains the declaration of bsearch. The second source line includes <stdio.h>, which contains the declaration of the function printf(). The third line includes the prototype of compare, which is the callback function used by bsearch:

```
#include <stdlib.h>
#include <stdio.h>
#include "compare.h"
```

An array of C strings is defined and initialized inside main(). The array is deliberately not sorted.

```
void main()
{
  /* define an array of pointers to char and initialize it */
  char * sarr[] = {"Kernighan", "Ritchie", "Koenig","Stroustrup"};
```

The following keys hold values that _lfind will look up in the array. The first key exists in the array; the second one does not.

```
char *pkey  = "Stroustrup";
char *pkey2 = "Stepanov";
```

A void pointer, p, stores the result of _lfind. Also, a variable num of type unsigned int is declared as an argument of _lfind.

```
void *p = NULL;
unsigned int num = 4; /* number of array elements */
```

_lfind is invoked twice. Here is the first invocation:

```
  printf ("\nlooking for %s...\n", pkey);

  p = _lfind( &pkey,      /* address of key */
              sarr,       /* address of array's beginning */
              &num,       /* number of elements in array */
              sizeof (char *), /* sizeof each element */
              compare);   /* pointer to user-defined comparison function */
```

The parameters passed to _lfind are the same as the parameters of bsearch, except for the third one. The first element is the address of a key _lfind has to look up (the address of a value to be located in the array). In this case, the sought array holds elements of type char *. A pointer to a char * is passed as the first argument. The second argument is the address of the array. The third argument is slightly different from bsearch: Instead of the number of total elements in the array, pass a pointer to an unsigned int that holds the number of total elements in the array. The fourth argument is the size of an element in the array. Finally, pass the address of the callback function. Again, it is the address of compare that you've used before.

The result returned from _lfind is stored in p. _lfind returns the address of the element that holds the value of the key, or null when the key does not exist in the array. Test the returned value and display a message accordingly:

```
if (p)
  printf("%s was found!\n", *(const char **) p);
else
  printf("requested item was NOT found\n");

printf ("\nlooking for %s...\n", pkey2);
```

_lfind looked for an element with the value "Stroustrup". This value exists in the array. In the second invocation of _lfind, use a key with the value "Stepanov". No element in the array holds this value, so you can expect to get null.

```
  printf ("\nlooking for %s...\n", pkey2);

  p = _lfind( &pkey2,   /* address of key */
              sarr,     /* address of array's beginning */
              &num,     /* number of elements in array */
              sizeof (char *), /* sizeof each element */
              compare);/* pointer to user-defined comparison function */
  if (p)
    printf("%s was found!\n", *(const char **) p);
  else
    printf("requested item was NOT found\n");
}
```

As expected, you get a null result this time.

COMPLEXITY
INTERMEDIATE

8.4 How do I...
Choose between _lfind and _lsearch?

Problem

I know how to use bsearch to find an element in a sorted array, and I also know I have to use _lfind to look up an element in an array that has not been sorted. However, I would like to know when I should use _lfind and when I should use _lsearch. Apparently, both these functions can be used to find an element in an array that has not been sorted.

Technique

_lsearch, like _lfind, performs a linear search on an array that doesn't have to be sorted in advance. The signature of _lsearch is identical to _lfind. Thus, these functions are pretty similar. However, there are three differences in their behavior when a key cannot be found in the array:

1. Unlike _lfind, which returns null when it cannot find a key, _lsearch appends that key to the end of the array.

2. _lsearch increments the number of array elements (the third argument) to reflect the fact that a new element has been added to the array.

3. After appending the new element and incrementing the number of elements, _lsearch returns a pointer to the newly added key.

The following program demonstrates how to use _lsearch.

Steps

1. Change to your base source directory and create a new subdirectory named LSEARCH_DEMO.

2. Start your source code editor and type the following code into a new file named MAIN.CPP:

```
#include <stdlib.h>
#include <stdio.h>
#include <search.h>

int __cdecl compare (const void* pfirst, const void * psecond)
      /* callback function */
{
 return (*(const char *) pfirst) - (*(const char *) psecond);
}

void main()
{

  char arr[] = {'a', 'b'};/* define and initialize */
                    /* an array of 2 chars */
  char key   = 'a';
  char key2  = 'c'; /* false key which does not exist in arr */
  void *p    = NULL; /* store the result of _lsearch */
  unsigned int num = 2; /* number of elements in arr */

  printf ("\nlooking for %c...\n", key);

/*first invocation. _lsearch finds 'a' in arr */
  p = _lsearch( &key,      /* address of key */
```

```
                    arr,       /* address of array's beginning */
                    &num,      /* number of elements in array */
                    sizeof (char), /* sizeof each element */
                    compare); /* pointer to user-defined */
                              /* comparison function */
        if (p)
          printf("%c was found!\n", *(char*)p);

        printf ("\nlooking for %c...\n", key2);

    /* second invocation. _lsearch can't find 'c' in arr */
    /* 'c' is appended to arr and num incremented */

      p = _lsearch( &key2,    /* address of key */
                    arr,       /* address of array's beginning */
                    &num,      /* number of elements in array */
                    sizeof (char), /* sizeof each element */
                    compare); /* pointer to user-defined */
                              /* comparison function */

      printf("%c was appended to arr\n", * (char*) p );
      printf("arr has %d elements \n", num );
      printf("the newly added element is: %c\n", arr[2] );

    }
```

3. Save MAIN.CPP.

4. Compile and link MAIN.CPP.

If you are not working in a Windows environment, your compiler might complain about the __cdecl specifier in the function compare. In that case, comment out or remove the specifier __cdecl from the definition of compare.

5. Run the program; the output should be as follows:

```
looking for a...
a was found!

looking for c...
c was appended to arr
arr has 3 elements
the newly added element is: C
```

How It Works

Let's look at MAIN.CPP. The first step is to define the appropriate version of compare, the callback function used by _lsearch.

```
int __cdecl compare (const void* pfirst, const void * psecond)
    /* callback function */
```

```
{
  return (*(const char *) pfirst) - (*(const char *) psecond);
}
```

An array of two characters is defined and initialized inside main(). Also define two keys to be looked up in the array, a **void** pointer to store the result of _lsearch, and an **unsigned int** that holds the number of array elements.

```
char arr[] = {'a', 'b'};/* define and initialize an array of 2 chars */
char key   = 'a';
char key2  = 'c'; /* false key which does not exist in arr */
void *p    = NULL; /* store the result of _lsearch */
unsigned int num = 2; /* number of elements in arr */
```

_lsearch is invoked with the key 'a'. This value exists in the array, so _lsearch returns a pointer to the address of the array element that holds the value 'a'.

```
/*first invocation. _lsearch finds 'a' in arr */
  p = _lsearch( &key,      /* address of key */
                arr,       /* address of array's beginning */
                &num,      /* number of elements in array */
                sizeof (char), /* sizeof each element */
                compare); /* pointer to user-defined comparison function */
  if (p)
    printf("%c was found!\n", *(char*)p);
```

The second invocation of _lsearch looks up the value 'c' in the array. This value does not exist in arr. Therefore, _lsearch appends 'c' to the end of the array, increments num, and returns a pointer to the newly added element:

```
/* second invocation. _lsearch can't find 'c' in arr */
/* 'c' is appended to arr and num incremented */

  p = _lsearch( &key2,    /* address of key */
                arr,      /* address of array's beginning */
                &num,     /* number of elements in array */
                sizeof (char), /* sizeof each element */
                compare); /* pointer to user-defined comparison function */

  printf("%c was appended to arr\n", * (char*) p );
  printf("arr has %d elements \n", num );
  printf("the newly added element is: %c\n", arr[2] );

}
```

Comments

When can _lsearch be useful? Suppose you need to compile a thesaurus of words that appear in some document. This process can be streamlined by using _lsearch. First, you declare an array of **char** *, in which every element represents a word. Then you retrieve the next word from the document and use _lsearch to look it up in the current array. If _lsearch doesn't find the word, it appends the missing word to the end of the array. This process is repeated until the entire document has been read. The resultant array contains all the words of the document.

The ANSI C standard does not define _lfind and _lsearch. If your code is to be ported to platforms other than Win32, you should consider judiciously the usage of nonstandard features in your programs. Remember also that the bsearch algorithm is more efficient because it uses a binary search to locate an element, whereas both _lsearch and _lfind use a linear search. _lsearch in particular is slower because it has to reallocate memory for the elements it appends to the array. For these reasons, you should prefer bsearch to _lfind or _lsearch whenever you have the choice.

COMPLEXITY
BEGINNING

8.5 How do I...
Generate a sequence of random numbers?

Problem

I need to generate a sequence of random numbers in my program.

Technique

The Standard C Library provides two functions for the purpose of random numbers generation: rand and srand. This How-To uses these functions to generate a sequence of random numbers.

Steps

1. Change to your base source directory and create a new subdirectory named RANDOM_DEMO.

2. Start your source code editor and type the following code into a new file named MAIN.CPP:

```cpp
#include <stdlib.h>
#include <stdio.h>

void main()
{
 int j = 0;
```

```
    for (; j < 5; j++)
     printf ("%d\n", rand() );

   }
```

3. Save MAIN.CPP.

4. Compile and link MAIN.CPP.

5. Run the program; it will display five different numbers on your screen. Write down these numbers.

6. Run the program once more; it should display the same five numbers that you wrote down.

How It Works

Let's look at MAIN.CPP. First, it includes the header <stdlib.h>, in which the function rand is declared. It also includes the header <stdio.h> to use printf.

```
#include <stdlib.h>
#include <stdio.h>
```

The body of main() is very simple. A loop control variable, j, is defined and initialized. Next, a for loop executes five times. On each iteration, the loop displays the value returned from the function rand. rand generates a sequence of pseudorandom numbers.

```
void main()
{
 int j = 0;

 for (; j < 5; j++)
  printf ("%d\n", rand() );

}
```

The term *pseudorandom* implies that the generated sequence is not really random; no matter how many times you execute the program, it generates exactly the same numbers. This is because rand has a set of values and a starting point. The default starting point is 1 and the generated sequence is between 1 and the macro RAND_MAX (defined in <stdlib.h> header). To create a unique sequence of numbers every time the program executes, you have to set a different starting point. You do that by using the function srand. To demonstrate that, add two changes to the source file MAIN.CPP:

1. #include the standard <time.h> header.

2. Add the following line immediately after the declaration of the variable j:

```
srand ( time(NULL) );
```

After these changes, MAIN.CPP should look like this:

```
#include <stdlib.h>
#include <stdio.h>
#include <time.h>
void main()
{
 int j = 0;
 srand ( time(NULL) ); //set starting-point

 for (; j < 5; j++)
  printf ("%d\n", rand() );
}
```

Now recompile and link MAIN.CPP. Run the program once and write down the generated numbers it displays. Run it once more. This time, a different sequence is generated.

The reason you get different sequences on every program run is that srand assigns a unique value to the starting point every time the program is executed. To create a unique value for srand, use the function time. time returns a long integer that holds the number of seconds elapsed since January 1, 1970.

TEMPL **INCLUDED ALGORITHMS**

9

THE STANDARD TEMPLATE LIBRARY'S INCLUDED ALGORITHMS

How do I...

9.1 Create classes for sequential containers?

9.2 Use predicates with sequence operations?

9.3 Repeat an action with all elements in a container range?

9.4 Compare two sequences?

9.5 Search for a sequence of values in a container?

9.6 Accumulate all container elements and create a sequence of accumulated sums?

9.7 Sort elements in a container using different sorting indexes?

9.8 Change the order of the container elements?

The Standard Template Library (STL) is a C++ component library developed by Alexander Stepanov and Meng Lee at the Hewlett-Packard laboratories. Algorithms is one of the sets of STL components. An *algorithm* is a computational procedure that applies to different containers.

STL algorithms are represented by template functions and provide copying, searching, sorting, merging, and other operations on data. Algorithms are not member functions; they are separate from the container classes.

The idea of separating data and algorithms might sound strange for a programmer used to the object-oriented approach to software design. Therefore, understanding the STL algorithms might be a serious challenge.

It is common now to combine STL algorithms into four groups: nonmutating operations, mutating operations, sorting and related operations, and generalized numeric operations. Tables 9.1 through 9.4 briefly describe the algorithms.

Table 9.1   Nonmutating Operations

ALGORITHM	DESCRIPTION
adjacent_find	Finds the consecutive duplicates in a range of elements
count, count_if	Counts the number of elements that satisfy a condition in a range of elements
equal	Compares two sequence ranges element by element
for_each	Applies a function to all elements in a range
find, find_if	Finds an element that equals a specified value or satisfies a certain condition
mismatch	Finds mismatches between two ranges of elements
search	Searches for the first match of a sub-sequence in a sequence of data

Table 9.2   Mutating Operations

ALGORITHM	DESCRIPTION
copy, copy_backward	Copies (or copies backward) a range of elements into another range
fill, fill_n	Fills a range of elements with a specified value
generate, generate_n	Generates values and fills a range with the values
partition, stable_partition	Moves the elements that satisfy a predicate before the other elements in a sequence

ALGORITHM	DESCRIPTION
random_shuffle	Randomly shuffles data in a range of elements
remove, remove_if, remove_copy, remove_copy_if	Removes elements from a range of elements
replace, replace_if, replace_copy, replace_copy_if	Replaces elements that satisfy specified conditions in a range of elements
reverse, reverse_copy	Reverses data in a range of elements
rotate, rotate_copy	Rotates data in a range of elements
swap, iter_swap, swap_ranges	Exchanges values or ranges in a sequence
transform	Performs a specified operation on a sequence, or two sequences, and copies the result into a new sequence
unique, unique_copy	Removes consecutive duplicates from a range of elements

Table 9.3 Sorting and Related Operations

ALGORITHM	DESCRIPTION
sort, stable_sort, partial_sort, partial_sort_copy	Sorts a range of elements (unstable, stable, or partial)
nth_element	Places an element in the location where it would be sorted
lower_bound, upper_bound, equal_range, binary_search	Finds bounds for, or location of, a value in a sorted range
merge, inplace_merge	Combines two sorted ranges in a single sorted range
includes, set_union, set_intersection, set_difference, set_symmetric_difference	Sets different operations on sorted ranges
push_heap, pop_heap, make_heap, sort_heap	Performs heap operations
min, max, min_element, max_element	Finds minimum and maximum of two arguments or in a specified range
lexicographical_compare	Lexicographically compares two ranges of elements
next_permutation, prev_permutation	Generates permutation of a range of elements

Table 9.4 Generalized Numeric Operations

ALGORITHM	DESCRIPTION
accumulate	Accumulates all elements in a range
inner_product	Calculates the inner product of the elements in two ranges
partial_sum	Calculates a generalized partial sum
adjacent_difference	Calculates the differences of adjacent elements

9.1 Create Classes for Sequential Containers

A sequential container in the STL is a container whose elements are arranged in a linear order. vector, deque, and list are examples of sequential containers. When developing a class based on the vector or on the list container, programmers might want to apply the algorithms to the container class. This How-To describes this process and shows the usage of count, find, and unique algorithms.

9.2 Use Predicates with Sequence Operations

An STL predicate is a unary function that returns a result representing the truth or the falsehood. The result should be convertible to the bool data type. The equality operator (==) is a simple example of a predicate. Nonmutating and mutating sequence operations, such as count or find, can be extended to the operations that compare the elements using predicates other than the equality operator. Usually, the extended version of the algorithm ends with _if, such as count_if and find_if. This How-To shows the usage of the _if as well as of the other functions with predicates.

9.3 Repeat an Action with All Elements in a Container Range

The for statement in C++ is a very common solution to perform an action on a range of elements. The elements usually can be accessed by using a pointer, and the for loop increments the pointer by performing a move to the next element. An analog of this operation is provided in the STL with the for_each algorithm. The algorithm accesses elements in a container sequentially in a specified range. The algorithm consecutively applies a function to the elements. This How-To shows an example of the usage of the for_each algorithm.

9.4 Compare Two Sequences

A comparison of two sequences is solved by a few algorithms. The equal and the mismatch algorithms are very similar. However, there is a major difference: The mismatch algorithm returns the iterator to the first element that is different in the sequences; the equal algorithm returns just true or false depending on the result of the comparison. This How-To provides an example of the two algorithms and describes their usage.

9.5   Search for a Sequence of Values in a Container

Another very common task programmers have to solve is the search for a sub-sequence within a sequence of elements. C and C++ have standard functions that help solve this task with strings as sequences of characters. The STL provides the search algorithms that can be applied to different containers. This How-To shows how you can search for a sequence of words in text.

9.6   Accumulate All Container Elements and Create a Sequence of Accumulated Sums

A quite common task in programming consists of calculating sums and accumulated sums for a sequence of data. The extension of this task can be an accumulation of data based on an operation other than addition. For example, calculating an accumulated product also happens very often. The STL functions, such as accumulate and partial_sum, can help programmers perform these common tasks. This How-To explores the accumulation of data in the STL.

9.7   Sort Elements in a Container Using Different Sorting Indexes

The sort algorithm in the Standard Template Library can have a different syntax. It can use a default relational operator for ordering the data or another function specified by the programmer. A class that can use the sort algorithm should provide certain features. This How-To creates a phone book class and then applies the sort algorithm to it. The sorting order is provided by the overloaded relational operator firs and then by the usei-defined LessThan function.

9.8   Change the Order of the Container Elements

It is very important to a programmer to be able to change the order of the sequence of elements. If the elements represent tasks in a queue, programs quite often rotate the elements—that is, take the first element and move it to the back of the queue. If the elements represent playing cards in a computer game, the programs need to shuffle the deck of cards. It might be necessary to reverse the order of the data elements for other applications. This How-To describes the rotate, reverse, and random_shuffle algorithms. These mutating algorithms represent common operations on data that change the order of the elements in a sequence.

The second part of the How-To describes the partition and the stable_partition algorithms. These algorithms move all elements that satisfy a certain predicate before other elements in the sequence. In addition, the stable_partition algorithm preserves the relative order in the parts of the sequence.

9.1 How do I...
Create classes for sequential containers?

Problem

I develop programs, such as parsers, for text processing. I want to maintain certain dictionaries as lists, for instance, a list of names. For the list of names, I want to create a fully operational class. However, the members of the `list` container don't support many operations, such as counting or finding elements based on certain criteria. On the other hand, some member functions of the list container provide the same functionality as some algorithms. For example, there is the `unique` member function and the `unique` algorithm, as well. Which functions should I use to create the class in a simple and elegant way?

Technique

The List and other sequential containers such as `vector` and `deque` have member functions that make container maintenance simple. These functions can be used to create the container, and add elements to the back, front (except `vector`), and middle of the container. You can get the elements from the back or front of the container and perform a few other operations. When creating a new class based on such a container, use member functions to support procedures specific to the class.

However, a few operations are not supported in the sequential containers. To find a certain element in a list of words or to count all elements that start with letter *s*, algorithms have to be used. In the Standard Template Library, algorithms are separated from the containers. During software design and development, these generic algorithms are applied to the specific needs of our class.

This How-To shows the creation of a class containing names. The class implementation is based on the list container. This How-To also compares the usage of certain algorithms and the usage of member functions.

Steps

1. Create a class declaration

Imagine you are developing a big application for text processing. The program is going to process English text. For the parsing and the keyword search, you would need a few data sets, such as prepositions or English names. To maintain the names, you must create a separate class that allows you to perform a few operations on the names, such as adding, searching, sorting, and removing duplicates.

First of all, you have to decide on the appropriate container for your needs. You want to do sequential operations that will process ranges of the data, such as "all names from Richard to Tom." Therefore, select sequential containers for the program. STL has three types of sequential containers: lists, vectors, and deques. (Some STL implementations also have slist and bit-vector containers; however, they are not common.) Choose the list container because it inserts the data faster than the vector or the deque. In STL, the list container represents a doubly linked list. An element on this list contains the pointers both to the next element and the preceding one.

The following code is the class declaration:

```
//persname.h

#include <list>
#include <string>
using namespace std;

class persname
{

public:
    persname();                    // constructor
    ~persname();                   // destructor

    // Add a new name
    void Add(string NewName);
    // Add a new name after an existing one
    void AddBefore(string NewName, string BeforeName);
    // Sort the names in alphabetical order
    void Sort(void);
    // Remove duplicate names from the sorted list
    void RemoveDuplicates(void);
    // Check is the name exists in the list
    bool NameExists(string TestName);

    // Count 'TestName' names
    int CountNames(string TestName);
    // Display all names
    void DisplayAll(void);

private:
    list <string> PName;

};
```

The private part of the class contains the list of strings. To support the strings as well as the STL lists, you must include the header files:

```
#include <list>
#include <string>
```

The Microsoft Visual C++ 5 compiler was used for this example. Depending on your compiler, you might change the header file names to `<list.h>` and `<string.h>` or some other names. You have to check your compiler reference to get the correct names.

In addition to the constructor and the destructor member functions, the public part of the class contains the following functions:

- `void Add(string NewName)` adds a new name of the **string** type to the end of the list.

- `void AddBefore(string NewName, string BeforeName)` adds a new name of the **string** type before the first occurrence of a specified name or to the back of the list if the specified name does not exist.

- `void Sort(void)` sorts all names in the list in ascending alphabetical order.

- `void RemoveDuplicates(void)` removes consecutive duplicate names from the list. The function is not supposed to remove all duplicates; it can do so only if the list is sorted.

- `bool NameExists(string TestName)` is one of the most important functions in the class. During a parsing procedure the function is executed to check words against the names in the list.

- `int CountName(string TestName)` counts the occurrences of `TestName` in the list.

- `void DisplayAll(void)` displays all names in the list to the computer screen.

These functions are just the first step in the class development. Later, you are going to create more functions to satisfy more needs of the class.

2. Class implementation

Your class implementation will be very simple. You can improve the class functionality by adding validation routines or improve the performance by changing the implementation according to the specifics of your compiler. One of the changes can be done if your version of STL supports the slist container (singly linked list). The singly linked list would perform better in this case because you don't need backward operations.

```cpp
// persname.cpp

#include <iostream>
#include <list>
#include <algorithm>
#include <string>
using namespace std;

#include "persname.h"

persname::persname()
{

}

persname::~persname()
{

}

// Add a new name
void persname::Add(string NewName)
{
    PName.push_back(NewName);

}

// Add a new name before an existing one or to the end
// of the list
void persname::AddBefore(string NewName, string BeforeName)
{
    list <string>::iterator SResult;

    SResult = find(PName.begin(), PName.end(), BeforeName);
    PName.insert(SResult, NewName);
}

// Sort the names in alphabetic order
void persname::Sort(void)
{
    PName.sort();
}

// Remove duplicate names from the sorted list
void persname::RemoveDuplicates(void)
{
    list <string>::iterator new_end;
```

```
    new_end = unique(PName.begin(), PName.end());
    PName.erase(new_end, PName.end());
}

// Check is the name exists in the list
bool persname::NameExists(string TestName)
{
    list <string>::iterator SResult;

    SResult = find(PName.begin(), PName.end(), TestName);
    if (SResult == PName.end()) return false;
    return true;

}

// Count all names
int persname::CountNames(string TestName)
{

    return count (PName.begin(), PName.end(), TestName);
}

// Display all names
void persname::DisplayAll(void)
{
    list <string>::iterator i;

    for (i = PName.begin(); i!=PName.end(); i++)
        cout << *i << endl;
}
```

This example was created using Microsoft Visual C++ version 5. If you
use the Borland C++ 5 compiler, you have to change the line

```
return count (PName.begin(), PName.end(), TestName);
```

in the `persname::CountNames` function to

```
int iCount;
count (PName.begin(), PName.end(), TestName, iCount);
return iCount;
```

Let's discuss the implementation of the member functions.

The `void Add(string NewName)` function takes a string argument and
pushes it to the end of the `PName` list. This operation helps to create the
lists rapidly without ordering the names. To implement it, use the
`push_back` member function of the list container. The member function is
common to all sequential containers and inserts a new element of an
appropriate type to the end of the container.

void AddBefore(string NewName, string BeforeName) inserts the NewName element before the first occurrence of the BeforeName element. If the BeforeName element does not exist, the function inserts the NewName element at the back of the list.

The two Add functions are void in this implementation. However, in a more sophisticated class the functions could return a value. For instance, true would be returned if the operation were successful and false if the operation failed.

void Sort(void) sorts all elements in the list. This brings up the first question: Should you use the sort member function of the list container to sort the names, or should you make the implementation with the sort algorithm of the Standard Template Library? No answer to this question is correct under all circumstances.

In this case, the choice to use the sort member function of the list container is determined by the limitations of the container. The container uses input/output, forward, and bidirectional iterators. However, the sort algorithm accepts only random-access iterators as its arguments.

Using the sort algorithm is appropriate when you want to make your solution more generic. For example, if you are not sure you selected the correct container and want to be able to change the container in the future, the sort algorithm will better solve this problem. You can apply the sort algorithm to different containers and changing the container would not change the persname::Sort member function.

On the other hand, using the sort member function of the list class is more efficient. Even if you developed a sort algorithm that works with bidirectional iterators, it is a good idea to keep using the sort member functions of the list container.

This Sort function sorts the data in ascending alphabetical order.

The RemoveDuplicates function removes the consecutive duplicates from the list of names. The function uses the unique algorithm to remove the duplicates. The algorithm is used instead of the unique member function so you will be able to extend the class functionality quickly.

The arguments of the unique algorithm specify the iterators to the first and last elements in the range that should be checked for duplicates. The algorithm returns an iterator that points to the end of the new list range.

Note that the **unique** algorithm does not truncate the unused elements after it removes the duplicates. Therefore, you have to apply the **erase** function that erases all elements of the list from the new end to the old end.

Pointing to the list elements is provided by the iterators. The iterator that points to the new end of the list is declared with the statement

```
list <string>::iterator new_end;
```

The iterators that point to the beginning and end of the list are the results of the **list** member functions **begin()** and **end()**. The functions exist for all sequential and associative containers.

The **NameExists** function uses the **find** algorithm to find the first occurrence of the specified name in the data range:

```
SResult = find(PName.begin(), PName.end(), TestName);
```

This algorithm accepts the range limits as the first two arguments. This class specifies the entire container as the range. The third argument is the value of the element to be found. The **find** algorithm compares the elements in the range with the specified value using the == operator of the data in the list. The return value is an iterator that points to the first occurrence of the specified element in the container. If the element with the specified value is not found, the resulting iterator points to the end of the range.

The **CountNames** function is the first iteration in creating a function that counts elements in a specified sub-sequence. The **CountNames** function returns the number of occurrences of a specified name in the list. The function uses the **count** algorithm on the entire sequence from **PName.begin()** to **PName.end()**.

In order to test this class, create the **DisplayAll** function that displays all elements in the list. The function runs a loop from the first to the last element in the list. Note that the **end()** member function points *after* the end of the list (or another container).

To use the algorithms, you must include the **<algorithm>** header file. For some compilers, the file can have **<algorithm.h>**, **<algo.h>**, or another name.

3. Testing the class

To test the **persname** class implementation, write a small program that executes all functions and displays the result.

```cpp
// This is the program to test
// persname class
// pntest.cpp

#include <iostream>
#include "persname.h"

int main()
{

    persname Names;

    Names.Add ("Andrew");
    Names.Add ("Peter");
    Names.Add ("Martin");
    Names.Add ("Andrew");
    Names.Add ("Andrew");
    Names.Add ("Margaret");

    Names.Sort();
    Names.DisplayAll();
    cout << endl;

    cout << "There are " << Names.CountNames("Andrew") <<
            " Andrews in the list" << endl;
    Names.RemoveDuplicates();
    cout << endl;

    Names.AddBefore("James", "Margaret");
    Names.DisplayAll();
    cout << endl;

    if (Names.NameExists("Peter")) cout << "Peter" << endl;
    if (Names.NameExists("peter")) cout << "peter" << endl;

return 0;
}
```

The program creates the list of names, sorts it, and displays it onscreen. The first output should show the names in the following order:

```
Andrew
Andrew
Andrew
Margaret
Martin
Peter
```

Then the program counts the number of Andrews in the list and shows

```
There are 3 Andrews in the list
```

The next step is to remove duplicates and to add James before Margaret. The output should show the new list:

```
Andrew
James
Margaret
Martin
Peter
```

Finally, check for the existence of the name Peter in the list. To do this, execute the NameExists method twice: the first time with the name Peter starting with a capital *P*, and the second time with the name peter starting with a small *p*. The output should show the line with the name only once:

```
Peter
```

Comments

Developing classes using STL is not a straightforward process. You have to decide the appropriate type of the container and whether to use algorithms or member functions. Sequential containers have some of the necessary functions. The selection of algorithms should be done thoroughly in order to allow extension of the class methods. The next How-To shows how you can extend the functionality of the class using STL predicates.

COMPLEXITY

ADVANCED

9.2 How do I...
Use predicates with sequence operations?

Problem

Sequence operations such as find, count, and unique use a comparison based on the == operator. The == operator is defined for the data type that is used in the container and it often does not cover my needs. I want to be able to find elements that satisfy certain criteria. For example, I want to find the elements that end with *er*, or count all elements that start with *M*. How do I use other functions than == operator with the sequential algorithms?

Technique

To extend the functionality of the **find**, **count**, and **unique** algorithms, specify certain predicates that will be used in the comparison instead of the equality operator (==). *Predicates* are unary functions that return a result representing true or false. The result should be convertible to the **bool** data type. You are going to create a few more methods using predicates for the class that maintains names for the text processing.

Steps

1. Create a method that uses a predicate with the **count** algorithm

In this How-To, you will learn to create a new method that counts all names in the list that start with the letters from *A* to *L*. One possible reason for doing this is to separate the set of names when it is becoming too big. To count the names, use the **count_if** algorithm that allows you to specify a function for selecting certain data.

The function should be a predicate—that is, a unary function whose result represents the truth or falsehood of some condition. In this example, the function will return **true** if the name starts with a letter from *A* to *L*. The function will be used in the new **CountNamesAL** method that is added to the **persname** class. The following code is added to the class definition that will be now in the file **persnam1.h**:

```
// Count names that start with 'A' to 'L'
int CountNamesAL(void);
```

The function definition is also added to the class and located in the file **persnam1.cpp**.

```
    // Count names that start with 'A' to 'L'
int persname::CountNamesAL(void)
{
    return count_if (PName.begin(), PName.end(),
                     bind2nd(less<string>(),"M"));
}
```

The **count_if** algorithm uses a new function **bind2nd**. It converts a binary function to a unary predicate. The result of the

```
bind2nd(less<string>(),"M")
```

is **true** if the element is lexicographically smaller than *M*. In other words, it will return **true** if the word starts with a letter from *A* to *L*.

Microsoft Visual C++ 5 was used to test this example. If you use Borland C++ 5, you must change the line with the **return** statement in the **CountNamesAL** function to

```
int iCount;
count_if (PName.begin(), PName.end(), bind2nd
➥(less<string>(),"M"), iCount);
return iCount;
```

To test this algorithm, the **main** program was modified slightly.

```
// This is the program to test
// persname class
// pn1test.cpp

#include <iostream>
#include "persnam1.h"

int main()
{

    persname Names;

    Names.Add ("Andrew");
    Names.Add ("Peter");
    Names.Add ("John");
    Names.Add ("Andrew");
    Names.Add ("Andrew");
    Names.Add ("Margaret");

    Names.Sort();
    Names.DisplayAll();
    cout << endl;

// The following code replaces the code in the previous example
    cout << "There are " << Names.CountNamesAL() <<
            " names starting from A to L" << endl;

return 0;
}
```

If you run the program, the output will be

```
There are 4 names starting from A to L
```

2. Create a method that uses a predicate with the **find** algorithm

You can use predicates with other algorithms such as **find**. The extended version of this algorithm also has the suffix **_if**. Let's write the function to find the first occurrence of the word that starts with a letter greater than *I*.

The new member function of the **persname** class is called FindNameJ. The FindNameJ declaration and definition follow:

```
// Find the first name that start with 'J'
string FindNameJ(void);
```

and

```
string persname::FindNameJ(void)
{
    list <string>::iterator i;

    i = find_if(PName.begin(), PName.end(),
                bind2nd(greater<string>(),"IZZZ"));
    return *i;
}
```

To start the search from the letter *J*, the code uses a trick. All words starting with *J* to *Z* are described as greater than IZZZ.

To test the member function, you can execute the following program:

```
// This is the program to test
// persname class
// pn1test.cpp

#include <iostream>
#include "persnam1.h"

int main()
{

    persname Names;

    Names.Add ("Andrew");
    Names.Add ("Peter");
    Names.Add ("John");
    Names.Add ("Andrew");
    Names.Add ("Andrew");
    Names.Add ("Margaret");

    Names.Sort();
    Names.DisplayAll();
    cout << endl;

// The following lines are new; they show the usage of FindNameJ
    cout << "The first name  starting with J is "
         << Names.FindNameJ() << endl;

    return 0;
}
```

The program should return

```
Andrew
Andrew
Andrew
Andrew
John
Margaret
Peter

The first name starting with J is John
```

3. Create a method that uses a predicate with the **unique** algorithm

There is no **_if** version of the **unique** algorithm. Instead, **unique** is an overloaded name. Another function accepts a binary predicate as an argument.

Let's write a program that removes all names starting with the same letter except the first one. The new member function of the **persname** class will have the following declaration and definition:

```
// Leaves one word per letter
void RemoveA (void);
```

and

```
class SameLetter:binary_function <string, string, bool>
{
public:
    bool operator()(const string& a, const string& b) {
        if (a.at(0) == b.at(0))
            return true;
        else
            return false;
    }
};

    // Leaves one word per letter
void persname::RemoveA (void)
{
    list <string>::iterator new_end;

    new_end = unique(PName.begin(), PName.end(), SameLetter());
    PName.erase(new_end, PName.end());
}
```

Because the **unique** algorithm does not truncate the list, the **erase** list member function must be used.

The class `SameLetter` defines the function object that specifies the new equality function. In the `unique` algorithm, two consecutive elements of the list are considered equal if the result of this function is `true`.

The `SameLetter` function is also called a *binary predicate.*

Comments

To increase the functionality of certain algorithms, you can use predicates to specify the criteria that the algorithm uses when processing data. A few algorithms change their names by adding the `_if` suffix. Other algorithms are overloaded and use the same names.

Predicates can be unary or binary depending on the number of arguments. A predicate is a function that results in truth or falsehood depending on certain conditions. Functions that change their names with `_if`, such as `count_if` and `find_if`, accept unary predicates. Functions that use overloaded names, such as `unique`, accept binary predicates.

The use of predicates dramatically increases the power of algorithms. It almost doubles their number and provides a programmer with the ability to embed his own functions in the standard algorithms.

COMPLEXITY

INTERMEDIATE

9.3 How do I...
Repeat an action with all elements in a container range?

Problem

I want to be able to apply a certain function to an entire container or to the range of a container. For example, I often have to convert an area from square feet to square meters and print the results. Do I have to use `for` loops or is there another way of coding?

Technique

The Standard Template Library has an analog of the C++ `for` statement. This is the `for_each` algorithm that can be applied to any sequential container. Moreover, the algorithm can work on any data structure that has a sequential order similar to an array.

The `for_each` algorithm applies the specified function in forward order, from the beginning to the end of the range. In this How-To, you will write a few examples to show the `for_each` algorithm functionality.

Steps

1. Using `for_each` algorithm with arrays

You want to create a program that converts square feet to square meters. The original C++ program is written with arrays and uses the standard C++ `for` statement.

```cpp
// fe1.cpp

#include <iostream>
#include <iomanip>
using namespace std;

int main()
{
    const double factor = 0.09290304;
    double area[]= {1200.0, 1080.78, 981.5, 224.70};

    for (int i = 0; i < 4; i++)
    {
        cout << setprecision(2) << setiosflags(ios::fixed) <<
            factor*area[i] << endl;
    }
return 0;

}
```

To use the STL `for_each` algorithm, you have to define the function you are going to use in the loop. Let's create the `PrintM` function that will convert the value in square feet to square meters and print the result.

Note that `for_each` is a nonmutative algorithm. It should not accept the functions that change the content of the container.

```cpp
// fe1.cpp

#include <iostream>
#include <iomanip>
#include <algorithm>
using namespace std;
```

```
void PrintM(double valueF)
{
    const double factor = 0.09290304;
    cout << setprecision(2) << setiosflags(ios::fixed) <<
        factor*valueF << endl;
}

int main()
{
    double areaF[]= {1200.0, 1080.78, 981.5, 224.70};

    for_each (areaF, areaF + 4, PrintM);
return 0;

}
```

The beginning and the end of the sorting range are **areaF** and **areaF+4**. Note that **areaF+4** points after the last element of the array.

The **<algorithm>** header file is required for all STL algorithms.

The output of the program should be

```
111.48
100.41
91.18
20.88
```

2. Change arrays to vectors

In order to provide more flexibility, replace the array in your implementation with the STL vector. The vector container is an expandable sequential container that is analogous to the C++ array. The main difference is that you don't have to specify the upper limit for the vector. It expands itself as the new element is being added.

```
// fe3.cpp

#include <iostream>
#include <iomanip>
#include <algorithm>
#include <vector>
using namespace std;

void PrintM(double valueF)
{
    const double factor = 0.09290304;
    cout << setprecision(2) << setiosflags(ios::fixed) <<
        factor*valueF << endl;
}
```

```
int main()
{
    vector <double> areaF;
    areaF.push_back(1200.0);
    areaF.push_back(1080.78);
    areaF.push_back(981.5);
    areaF.push_back(224.70);

    for_each (areaF.begin(), areaF.end(), PrintM);
return 0;

}
```

In order to use vectors in this program, you must include the `<vector>` header file. Also, the vector initialization was changed. The vector is initialized using the **push_back** function.

Because you haven't changed the data type of the data, don't make changes in the **PrintM** function. Therefore, the **for_each** function remained the same too.

3. Trying to change the class with the nonmutating algorithm

As noted before, the data should not be changed with a nonmutating algorithm. This is specified in the STL standard. However, not all compilers check that the function used in the **for_each** algorithm does not change the data. If you try to replace the **PrintM** function with the following one

```
void PrintM(double &valueF)
{
    const double factor = 0.09290304;
    valueF = factor*valueF;
    cout << setprecision(2) << setiosflags(ios::fixed) <<
        valueF << endl;
}
```

you won't get any warnings if you run Microsoft Visual C++ 5. The code will be compiled and the main function

```
// fe1.cpp

#include <iostream>
#include <iomanip>
#include <algorithm>
using namespace std;
```

```
int main()
{
    double areaF[]= {1200.0, 1080.78, 981.5, 224.70};

    for_each (areaF, areaF + 4, PrintM);
    for (int i= 0; i < 4; i++) cout << areaF[i] << endl;

return 0;

}
```

will produce the output

```
111.48
100.41
91.18
20.88
111.48
100.41
91.18
20.88
```

that confirms the changes.

Comments

STL provides a general algorithm that replaces the **for** loop for the containers. The **for_each** algorithm applies a specified function to a range of a container. Even if the range is specified with the iterators that point to the beginning and to the end of it, and if you don't know the number of elements in the range, the **for_each** algorithm can handle such an approach.

The **for_each** algorithm has a linear complexity, which means it executes the function a number of times proportional to the length of the range.

COMPLEXITY
INTERMEDIATE

9.4 How do I...
Compare two sequences?

Problem

One common problem I have to solve while working with the STL containers is comparing two ranges of sequences. What algorithms should I use to compare the ranges? What is the difference between the **equal** and the **mismatch** algorithms?

Technique

The equal and mismatch algorithms carry out the same task. They compare the ranges of sequences and find whether the ranges differ. The behavior of the two algorithms is very similar. The difference between them is that equal simply returns false if the two ranges differ. The mismatch algorithm returns the first location where they differ.

This How-To discusses how the two algorithms are properly used.

Steps

1. Using the equal algorithm

Consider an example of data sets of integers for an interactive computer game. You want to maintain the integers in the vector and consider the vector a pattern for matching with other data structures. For example, you want to know if the incoming data differs from the pattern that you maintain.

In the program, keep the pattern in the pattern vector. Read the incoming data in the inData vector, and compare the data with pattern. You must make a few assumptions. First, in order to make the program simpler, don't read the data. Instead, hardcode the inData initialization. Second, assume that you already know that the proper range that could match the incoming data starts with the pattern[1] element. You also know that the length of inData will not exceed the length of the rest of pattern.

```
// equal_a.cpp

#include <iostream>
#include <vector>
#include <algorithm>
using namespace std;

int main()
{
    vector <int> pattern;
    vector <int> inData;

    vector <int>::iterator i;

    pattern.push_back(12);
    pattern.push_back(25);
    pattern.push_back(33);
    pattern.push_back(49);
```

```
inData.push_back(25);
inData.push_back(33);
inData.push_back(48);

i = pattern.begin();
i++;
if (equal(i, pattern.end(), inData.begin()))
    cout << "The ranges are equal" << endl;
else
    cout << "The ranges are not equal" << endl;

return 0;
}
```

The most interesting lines in this very short program are

```
i = pattern.begin();
i++;
if (equal(i, pattern.end(), inData.begin()))
```

The first line creates an iterator that helps to walk through the **pattern** vector. The second line increments the iterator. (In a bigger program, you would write some code that finds the beginning of the range in the pattern that would be checked against **InData**.) The third line uses the **equal** algorithm with three arguments. The first argument points to the beginning of the pattern. It should start with the second element of the **pattern** vector, where the **i** iterator points now. The second argument points after the end of the range, and the **end()** member function of the **vector** container is used for this purpose. The third argument points to the beginning of the second range, which is compared with the first one. You will use the **begin()** function of the vector container.

The output will show

```
The ranges are not equal
```

2. Using the **mismatch** algorithm

In the previous example, you were not interested in finding the difference between the two ranges. The knowledge that the incoming range was the same or was different from the pattern was sufficient. Now you want to know which element makes this difference. For that reason, you are going to change the **equal** algorithm to the **mismatch** algorithm.

```
// equal_a.cpp

#include <iostream>
#include <vector>
#include <algorithm>
using namespace std;

int main()
{
    vector <int> pattern;
    vector <int> inData;

    vector <int>::iterator i;

    pattern.push_back(12);
    pattern.push_back(25);
    pattern.push_back(33);
    pattern.push_back(49);

    inData.push_back(25);
    inData.push_back(33);
    inData.push_back(48);

    i = pattern.begin();
    i++;

    pair<int*, int*> result;
    result= mismatch(i, pattern.end(), inData.begin());

    if (equal(i, pattern.end(), inData.begin()))
        cout << "The ranges are equal" << endl;
    else
        cout << "The different values are: " <<
                *(result.first) << " and " <<
                *(result.second) <<  endl;

    return 0;
}
```

This example was written using the Microsoft Visual C++ version 5 compiler. If you use the Borland C++ 5 compiler, you have to include the <utility> header file for **pair** definition.

Running the application now will show

```
The different values are 48 and 49
```

The syntax of the **mismatch** algorithms is interesting. In order to execute it, you wrote the two lines:

```
pair<int*, int*> result;
result= mismatch(i, pattern.end(), inData.begin());
```

The first line defines a pair of two variables of the type `int*`. In general, the pair is heterogeneous—the types of the variables shouldn't be the same. A pair is similar to a structure: the first member in the pair is referenced as `result.first`, and the second member is referenced as `result.second`, where `result` is the name of the pair.

`pair` allows you to return the two values. The `mismatch` algorithm also returns two values: the first occurrence of the different elements in the ranges. If no such difference exists, the first member of the `mismatch` algorithm result points after the end of the first range.

3. Comparison of the two cases

The `equal` and `mismatch` algorithms solve the same problem. Both algorithms compare two ranges element by element. Using the `equal` algorithm can be simpler because it does not need to define a pair of resulting values. The `mismatch` algorithm returns the different values that might be necessary for later use in the program.

Comments

Matching a range of data against another range of data is a very common task in programming. The `equal` and `mismatch` algorithms provide this matching capability.

COMPLEXITY
INTERMEDIATE

9.5 How do I...
Search for a sequence of values in a container?

Problem

For text processing applications, user interface design, and other data parsing, I have to search for sub-sequences of data in sequences such as texts. I already know how I can search for a word in a sequence of characters. Can I search for a sequence of words in a text if the texts are vectors of words?

Technique

The STL provides the **search** algorithm that searches for a range of data in another range of data. The data should be of the same type. This How-To describes an example that searches a sequence of words. The program keeps the words in the vector container with the elements of the **string** type.

Another example extends the algorithm capabilities. The example shows how you can use the **search** algorithm to compare the elements by applying a special function. This How-To will search for a sub-sequence of words that start with the same letters as the specified sequence of words.

Steps

1. Applying the **search** algorithm

In this How-To, you will create a program that searches for a word combination in a quote from Oscar Wilde: "All art is quite useless." The first search will be done for the sequence **quite useless**.

```cpp
// search.cpp

#include <algorithm>
#include <string>
#include <vector>
#include <iostream>
using namespace std;

int main()
{
    vector <string> MainText;
    vector <string> TempString;

    vector <string>::iterator i;

    MainText.push_back("All");
    MainText.push_back("art");
    MainText.push_back("is");
    MainText.push_back("quite");
    MainText.push_back("useless");

    TempString.push_back("quite");
    TempString.push_back("useless");

    i = search (MainText.begin(), MainText.end(),
            TempString.begin(), TempString.end());
    if (i == MainText.end())
       cout << "The substring is not found" << endl;
    else
       cout << "The substring is found" << endl;
```

```
    return 0;

}
```

The programming example given here is much simpler than a real program. To maintain the sentence "All art is quite useless," the MainText vector is defined and filled in with the push_back function. The word combination quite useless is being kept in another vector, TempString. Both vectors have elements of the string data type; therefore, the following header files were included:

```
#include <vector>
#include <iostream>
```

This example was created using Microsoft Visual C++ version 5. If you use other compilers or older versions of the Microsoft compiler, you might have to include the <algorithm.h>, <string.h>, <vector.h>, and <iostream.h> header files.

The search algorithm in its simplest version takes four arguments. The first two arguments specify the data range in the main sequence. In this example, you want to search from the very beginning to the very end of MainText. The second pair of the arguments specifies the range of the sequence to search for.

The result of the search algorithm is an iterator that points to the beginning of a sub-sequence in the main sequence that is equal to the second sequence. In this example, the i iterator points to the element of the main sequence that contains the word quite. If the search algorithm fails, the result would point after the end of the main sequence.

If you run the program, it will show

```
The substring is found
```

on the computer screen.

2. Applying the search algorithm with a special comparison function

A simple search uses the equality operator or an overloaded equality operator to compare the sequences. If you want to make the search more sophisticated, you can specify another binary function for the comparison.

This case, you search for the word combination that starts with the same letters as the given word combination. In other words, the equality operator will be replaced with the following function:

```
#include <functional>
class WordCompare:binary_function <string, string, bool>
{
public:
    bool operator()(const string& a, const string& b) {
        if (a.at(0) == b.at(0))
            return true;
        else
            return false;
    }
};
```

For `binary_function` support, you have to include the `<functional>` header file.

Change the word combination you want to use as a search pattern. Search for the sub-sequence that starts with the same letters as the word combination `quite unique`.

```
// search.cpp

#include <algorithm>
#include <string>
#include <vector>
#include <functional>
#include <iostream>
using namespace std;

class WordCompare:binary_function <string, string, bool>
{
public:
    bool operator()(const string& a, const string& b) {
        if (a.at(0) == b.at(0))
            return true;
        else
            return false;
    }
};

int main()
{
    vector <string> MainText;
    vector <string> TempString;

    vector <string>::iterator i;

    MainText.push_back("All");
    MainText.push_back("art");
    MainText.push_back("is");
    MainText.push_back("quite");
    MainText.push_back("useless");
```

```
TempString.push_back("quite");
TempString.push_back("unique");

i = search (MainText.begin(), MainText.end(),
        TempString.begin(), TempString.end(), WordCompare());
if (i == MainText.end())
    cout << "The substring is not found" << endl;
else
    cout << "The substring is found" << endl;

return 0;

}
```

If the program is run, the output will be

```
The substring is found
```

because the sentence "All art is quite useless" has a word combination
`quite useless` that starts with the same letters as `quite unique`.

The `search` function in this example accepts five arguments. The last one
is the function object that defines the comparison procedure.

Comments

The `search` algorithm is a powerful tool that can be used to search within data
containers. The search procedure can be expanded by the usage of a function
object that specifies the comparison procedure.

COMPLEXITY
INTERMEDIATE

9.6 How do I...
Accumulate all container elements and create a sequence of accumulated sums?

Problem

I want to accumulate data for my accounting program as a simple sum and as
an accumulated sum. In other words, I want to create a sequence of partial
sums in the given sequence. For another program, I want to be able to calculate
products of the given values and accumulate them. Is there a standard function
in the STL that helps me perform this task?

Technique

The STL has a few algorithms that can accumulate data. The algorithms discussed in this section are the **accumulate** and the **partial_sum** algorithms. The modifications of the algorithms can use functions other than addition, which increases their applicability.

The syntax of the algorithms is simple enough to allow a user to implement them intuitively. This How-To discusses a few examples of the implementation of these two algorithms.

Steps

1. Accumulating data using addition

The first example creates a sum for a set of transactions. The transactions are represented with a vector container. The program simply calculates the sum and shows it on the screen.

```
// accum.cpp

#include <iostream>
#include <algorithm>
#include <numeric>
#include <vector>
using namespace std;

int main()
{
    vector <float> Transaction;
    float InitValue= 0.0;
    float ResultSum;

    Transaction.push_back(18.56);
    Transaction.push_back(-100.00);
    Transaction.push_back(123.01);
    Transaction.push_back(7610.23);
    Transaction.push_back(-507.65);

    ResultSum = accumulate (Transaction.begin(),
    ➥Transaction.end(), InitValue);

    cout << "The balance of the transations is "
        << ResultSum << endl;

    return 0;
}
```

The program needs to include a few header files. `<iostream>` for the cout, `<vector>` for the vector container support, and `<algorithm>` for the usage of STL algorithms are files that you already used. However, in this example you also need the `<numeric>` header file that supports numeric algorithms, such as the **accumulate** algorithm. The compiler directive

```
using namespace std;
```

is the usual addition to these standard header files.

The `Transaction` vector of **float** values will contain all transaction amounts for your calculations. Initialize the vector using the **push_back** member function of the vector container.

The accumulated value has two components. The first is the initial value kept in the **ResultSum** variable. Set this value to **0.0**. Under different circumstances, the value can be other than zero (usually it keeps the balance of the previous financial period). The second component of the accumulated value is the sum of the vector's values. The **accumulate** algorithm takes the first iterator in the range, which is `Transaction.begin()` in this example, and takes all the values up to the last iterator, which is `Transaction.end()`. If there is no data in the container, the algorithm will return the initial value. Therefore, the existence of the initial value is quite important for the algorithm's reliability.

Finally, when the program is running it shows the string

```
The balance of the transations is 7144.15
```

The result represents the balance of the transaction set.

2. Accumulating data using subtraction

For the same accounting application, change the task slightly. Now, calculate expenses by subtracting them from the initial value. To do that, you must make a few changes to the program.

```
// accum.cpp

#include <iostream>
#include <algorithm>
#include <numeric>
#include <vector>
#include <functional>
using namespace std;
```

```
int main()
{
    vector <float> Transaction;
    float InitValue= 10000.0;
    float ResultSum;

    Transaction.push_back(18.56);
    Transaction.push_back(100.00);
    Transaction.push_back(123.01);
    Transaction.push_back(7610.23);
    Transaction.push_back(507.65);

    ResultSum = accumulate (Transaction.begin(),
    ➥Transaction.end(), InitValue, minus <float>());

    cout << "The balance of the transations is "
         << ResultSum << endl;

    return 0;
}
```

First of all, based on the task, change the initial value and make all transaction amounts positive. To calculate the result, use the **accumulate** algorithm with the fourth argument that specifies the calculations. The fourth argument can be any function object. Note that the algorithm consequently takes the values and applies the function to the result. In this case the steps in the processing of the algorithms are

1. Result1 = InitValue–Value1

2. Result2 = Result1–Value2

3. Result3 = Result2–Value3

4. Result4 = Result3–Value4

5. Result5 = Result4–Value5

where **Result1** to **Result5** are the internal intermediate values, and **Value1** to **Value5** are the values of the **Transaction** vector elements.

To calculate the result, use the **minus** function from the STL. The function is defined in the **<functional>** header file; therefore, you have to include it into your code.

If you run the program it will show

```
The balance of the transations is 1640.55
```

The result represents the rest of the funds after the expenses are calculated.

3. Creating accumulated sums

Now create another container that will keep the accumulated sums. In other words, keep the values **Value1**, **Value1+Value2**, **Value1+Value2+Value3**, and so on.

```
// accum.cpp

#include <iostream>
#include <algorithm>
#include <numeric>
#include <vector>
using namespace std;

int main()
{
    vector <float> Transaction;
    vector <float> Sums(5);
    vector <float>:: iterator i;

    Transaction.push_back(18.56);
    Transaction.push_back(-100.00);
    Transaction.push_back(123.01);
    Transaction.push_back(7610.23);
    Transaction.push_back(-507.65);

    partial_sum (Transaction.begin(), Transaction.end(),
    ➥Sums.begin());

    for (i = Sums.begin(); i!= Sums.end(); i++)
        cout << *i << endl;

    return 0;
}
```

The program works with the two vector containers. The first one is the **Transaction** vector from the first example in this section. The vector is initialized by the **push_back** vector function. The second container, **Sums**, is intended to keep the accumulated sums. It is created in such a way that the constructor makes space for the first five elements in it:

```
vector <float> Sums(5);
```

This is a very important point. If you did not create the elements in the vector, your program would crash because the algorithm that you use does not create new elements; it just fills in the existing ones.

To create the sums, use the **partial_sum** algorithm. The algorithm has three arguments. The first two arguments specify the range of the container data to process, the third argument specifies the beginning of the output container.

The output of the program is

```
18.56
-81.44
41.57
7651.8
7144.15
```

No wonder the last line results in the same value as the first example in this How-To.

4. Creating accumulated products

Similar to the previous example, this example will accumulate the values. However, now you create products in the output vector. The program will calculate the values 1, 1*1/2, 1*1/2*1/3, and so on, and move them in the **Products** vector.

```cpp
// accum.cpp

#include <iostream>
#include <algorithm>
#include <numeric>
#include <functional>
#include <vector>
using namespace std;

int main()
{
    vector <float> SourceValues;
    vector <float> Products(5);
    vector <float>:: iterator i;

    SourceValues.push_back(1.);
    SourceValues.push_back(1./2.);
    SourceValues.push_back(1./3.);
    SourceValues.push_back(1./4.);
    SourceValues.push_back(1./5.);

    partial_sum (SourceValues.begin(), SourceValues.end(),
                    Products.begin(), multiplies <float>());

    for (i = Products.begin(); i!= Products.end(); i++)
        cout << *i << endl;

    return 0;
}
```

This example works with the Microsoft Visual C++ version 5 compiler. If you use the Borland C++ 5 compiler, you have to change the `multiplies` function object to the `times` function object. Currently, the STL considers `times` obsolete.

The program uses the `partial_sum` algorithm with the four arguments. The first two arguments specify the range that is processed for the source data container. The third parameter specifies the first element of output container. Note that you have to make some space for the output data because the `partial_sum` function does not create the new output elements, it uses the existing ones instead.

The output of the program is

```
1
0.5
0.166667
0.04166667
0.0833333
```

The values may slightly differ for different compilers.

Comments

The `accumulate` and the `partial_sum` algorithms belong to the group of generalized numeric algorithms in the Standard Template Library. The `accumulate` algorithm calculates a sum of the values of the given container elements. A version of the algorithm can apply functions other than addition to the values in the container. The `partial_sum` algorithm creates the consecutive sums of the elements of the given container. Using functions other than addition can also extend the functionality of this algorithm.

COMPLEXITY
ADVANCED

9.7 How do I...
Sort elements in a container using different sorting indexes?

Problem

I often create containers of different user-defined types. To maintain phone books, I use a special class that describes a phone book entry. For some applications, the entries can be very complicated and contain many fields. I want to perform many operations with the phone book; I want to sort the data using different fields. Can I specify different fields as sorting keys without changing my class?

Technique

To sort a data container, you have to define a few parameters: the container itself, the subset of the container that should be sorted, and the sorting order. To define the sorting order you need to define the greater-than (or less-than) relational operator on the container elements. In other words, you should always be able to say whether an element is greater than another element.

You are going to apply the **sort** algorithm to the class that specifies phone book entries and enables simple manipulations with the class data. To change the sorting keys, the program will change the less-than function from the < operator to another one.

Steps

1. Declaring the data and relational operations

First of all, let's write the phone book class declaration.

```
// PhBook.h - this is a header file with
// declaration of PhBook class

#include <string>
using namespace std;

class PhBook
{
public:
    PhBook();                // default constructor
    PhBook(string InLastName, string InFirstName,
            string City, string AreaCode, string Phone);
    ~PhBook();               // destructor

    //Often used comparison operators
    bool operator==(const PhBook) const;
    bool operator>(const PhBook) const;
    bool operator<(const PhBook) const;

    //Seldom used comparison functions
    bool Equal(const PhBook) const;
    bool GreaterThan(const PhBook) const;
    bool LessThan(const PhBook) const;

    //Display functions
    void DisplayPhone() const;
    void DisplayCity() const;
```

```
private:
    string LastName;
    string FirstName;
    string City;
    string AreaCode;
    string Phone;

};
```

The phone book entry described in the class is not very complex. It consists of last name, first name, city, area code, and phone fields. Real phone books might also have middle names or initials, addresses, phone extensions, fax numbers, sometimes email addresses, and many other fields. The code specified **string** as a data type for all fields. You could use a numeric data type for area codes or phone numbers, but it does not make sense because you are not doing arithmetic operations on them. The **string** data type needs the **string** include file that comes with the Microsoft Visual C++ compiler. Other compilers might use other include files such as **string.h** or **cstring.h**.

Besides two constructors and a destructor, the class declaration specifies overloaded equality and relational operators: ==, <, and >. A complete class declaration needs three more overloaded operators: !=, >=, and <=.

The overloaded operators are used to provide comparison algorithms for the most common operations, such as comparison of last names and first names only. To perform more precise routines, declare three member functions: **Equal**, **GreaterThan**, and **LessThan**. The functions are similar to the equality and relational operators, but they are used to compare all fields in two phone book entries.

Finally, you declared display functions. The first function, **DisplayPhone**, is intended to display the name and the phone number including the area code of phone book entries. The second function, **DisplayCity**, will show the name and the city of the entries.

2. Defining the class member functions

The class definition is located in a separate file, **phbook.cpp**. The constructors simply initialize the private data members, and the destructor is empty.

```
// PhBook.cpp
// PhBook class definition

#include <iostream>
#include <string>
using namespace std;
```

```cpp
#include "phbook.h"

PhBook::PhBook()
{
    LastName= "";
    FirstName= "";
    City= "";
    AreaCode= "";
    Phone= "";

}

PhBook::PhBook(string InLastName, string InFirstName,
            string InCity, string InAreaCode, string InPhone)
{
    LastName= InLastName;
    FirstName= InFirstName;
    City= InCity;
    AreaCode= InAreaCode;
    Phone= InPhone;

}

PhBook::~PhBook()
{
}

bool PhBook::operator==(const PhBook InPhBook) const
{
if (LastName != InPhBook.LastName) return false;
if (FirstName != InPhBook.FirstName) return false;

return true;

}

bool PhBook::operator>(const PhBook InPhBook) const
{
    if (LastName > InPhBook.LastName) return true;
    if (LastName < InPhBook.LastName) return false;
    if (LastName == InPhBook.LastName)
    {
        if (FirstName > InPhBook.FirstName) return true;
        else return false;
    }

return true;
}

bool PhBook::operator<(const PhBook InPhBook) const
{
    if (LastName < InPhBook.LastName) return true;
    if (LastName > InPhBook.LastName) return false;
    if (LastName == InPhBook.LastName)
```

```
        {
            if (FirstName < InPhBook.FirstName) return true;
            else return false;
        }
    return false;
    }

    bool PhBook::Equal(const PhBook InPhBook) const
    {
    if (LastName != InPhBook.LastName) return false;
    if (FirstName != InPhBook.FirstName) return false;
    if (City != InPhBook.City) return false;
    if (AreaCode != InPhBook.AreaCode) return false;
    if (Phone != InPhBook.Phone) return false;

    return true;
    }

    bool PhBook::GreaterThan(const PhBook InPhBook) const
    {
        if (LastName > InPhBook.LastName) return true;
        if (LastName < InPhBook.LastName) return false;
        if (LastName == InPhBook.LastName)
        {
            if (FirstName > InPhBook.FirstName) return true;
            if (FirstName < InPhBook.FirstName) return false;
            if (FirstName == InPhBook.FirstName)
            {
                if (City > InPhBook.City) return true;
                if (City < InPhBook.City) return false;
                if (City == InPhBook.City)
                {
                    if (AreaCode > InPhBook.AreaCode) return true;
                    if (AreaCode < InPhBook.AreaCode) return false;
                    if (AreaCode == InPhBook.AreaCode)
                    {
                        if (Phone > InPhBook.Phone) return true;
                        if (Phone < InPhBook.Phone) return false;
                        if (Phone == InPhBook.Phone) return true;
                        else return false;
                    }
                }

            }
        }
    return false;
    }

    bool PhBook::LessThan(const PhBook InPhBook) const
    {
        if (LastName < InPhBook.LastName) return true;
        if (LastName > InPhBook.LastName) return false;
        if (LastName == InPhBook.LastName)
```

```
    {
        if (FirstName < InPhBook.FirstName) return true;
        if (FirstName > InPhBook.FirstName) return false;
        if (FirstName == InPhBook.FirstName)
        {
            if (City < InPhBook.City) return true;
            if (City > InPhBook.City) return false;
            if (City == InPhBook.City)
            {
                if (AreaCode < InPhBook.AreaCode) return true;
                if (AreaCode > InPhBook.AreaCode) return false;
                if (AreaCode == InPhBook.AreaCode)
                {
                    if (Phone < InPhBook.Phone) return true;
                    if (Phone > InPhBook.Phone) return false;
                    if (Phone == InPhBook.Phone) return true;
                    else return false;
                }
            }
        }
    }
    return false;
}

void PhBook::DisplayPhone() const
{
    string FullName, FullPhone;
    FullName = LastName + ", " + FirstName;
    FullPhone = "(" + AreaCode + ")" + Phone.substr(0,3)
           + "-" + Phone.substr(3,4);
    cout << FullName << ": " << FullPhone << endl;
}

void PhBook::DisplayCity() const
{
    string FullName;
    FullName = LastName + ", " + FirstName;
    cout << FullName << ": " << City << endl;
}
```

This example uses two sets of comparison functions. The first set is presented by overloaded equality and relational operators (==, >, and <). These functions compare the last name and the first name fields in the phone book entries; this set of functions is used most often. The second set is presented by member functions Equal, GreaterThan, and LessThan. The functions compare all fields in the phone book record and are intended to be used rarely. Therefore, less convenient names are designated for these functions.

To initialize the objects of the PhBook class, use the constructor

```
PhBook::PhBook(string InLastName, string InFirstName,
               string InCity, string InAreaCode, string InPhone)
```

To display the objects on the computer screen, use the DisplayPhone and DisplayCity functions.

3. Preparing simple sorting

For sorting, the last and first names of a person are considered as one entity. The phone book is not usually sorted by last names only, and I can barely imagine that somebody wants to sort the phone book by first names. In the first example, you want to sort phone book entries by last name and then by first name. You want to arrange the entries in alphabetical order, and are not interested in the fields other than the name fields.

In other words, it is sufficient to use the overloaded operator < to specify the sorting order. For the objects defined as

```
PhBook A, B;
```

if

```
A < B
```

is true, the A object should be before the B object in the sorted sequence of PhBook objects.

The sort algorithm, which uses the < relational operator (or overloaded < operator) to determine the ordering, has a quite simple syntax:

```
void sort(RandomAccessIterator first,
➥RandomAccessIterator last);
```

The first and the last random access iterators specify the range in the data container that should be sorted. The assumptions that the algorithm makes are

- The container has random access to its elements between the two iterators. It is common to specify the range with the notation [first, last).

- The operator < is defined for the class. The sort algorithm uses this operator to determine the ordering in the container.

For the sort algorithm, you have to include the file algorithm, which works fine with Microsoft Visual C++. Other compilers might need algorithm.h, algo.h, or other header files.

4. Testing the sorting

The following programming code shows how you can apply the simple version of the **sort** algorithm to sort vectors using the overloaded < operator to specify the sorting order.

```cpp
// phbtest.cpp

#include <iostream>
#include <vector>
#include <algorithm>
using namespace std;

#include "phbook.h"

int main()
{

    vector <PhBook> MyPhoneBook;

    // initialize phone book lines
    PhBook PBLine1("Smith", "Robert", "Portland, OR", "503",
                ➡"2027656");
    PhBook PBLine2("Smith", "John", "Seattle, WA", "206",
                ➡"7681290");
    PhBook PBLine3("Barney", "Tom", "Eugene, OR", "541",
                ➡"7682322");
    PhBook PBLine4("Anderson", "Peter", "San Diego, CA", "619",
                ➡"5451551");
    PhBook PBLine5("Smith", "John", "New York, NY", "212",
                ➡ "1234567");

    // set up vector values
    MyPhoneBook.push_back (PBLine1);
    MyPhoneBook.push_back (PBLine2);
    MyPhoneBook.push_back (PBLine3);
    MyPhoneBook.push_back (PBLine4);
    MyPhoneBook.push_back (PBLine5);

    sort(MyPhoneBook.begin(), MyPhoneBook.end());

    // display the vector after sorting
    vector<PhBook>::iterator i;
    for (i = MyPhoneBook.begin(); i != MyPhoneBook.end(); ++i)
        i->DisplayPhone();

    return 0;

}
```

In addition to the **algorithm** header file, you have to include the **vector** header file, which supports vector containers.

The program defines the MyPhoneBook vector and adds five lines to it. The lines are added to the back of the container using **push_back** functions. To specify the sorting range, use **begin** and **end** functions that return iterators setting up all elements of the container for the sorting. The following line applies the **sort** algorithm:

```
sort(MyPhoneBook.begin(), MyPhoneBook.end());
```

The sorted vector is displayed using the **DisplayPhone** member function of the **PhBook** class:

```
vector<PhBook>::iterator i;
for (i = MyPhoneBook.begin(); i != MyPhoneBook.end(); ++i)
    i->DisplayPhone();
```

All elements of the vector are displayed in the natural order. The range is specified with iterators that start from **MyPhoneBook.begin()** and finish with **MyPhoneBook.end()**. The latter iterator points beyond the last element in the container.

The output of the program shows that the algorithm sorted the phone book entries using only the name fields:

```
Anderson, Peter: (619)545-1551
Barney, Tom: (541)768-2322
Smith, John: (206)768-1290
Smith, John: (212)123-4567
Smith, Robert: (503)202-7656
```

The output that was produced on my computer with Microsoft Visual C++ version 5 kept the original order of the equal records

```
Smith, John: (206)768-1290
Smith, John: (212)123-4567
```

However, this behavior is not necessary. To make sure that the relative order of equal elements remains unchanged, use the **stable_sort** algorithm instead of the **sort** algorithm:

```
stable_sort(MyPhoneBook.begin(), MyPhoneBook.end());
```

5. Determine the ordering by other means than the < operator

Very often, you will want to sort the records in your phone book in another order. You might want to sort the records by cities first, and then by names or by area codes. Let's write a program that sorts the phone book according to the **LessThan** function in the **PhBook** class.

The STL requires that the ordering function is defined with a function object—a class that defines the function-call operator (`operator()`).

```
class NameCompare:binary_function <PhBook, PhBook, bool>
{
public:
    bool operator()(const PhBook& a, const PhBook& b) {
        return (a.LessThan(b));
    }
};
```

In order to use `binary_function`, you have to include the `<functional>` header file.

Now you can change the `sort` statement in the `phbtest` program.

```
// phbtest.cpp

#include <iostream>
#include <vector>
#include <algorithm>
#include <functional>
using namespace std;

#include "phbook.h"

class NameCompare:binary_function <PhBook, PhBook, bool>
{
public:
    bool operator()(const PhBook& a, const PhBook& b) {
        return (a.LessThan(b));
    }
};

int main()
{

    vector <PhBook> MyPhoneBook;

    // initialize phone book lines
    PhBook PBLine1("Smith", "Robert", "Portland, OR", "503",
                ➥"2027656");
    PhBook PBLine2("Smith", "John", "Seattle, WA", "206",
                ➥"7681290");
    PhBook PBLine3("Barney", "Tom", "Eugene, OR", "541",
                ➥"7682322");
    PhBook PBLine4("Anderson", "Peter", "San Diego, CA", "619",
                ➥"5451551");
    PhBook PBLine5("Smith", "John", "New York, NY", "212",
                ➥"1234567");
```

```
                    // set up vector values
                    MyPhoneBook.push_back (PBLine1);
                    MyPhoneBook.push_back (PBLine2);
                    MyPhoneBook.push_back (PBLine3);
                    MyPhoneBook.push_back (PBLine4);
                    MyPhoneBook.push_back (PBLine5);

                    // sort the vector
                    sort(MyPhoneBook.begin(), MyPhoneBook.end(), NameCompare());

                // display the vector after sorting
                for (int i = MyPhoneBook.begin(); i != MyPhoneBook.end(); ++i)
                    i->DisplayCity();

                return 0;
        }
```

Comments

In order to implement a sorting order for a class, you have to do just a few steps:

- Create the class that has random access to its elements.

- Define the < operator on the class data. This provides you with the default sorting order for the **sort** algorithm.

If you want to use a sorting order other than specified with the < operator:

- Develop a member function that specifies the sorting order in the class.

- In the module that calls the **sort** algorithm write the code for a function object; that is, a class that defines the function-call operator (operator()).

- Apply the function object to the **sort** function.

Other amendments to the program could be to use other **sort** algorithms that provide stable or partial sorting.

9.8 How do I...
Change the order of the container elements?

Problem

For virtually all large applications with STL containers and even simpler data structures, I want to reorder the sequence of elements. I want to shuffle the data randomly and order the elements according to certain rules. What types of data reordering are implemented in the STL? Which algorithms can I use to reorganize my data?

Technique

STL algorithms that change the data container are called *mutating algorithms*. A few mutating algorithms can reorder container elements. The algorithms change the sequence of elements in a container or another data structure without changing the element values. This How-To discusses the **rotate**, **reverse**, and **random_shuffle** algorithms.

Two more complicated algorithms are the **partition** and the **stable_partition** algorithms. The algorithms apply a predicate to a given sequence. If the predicate returns **true** for an element, the element goes to the beginning of the sequence. If the predicate returns **false**, the element goes to the end of the sequence. In other words, the algorithms reorder the sequence in such a way that the elements that satisfy the predicate precede the elements that don't satisfy the predicate. The **stable_partition** algorithm also keeps the relative order in both parts of the reordered sequence.

Steps

1. Rotating a sequence

To rotate a sequence of elements, let's first create the sequence. This example uses a simple container, a vector of integers. To support the STL container, you have to include the **<vector>** header file. I used the Microsoft Visual C++ 5 compiler; therefore, you should provide the **using namespace std;** directive as well.

```
#include <vector>
using namespace std;
```

The following code defines the `VectExample` vector and fills it in with four elements: 1, 2, 6, 7.

```
// Vector definition
vector <int> VectExample;

    // Filling in the container
    VectExample.push_back (1);
    VectExample.push_back (2);
    VectExample.push_back (6);
    VectExample.push_back (7);
```

To rotate the given sequence on integers, use the **rotate** algorithm. The **rotate** algorithm takes three iterators as arguments. The first argument specifies the beginning of the sequence. The second argument specifies the starting location of the rotating elements, the last argument specifies the end of the sequence. For example, if the algorithm is specified as

```
rotate (First_Iterator, Middle_Iterator, Last_Iterator)
```

the algorithm will move the `*Middle_Iterator` element to the `First_Iterator` position, the `*(Middle_Iterator + 1)` element to the `First_Iterator + 1` position, and so on.

In this example, you want to move the first element to the back of the sequence. To do so, you have to move the second element to the first position, the third element to the second position, and so forth. The following code does just that:

```
// Temporary iterator definition
vector <int>::iterator iTemp;
// Rotate the sequence: move the first element
// to the end
iTemp = VectExample.begin();
iTemp++;
rotate (VectExample.begin(), iTemp, VectExample.end());
```

This code assigned the iterator to the beginning of the vector to the `iTemp` temporary iterator, and then moved the iterator to the second element by executing the `++` operator.

2. Reversing the order of a sequence

The same example will be used to discuss the **reverse** algorithm. This algorithm reverses a range of elements. The algorithm takes two parameters: the iterator that points to the beginning of the range and the iterator that points the end of the range.

In this example, you want to reverse the order of the whole sequence. Therefore, use the `begin()` and the `end()` functions of the vector.

The code looks very simple:

```
// Reverse the order of the elements
reverse (VectExample.begin(), VectExample.end());
```

and it certainly is.

3. Randomly shuffling a sequence

When I read about shuffling the data, the first thing I think about is a gambling application. However, shuffling the data is much more important. It is used in modeling physical processes, in mathematical calculations, and in estimation of missile trajectories, among other things.

The STL uses the `random_shuffle` algorithm to randomly shuffle the data. The algorithm yields uniformly distributed results; that is, the probability of any particular ordering is $1/N!$. The simple version of the algorithm takes two arguments: the iterators that specify the beginning and the end of the range. The more advanced version of the algorithm needs one more argument: the random number generator, a special function object.

This example shows the simple version of the algorithm that uses the internal random number generator:

```
// Randomly shuffle the sequence
random_shuffle (VectExample.begin(), VectExample.end());
```

The example shuffles the data in the entire vector.

4. Testing the `rotate`, `reverse`, and `random_shuffle` algorithms

Now you are ready to write a small program that uses all the algorithms. To display the result of an algorithm, the program will use the following code:

```
for (i= VectExample.begin(); i != VectExample.end(); ++i)
    cout << *i << endl;
```

where `i` is an iterator defined as

```
vector <int>::iterator i;
```

Last but not least, include the **<algorithm>** header file to your program.

```cpp
// order.cpp

#include <iostream>
#include <algorithm>
#include <vector>
using namespace std;

int main()
{
    // Vector and iterators definition
    vector <int> VectExample;
    vector <int>::iterator i;
    vector <int>::iterator iTemp;

    // Creating the container
    VectExample.push_back (1);
    VectExample.push_back (2);
    VectExample.push_back (6);
    VectExample.push_back (7);

    cout << "Original sequence:" << endl;
    for (i= VectExample.begin(); i != VectExample.end(); ++i)
        cout << *i << endl;

    // Rotate the sequence: move the first element
    // to the end
    iTemp = VectExample.begin();
    iTemp++;
    rotate (VectExample.begin(), iTemp, VectExample.end());
    cout << "Rotated sequence:" << endl;
    for (i= VectExample.begin(); i != VectExample.end(); ++i)
        cout << *i << endl;

    // Reverse the order of the elements
    reverse (VectExample.begin(), VectExample.end());
    cout << "Reversed sequence:" << endl;
    for (i= VectExample.begin(); i != VectExample.end(); ++i)
        cout << *i << endl;

    // Randomly shuffle the sequence
    random_shuffle (VectExample.begin(), VectExample.end());
    cout << "Shuffled sequence:" << endl;
    for (i= VectExample.begin(); i != VectExample.end(); ++i)
        cout << *i << endl;

    return 0;
}
```

The `random_shuffle` algorithm can produce different results depending on the internal random number generator. The rest should show the same lines for all compilers. After I compiled the program with the Microsoft Visual C++ 5 compiler and ran the program, my computer showed the following result:

```
Original sequence:
1
2
6
7
Rotated sequence:
2
6
7
1
Reversed sequence:
1
7
6
2
Shuffled sequence:
7
2
1
6
```

5. Reordering a sequence according to a predicate

In this example, let's separate odd numbers from even numbers. To see how to move the odd numbers before the even numbers, examine the following program:

```cpp
// part.cpp

#include <iostream>
#include <algorithm>
#include <vector>
#include <functional>

using namespace std;

int main()
{
    // Vector and iterators definition
    vector <int> VectExample;
        vector <int>::iterator i;

    // Creating the container
    VectExample.push_back (1);
    VectExample.push_back (2);
    VectExample.push_back (6);
    VectExample.push_back (7);
```

```
    cout << "Original sequence:" << endl;
    for (i= VectExample.begin(); i != VectExample.end(); ++i)
        cout << *i << endl;

    partition (VectExample.begin(), VectExample.end(),
                bind2nd(modulus<int>(), 2));
    cout << "Odd numbers first:" << endl;
    for (i= VectExample.begin(); i != VectExample.end(); ++i)
        cout << *i << endl;

    return 0;
}
```

The program creates the same vector as in the previous example. The odd
vector elements are separated from the even elements using the
partition algorithm. The algorithm takes three arguments. The first and
the second arguments specify the sequence range. In this case, you want
to apply the algorithm to the whole vector from **VectExample.begin()** to
VectExample.end(). The third argument specifies the predicate. Apply
the **modulus** operation that returns **0** (**false**) if the element is even and
1 (**true**) if the element is odd.

My compiler produced the following result:

```
Original sequence:
1
2
6
7
Odd numbers first:
1
7
6
2
```

The result might vary for other compilers. However, the important thing
is that the **partition** algorithm does not preserve the relative order of the
even and odd elements. In the original sequence, 2 precedes 6. In the
result sequence, 2 follows 6.

To preserve the order, you can use the **stable_partition** algorithm. If
you change the statement with the **partition** algorithm in the
example to

```
stable_partition (VectExample.begin(), VectExample.end(),
                bind2nd(modulus<int>(), 2));
```

the result will be

```
Original sequence:
1
2
6
7
Odd numbers first:
1
7
2
6
```

Comments

The mutating algorithms include a few reordering algorithms. This How-To discusses their use with the Microsoft Visual C++ 5 compiler. The Borland C++ 5 compiler uses the same syntax of the algorithms and the same filenames for the header files. However, other compilers might use `<algorithm.h>` or `<algo.h>` instead of the `<algorithm>` header file, and `<vector.h>` instead of the `<vector>` file.

PART IV
ERROR HANDLING

C-STYLE ERROR HANDLING

10

C-STYLE ERROR HANDLING

How do I...

10.1 Handle runtime errors in my programs?

10.2 Use the Standard C Library functions `perror` and `strerror` and the predefined C macros to report runtime errors in my programs?

10.3 Use `assert` to catch errors in my code when running in debug mode?

10.4 Use `raise` and `signal` to indicate errors in my programs?

10.5 Use `abort` to terminate my application if a serious error occurs?

10.6 Use `exit` and `atexit` together to perform some action when my program terminates normally?

10.7 Detect errors that occur when reading from or writing to a file using the file functions provided with the Standard C Library?

10.8 Use `setjmp` and `longjmp` to maintain state when handling errors?

10.9 Use a C++ class to handle runtime errors in a more maintainable fashion?

By now, you're an expert C++ programmer. Although this might be true, you have no doubt run into errors in your code. Even the most knowledgeable C++ programmer has to account for situations for which he or she has no control. These errors might be caused by users entering incorrect data or problems with other systems on which your program is dependent. In any case, many problems are bound to arise in the process of executing your program.

That is where error handling comes into play. When designing and coding your application, you must take into account these situations that might arise. When these problems occur, your code has to take care of them. Should it display a message for the user, write a message to a log file, or abort the program completely? The decision of what to do is totally up to you as the designer and developer of the application. Your decision will depend on the specific situation at hand.

Although determining what to do and when to do it are decisions you will have to make on your own, knowing how to do it is the purpose of this chapter. This chapter will discuss ways to handle errors that will work in C and C++ programs and some ways that do not work well in C++ programs. Although this is a C++ book, C-type error-handling techniques are discussed so you will know what you are dealing with if you run into them in older C and C++ programs.

10.1 Handle Runtime Errors in My Programs

This How-To covers the basic method used to handle runtime errors in C programs—returning error codes from functions or methods. This method will be applied to C++ in the sample code fragments that are presented.

10.2 Use the Standard C Library Functions perror and strerror and the Predefined C Macros to Report Runtime Errors in My Programs

The Standard C Library provides many functions to assist you when handling errors from Standard C Library routines you might be using in your C++ programs. This How-To will introduce you to two of these functions: perror and strerror. This How-To also discusses the purpose behind the errno global variable and some predefined macros that can be used when reporting errors.

10.3 Use assert to Catch Errors in My Code When Running in Debug Mode

After developing your application, it is necessary to test it before you release your final product. When testing, you want to be alerted to any crucial errors that have occurred. This How-To will discuss how to use the Standard C debugging utility **assert** to test conditions in your code and raise errors if those conditions are not met.

10.4 Use `raise` and `signal` to Indicate Errors in My Programs

When a serious error occurs, returning an error code from a function might not be the best thing to do. This How-To will talk about how to use the Standard C functions **raise** and **signal** to handle errors in your programs.

10.5 Use `abort` to Terminate My Application If a Serious Error Occurs

In the unfortunate situation in which a serious error occurs and you can't recover from it, it might be necessary to terminate your application. This How-To will discuss how to use the **abort** function to terminate your application. This How-To will also discuss how to perform some action, such as clean up, when your application terminates abnormally.

10.6 Use `exit` and `atexit` Together to Perform Some Action When My Program Terminates Normally

When your application is terminated normally, you might wish to perform some action, such as writing a log to a file. This How-To will talk about how to use **exit** to terminate your application normally and **atexit** to specify a function to be called whenever your application terminates normally.

10.7 Detect Errors That Occur When Reading from or Writing to a File Using the File Functions Provided with the Standard C Library

Errors can occur in the process of reading from or writing to a file when using the file functions included with the Standard C Library. This How-To will show you how to detect whether an error has occurred when reading or writing to a file by using the **ferror** function.

10.8 Use `setjmp` and `longjmp` to Maintain State When Handling Errors

Another way to handle errors in programs is by performing non-local jumps. When doing so, you need to save the state of the stack environment. This How-To will discuss how to perform non-local jumps and save the stack environment using **setjmp** and **longjmp**. The How-To will discuss why it is not safe to use these functions in C++ programs.

10.9 Use a C++ Class to Handle Runtime Errors in a More Maintainable Fashion

Returning error values from functions is a very efficient way to handle errors. However, the meanings of the return values of many different functions can be very difficult to keep track of. They are also very difficult to maintain, especially if you are not the original developer of the code and the comments are nonexistent or poorly written. This How-To will discuss how to create your own C++ class to use when reporting errors from functions or methods.

COMPLEXITY

BEGINNING

10.1 How do I...
Handle runtime errors in my programs?

Problem

I want to be able to handle errors that occur in my programs and either recover from them or report them and exit my program gracefully. How can I do this in C and C++ programs?

Technique

This How-To will discuss the basic method used to handle runtime errors in C programs—returning error codes from functions or methods.

When an error is encountered in a typical function, the best thing to do is to handle the error and proceed. However, this might not be possible. For example, if you allocate some memory using `malloc`, `calloc`, or `new`, and your system is out of memory, you might not be able to continue execution of your program. In some cases, you might be able to free some memory that is not being used and continue.

But what if you are calling a function that runs into an error such as a problem allocating memory or in accessing a database? If that function does not return a code to indicate the success or failure of the function, how will callers of the function be able to determine what action to take?

Worse yet, what if the function allocating the memory or accessing the database just decides to shut down the application if an error occurs? This could be disastrous.

Most applications must be able to recover from errors. Many real-time systems, such as point-of-sale systems in stores, access databases to get up-to-the-minute information, such as product prices or information. Therefore, it is important for functions that make up an application to return values that indicate the success or failure of the function. Using these return codes, callers of this function will have the chance to recover from an error. In a case in which recovery is not possible, at least the caller will be able to write to a log file and shut down the application gracefully.

Steps

1. Analyze each function in your application and determine the set of return codes for each function. For example, in the point-of-sale system, a function that adds records to a database (**addRecord** for example) might return the values listed in Table 10.1.

Table 10.1 Return Values from the addRecord Function

RETURN VALUE	DESCRIPTION
-1	Database could not be opened.
-2	Record could not be added.
0	Record added successfully.
1	Duplicate record added

2. Trap error conditions in your functions. This means it might be necessary to test the return values of other functions your function is calling. For example, in the **addRecord** function, one necessary step that might need to be taken is opening the database. If the database cannot be opened, the caller might wish to attempt this operation again on a backup database. Therefore, the **addRecord** function must tell the caller that an error has occurred. The following is code that would appear in the **addRecord** function. This code tests the opening of a database and returns -1 as indicated in Table 10.1.

```
if (open(databaseName) < 0)
    return -1;
```

3. Maintain return values throughout your function. Your function might perform many actions. Because it's best to return from a function in only one place, return error and success values only at the end of your function. The **addRecord** function will open the database, search for an existing record, and add the record to the database. This application allows duplicate records to be added to the database. However, if a duplicate record is found, **addRecord** tells the caller by returning a success code of 1 as indicated in Table 10.1. The following is the entire code for the **addRecord** function. This function just happens to be a method in the **ProductDatabase** class.

```
int ProductDatabase::addRecord(DatabaseType dbType,
                               const ProductRecord& record)
{
    int retVal = 0;
    bool openedByMe = false;

    // Open the database if it's not already open.
    if (_hDatabase == NULL)
    {
        if (open(_databases[dbType]) < 0)
        {
            retVal = -1;
        }

        openedByMe = true;
    }

    if (retVal == 0 && _hDatabase != NULL)
    {
        if (findProduct(record.prodNumber()) == 0)
            retVal = 1;

        // Attempt to add the record;
        //
        if (fprintf(_hDatabase, "%ld %s\n", record.prodNumber(),
        ➥record.prodName()) == 0)
            retVal = -2;

        // Close the database.
        if (openedByMe)
            close();
    }

    return retVal;
}
```

4. Handle the error returned from the function. The following code calls the **addRecord** function and then tests the return value. It then displays a message to tell the user what happened.

```
void main()
{
    ProductDatabase db("c:\\databases\\primary.db",
                       "c:\\databases\\secondary.db");

    Product product("Joe's Best Detergent");
```

```
        int retVal;
        retVal = db.addRecord(ProductDatabase::Primary, product);

        if (retVal == -1)
        {
           cout << "Error opening Primary database."
                << endl;

           retVal = db.addRecord
        ➥(ProductDatabase::Secondary, product);

           if (retVal == -1)
           {
              cout << "Error opening Secondary database."
                   << endl;
           }
        }

        if (retVal != -1)
        {
           if (retVal == -2)
           {
              cout << "Error adding record number "
                   << product.prodNumber() << endl;
           }
           else if (retVal == 1)
           {
              cout << "Added duplicate record number "
                   << product.prodNumber() << endl;
           }
           else
           {
              cout << "Added record number "
                   << product.prodNumber() << endl;
           }
        }
    }
```

How It Works

The `addRecord` method belongs to the `ProductDatabase` class, which is a class that contains functions to open and close a database as well as add, retrieve, and delete records. This class maintains two databases. If the first database fails, the second one will be used. In this simple example, the databases are just flat files.

To create an instance of the class, the code must pass the names of the databases to be used for the primary and secondary databases. The constructor for the `ProductDatabase` class does not open the databases; it just stores the names in an array. This is a real-time system, so the databases should not be open longer than they have to be.

Next, the code creates an instance of the **Product** class. This is a very simple class that represents a product to be added to the database.

Then call the **addRecord** method passing the enumerated value **Primary** and the product that was just created. The **Primary** enumerated type tells **addRecord** which database to use when adding the record.

The **addRecord** method first checks to see whether the database is already open by checking to see whether the database handle member variable, **_hDatabase**, is **null**. The **addRecord** method can be called from a method that already has the database open. For this reason, you don't need to open it if it is already open.

Next, **addRecord** attempts to open the database indicated by the enumerated type that was passed to this function. As mentioned previously, the database names are kept in an array. The enumerated type indicates the position in the array of the database to open. If the **open** operation fails, **-1** is stored in the local integer, **retVal**, which will be returned to the caller.

If the database was opened, **addRecord** tries to find a duplicate record in the database. Because this system allows duplicate records to be added to the database, this operation is just for reporting purposes. In systems that do not allow duplicate records, this would be an error condition. If a duplicate record is found, **retVal** is set to a value of **1**. This is a warning code that tells the caller that a duplicate record was added to the database.

Then, an attempt is made to add the record to the database by calling a database-specific function to add the record. In this sample code, the database is a flat file, so simply call **fprintf** to write the database record to the file. If this function fails, **retVal** is set to **-2**. You might wish to set **retVal** to the return value of the database-specific function you decide to use.

If the database was opened in the **addRecord** method and not by the caller, the database is closed.

Finally, **retVal** is returned to the caller to indicate the success or failure of the **add** operation.

Going back to the calling function, **main**, you'll see that the code tests the value returned from the call to **addRecord** and displays a message indicating the success or failure of the operation. If the return value indicates that the Primary database could not be opened (**-1**), the program attempts the operation again on the Secondary database.

The preceding code demonstrates how to handle errors in your programs. To see this code in action, compile and run the sample code for this chapter that is included on the CD that comes with this book.

Comments

One thing to note about returning error codes from functions is that these return values are the decision of the developer of that particular function. This means return values from a function developed by one person might be totally different values than a function developed by another person. As you can see, the situation can become very confusing very fast.

For that reason, it is a good idea to develop a set of standards for return values that all developers on a project can follow. One possibility is to use negative return values to indicate an error condition, **0** to indicate success, and positive values to indicate success with warnings.

But this still doesn't fix the problem completely. A return value of -1 from one method might mean something different than a return value of -1 from another method. Therefore, it is good practice to create your error codes as #defines or constants and group them all in a single header file that is used in every file in your application. That way, return values mean the same thing no matter which method or function they come from.

As an alternative, you might wish to store your error and success codes along with their descriptions in a database that can be accessed by reporting programs. You can then generate meaningful reports from log files that contain only numeric codes.

Another standard that can be employed is using an error class for the return value of a function or method. This error class can take care of maintaining return values and providing methods that create human-readable versions of these values. An example of such a class will be discussed later in this chapter.

COMPLEXITY
BEGINNING

10.2 How do I...
Use the standard C library functions perror and strerror and the predefined C macros to report runtime errors in my programs?

Problem

I want to be able to handle errors that occur in the Standard C Library functions I am calling in my program. Is there anything provided by the Standard C Library that will help me do this?

Technique

In order to handle errors that are returned from functions, you have to know what those error values mean. This is easy if the return values are coming from functions you have created. But what if you are using the Standard C Library and wish to report errors returned from functions in this library in a manner that is understandable to everyone?

You could look up the error code for each function you are calling and insert `if` statements in your code to test for each error. Then, you could write a descriptive message to the standard output or a log file based on the error code.

As you might imagine, this is quite cumbersome. You'll need one `if` statement for each error code. To make things easier, you could just write the error code to your log file or to the screen and then look up the error manually.

Again, this still requires a lot of work. Isn't there a better way? Fortunately, there is. The Standard C Library maintains a global variable called **errno** to report error codes. Also, it provides a function to print a descriptive error to the screen—**perror**. The Standard C Library also provides the **strerror** function to enable you to create human-readable error messages. Finally, a number of macros are provided to help make error messages from Standard C Library functions more readable. The following sections will show you how to use each of these facilities and how they work.

Steps

1. Clear the global **errno** variable by setting it to **0**.

2. Call a Standard C Library function that might generate an error.

3. Test the return value of the function you called to see if it was successful or failed.

4. Call `perror` if the Standard C Library function failed.

5. Pass a string to `perror` that you want to be displayed along with the description of the return value.

```
perror("Could not open file");
```

6. Call `strerror` to create an error message string that you can print out to the screen or write to a file.

7. Pass the **errno** variable for which you want to create a description to `strerror`.

```
printf("Could not open file: %s\n", strerror(errno));
```

8. Use any of the special built-in macros provided in ANSI C implementations to help you locate the error at runtime. See Table 10.2 for a list of the provided macros and what they mean.

Table 10.2 Built-in ANSI C Macros

MACRO	DESCRIPTION
__DATE__	The date the source file was compiled in the form Mmm dd yyyy. For example, Oct 4 1998.
__FILE__	The name of the current source code file.
__LINE__	Decimal integer representing the current line number in the source file.
__STDC__	This macro can be used to determine whether the compiler is ANSI C compliant.
__TIME__	The time the source file was compiled in the form hh:mm:ss.

9. The following is a sample code snippet that attempts to open a file that does not exist.

```c
#include <stdio.h>
#include <string.h>
#include <errno.h>

void main()
{
   FILE* fptr;

   errno = 0;
   fptr = fopen("NoSuchFile", "r");

   if (fptr == NULL)
   {
      perror("(perror)   - Could not open NoSuchFile");

      printf("\n%s \n\t file:  %s\n\t date:  %s\n\t time:
➥%s\n\t error: %s\n",
            "(strerror) - Could not open NoSuchFile ",
            __FILE__, __DATE__, __TIME__, strerror(errno));
   }
   else
   {
      fclose(fptr);
   }
}
```

10. The following is the output from this sample program:

```
(perror)  - Could not open NoSuchFile: No such file or directory

(strerror) - Could not open NoSuchFile
           file:  printerr.c
           date:  Oct  4 1998
           time:  13:31:24
           error: No such file or directory
```

How It Works

The Standard C Library functions use the global variable `errno` to hold error codes. These error codes are typically defined in the `errno.h` header file. All error codes are positive integers and the Standard C Library routines should not clear the `errno` variable. That is the reason for step 1, the clearing of `errno`.

For efficiency and performance purposes, the values of `errno` are usually stored in an array of string pointers called `sys_errlist`. The maximum number of elements in the `sys_errlist` array is indicated by the value of a global variable named `sys_nerr`. The names of the `sys_errlist` array and `sys_nerr` variable might be slightly different depending on the compiler you are using.

To obtain the description of the error value in `errno`, `perror` and `strerror` retrieve the string at the position in the array indicated by `errno`. They are able to do this because the `sys_errlist` array is indexed by the `errno` variable.

The preceding sample code attempts to open a file that does not exist. If the returned file pointer is `null`, which it should be, the code proceeds to print the error. The error is printed in two different ways. First, `perror` is used to print a short message along with the error. Next, `strerror` along with some of the predefined ANSI C macros are used to print a more descriptive message. The `perror` function prints its description to `stderr`, which is usually defined to be the console window.

Comments

As you can see, the way the Standard C Library handles errors is very efficient and maintainable. Also, it ensures that the error values are consistent across all functions in the library.

You could do something similar in your applications by creating your own version of the `errno.h` file and `sys_errlist` array. The only downside to this approach is that you have to recompile your application every time you add an error code.

An alternative to keeping these error codes in a header file is to keep them in a database. When your application starts, it can load an array with all the error codes and descriptions in the database. Your startup time will be longer, but your execution time will not change. I feel that the advantages of this approach far outweigh the minimal increase in startup time.

COMPLEXITY
BEGINNING

10.3 How do I...
Use assert to catch errors in my code when running in debug mode?

Problem

I want to be able to catch errors in my code before I ship my application. Is anything provided with the Standard C Library that will help me catch errors before my application is released?

Technique

Before releasing your application for general use, it is imperative that it goes through rigorous testing. In order to catch errors when you are testing, it is important that your code tests different conditions and reports anomalies to the tester. Also, if an anomalous condition occurs, you will want to terminate your program so you can investigate why the problem occurred. Executing your application in this context is referred to as running your application in debug mode.

However, when your product is released, you don't want your application to terminate if an anomalous condition occurs. In that situation, your application might be able to write a log message to a file and continue executing.

The Standard C Library provides the **assert** function that can be used to test the validity of an expression. This expression can be anything that can be evaluated to true or false, such as whether a pointer is **null**. If the expression is false, **assert** prints a diagnostic message and aborts the program. You can then use this diagnostic message to investigate the cause of the error condition.

Steps

1. Determine conditions in your code that you want to test, such as a pointer not being null.

2. Include assert.h in your source code file.

```
#include <assert.h>
```

3. Use the assert function to test the condition.

```
FILE* fptr = NULL;

fptr = fopen("NoSuchFile", "r");
assert(fptr != NULL);

fclose(fptr);
```

4. If the condition evaluates to false, assert will print a diagnostic message and abort the program.

```
Assertion failed: fptr != NULL, file assert.c, line 9
```

How It Works

The assert function takes as input an integer variable that evaluates to true (not equal to 0) or false (0). If the value is false, assert prints a diagnostic message and aborts the program by calling the abort function in ANSI C implementations or exit in traditional C implementations. These functions are discussed later in this chapter. The diagnostic message includes the name of the file and the line number at which the error occurred.

When you are ready to release your program for general use, you can turn off assertions by defining the macro NDEBUG either in your code or on the command line when compiling. To include this in your code, just add the following line to an include file that is included in all your source code files.

```
#define #NDEBUG  1
```

Including this macro on the command line when compiling will be different for each compiler. Therefore, check the documentation for your compiler for instructions about how to do this.

Comments

Using assert in your code can greatly aid in documentation for those who are maintaining your program and is also very helpful when debugging. When you have finished testing your program, you can then simply turn off assertions by defining the NDEBUG macro. Assertions in your code have no runtime overhead when they have been disabled by defining the NDEBUG macro.

10.4 How do I...
Use raise and signal to indicate errors in my programs?

Problem

Is there any way to handle runtime errors in my program other than returning error codes from functions?

Technique

In certain situations, returning an error code is just not possible, such as when a user interrupts the program by pressing Ctrl+C. In these situations, an error is triggered or *raised* by the computer's error detection mechanism. This error is raised by the system and often will cause your application to terminate.

When this error occurs, you might wish to try to recover or you might want to perform some clean up and exit gracefully. Fortunately, the Standard C Library provides the **signal** function that can be used to catch the errors raised by the system. When the error is raised, the function you specify in a call to **signal** will be executed.

But what if you want to do something similar to this in your code? Is it possible for you to raise an error in your code? The Standard C Library provides the **raise** function for just this reason.

Using **raise** and **signal** together, you can implement an alternative error handling technique. The sections that follow will show you how to do this and how it works.

Steps

1. Include **stdio.h** for the **printf** function and **stdlib.h** for the **exit** function. (The **exit** function will be discussed later in this chapter.)

```
#include <stdio.h>
#include <stdlib.h>
```

2. Include **signal.h** in your code.

```
#include <signal.h>
```

3. Define the prototype for the previous **SIGINT** signal handler and your new **SIGINT** signal handler. **SIGINT** is raised whenever the user presses Ctrl+C.

```
void (*PrevInterruptHandler)(int);
void InterruptHandler(int);
```

4. If you are going to raise signals yourself, define any additional signal handler functions. This sample will raise the **SIGTERM** signal. Define the previous and new signal handlers for **SIGTERM**.

```
void (*PrevTerminateHandler)(int);
void TerminateHandler(int);
```

5. Inside the **main** function, set the signal handler functions for the **SIGINT** and **SIGTERM** signals.

```
PrevInterruptHandler = signal(SIGINT, &InterruptHandler);
PrevTerminateHandler = signal(SIGTERM, &TerminateHandler);
```

6. Also inside **main**, test the values of **PrevInterruptHandler** and **PrevTerminateHandler**. Print a diagnostic message if either is equal to **SIG_ERR**.

```
if (PrevInterruptHandler == SIG_ERR)
   printf("Could not set SIGINT signal handler\n");

if (PrevTerminateHandler == SIG_ERR)
   printf("Could not set SIGTERM signal handler\n");
```

7. Enter some code in **main** that will prompt the user for input.

```
printf("Enter a string.  Enter Ctrl+C to quit: ");
scanf("%s", str);
```

8. Implement the **InterruptHandler** function. This function will print a diagnostic message when the user presses Ctrl+C. It will then reset the previous interrupt handler and raise the **SIGTERM** signal.

```
void InterruptHandler(int sig)
{
   printf("\n\nHandled SIGINT signal (%d).\n", sig);

   if (signal(SIGINT, PrevInterruptHandler) == SIG_ERR)
      printf("Could not reset previous SIGINT signal handler\n");

   raise(SIGTERM);
}
```

9. Implement the **TerminateHandler** function. This function will print a diagnostic message and exit the program using the **exit** function that is discussed later in this chapter.

```
void TerminateHandler(int sig)
{
   printf("Handled SIGTERM signal (%d). Exiting program.\n", sig);

   if (signal(SIGTERM, PrevTerminateHandler) == SIG_ERR)
      printf("Could not reset previous SIGTERM signal handler\n");

   exit(0);
}
```

10. The following is the output for this sample program:

```
Enter a string.  Enter Ctrl+C to quit:

Handled SIGINT signal.
Handled SIGTERM signal. Exiting program.
```

How It Works

Each implementation of the Standard C Library defines a set of signals in the signal.h header file. The name of each signal begins with the letters SIG. Signals are raised in response to user actions, the computer's error-detection facility, or manually by calling the **raise** function. See Table 10.3 for a list of some standard signals.

Table 10.3 Standard Signals

SIGNAL	DESCRIPTION
SIGABRT	Terminates the program. This signal indicates abnormal program termination as might be caused by a call to abort.
SIGFPE	Floating-point error such as one caused by dividing by zero.
SIGINT	Illegal computer instruction.
SIGEGV	Invalid memory access.
SIGTERM	Termination signal sent to the program from a user or another application.

The sample code in the "Steps" section sets a signal handler function for the SIGINT signal that is raised when the user presses Ctrl+C. Also, the code is going to raise a signal so it has to set the handler function for that signal. The SIGTERM signal will be raised when the handler for SIGINT is called.

The signal handlers that you set must be defined to take an integer input parameter and return **void**. In some implementations, handler functions for floating-point exceptions (SIGFPE) take an optional second parameter that indicates the type of floating-point exception that has occurred.

After setting the handlers for each signal, the code checks the value of the return code for the **signal** function. The **signal** function will return a pointer to the previous handler function that should be reset at some later point in the program. If the value of the previous handler function is SIG_ERR, which is -1 in most implementations, the **signal** function failed to set the new signal handling functions. No signal handling functions have previously been set, so the values returned from **signal** should be **null**.

If you want a specific signal to be ignored, you can pass the special value
`SIG_IGN` to the `signal` function. In addition, if you want a signal to revert back
to its default action, you can pass the special value `SIG_DFL` to the `signal`
function.

When the user presses Ctrl+C, the interrupt signal `SIGINT` is fired by the
system. Because you have set a handler function for this signal, the
`InterruptHandler` function is called when this occurs. This function prints a
diagnostic message and then calls the `raise` function to raise the `SIGTERM`
signal. When this signal is raised, the `TerminateHandler` function is called.
This function prints a diagnostic message and exits the program.

Each of the signal handlers resets the previous signal handler. This might not
always be necessary, especially in this case, because you will be immediately
exiting the program. In fact, the value of the previous signal handlers should be
a `null` pointer because you have not previously set any signal handlers for these
signals. This code is provided to show you how to reset previous signal
handlers if you want to temporarily set a signal handler.

If a handler function returns, execution continues at the point of
interruption. However, if the signal was raised by a call to the `abort` function,
ANSI C–compliant programs are terminated. If the handled signal was `SIGFPE`,
the behavior upon return from the handler is undefined.

If you don't set a handler function for a signal or specify one of the special
values, the signal has a default action. Table 10.4 lists the default action for
each of the standard signals listed in Table 10.3.

Table 10.4 Default Action for the Standard Signals

SIGNAL	ACTION
SIGABRT	Terminates the program.
SIGFPE	Terminates the program.
SIGINT	Terminates the program.
SIGEGV	Terminates the program.
SIGTERM	Ignored.

Comments

By using `raise` and `signal`, you can implement an alternative error handling
technique into your programs. Instead of returning errors from functions, you
can set handler functions that are called when a signal is raised. This also allows
you to perform such actions as freeing memory when your program is
abnormally terminated.

When compiling the preceding sample code, you might experience warnings if you are using a compiler that is not ANSI C–compliant or does not support the latest features of the C++ language.

COMPLEXITY
BEGINNING

10.5 How do I...
Use abort to terminate my application if a serious error occurs?

Problem

I have run into a serious error condition from which I cannot recover in my program. How can I terminate my application? Is there any way to execute a body of code when my program is terminated?

Technique

In the unfortunate situation in which a serious error occurs and you can't recover from it, it might be necessary to terminate your application.

The Standard C Library provides the **abort** function that enables you to terminate your application abnormally.

When this abnormal termination occurs, you might wish to perform some action, such as freeing memory. Using the **signal** function described earlier, you can specify a function that is called when the program is abnormally terminated.

The following sections will discuss how to use **abort** to terminate your application and how to use **signal** to execute a function when **abort** is called.

Steps

1. Include stdio.h for the printf function and stdlib.h for abort, free, and malloc.

```
#include <stdio.h>
#include <stdlib.h>
```

2. Include signal.h in your code.

```
#include <signal.h>
```

3. Define the prototype for the previous **SIGABRT** signal handler and your new **SIGABRT** signal handler.

```
void (*PrevAbortHandler)(int);
void AbortHandler(int);
```

4. Define a global variable to hold some memory.

```
char* str;
```

5. Inside the **main** function, enter code to handle the **SIGABRT** signal, allocate some memory, and then call **abort**.

```
void main()
{
    PrevAbortHandler = signal(SIGABRT, &AbortHandler);

    if (PrevAbortHandler == SIG_ERR)
        printf("Could not set SIGABRT signal handler\n");
    else
    {
        str = (char*)malloc(10);
        abort();
    }
}
```

6. Implement the handler function for the **SIGABRT** signal. This function will print a diagnostic message, reset the previous **SIGABRT** handler function, and free the memory that was allocated in **main**.

```
void AbortHandler(int sig)
{
    printf("\nHandled SIGABRT signal (%d). Cleaning
    ➥up allocated memory\n", sig);

    free(str);
}
```

7. The following is the output from this sample program:

```
Handled SIGABRT signal. Cleaning up allocated memory
```

How It Works

When called, **abort** prints the message **abnormal program termination**, and then raises the **SIGABRT** signal. If you have set a signal handler for **SIGABRT**, your handler function will be called.

The code listed in the "Steps" section sets a handler function for the **SIGABRT** signal. Then it allocates some memory and calls **abort**. The handler function, **AbortHandler**, is then called. This function prints a diagnostic message and then frees the memory that was allocated in **main**. When **AbortHandler** returns, the program is terminated.

Comments

Using abort in your programs is an easy way to terminate your application if a condition occurs from which you cannot recover. Setting a handler function for SIGABRT allows you to perform some action when your program is aborted, such as cleaning up previously allocated memory. This means any time your program is aborted, whether or not you are the one calling abort, you can be assured that all allocated resources have been freed.

COMPLEXITY
BEGINNING

10.6 How do I...
Use exit and atexit together to perform some action when my program terminates normally?

Problem

I would like to exit my application and return a code from my application. Also, I would like a function to be executed automatically when my application terminates. How can I do this?

Technique

In order to exit your application, you can use the abort function as mentioned earlier. However, abort is usually used for abnormal program termination.

Therefore, the Standard C Library provides the exit function that can be used to exit your program. This function can also be used to return error or success codes from your application. In addition, the atexit function is provided to enable you to specify a function that will be called any time the exit function is called.

The following sections describe how to use exit and atexit and how they work.

Steps

1. Include stdio.h for the printf function and stdlib.h for atexit and exit.

```
#include <stdio.h>
#include <stdlib.h>
```

2. Define the prototype for a function that will be called when exiting the program normally.

```
void FinalCleanup(void);
```

3. Define a global variable that will be used to hold some memory.

```
char* str;
```

4. Inside `main`, enter code to set the function called when the program exits, allocate some memory, and call `exit`.

```
void main()
{
    int retVal = atexit(FinalCleanup);

    if (retVal != 0)
        printf("Could not set exit function\n");
    else
    {
        str = (char*)malloc(10);
        exit(1);
    }
}
```

5. Implement the `FinalCleanup` function. This function will print a diagnostic message and free the memory previously allocated in `main`.

```
void FinalCleanup(void)
{
    printf("\nCleaning up allocated memory.\n");

    free(str);
}
```

6. The following is the output for this sample program:

```
Cleaning up allocated memory.
```

How It Works

The `exit` function causes the program to be terminated normally. Unlike `abort`, `exit` does not print a diagnostic message. You can return an exit status code to the operating system or the caller of your program by specifying that exit status when you call the `exit` function.

You can register a function that will be called when `exit` is called or `main` returns by using the `atexit` function. The function you register with `atexit` must take no input parameters and return `void`. Anytime the program exits normally, your registered function will be called. You can register multiple functions with `atexit` and you can register the same function more than once. If you have called `atexit` multiple times, the registered functions are called in reverse order of their registration. In other words, the functions are executed in last-in first-out (LIFO) order.

The `exit` function will perform clean up before exiting. On ANSI C–compliant compiler implementations, all functions registered with `atexit` are called in reverse order of their registration. Then, all output streams are flushed and all open streams are closed. Next, files that were previously created using the `tmpfile` Standard C Library routine are removed. Finally, control is returned to the operating system or caller of this program with the return value specified in the call to `exit`.

The sample code listed in the "Steps" section registers the `FinalCleanup` function with `atexit`. When the program exits normally, `FinalCleanup` is called. It then prints a diagnostic message and frees memory that was previously allocated in `main`.

Comments

Using the `exit` function, you can return status or error codes to the operating system or to other programs. Using the `atexit` function, you can be sure all resources are freed when exiting your program normally. As you can see, if you use the techniques presented in this How-To and How-To 10.5 together, you can almost always be sure resources are freed whether your program exits normally or abnormally.

COMPLEXITY
INTERMEDIATE

10.7 How do I...

Detect errors that occur when reading from or writing to a file using the file functions provided with the Standard C Library?

Problem

When working with files, is there any way to detect errors that occur when reading from or writing to a file?

Technique

The functions for dealing with a file provided by the Standard C Library typically deal with the file as a stream. The `ferror` function can be used to test the stream for a read or write error.

The following section discusses how to test a file stream for a read or write error and how it works.

Steps

1. Include `stdio.h` for standard I/O operations and `errno.h` in order to have access to the `errno` variable.

```
#include <stdio.h>
#include <errno.h>
```

2. The code in the remaining steps should be placed in `main`.

3. Declare variables to hold the file pointer of an open file, the data read from a file stream, the number of bytes read, and an err value that will be returned from `ferror`.

```
FILE *fptr;
char  buf[81];
int   errVal;
```

4. Clear the `errno` variable and open a file for write-only access.

```
errno = 0;
fptr = fopen("NewFile", "w");
```

5. If the open failed, print an error message. Otherwise, attempt to read from the file that is open for write-only access. Test for an error condition using `ferror` and print a message if the read operation failed. Finally, clear the error condition and close the file.

```
if (fptr == NULL)
     perror("Could not open NewFile");
else
{
   errno = 0;
 fread(buf, sizeof(char), sizeof(buf), fptr);

   errVal = ferror(fptr);
   if (errVal)
   {
      printf("Error %d reading stream\n", errVal);
      clearerr(fptr);
   }

   fclose(fptr);
}
```

6. The following is the output for this sample program:

```
Error 32 reading stream
```

How It Works

The `ferror` function tests for an error condition that might have occurred when reading from or writing to a stream. It will return the error status to the caller. If the error status is not equal to **0**, an error has occurred. The `ferror` function will continue to return errors unless the `clearerr` function is called. Closing the stream with `fclose` will also clear the error condition.

The sample code in the "Steps" section opens a file for write-only access and attempts to read from it. This will cause an error to occur. The `ferror` function is called to test for an error. A diagnostic message is printed if there is an error. Next, `clearerr` is called to clear the error condition.

Comments

The `ferror` function is very useful when testing the status of a read or write operation to a file stream. However, if you are going to make repeated calls to `ferror`, remember to call `clearerr` each time.

COMPLEXITY

INTERMEDIATE

10.8   How do I...
Use `setjmp` and `longjmp` to maintain state when handling errors?

Problem

Is there another way to handle errors in my code instead of returning error values from functions or using `raise` and `signal`?

Technique

Another way to handle error conditions in your code is to perform what are known as non-local jumps. This means if an error occurs in a function, you can jump to a particular line of code. Typically, that line of code is just prior to where the function was originally called.

Using the `setjmp` and `longjmp` functions provided with the Standard C Library, you can perform non-local jumps to handle error conditions and still maintain the state of the caller's stack environment. This means when control is set back to the calling function, its local variables still have the same values.

This How-To will discuss how to use `setjmp` and `longjmp` together to perform error handling. This How-To will also discuss how they work and why it is not safe to use these functions in C++ programs.

Steps

1. Include `stdio.h` for standard I/O operations.

```
#include <stdio.h>
```

2. Include `setjmp.h` for the `setjmp` and `longjmp` functions and the `jmp_buf` typedef.

```
#include <setjmp.h>
```

3. Define the prototype for a function that you will call from `main`.

```
void DoSomeWork(void);
```

4. Define a global jump buffer environment variable using the `jmp_buf` typedef.

```
jmp_buf Env;
```

5. Inside `main`, call `setjmp` to record the stack environment. Then call the function defined in step 3.

```
void main()
{
    int retVal = setjmp(Env);

    if (retVal != 0)
        printf("Call to setjmp returned: %d\n", retVal);
    else
        DoSomeWork();
}
```

6. Implement the `DoSomeWork` function. This function attempts to open a file that does not exist. If the open fails, it calls `longjmp` to cause the program to return from the call to `setjmp` again.

```
void DoSomeWork(void)
{
    FILE* fptr = fopen("NoSuchFile", "r");
```

```
    if (fptr == NULL)
    {
       printf("Calling longjmp\n");
       longjmp(Env, -1);
    }
}
```

How It Works

The setjmp function records the current state of the stack environment. The jmp_buf typedef is an implementation-defined array. After recording the current stack environment, setjmp returns 0.

A call to longjmp will restore the stack environment that was saved when setjmp was called. When calling longjmp, you specify the variable used to save the stack environment and a return code. Calling longjmp causes the program to return from setjmp, again returning the return code that was given to longjmp as the second parameter. When setjmp returns, all variables, except register variables, that are accessible by the function calling setjmp have the same values they had when the longjmp function was called.

The sample code in the preceding "Steps" section first calls setjmp to save the current state. The return value from this first call to setjmp is 0, so you call the DoSomeWork function. This function attempts to open a file that does not exist. If the open fails, DoSomeWork calls longjmp and passes to it the stack environment previously saved and a return code of -1. This causes setjmp to be returned from again. This time the return value from setjmp is -1. Therefore, the program exits.

Comments

Using setjmp and longjmp, you can implement another form of error handling in your programs. However, you should not use setjmp and longjmp in C++ programs. These functions do not support the semantics of C++ objects. That means destructors for objects will not be called when longjmp is called. In C++ programs, you should use the C++ exception-handling constructs that are talked about in Chapter 11, "Exception Handling in C++."

10.9 How do I...
Use a C++ class to handle runtime errors in a more maintainable fashion?

Problem

I understand the importance of error handling in my programs. I also understand how to return values from functions. Is there a better way to keep track of error information in my programs?

Technique

Returning error values from functions is a very efficient way to handle errors. However, the meanings of the return values of many different functions can be very difficult to keep track of. They are also very difficult to maintain, especially if you are not the original developer of the code and the comments are poorly written or nonexistent.

This section provides a sample class called **ErrorClass** that can be used as the return value for a function. This class takes care of maintaining error codes and provides human-readable descriptions. You can then modify this class to suit your own needs.

Steps

This section discusses how to use this sample class in your programs. The actual class itself will be discussed in the "How It Works" section.

1. Create a file that contains descriptions of all the errors you will encounter in your program. Here is an example of an error file called **errors.txt**.

```
Error opening file
Error reading file
Floating-point exception
Unable to open database
Database query failed
Drive is full
Web page not found
```

2. Create a header file that contains macros for your error codes. Here is an example of a header file that holds all the error codes for a program. You should name this file **errors.h**.

```
#define OPNERR       0  // Error opening file
#define READERR      1  // Error reading file
#define FPERR        2  // Floating-point exception
#define DBOPNERR     3  // Unable to open database
#define DBQERR       4  // Database query failed
#define DRVFULLERR   5  // Drive is full
```

3. Create a global instance of the **ErrorClass** class.

```
ErrorClass ec;
```

4. When your program starts, load the description of your errors from an error file. If loading the errors fails, you might want to exit the program.

```
if (ec.loadErrors(ERROR_FILE) == false)
{
   cout << "Error loading error file" << endl;
   exit(-1);
}
```

5. When an errors in a function, set the current error code.

```
ec.currentError(OPNERR);
```

6. You can provide a human-readable description of the error by calling one of the two overloaded **description** functions. The first one provides a description of the current error state. The second one provides a description of the specified error code. You can pass one of these functions to **printf** or **cout** to display descriptive error information.

```
cout << "Error in function: " << ec.description() << endl;
```

7. If you are passing the error object around in your program, you can check the current error state by using the **isError** function.

```
if (ec.isError())
   cout << "Error in function: " << ec.description() << endl;
```

How It Works

The **ErrorClass** class maintains an array of error descriptions that are read from an error file. These error messages are sequential starting at 0 and going as high as 100 for this small example. The class definition of the **ErrorClass** class is provided in Listing 10.1 and the implementation file (**.cpp**) is given in Listing 10.2. This sample code is also provided on the CD that comes with this book. The important methods of this class will be discussed in turn.

Listing 10.1 ErrorClass Class Definition File

```
//
// ErrorClass.h - definition of ErrorClass class
//

#include <iostream.h>

#define ERRDESC_SIZE  81
#define MAX_ERRNUM    100

class ErrorClass
{
public:
   ErrorClass();
   virtual ~ErrorClass();

   // Utility methods
   const char* description() const;
   const char* description(int errorNumber) const;

   void currentError(int errorNumber);
   int  currentError(void) const;

   bool isError() const;
   bool loadErrors(const char* errorFile);

protected:
   int  _currentError;
   bool _openError;
   char _errors[MAX_ERRNUM][ERRDESC_SIZE];
};
```

Listing 10.2 ErrorClass Class Implementation

```
//
// ErrorClass.cpp - implementation of ErrorClass class
//

#include <stdio.h>
#include <stdlib.h>
#include <string.h>
#include "ErrorClass.h"

ErrorClass::ErrorClass()
   : _currentError(-1),
     _openError(false)
{
}

ErrorClass::~ErrorClass()
{
}

const char* ErrorClass::description() const
{
```

```
      return description(_currentError);
   }

   const char* ErrorClass::description(int errorNumber) const
   {
      if (_openError)
         return "Error loading errors list";

      if (_errors[0][0] == '\0' ¦¦ errorNumber >= MAX_ERRNUM)
         return "";

      return _errors[errorNumber];
   }

   void ErrorClass::currentError(int errorNumber)
   {
      _currentError = errorNumber;
   }

   int ErrorClass::currentError() const
   {
      return _currentError;
   }

   bool ErrorClass::isError() const
   {
      if (_openError)
         return true;

      return (_currentError >= 0);
   }

   bool ErrorClass::loadErrors(const char* errorFile)
   {
      FILE* fptr = fopen(errorFile, "r");

      if (fptr == NULL)
      {
         _openError = true;
         return false;
      }
      else
      {
         _openError = false;

         for (int j = 0; !feof(fptr); j++)
         {
            char buf[ERRDESC_SIZE];

            // Read the error descriptions from the
            // error file.  The error descriptions must
            // be in sequential order.
            //
            if (fgets(buf, ERRDESC_SIZE, fptr) != NULL)
               strcpy(_errors[j], buf);
         }
```

continued on next page

continued from previous page

```
        fclose(fptr);
    }

    return true;
}
```

The first important method of this class you will use after constructing an **ErrorClass** object is the **loadErrors** method. This method first opens the specified error file. Then it reads each line of the file and populates the **_errors** array. The **_errors** data member is just an array that can hold up to 100 strings. You might want to implement **_errors** another way, such as an STL map class that maps error codes to their descriptions. Also, you might want to store your error codes and descriptions in a database.

After the errors are loaded into the array, you can set the current error state by using the overloaded **currentError** method that takes an integer as its input parameter. You can retrieve the current error state at a later time by calling the other **currentError** method.

You can check to see whether an error has occurred at any time by calling the **isError** method. This method returns true if there was an error opening the error file, as represented by the **_openError** data member, or if the **_currentError** data member is greater than or equal to **0**. It will return false otherwise.

Next, to obtain a human-readable description of an error, you can use the two overloaded **description** methods. The one that takes no input parameters simply passes the **_currentError** data member to the **description** method that takes an integer parameter. This **description** method returns the string that is stored in the **_errors** array at the position indicated by the error number.

Listing 10.3 lists the driver program that is included to demonstrate how to use the **ErrorClass** class.

Listing 10.3 Driver Program for the ErrorClass Class

```
//
// driver.cpp - Driver for ErrorClass class.
//

#include <iostream.h>
#include <stdlib.h>
#include "ErrorClass.h"
#include "errors.h"

#define ERROR_FILE    "errors.txt"

const ErrorClass& DoSomething();

// Global error object
ErrorClass ec;
```

```
void main()
{
   if (ec.loadErrors(ERROR_FILE) == false)
   {
      cout << "Error loading error file" << endl;
      exit(-1);
   }

   ErrorClass ec = DoSomething();

   if (ec.isError())
      cout << "Error in DoSomething: " << ec.description() << endl;
}

const ErrorClass& DoSomething()
{
   ec.currentError(OPNERR);
   return ec;
}
```

In order to use **ErrorClass**, a little preparation has to be done. First, you must create a file that contains all the error descriptions in sequential order. Next, you might want to create a header file that contains macros for each of these errors. This will make your code easier to read and maintain.

Next, you have to construct an **ErrorClass** object. This object can be global to your program or local to a function that is setting an error.

Then you must load the error descriptions from the error file by calling the **loadError** method. If the errors are loaded successfully, you can then set the current error using the **currentError** method and obtain the description of the error using the **description** method.

The driver code in Listing 10.3 calls a function to perform some action. This function sets the current error to **OPNERR** and returns a reference to the global **ErrorClass** object. If you create an **ErrorClass** object locally in a function, you must pass a copy of the object back to the caller. If you pass back a reference to the local object, your program will crash when the caller tries to use it. This is because the local object was destroyed when control was returned to the caller (that is, when it went out of scope).

Comments

Using a class such as **ErrorClass** gives you an easy way to provide descriptive information about errors that occur in your program. You can print these descriptions to the standard output or to a log file for later research. I encourage you to change this class to fit the needs of your program.

CHAPTER 11
EXCEPTION HANDLING IN C++

11

EXCEPTION HANDLING IN C++

How do I...

11.1 Utilize the exception handling mechanism to process potential error conditions?

11.2 Use the various catch constructs such as multiple catch clauses, catch ordering, and the rethrowing of exceptions?

11.3 Implement and use an exception class?

11.4 Specify exceptions that a function will throw?

11.5 Handle exceptions that are not caught or not expected?

How-To 1.7 demonstrated the use of the exception handling mechanism offered by the C++ Standard. That How-To is a basic introduction into the use of exception handling. This chapter will explore the world of exception handling in more detail.

The exception handling mechanism furnished by the Standard provides a common and standard interface for handling program anomalies. Without exception handling, error handling is performed using return values from functions and global status variables. Every developer has her own style of handling errors, leading to inconsistency among applications and library packages. In this chapter, you will see various ways to apply the exception handling mechanisms.

One word of caution about this chapter: If you are using a compiler that does not support exception handling, the examples will not compile and execute as expected. If you have been putting off upgrading your compiler, now is the time to do it.

11.1 Utilize the Exception Handling Mechanism to Process Potential Error Conditions

Error handling is an important feature for the success of an application. Invalid input, access to hardware that is not available, and other program anomalies must be tested for and handled gracefully. This How-To gives a review of the C++ exception handling mechanism. The exception handling mechanism provided by the C++ Standard is a standardized process for handling exceptions at runtime.

11.2 Use the Various catch Constructs Such As Multiple catch Clauses, catch Ordering, and the Rethrowing of Exceptions

The C++ exception handling mechanism is a very robust and standardized way to handle program anomalies. Multiple catch clauses provide a means to handle more than one exception type thrown from a try block. The ordering and rethrowing of catch clauses can be important. In this How-To, you will see how to set up multiple handlers and how to rethrow exceptions.

11.3 Implement and Use an Exception Class

The throwing of exception types can include native types such as int and char* and user-defined types. User-defined exception types provide a more robust mechanism for the capturing and reporting of exceptions. In this How-To, you will see how to declare, define, throw, and catch exception class objects.

11.4 Specify Exceptions That a Function Will Throw

Exception handling is an important feature of the C++ language. The exception handling mechanism provides a robust method for handling errors at runtime. Yet, for the developer, knowing all the exceptions a function will throw can sometimes be guesswork. Exception specifications provide a mechanism to reveal the exceptions a function will or will not throw.

11.5 Handle Exceptions That Are Not Caught or Not Expected

Although the exception handling mechanism is very robust and allows you to handle exceptions of any type, the unexpected exception is indeed difficult to handle. In this How-To, you will see how to incorporate code to manage unexpected exceptions.

COMPLEXITY

BEGINNING

11.1 How do I...
Utilize the exception handling mechanism to process potential error conditions?

Problem

I need to incorporate exception handling into my programs. I have read that the C++ language Standard provides a standard facility to handle exceptional conditions at runtime. How can I get a good overview of exception handling in C++?

Technique

This How-To begins by providing a straightforward example that demonstrates various uses of the exception handling mechanism. This How-To will only scratch the surface of exception handling; the How-Tos that follow will address specific issues and advanced features of the C++ exception handling mechanism.

Steps

1. Create a new directory named **EXCEPTH** under your base source directory and make **EXCEPTH** the current directory.

2. Start up your source code editor and type in the following source code, exactly as shown.

```
// filename: excepth.cpp - program to demonstrate
// basic exception handling in C++
#include <iostream>
using namespace std ;
```

```cpp
const int DB_OK = 0 ;
const int DB_NOT_INIT = -1 ;
const int DB_ACCESS_ERROR = -2 ;

int dbInit( ) ;
int dbOpen( const char *fname ) ;
int dbGetData( int field, char *data ) ;
int dbClose( int handle ) ;

void dbInitEH( ) ;
int  dbOpenEH( const char *fname ) ;
void dbGetDataEH( int field, char *data ) ;
void dbCloseEH( int handle ) ;

int main( )
{
    // manipulating a database,
    // traditional error handling.
    if( dbInit( ) == DB_OK )
    {
        int theHandle = dbOpen( "test.dat" ) ;

        if( theHandle > 0 )
        {
            char data[ 30 ] ;

            if( dbGetData( 1, data ) == DB_OK )
                cout << "Data is: " << data << endl ;
            else
                cout << "Error getting data" << endl ;

            if( dbClose( theHandle ) != DB_OK )
                cout << "Error closing dB" << endl ;
        }
        else
            cout << "Error opening DB" << endl ;
    }
    else
        cout << "Error initializing DB" << endl ;

    // manipulating a database,
    // the exception handling way
    try {
        char data[ 30 ] = "" ;

        dbInitEH( ) ;
        int theHandle = dbOpenEH( "test.dat" ) ;

        dbGetDataEH( 1, data ) ;
        cout << "Data is: " << data << endl ;
        dbCloseEH( theHandle ) ;
    }
    catch( int v ) {
        cout << "Error with DB: " << v << endl ;
    }
```

```
        return( 0 ) ;
    }

int dbInit( )
{
    return( DB_OK ) ;
}

int dbOpen( const char *fname )
{
    return( 2 ) ;
}

int dbGetData( int field, char *data )
{
    int i = 0 ;
    for( ; i < 10; i++ )
        data[ i ] = i + 48 ;
    data[ i ] = 0x00 ;

    return( DB_OK ) ;
}

int dbClose( int handle )
{
    return( DB_OK ) ;
}

void dbInitEH( )
{
}

int dbOpenEH( const char *fname )
{
    return( 2 ) ;
}

void dbGetDataEH( int field, char *data )
{
    int ret = DB_ACCESS_ERROR ;

    throw( ret ) ;
}

void dbCloseEH( int handle )
{
}
```

3. Save the file, naming it **EXCEPTH.CPP**. Then exit the editor and return to the command line.

4. At the command line, type the command required to compile and link the program. For example, if you are using Microsoft Visual C++, you type **cl first.cpp**. If you are using DJGPP, type **gcc excepth.cpp**. The compiler and linker will run and (if you typed all source text correctly) return to the command line without any error messages.

5. At the command prompt, run the final executable (called **excepth**). If you are on a UNIX system and you do not see a file named **excepth**, look for a file named **a.out**; if you find this filename, execute it. You should see the following output on your screen:

```
Data is: 0123456789
Error with DB: -2
```

The next section, "How It Works," will discuss how this program operates.

How It Works

After the two source comment lines, you see the include directive for **iostream**. On the next line is the **using** directive, effectively making all names visible in namespace **std** into the current scope.

The next three lines of code declare and define three constant values.

```
const int DB_OK = 0 ;
const int DB_NOT_INIT = -1 ;
const int DB_ACCESS_ERROR = -2 ;
```

These values are used as status codes for the "dummy" database functions. These values are representative of some well-known Indexed Sequential Access Methods (ISAM) C libraries. Not that the values themselves match the libraries' codes, but rather the logic of using negative integer values to represent error codes.

The next four lines

```
int dbInit( ) ;
int dbOpen( const char *fname ) ;
int dbGetData( int field, char *data ) ;
int dbClose( int handle ) ;
```

are function declarations representing traditional C-style ISAM functions. This program does not actually access any data files, but simulates the logic of doing so. The functions are described in more detail later in this section.

The next four source lines

```
void dbInitEH( ) ;
int  dbOpenEH( const char *fname ) ;
void dbGetDataEH( int field, char *data ) ;
void dbCloseEH( int handle ) ;
```

declare four functions oriented around exception handling. The function names match the previous function names with the string **EH** appended to the names.

The EH designates that these functions utilize exception handling. Also, notice that all but one of these functions return **void**, whereas the previous four functions return an **int**.

Now, let's take a step back and examine the following section of code. Notice all the **if-else** statements; this code is almost hard to follow. You really have to pay attention to what is happening here.

```
if( dbInit( ) == DB_OK )
{
    int theHandle = dbOpen( "test.dat" ) ;

    if( theHandle > DB_OK )
    {
        char data[ 30 ] ;

        if( dbGetData( 1, data ) == DB_OK )
            cout << "Data is: " << data << endl ;
        else
            cout << "Error getting data" << endl ;

        if( dbClose( theHandle ) != DB_OK )
            cout << "Error closing DB" << endl ;
    }
    else
        cout << "Error opening DB" << endl ;
}
else
    cout << "Error initializing DB" << endl ;
```

The first line in this section of code calls the **dbInit()** function to initialize the database. The return value from that function specifies whether the initialization is successful. Otherwise, the associated **else** reports an error.

The next line declares an integer to hold the handle associated with the file to be opened. Notice that the **dbOpen()** function returns a non-zero, positive value to indicate success. The logic of this function call and the logic of the previous one are not consistent with each other.

The **if** statement that follows checks that the return from **dbOpen()** is greater than zero; otherwise, the associated **else** displays an error message.

The first line in this **if** block declares an array of **char** named **data**. This variable is used by the function call within the **if** statement that follows:

```
if( dbGetData( 1, data ) == DB_OK )
```

This example prints out the value of the variable as a result of the function call. A real database application might perform some operations on the data, expanding the **if** code block. Notice that the associated **else** displays an error to the user if the function call is unsuccessful.

The next **if** block makes a function call to close the data file. If the close is unsuccessful, an error message is displayed to the user.

Take one more look at the previous block of code. All it does is simply initialize, open, retrieve from, and close a data file. A lot of "extra" code is lying around taking up space, wouldn't you say? Notice that the code always has to take one route if the function call is successful and another route if the function call fails for any reason. This tends to clutter the source code with a never-ending string of **if-else** statements. Another option is to use a global status variable, but this does not cut down on the **if-else** dilemma. As a matter of fact, this method tends to make the code look worse because you have to make the function call and then check the status variable.

Okay, let's move on to the next section of code:

```
try {
    char data[ 30 ] = "" ;

    dbInitEH( ) ;
    int theHandle = dbOpenEH( "test.dat" ) ;

    dbGetDataEH( 1, data ) ;
    cout << "Data is: " << data << endl ;
    dbCloseEH( theHandle ) ;
}
catch( int v ) {
    cout << "Error with DB: " << v << endl ;
}
```

Now there's a clean-looking block of code. Notice that the **dbInitEH()**, **dbOpenEH()**, **dbGetDataEH()**, and **dbCloseEH()** function calls are encased within a **try** block. No checks are made for success or failure for each function call—no need to clutter the code with **if-else** blocks. The previous block of code constitutes 14 lines of code; this section of code occupies 9 lines of code. Any errors caught in any of the function calls are caught by the associated **catch** clause.

This is the real intent of exception handling: to separate the recognition and handling of a program anomaly. Let's take a second look at the previous section of code and discuss the **try** block and **catch** clause.

A **try** block is introduced with the **try** keyword followed by the block of code to be executed. The **try** block can be a single statement or a series of statements encased within a left and right brace. It is recommended that you always use the left and right brace as a visual aid and for future maintenance efforts.

All statements within a **try** block are executed unless one of the statements throws an exception. If any exception is thrown, control is transferred to the **catch** clause. If a **catch** clause cannot be found to handle the exception within the current scope, the exception handling mechanism searches up the call chain, attempting to locate a **catch** clause that can handle the exception. If control must leave the current scope, say to a function block, the stack is unwound and any objects created are properly destroyed. Control is then returned to the calling block so the exception can be handled. Note that any objects created on the free store will not be destroyed.

If no exception handler is found and control has reached the `main` function, the `terminate()` function, found within the standard library, is invoked. The default action of the `terminate()` function is, of course, to terminate the program.

A `try` block is the same as any other C++ block. You can declare variables, call other functions, execute loop statements, and so on and so forth. Remember that any variables declared will not be accessible outside the `try` block. Although not an absolute requirement, you should follow a `try` block with one or more `catch` clauses that can handle any exceptions that might be thrown.

Let's take a closer look at the `catch` clause:

```
catch( int v )
```

A `catch` clause consists of the keyword `catch`, followed by an argument of some type. The previous `catch` clause will handle an exception of type `int` that is thrown within the preceding `try` block. The argument to a `catch` clause can be a native type such as `int` or `char*`, or it can be a user-defined type.

You can specify one or more `catch` clauses following a `try` block. There is a special-case `catch` clause, known as the catch-all clause. It looks like this:

```
catch( ... )
```

The catch-all `catch` clause must be the last `catch` clause among multiple `catch` clauses. This `catch` clause will catch any exception thrown. I have seen application code in which every `try` block is followed by a catch-all catch clause. In my opinion, this style of exception handling should not be implemented. The exceptions to be caught should be explicitly stated. The catch-all `catch` clause should be used only in situations in which you do not specifically know the type of exceptions that might be thrown.

Let's examine the function definitions that follow the `main` function. The majority of these function definitions are rather trivial, so I will move through the descriptions quickly.

The first function, `dbInit()`, pretends to initialize a database and simply returns a success value. Next is the function `dbOpen()` that fakes database open functionality; it simply returns a positive, non-zero handle to the calling function. Moving the source file, you come upon the next function, `dbGetData()`. This function provides some functionality, even if minimal; it simply assigns each ASCII digit, 0–9, to the character array passed in (actually a pointer). Finally, the function returns a success value to the calling function. You arrive at the function **dbClose()**, which simulates the closing of a database file; it merely returns a success value.

The previous set of function definitions represents the traditional style of a function returning a result value. Although these functions return only a simple value to designate success or failure, the code required at the call site can become tedious and excessive. You can witness this with just the minimal code in this How-To.

The next set of function definitions is different than the previous set. One function within this set uses the third component of exception handling, the **throw** statement.

```
void dbGetDataEH( int field, char *data )
{
    int ret = DB_ACCESS_ERROR ;

    throw( ret ) ;
}
```

Move forward through the code to the **dbGetDataEH()** function definition. Notice that an error code mnemonic is assigned to the **ret** integer variable. The next line of code in the function is a **throw** statement. The argument supplied to the **throw** statement is an **int** variable. You can supply any data type, either simple or user defined. This function is called within the **try** block within the main function. Because this function throws an exception, control is immediately transferred to the **catch** clause that follows:

```
    dbGetDataEH( 1, data ) ;
    cout << "Data is: " << data << endl ;
    dbCloseEH( theHandle ) ;
}
catch( int v ) {
    cout << "Error with DB: " << v << endl ;
}
```

This exception handler manages exceptions of type **int**.

If a statement raises an exception, any statements that follow will not be executed. In this example, the **cout** and the **dbCloseEH()** call are not executed.

Comments

This How-To has taken a quick look at the basics of exception handling. With these basics, you can begin to reap the benefits of exception handling.

An additional benefit of exception handling is a more logical grouping of code. Developers tend to group logical sections of code within **try** blocks, thereby producing source code that is more readable, robust, and maintainable.

The How-Tos that follow will delve into more detail concerning exception handling.

COMPLEXITY
INTERMEDIATE

11.2 How do I...
Use the various catch constructs such as multiple catch clauses, catch ordering, and the rethrowing of exceptions?

Problem

I understand that multiple catch clauses can be provided to handle exceptions thrown from a try block. I am unsure if ordering of catch clauses is important and want to know if an exception caught can be rethrown by a catch clause.

Technique

The technique required to organize multiple catch clauses is quite easy. The tricky part is to understand any exceptions that require handling.

The following source code demonstrates how to apply the use of multiple catch clauses, including the catch-all clause. The technique required to rethrow exceptions is also shown.

Steps

1. Change to your base source directory and create a new directory named CATCH. Next, start your code editor and type in the following source code:

```
// catch.cpp - demonstrates the use
// of multiple catch clauses
#include <exception>
#include <iostream>
using namespace std ;

void rethrowFunc( int i ) ;
void throwFunc( int i ) ;

int main( )
{
    for( int i = 0; i < 6; i++ )
    {
        try {
            rethrowFunc( i ) ;
        }
```

```
            catch( int v ) {
                cout << "Int caught: " << v << endl ;
            }
            catch( float f ) {
                cout << "Float caught: " << f << endl ;
            }
            catch( double d ) {
                cout << "Double caught: " << d << endl ;
            }
            catch( char *s ) {
                cout << "Char* caught: " << s << endl ;
            }
            catch( ... ) {
                cout << "Other exception caught" << endl ;
            }

    }// for loop

    return( 0 ) ;
}

void rethrowFunc( int i )
{
    try {
        throwFunc( i ) ;
        cout << "rethrowFunc()" << endl ;
    }
    catch( int v ) {
        throw ;
    }
    catch( float f ) {
        throw ;
    }
    catch( double d ) {
        throw ;
    }
    catch( char *s ) {
        throw ;
    }
    catch( ... ) {
        throw ;
    }
}

void throwFunc( int i )
{
    int x = 5, y = 0, r = 0 ;

    switch( i )
    {
    case 0:
        throw( int(5) ) ;
        break ;
```

```
            case 1:
                throw( float(10.5) ) ;
                break ;
            case 2:
                throw( double(21.0) ) ;
                break ;
            case 3:
                throw( "an exceptional string" ) ;
                break ;
            default:
                r = x / y ;
                break ;
        }
    }
```

2. Save the file as **CATCH.CPP**. Next, exit out of the editor, return to the command line, and run the compiler and linker, naming **CATCH.CPP** as the input file.

3. Run the **CATCH** program. The following should be displayed:

```
Int caught: 5
Float caught: 10.5
Double caught: 21
Char* caught: an exceptional string
Other exception caught
Other exception caught
```

The source code will be examined in detail in the following section.

How It Works

Starting at the top of the file, you will find two **include** directives and a **using** directive. Next, you will see function declarations for **rethrowFunc()** and **throwFunc()**. The purpose of the **throwFunc()** function is to throw different types of exceptions. The **rethrowFunc()** function's purpose is to catch exceptions thrown by **throwFunc()** and to then rethrow the exceptions. These two functions are examined in more detail later in this section. But first, let's continue our journey into the main function.

The first statement in **main** is a **for** loop. The **for** loop provides the logic to iterate through all the exceptions to **throw** without excessive lines of code. The first block of code within the **for** loop is the **try** block:

```
try {
    rethrowFunc( i ) ;
}
```

As the code begins its journey down the loop, it enters the **try** block and encounters the call to **rethrowFunc()**. The function is passed the value of **i** as its argument. Let's take a quick diversion to **rethrowFunc()**'s definition. This discussion will only look at the first few lines, as follows:

```cpp
void rethrowFunc( int i )
{
    try {
        throwFunc( i ) ;
        cout << "rethrowFunc()" << endl ;
    }
//...
```

The first logical block of code in this function is another **try** block. This **try** block is independent of the **try** block found in the **main** function. The only statement found within the **try** is a call to the function **throwFunc()**. Notice that the original value of **i** from **main** is again passed to **throwFunc()**. Because program flow is again being redirected, let's divert our attention to the definition of **throwFunc()**.

The body of **throwFunc()** follows:

```cpp
void throwFunc( int i )
{
    int x = 5, y = 0, r = 0 ;

    switch( i )
    {
    case 0:
        throw( int(5) ) ;
        break ;
    case 1:
        throw( float(10.5) ) ;
        break ;
    case 2:
        throw( double(21.0) ) ;
        break ;
    case 3:
        throw( "an exceptional string" ) ;
        break ;
    default:
        r = x / y ;
        break ;
    }
}
```

The first statement in the function declares three integers for use in a subsequent expression within the function. Next you find a **switch** statement, its argument being the argument to the function. Remember that this argument is the original value of the integer used in the **for** loop in **main**. This provides a unique value to switch on, so that a different throw can be demonstrated. Depending on the value, a different **case** statement is executed.

This function will throw one of five types of exceptions: int, float, double, char*, or divide-by-zero. The last one, divide-by-zero, is defined by the Standard; it is why the **exception** header file was included. Take a look at the **default** block; if you examine the values of the variables, this expression divides 5 by 0, obviously a mathematical no-no. The reason I added this line of code will be obvious later in this section. Beyond the **switch** and **throw** statements, not much else happens in this function. Although simple, it provides the logic required to rethrow exceptions and demonstrate multiple **catch** clauses. Let's now return to the **rethrowFunc()** function definition. Here it is again in its entirety:

```
void rethrowFunc( int i )
{
    try {
        throwFunc( i ) ;
        cout << "rethrowFunc()" << endl ;
    }
    catch( int v ) {
        throw ;
    }
    catch( float f ) {
        throw ;
    }
    catch( double d ) {
        throw ;
    }
    catch( char *s ) {
        throw ;
    }
    catch( ... ) {
        throw ;
    }
}
```

Pay particular attention to the **cout** statement. If you recall the output of this program, this statement is never executed. Again, here is the output:

```
Int caught: 5
Float caught: 10.5
Double caught: 21
Char* caught: an exceptional string
Other exception caught
Other exception caught
```

Remember that because **throwFunc()** throws an exception, any statement following the call to **throwFunc()** within the **try** block will not be executed. Control will instead be diverted to the **catch** clause that can handle the exception.

Look again at the previous function definition. Notice that each **catch** clause contains a single **throw** expression. This is referred to as a rethrow expression. When the exception mechanism encounters a **throw** expression within a **catch** clause, the same exception will be thrown again. You should provide rethrow logic any time you think the exception should be handled further up the call chain.

You have to be cautious when dealing with rethrow logic. If, for example, you modify the exception object and then execute a `throw` expression, the changes to the object might not be what you expect. A nonreference object that is passed as an argument to a `catch` clause will get a *copy* of the original object. Therefore, if you modify the object, you will modify only the local copy. The following example demonstrates this:

```
catch( int val ) {
    val = 32000 ;
    throw ;
}
```

The argument variable `val` is assigned the value `32000`, but it is the local copy that gets the new value, not the original object thrown. Therefore, when the `throw` expression is executed, the original object will be thrown back up the call chain. If you need to modify the original object, you should pass by reference, as the following code snippet shows:

```
catch( int & val ) {
    val = 32000 ;
    throw ;
}
```

The last `catch` clause in the `rethrowFunc()` is called the catch-all `catch` clause and it looks like this:

```
catch( ... ) {
//...
}
```

The ellipsis is required; this signature makes it visually apparent as to the functionality of this `catch` clause. The catch-all `catch` clause must be the last handler if more than one `catch` clause exists. The catch-all clause can catch any exception. Don't take this as an invitation to use the catch-all clause after every `try` block.

You have seen how the rethrow expression is used as demonstrated within the `rethrowFunc()` function. Because every `catch` clause within this function rethrows its exception, you can return to the main function. Again, you find the same `catch` clauses after the `try` block in `main`, including a catch-all clause. The `for` loop iterates six times, each iteration in turn realizing a different exception. The output of the program confirms this:

```
Int caught: 5
Float caught: 10.5
Double caught: 21
Char* caught: an exceptional string
Other exception caught
Other exception caught
```

Notice that the `Other exception caught` text occurs twice in succession. This text is displayed as a result of the catch-all `catch` clause. The exception thrown in this case is a divide-by-zero exception. This exception is generated, if you recall, in the `default` case within the `throwFunc()` function.

Comments

In the previous section, I mentioned that you shouldn't blindly apply catch-all `catch` clauses after every `try` block. However, there are a couple of good reasons why you might want to use a catch-all clause. One reason is that you might not know all the exceptions that might be thrown by some function call or statement within a `try` block. Another reason might be that you must release some resource within a function. If some statement generates an exception and you don't have a `catch` clause to handle it, the catch-all will handle it and you can release the resource there. The following example demonstrates this:

```
void func()
{
    char *buf = new char[ 30000 ] ;
    try {
        functionCall( ) ;
    }
    catch( char *s ) {
        // code to handle char* exception
    }
    catch( ... ) {
        delete [] buf ;
    }
}
```

How can you be sure that `functionCall()` only throws a `char*` exception? Well, you might know it and then again, you might not. You might be dealing with invalid or out-of-date documentation. The catch-all `catch` clause ensures that a memory leak does not occur under this circumstance.

COMPLEXITY

INTERMEDIATE

11.3 How do I...
Implement and use an exception class?

Problem

I have been using exception handling in my applications and find the use of native types to be restrictive and uninformative. Is there a way to use a class as an exception type? And if so, how can I implement such a class type?

Technique

In this How-To, a simple application is used to demonstrate the use of an exception class. The use of an exception class is preferred over simple types because a class is more expressive.

Steps

1. Change to your base source directory and create a new directory named EXCLASS.

2. Next, start your text editor and type the following source code, exactly as shown below:

```cpp
// exclass.cpp - program to demonstrate the
// use of an exception class
#include <iostream>
using namespace std ;

class MathError
{
public:
    MathError( ) : x(0), y(0) {
    }

    MathError( int x, int y ) : x(x), y(y) {
    }

    void message( ) {
        cout << "MathError exception caught:" << endl ;
        cout << "x==" << x << ", y==" << y << endl ;
    }
private:
    int x, y ;
} ;

int divide( int x, int y ) throw( MathError ) ;

int main()
{
    int x = 5, y = 0, result = 0 ;

    try {
        result = divide( x, y ) ;
    }
    catch( MathError &m ) {
        m.message() ;
    }

    return 0 ;
}
```

```
int divide( int x, int y ) throw( MathError )
{
    if( y == 0 )
        throw MathError( x, y ) ;

    return( x / y ) ;
}
```

3. Save the file as **EXCLASS.CPP** and exit the editor to the command line.

4. Compile and link the **EXCLASS.CPP** source file.

5. Run the program; the output should be as follows:

```
MathError exception caught:
x==5, y==0
```

How It Works

Begin your use of an exception class by examining the source code. Starting at the top of the file, you will find an **include** directive and immediately following that a **using** directive.

Next, you come upon the declaration of a class named **MathError**, as follows:

```
class MathError
{
public:
    MathError( ) : x(0), y(0) {
    }

    MathError( int x, int y ) : x(x), y(y) {
    }

    void message( ) {
        cout << "MathError exception caught:" << endl ;
        cout << "x==" << x << ", y==" << y << endl ;
    }
private:
    int x, y ;
} ;
```

This class serves as an exception class. An exception class is used to capture pertinent information about an exception condition. An exception class is used by an application to create objects of that type. In the **MathError** class, you will find two constructors and a member function named **message()**. The default constructor is defined inline as is the constructor taking two **int** arguments.

The **message()** member function prints out an informational message to include the values of the instance variables. Within the **private** section, you will find the declarations for two **int** variables. These variables are used to hold information about a particular exception.

The line of code following the `MathError` class declaration is a function declaration for `divide()`:

```
int divide( int x, int y ) throw( MathError ) ;
```

Notice the exception specification for the `divide()` function; this function states that it will throw an exception of type `MathError` and only `MathError`. If you are unfamiliar with exception specifications, refer to How-To 11.4.

Next, you come to the `main` function. Starting with the first line of code within `main`, you will see the declaration of three integer variables.

Following the variable declarations, you come upon the `try-catch` section of code shown here:

```
try {
    result = divide( x, y ) ;
}
catch( MathError &m ) {
    m.message() ;
}
```

The `try` block consists of a single statement, a call to the function `divide()`. The `divide()` function is passed two integer arguments and the result of the call is returned to the variable `result`.

Now turn your attention to the definition of `divide()` shown here:

```
int divide( int x, int y ) throw( MathError )
{
    if( y == 0 )
        throw MathError( x, y ) ;

    return( x / y ) ;
}
```

Again, you will notice the exception specification for the function. Within the function, the first line checks to see whether the denominator, represented by `y`, is zero. If `y` is zero, an exception of type `MathError` is thrown, otherwise the `return` statement is executed, returning the result of the expression `x/y`.

Take note of the `throw` expression in `divide()`. An object of type `MathError` is created, although it is not explicitly shown. The compiler creates a hidden temporary for the constructor call. Next, a copy of this temporary is created and passed to the exception handler. The temporary is then destroyed, even before the exception handling mechanism begins its search for a handler.

Let's now return to the `main` function to continue the journey. Turn your attention to the `catch` clause because the `divide()` function throws an exception. The `catch` clause follows:

```
catch( MathError &m ) {
    m.message() ;
}
```

The argument to a **catch** clause can be an object or a reference to an object. If you decide to rethrow an exception, you should consider using a reference as the argument. The most compelling reason is that if you alter the exception object, the changes are reflected in the rethrow of the object. If an object is passed, you operate on only the local object passed in to the **catch** clause. The following code snippet should illuminate this fact:

```
catch( MathError m ) {
    m.setMessage( "Divide by zero exception" ) ;
    throw ;
}
```

In this version, the exception object is a copy of the original object thrown. The call to the member function **setMessage()** is executed to change the internal message that the exception class will eventually display. The problem with this version is that m is a local object to the **catch** clause block. This object will cease to exist when the **throw** is encountered. The next **catch** clause that handles this exception will not get the altered object. To remedy this problem, you must make m a reference, as shown here:

```
catch( MathError &m ) {
    m.setMessage( "Divide by zero exception" ) ;
    throw ;
}
```

Now, the call to **setMessage()** will operate on the original object, so the next handler to receive the object will realize the changes made in this catch clause.

Comments

You should always consider providing an exception class rather than a simple type. The main reason is that simple types such as **int** and **double** do not provide sufficient information in processing an exception condition. An exception class provides a level of detail required to sufficiently handle and report an exception to users.

In this How-To, you saw how to create an exception class and use it. A more robust exception class might write information to a log file or capture additional information about an exception or the environment of the user. The possibilities are limited only by your imagination.

11.4 How do I...
Specify exceptions that a function will throw?

Problem

I have been using the C++ exception handling mechanism and want to know how I can specify the exceptions thrown by a function. Isn't there a way to do this without relying on source code comments or documentation?

Technique

This can be a source of confusion to many developers. I have been approached with this question on numerous occasions. This How-To will demonstrate the use of exception specifications.

Steps

1. Change to your base source directory and create a new directory named SPEC.

2. Start your editor and type in the following source code:

```
// spec.cpp - program to demonstrate
// exception specifications
#include <exception>
#include <iostream>
using namespace std ;

void func1( int val ) throw( int, char* ) ;
void func2( void ) throw( float ) ;
void func3( void ) throw( ) ;

int main()
{
    for( int i = 0; i < 3; i++ )
    {
        try {
            switch( i ) {
            case 0 :
                func1( 0 ) ;
                break;

            case 1 :
                func2( 1 ) ;
                break;
```

```
                    case 2 :
                        func3( ) ;
                        break;
                }
            }
            catch( int val ) {
                cout << "int caught: " << val << endl ;
            }
            catch( float val ) {
                cout << "float caught: " << val << endl ;
            }
            catch( char *val ) {
                cout << "char* caught: " << val << endl ;
            }
        }// for

        return 0 ;
    }

    void func1( int val ) throw( int, char* )
    {
        if( val == 0 )
            throw( int(20) ) ;
        else
            throw( "exceptional string!" ) ;
    }

    void func2( ) throw( float )
    {
        throw( float(10.5) ) ;
    }

    void func3( ) throw( )
    {
    }
```

3. Save the file as **SPEC.CPP** and exit the editor to the command line.

4. Compile and link the **SPEC.CPP** source file.

5. Run the program; the output should be as follows:

```
int caught: 20
char* caught: exceptional string!
float caught: 10.5
```

How It Works

Let us start at the beginning of the source file. Moving past the **include** and **using** directives, the next section of code is as follows:

```
void func1( int val ) throw( int, char* ) ;
void func2( void ) throw( float ) ;
void func3( void ) throw( ) ;
```

These are, of course, function declarations. I am sure you have noticed something quite different about these declarations, namely the exception specifications.

The first two exception specifications are obvious: func1() can throw only an int or a char* and function func2() can throw only a float. What exceptions will the function func3() throw? That is not so obvious. Let's think about this one: The exception specification is empty, right? That must mean this function guarantees not to throw any exceptions. The assumption proves to be correct; func3() guarantees to not throw an exception.

You should be thinking about this fact whenever you are designing and coding functions and member functions. If the applications you are building utilize the exception handling facilities, you should consider marking all your functions with an exception specification. Attention to detail, although tedious, eventually pays off—the intent of your code becomes much clearer.

How about functions not marked with an exception specification? Well, those functions have free rein concerning the throwing of exceptions. Quite literally, a function without an exception specification can throw any and all conceivable exceptions. It is my opinion that you are better off using exception specifications for functions that do and do not throw exceptions. The developers who will maintain your code will thank you also.

As you move down through the source code, you come upon the main function. Inside main, you come upon the for loop used to call one of the three functions previously declared. The functions are called one at a time, within the try block. The section of code follows:

```
for( int i = 0; i < 3; i++ )
    {
        try {
            switch( i ) {
            case 0 :
                func1( 0 ) ;
                break;

            case 1 :
                func1( 1 ) ;
                break;

            case 2 :
                func2( ) ;
                break;
            }
        }
    }
```

For each iteration of the for loop, the try block is entered and based on the value of i, the proper case is selected within the switch. A call is made to either func1() or func2(); in both cases, an exception is thrown. In the case of func1(), an exception of type int or char* is thrown depending on the value the argument passed.

Moving past the **try** block, you find three **catch** clauses. Each **catch** clause is designated to handle a different exception type. The catch-all **catch** clause could have been added to the list, but would have never realized its value because the code is handling all types of exceptions. In essence, the programs has been designed and coded for the known exceptions. In situations in which you don't know all the exceptions thrown, you should put up your guard by providing the catch-all handler. In any event, within each **catch** clause, a **cout** statement is executed to acknowledge the receipt of the exception.

As you move down the source file past the **main** function, you find the definition for **func1()**. You can see that the exception specification is again specified; this is in addition to the function's declaration. The logic for the function is simple: If the value is **0**, throw an **int**; otherwise, throw a **char***.

The definition for **func2()** is found next within the source code. Again, you see the exception specification as part of the signature. This function merely throws a **float**.

Finally, the definition for **func3()** is encountered. If you recall, this function guarantees to not throw an exception. As you can see by the empty definition, the guarantee is fulfilled.

Comments

Utilizing exception specifications leads to readable and maintainable source code. The use of exception specifications also provides a form of self-documenting code. The other option you have is to furnish comments at the declaration and definition for a function that throws exceptions. The problem with that is the lack of consistency; someone might add an exception within the definition and forget to document the declaration.

Once again, an exception specification follows a function's argument list and consists of the keyword **throw**, followed by a list of exception types encased within parentheses. If the exception list is empty, the function guarantees not to throw an exception.

What if a function throws an exception not specified within the exception specification list? You might think the compiler could catch the various exceptions thrown by examining the **throw** statements. In reality, the compiler isn't quite that smart. The following example illustrates that fact:

```
void f() throw( int )
{
    int i, j , k ;
    //...
    k = i / j ;
    //...
}
```

This function definition states that the function will only throw an exception of type int. The problem is that a divide-by-zero exception could be thrown; the compiler can't possibly know this. I'm sure a compiler vendor can provide a compiler switch to produce a warning message whenever it encounters a division expression. However, I assume most developers would turn that switch off, especially if developing an accounting package. The point is that you should not rely on the exception specification to tell you all the exceptions a function will throw.

What if a function throws an exception not listed within the exception specification? The library function unexpected() is called. This will happen only if the function does not handle the unknown exception. For example, you might provide the catch-all catch clause for this purpose. The default action for unexpected() is to invoke the library function terminate(). It might be in your best interest to override unexpected() so you can control its behavior. How-To 11.5 explains how to handle this situation.

COMPLEXITY
INTERMEDIATE

11.5 How do I...
Handle exceptions that are not caught or not expected?

Problem

The applications I am writing include exception handling, but exceptions are still being thrown. Is there any way that the application can process unhandled exceptions gracefully?

Technique

In this How-To, you will see how to handle exceptions that are not handled or unexpected. Although you might provide exhaustive measures to handle exceptions, there will be instances in which exceptions are missed. The example provided here will help alleviate uncaught exceptions.

Steps

1. Move to your base source directory and create a new subdirectory named UNEXPECT.

2. As usual, start your favorite text editor and type in the following source code:

```cpp
// unexpect.cpp - program to demonstrate the
// handling of unexpected exceptions
#include <iostream>
#include <cstdlib>
using namespace std ;

typedef void(*pUnExp)() ;

class ErrorClass
{
public:
    ErrorClass() ;
    void message() { cout << "ErrorClass" << endl ; }
} ;

void func( void ) throw( ErrorClass ) ;

void unexpectedHandler( )
{
    cout << "Unexpected handler!" << endl ;
    exit( 1 ) ;
}

int main()
{
    pUnExp oldHandler2 = set_terminate( unexpectedHandler ) ;

    try {
        func( ) ;
    }
    catch( ErrorClass &e ) {
        e.message() ;
    }

    return 0 ;
}

void func(   ) throw( ErrorClass )
{
    throw( double(10.0) ) ;
}
```

3. Save your work in a file named UNEXPECT.CPP and exit the editor back to the command line.

4. Next, execute the compiler and linker on the source file UNEXPECT.CPP. If your compiler does not support the **cstdlib** header, include **stdlib** instead.

5. Now, run the program. The output should be as follows:

```
Unexpected handler!
```

How It Works

Begin your exploration of unexpected exceptions at the top of this source file. The sixth line of code provides a **typedef** to the declaration of the error handler as shown here:

```
typedef void(*pUnExp)() ;
```

This **typedef** says that **pUnExp** is a pointer to a function taking no arguments and returning nothing.

The next block of code declares a class named **ErrorClass**. It is used as an exception class to process exceptions. **ErrorClass** contains a default constructor and a member function **message()** to print out a diagnostic message.

The next line of code is a function declaration for **func()** as shown:

```
void func( void ) throw( ErrorClass ) ;
```

This function declaration also includes an exception specification. The exception specification states that **func()** will throw an exception of type **ErrorClass**.

Next, you come to the function definition **unexpectedHandler()**. This function is used to process unexpected exceptions. The function contains two statements: **cout** and **exit()**. You should provide appropriate functionality required to process unexpected exceptions; this code provides a basic example.

The first line of code in the **main** function is a call to the **set_terminate()** library function. This call will set the function **unexpectedHandler()** to handle unexpected exceptions. The return from **set_terminate()** is the address of the most current handler.

The next block of code consists of a **try-catch** code section. A call to **func()** is made within the **try** block. The only handler defined consists of the **catch** clause accepting an exception object of type **ErrorClass**.

Let's turn our attention to the definition of **func()**. The definition follows:

```
void func(   ) throw( ErrorClass )
{
    throw( double(10.0) ) ;
}
```

Notice that the exception specification specifies that this function will only throw exceptions of type **ErrorClass**. But hold on a minute—what do you see in the body of the function? The **throw** expression throws a **double**.

However, there is no need to worry because the application is prepared to process unexpected exceptions as the following shows:

```
Unexpected handler!
```

You might have expected to see the following message:

```
ErrorClass
```

This is the message displayed from the **ErrorClass**'s member function **message()**. Indeed, the **catch** clause in the **main** function contains the call:

```
e.message().
```

Because the exception thrown is not of type **ErrorClass**, this **catch** clause never gets the opportunity to handle the exception. Instead, the exception handling mechanism looks up the address of the current unexpected handler and invokes the function **unexpectedHandler()**, which is defined within this application.

Comments

Considering most applications these days exceed 100,000 lines of code, it is imperative that you take a defensive stance when designing and developing applications. Exception handling is a feature you should be utilizing. Unexpected exceptions can take you by surprise if your application is not prepared to handle the unexpected. This How-To introduced you to handling unexpected exceptions. With this knowledge, you are in a better position to express your defensive programming position.

PART V
MEMORY MANAGEMENT

NEW AND DELETE VERSUS MALLOC() AND FREE()

NEW AND DELETE VERSUS MALLOC() AND FREE()

How do I...

12.1 Use `new` and `delete` with the C `malloc()` and `free()` routines?

12.2 Use other C `mem...` routines on objects allocated with `new`?

12.3 Find out how much memory my structures and classes really take?

12.4 Prevent memory leaks caused by not using `delete[]` to delete arrays?

12.5 Override the `new` or `delete` operators for my classes?

12.6 Overload the `new` and `delete` functions for arrays?

This chapter compares and contrasts the differences between the C++ `new` and `delete` operators and the C functions `malloc()` and `free()`, and their place in C++ memory management.

As with the I/O libraries, programmers must often resolve (or at least be aware of) problems that can occur when old and new techniques are used side-by-side. These situations can occur when older C++ Standard (or non-standard, or worst of all, poorly written) code or legacy C code has to be integrated with new programs and code. This is common—many companies still use old libraries developed in C with their C++ programs.

Both the C++ operators and the C functions are part of a memory management system that is part of your compiler's runtime library. Many compiler vendors extend these libraries, and others (as well as third parties) provide tools to troubleshoot the use of the libraries (such as Inprise's Borland CodeGuard provided with the Borland C++ compilers).

This chapter addresses some common issues involving the use of the `new` and `delete` operators, as well as potentially tricky operating system and compiler issues.

12.1 Use `new` and `delete` with the C `malloc()` and `free()` Routines?

Often programmers find themselves having to work with or integrate existing C code into their C++ programs. This How-To discusses possible issues with doing this.

12.2 Use Other C `mem...` Routines on Objects Allocated with `new`

Although C++ provides built-in replacements for `malloc()` and `free()`, other memory functions are often needed. Some pointers to possible problems (no pun intended) are discussed in this How-To.

12.3 Find Out How Much Memory My Structures and Classes Really Take

There is a lot more to calculating the sizes of structures and classes than first meets the eye. Considerations such as the operating system and compiler settings can have far-reaching effects.

12.4 Prevent Memory Leaks Caused By Not Using `delete[]` to Delete Arrays

This How-To is a discussion of memory debugging tools and techniques.

12.5 Override the new or delete Operators for My Classes

This How-To shows how to overload the new and delete operators to implement a simple memory statistics keeper.

12.6 Overload the new and delete Functions for Arrays

Building on the statistics keeper from the preceding How-To, this How-To discusses some additional issues for overloading the array handling versions of new and delete.

COMPLEXITY

INTERMEDIATE

12.1 How do I...

Use new and delete with the C malloc() and free() routines?

Problem

Many programming books state that using new and delete along with malloc() and free() related C routines is a bad idea. Is it really unsafe?

Technique

For most modern C++ compilers and runtime libraries, using both is quite safe. However, the reason all the programming books and instructors preach so fervently against the use of malloc() and free() is that the code you write—intended to be rather "pure" C++ code—should, of course, be free of any C language baggage.

Other arguments used against using both the C-style memory allocations and C++'s new and delete operators are error-handling issues in the new versions of C++. If new fails, it will no longer return null; instead, it will throw an exception. This has the effect of somewhat simplifying the code because it is not filled with if statements that check for failed allocations. Instead, your code can concentrate on getting the job done. If your program needs to deal with these exceptions rather than terminate, enclosing all code in a try { ... } catch sequence will allow you to keep all error handling in one place. (See Chapter 11, "Exception Handling in C++.") Naturally, the C allocation functions still return null if they fail, so code using them could very well end up being tougher to read and maintain.

In reality, most modern C++ memory managers used by the `new` and `delete` operators are in fact the same memory managers that C's `malloc()` and `free()` routines use. However, there are some differences in how the different ways of allocating memory are handled for each method, so the "Steps" section has some relatively simple rules to follow when you're working (or have to work) with C memory.

Steps

Intermingling the C and C++ ways of allocating and freeing memory is not recommended, although most compilers' runtime libraries handle the combination correctly.

Check your code against these simple rules when both have to be used:

1. Never use `free()` to de-allocate memory allocated with `new`.

2. Never use `delete` to free memory allocated with `malloc()`.

That's it. These are simple but important rules to validate your code. This is really a compiler or runtime library issue more than a language issue. Officially, the two are not supposed to be mixed, but most compilers keep them as compatible as possible to minimize complaints.

COMPLEXITY

INTERMEDIATE

12.2 How do I...
Use other C mem... routines on objects allocated with new?

Problem

A plethora of functions is available in the C header files `string.h` and `mem.h`. Functions such as `memcpy()` and `memmove()` are handy, and it would be nice to confirm whether it is possible to use them in C++.

Technique

Yes, it's possible to use the C memory manipulation functions. Most of the `mem...` functions take `void` pointers as arguments, which are generic memory references that are not managed by the memory manager.

For instance, this C++ code snippet is perfectly valid, assuming that the header files are C++ safe. (That is, that they have been appropriately modified for use with a C++ compiler. It's safe to say that all header files that come with your C++ system are correct.)

```
#include <string.h>

...

char* MyMemory = new char[1500];
memset(MyMemory, 0, 1500);
delete[] MyMemory;
```

Of course, production code would wrap the allocation in a `try { ... }` `catch` sequence to make sure the call to **new** was successful before calling `memset()`.

How It Works

After a pointer exists, functions that do not have anything to do with memory allocation or de-allocation work the same way they did in C.

Comments

It is useful to peruse the header files for the C functions you want to use in your programs, because many compiler vendors have extended the C++ versions to include default arguments. Because C++ implements much stricter type checking than C, it's also useful to know the specific types. Unlike C, for instance, the **char** and **int** types cannot be interchanged, and doing so will cause some compiler warning messages.

COMPLEXITY

INTERMEDIATE

12.3 How do I...
Find out how much memory my structures and classes really take?

Problem

Sometimes it is not readily apparent how much actual memory an object uses. This is especially important to understand when moving data formats between 16- and 32-bit platforms.

Technique

Instantiated classes take the same amount of space as all their data members, which is system dependent. On 32-bit systems, each `integer`, `unsigned int`, and pointer takes 4 bytes, `char`s take 1 byte, unicode `char`s take 2 bytes, and `float`s are 4 bytes, `double`s are 8 bytes, and `long double`s are 10 bytes on Intel processor machines.

This is by no means the end of it. The byte alignment setting on your compiler modifies the real amount of memory your structures and classes take. Some compilers default to specific settings, and others allow complete control over this setting.

Byte Alignment

Your compiler will likely have settings for byte alignment. These options can increase the performance of your programs on some processors, because most processors incur a sometimes-significant performance penalty when they are fetching data that does not end on their alignment boundary.

For instance, the Intel 486 processor uses a 32-bit data bus. When fetching a 16-bit integer (an `int` in DOS and 16-bit Windows), it actually fetches the whole 32 bits of memory. Further, from the processor's point of view the memory is actually divided into 1/4 of the actual bytes of memory available (4 bytes = 2 16-bit words). Even the 32-bit Intel processors refer to one 32-bit value as a double word or DWORD, and the processor can only retrieve data based on these boundaries.

This might not seem significant at first glance, but take a moment to think through the following example.

If the integer is a structure or class like this

```
struct {
    char MyChar ;
    long int myLongInt ;
} MyStruct ;
```

when your program is byte-aligned (the smallest granularity possible on a PC), the computer (assuming it is a 386DX or later processor) will fetch the 32-bit region containing `MyChar` when the member is referenced. It will then shuffle the bits around appropriately to allow your program to work with the variable. One time out of four the structure will line up correctly, but the rest of the time the computer will have to do some work to make it possible for this variable to be worked with.

When fetching `MyLongInt`, there is a 50% percent chance the system will have to fetch only one 32-bit word to get all of `MyLongInt`. The other 50% of the time, it will have to do 2 fetches—first it gets the least significant bytes, and then the most significant bytes, and then shuffles the data to get one 32-bit integer. If you think this has to be slower, you're absolutely right. It adds a lot of overhead.

There are other byte-alignment issues as well. Most code starting points (for example, functions) perform best when started on these 4-byte boundaries, and little performance gains can add up quickly.

If the structure were aligned on a 4-byte boundary, `MyChar` would start on a 4-byte boundary, and `myLongInt` would also, and there would be 24 bits of wasted space between the two, meaning the actual `struct` would be 8 bytes, rather than 5 bytes in size.

With the preceding in mind, envision the following development scenario: Two groups of developers have to make binary files transportable between their respective applications. To that end, they share some header files that define the structures the programs use. If one group used 2-word (4 bytes) byte alignment in its compiled application, and the other one did not, their structure sizes are not likely to match when the data is read back from the file. The result will likely be that some poor programmer has to dig through code that might be just fine, only to discover at some point that the actual structure sizes written to disk differ.

How can a programmer account for this? For the most part, it involves some knowledge about the development system and operating system in use. Just knowing C++ is not enough when these machine- and OS-dependent issues come into play. If you're working with outside code, especially executables, it's tough to find out what the byte alignment setting was.

Making Your Structure Work with All Settings

The most common way to make your structure work with all settings is to byte-pad structures to make sure (for the PC architecture) they take up some multiple of 4 bytes. This ensures the alignment will be the same for compilers using any of the three settings for compilation. A more alignment-safe structure would look like this:

```
struct {
    char MyChar ;
    char[3]/* reserved */ ;
    long int myLongInt ;
} MyStruct ;
```

Some compilers might insist that you name the second data member, but most don't.

You should watch for structure alignment issues when working with binary files, binary data transfers, operating system, and even lower level structures. Mismatched byte-alignment settings cause all sorts of bugs (in the form of garbage values) to creep into your programs.

Steps

Probably the easiest way is to use the `sizeof()` operator to return the size of the objects that are being worked with.

For example, to output the size of a previously declared class `MyClass`, use

```
cout << "Size of myclass: " << sizeof( MyClass) << endl ;
```

If this seems like too much work, try adding up the data member according to the sizes above.

This will also show possible byte-alignment problems. Anytime your structure or class contains `char`s, a little flag should go up to ensure the structure is byte-alignment safe. I call this *defensive coding*, and it can save you a lot of long hours and lost sleep.

COMPLEXITY

INTERMEDIATE

12.4   How do I...

Prevent memory leaks caused by not using `delete[]` to delete arrays?

Problem

Using the `delete` operator on an array does not delete all the memory allocated for the array. `delete[]` must be used instead.

Technique

A memory debugger such as Inprise's venerable Borland CodeGuard tool can be invaluable as a safety check for your code. Other systems and compilers either come with their own memory-debugging library or have one available for them.

Source code analyzers can often detect these errors, too—tools such as lint can be very useful for finding all sorts of possible problems with code.

Steps

Check your code for any statements that allocate arrays with `new`, and find the corresponding `delete` statement.

Whenever an array is allocated with `new`, the actual operator used is `new[]`. Unfortunately, most documentation and programmers' texts do not distinguish between the two for fear of confusing beginning programmers.

Allocating an array like this

```
char* myArray = new char[45] ;
```

calls `new[]`, although the brackets appear later on. Free the storage allocated this way:

```
delete[] myArray ;
```

The steps for this How-To are relatively simple:

1. Find all occurrences of **new** in your code. Utilities such as **grep** are useful for this.

2. Check to see if these **new** operators allocate arrays.

3. Ensure that the **delete[]** operator is used to delete the arrays.

How It Works

The **delete[]** syntax is used to explicitly inform the memory manager that an entire section is to be deleted. Although most memory managers do keep detailed information on the memory allocated, calling plain **delete** for an array deletes the first location of the array, and nothing else, by definition.

Some memory managers are smarter than this, but at times they will have compatibility problems with some C++ code that exploits this "feature."

COMPLEXITY

ADVANCED

12.5 How do I...
Override the new or delete operators for my classes?

Problem

There are lots of possible reasons you would want to override the standard **new** and **delete** operators for a class or even an entire program.

Here is a short list of things that can be accomplished by overloading the **new** and **delete** operators (this is by no means complete):

- Debugging your program's memory management.

- Taking advantage of operating system–specific routines that might be more efficient than the compiler's included memory allocation routines.

- Gathering statistics for memory allocation and deallocation in your program for performance or efficiency reasons.

Technique

Overriding the `new` and `delete` operators for classes is achieved very much the same way any other operator is overloaded. The only thing that really needs to be known is the number of bytes to be allocated for the `new` operator:

```
void* myclass::operator new(size_t bytes_to_allocate)
```

The function must return a pointer of type `void`, and takes a `size_t` argument (usually defined as a 32-bit `int` in the file `stddef.h`, which you might have to include) to indicate the size of the object. This is the same number returned by the built-in function `sizeof()`.

The `delete` operator does not return anything; it takes a `void` pointer and `size_t` as arguments.

```
void myclass::operator delete(void* obj, size_t size)
```

Again, `size_t` is defined in `stddef.h`, and this will likely need to be included in your program.

There is quite a caveat attached to this technique, however. Remember the previous discussion of the operator `delete[]`? The technique shown here does not overload this operator, nor the `new[]` version thereof. That means the overloading technique is only really useful for some debugging and statistics work. Granted, everyone uses STL vector classes now, right? (Now there's a subtle hint…)

Allocating the memory is also possibly tricky—it is easiest to allocate the space using an array of `char`. However, some platforms, such as Unicode-based systems, do not use 1-byte characters. Production code should determine the size of a `char` before allocating the memory to ensure that twice the memory needed is not allocated by accident.

Steps

For this example, a simple memory allocation counter will be implemented—it will keep track of the total bytes allocated, deleted, and the number of calls to `new` and `delete` operators. You might be surprised at the execution results because allocating an array of these objects does not show in the statistics.

1. Create a class that contains statistics or information you want to keep track of. In this case, it will be just bytes allocated, de-allocated, and the number of calls to `new` and `delete`. These are by no means the only things that can be dealt with this way. The following code shows the class to keep memory statistics:

```
class MemStats
{
    private:
```

```cpp
unsigned    BytesAllocated ;
unsigned BytesDeleted ;
unsigned    CallsToNew ;
unsigned    CallsToDel ;

fstream    StatsFile;

public:

MemStats() :      BytesAllocated(0), BytesDeleted(0),
                  ➥CallsToNew(0), CallsToDel(0)
{
   StatsFile.open( "memstats.txt", ios::out ) ;
    if( !StatsFile )
       throw runtime_error( "Could not open memstats.txt" ) ;
}

MemStats( const string& filename ) : BytesAllocated(0),
➥BytesDeleted(0), CallsToNew(0), CallsToDel(0)
{
   StatsFile.open( filename.c_str() , ios::out ) ;
    if( !StatsFile )
       throw runtime_error( "Could not open user-defined
                              ➥file." ) ;
 }

// these functions can be expanded to do all sorts of other
//  things, like print more info into the output file, time
//  and date, etc. or keep track of the allocated chunks of
//  memory in an associative array.


void newcalled( size_t size )
{
    CallsToNew++ ;
   BytesAllocated += size ;
}

void delcalled( size_t size )
{
    CallsToDel++ ;
   BytesDeleted += size ;
}

 ~MemStats()
 {
     StatsFile      << endl
           << " Memory allocation statistics : " << endl
           << "  (the numbers below should match)" << endl
           << endl
           << " Bytes Allocated : " << BytesAllocated << endl
           << " Bytes Deleted :   " << BytesDeleted << endl
           << " Calls to new :    " << CallsToNew << endl
           << " Calls to delete : " << CallsToDel << endl
           << endl ;
```

```
            StatsFile.close() ;      // explicitly close file to make
                                     // doubly sure.
        }
} ;
```

Note that all the functions are inlined in order to not excessively impact the performance of the code being profiled.

2. For the class you want to monitor, overload the respective `new` and `delete` functions. After the statistics are updated, the easiest way to actually allocate the memory for most situations is to call the global operators to allocate and de-allocate memory. To call a global operator, use the member-of operator (`::`) without a scope name, that is, `::new`. You must also make the statistics-keeping object accessible to the `new` and `delete` functions of your class. In this case, using a global variable was convenient, but it could just as easily have been a data member of the class. The following code shows the overloaded `new` and `delete` functions:

```
void* operator new( size_t size )
    {
        stats.newcalled( size ) ;
        return (void*) ::new char[size] ; // allocate specified
                    // number of bytes with the actual new operator
    }

    void operator delete( void* mem, size_t size )
    {
        stats.delcalled( size );
        ::delete[] mem ;
    }
```

3. When allocating memory with code like this

```
::new char[size]
```

be sure to use the proper version of `delete` to free the memory:

```
::delete[] mem
```

It is easy to become confused when implementing the singular version of `new` and `delete` that actually allocates an array of data.

4. It's important to remember that byte sizes are not the same across platforms; a DOS `char` type is 1 byte, but some systems (such as Unicode) use 2-byte characters. When overloading `new` and `delete` in production code, it is important to write code to make this distinction to prevent your program from using two (or more) times the amount of memory it should.

How It Works

After the new and `delete` operators are overloaded, single calls to allocate an instance of the class will be processed through the overloaded functions. The key thing to remember is that allocating arrays of that class will *not* call the overloaded new and `delete` functions. These are allocated though the global new[] and `delete[]` operators, which are not guaranteed to be overloadable on all C++ compiler implementations.

Comments

It is absolutely critical to remember to deallocate memory properly in the `delete` operator, or risk memory leaks in your program. The operating system or runtime library will clean up after your program when it terminates, but there is nothing more frustrating than watching 10 or more hours of calculations go down the drain because the program ran out of memory.

COMPLEXITY
ADVANCED

12.6 How do I...
Overload the new and delete functions for arrays?

Problem

Now that I know how to overload the singular new and `delete` operators, it would be nice to overload the array-based new[] and `delete[]` operators, too.

Technique

Overloading the array allocation and de-allocation routines for a class is compiler dependent. Some compiler versions (namely Borland C++ 5) do not pass the correct array size to the `delete[]` operator, for instance, making accurate statistics keeping difficult. The sample code is located in the newdel\ex2 subdirectory, with pre-compiled executables from the DJGPP and Borland compilers.

The function prototypes for new[] and `delete[]` operators are as follows:

```
void* myclass::operator new[]( size_t size )

void  myclass::operator delete[]( void* data, size_t size )
```

The size_t argument for `delete[]` is optional on some C++ compilers.

Steps

It's probably worth trying to compile the sample program with your compiler to make sure the new[] and delete[] operators are overloadable and implemented correctly. Also, note that the sample code in this How-To is based completely on the code from the previous How-To, with the additional operator overloaded.

1. Create a class to keep your statistics. The sample program keeps track of bytes allocated and deleted and calls to new, delete, new[], and delete[]. The following is the code for keeping the memory statistics. Note the modifications from the previous How-To.

```
class MemStats
{
    private:

    unsigned    BytesAllocated ;
    unsigned BytesDeleted ;
    unsigned    CallsToNew ;
    unsigned    CallsToDel ;
    unsigned CallsToNewArray ;
    unsigned CallsToDelArray ;

    fstream    StatsFile;

    public:

    MemStats() :      BytesAllocated(0), BytesDeleted(0),
                      ➥CallsToNew(0), CallsToDel(0),
                      ➥CallsToNewArray(0),
                      ➥CallsToDelArray(0)
    {
       StatsFile.open( "memstats.txt", ios::out ) ;
        if( !StatsFile )
           throw runtime_error( "Could not open memstats.txt" ) ;
    }

    MemStats( const string& filename ) : BytesAllocated(0),
                  ➥BytesDeleted(0), CallsToNew(0),
                  ➥CallsToDel(0), CallsToNewArray(0),
                  ➥CallsToDelArray(0)
    {
       StatsFile.open( filename.c_str() , ios::out ) ;
        if( !StatsFile )
           throw runtime_error( "Could not open user-defined
                                  ➥ file." ) ;
     }

    // these functions can be expanded to do all sorts of other
    // things, like print more info into the output file, time
    // and date, etc. or keep track of the allocated chunks of
    // memory in an associative array.
```

```
void newcalled( size_t size )
{
   CallsToNew++ ;
   BytesAllocated += size ;
}

void newarraycalled( size_t size )
{
   CallsToNewArray++ ;
   BytesAllocated += size ;
}

void delcalled( size_t size )
{
   CallsToDel++ ;
   BytesDeleted += size ;
}

void delarraycalled( size_t size )
{
   CallsToDelArray++ ;
   BytesDeleted += size ;
}

~MemStats()
{
   StatsFile    << endl
        << " Memory allocation statistics : " << endl
        << "  (the numbers below should match)" << endl
        << endl
        << " Bytes Allocated : " << BytesAllocated << endl
        << " Bytes Deleted :   " << BytesDeleted << endl
        << " Calls to new :    " << CallsToNew << endl
        << " Calls to new[] :  " << CallsToNewArray << endl
        << " Calls to delete : " << CallsToDel << endl
        << " Calls to delete[]:" << CallsToDelArray << endl
        << endl ;
   StatsFile.close() ;    // explicitly close file to make
                          // doubly sure.
}
} ;
```

2. Overload the new, delete, new[], and delete[] operators for the class
you want to monitor. Depending on what needs to be tracked, not all the
functions need to be implemented or defined. The following listing shows
the implementation of the overloaded new, new[], delete, and delete[]
operators:

```
class MemStats
{
   private:

   unsigned    BytesAllocated ;
   unsigned BytesDeleted ;
   unsigned    CallsToNew ;
```

```
unsigned    CallsToDel ;
unsigned CallsToNewArray ;
unsigned CallsToDelArray ;

fstream    StatsFile;

public:

MemStats() :      BytesAllocated(0), BytesDeleted(0),
                  ➥CallsToNew(0), CallsToDel(0),
                  ➥CallsToNewArray(0),
                  ➥CallsToDelArray(0)
{
   StatsFile.open( "memstats.txt", ios::out ) ;
    if( !StatsFile )
       throw runtime_error( "Could not open memstats.txt" ) ;
}

MemStats( const string& filename ) : BytesAllocated(0),
                  ➥BytesDeleted(0), CallsToNew(0),
                  ➥CallsToDel(0),
                  ➥CallsToNewArray(0),
                  ➥CallsToDelArray(0)
{
   StatsFile.open( filename.c_str() , ios::out ) ;
    if( !StatsFile )
       throw runtime_error( "Could not open user-defined
                            ➥file." ) ;
 }

// these functions can be expanded to do all sorts of other
// things, like print more info into the output file, time
// and date, etc. or keep track of the allocated chunks of
// memory in an associative array.


void newcalled( size_t size )
{
   CallsToNew++ ;
   BytesAllocated += size ;
}

void newarraycalled( size_t size )
{
   CallsToNewArray++ ;
   BytesAllocated += size ;
}

void delcalled( size_t size )
{
   CallsToDel++ ;
   BytesDeleted += size ;
}
```

```
                void delarraycalled( size_t size )
                {
                   CallsToDelArray++ ;
                   BytesDeleted += size ;
                }

                ~MemStats()
                {
                   StatsFile      << endl
                         << " Memory allocation statistics : " << endl
                         << "  (the numbers below should match)" << endl
                         << endl
                         << " Bytes Allocated : " << BytesAllocated << endl
                         << " Bytes Deleted :   " << BytesDeleted << endl
                         << " Calls to new :    " << CallsToNew << endl
                         << " Calls to new[] :  " << CallsToNewArray << endl
                         << " Calls to delete : " << CallsToDel << endl
                         << " Calls to delete[]:" << CallsToDelArray << endl
                         << endl ;
                   StatsFile.close() ;    // explicitly close file to make
                                          // doubly sure.
                }
            } ;
```

3. When implementing the new and new[] functions, the easiest way to get them to return memory is to call the global operator ::new[] to allocate an array of char. It is also possible, of course, to call your operating system–specific memory allocation functions. There might be type size issues here; a char is not necessarily one byte on all platforms.

4. Remember that if you have allocated memory in the new and new[] functions, you must use ::delete[] to free the memory in your delete operators, even on the singular delete function. After all, the memory was allocated by new[], not new. This entire process is hidden from users of the class.

How It Works

The C++ compiler will automatically call the overloaded functions instead of the built-in ones.

Comments

The quality and details of the delete[] and new[] operators vary significantly between compiler vendors. Try running the sample code to see what your compiler generates. All sample listings here are initially compiled with Borland C++, and are tested with DJGPP (a GNU compiler for DOS, including a 32-bit DOS extender). The program leaves the memory statistics in the file memstats.txt, and the results vary between even these two compilers. The following listing shows the memstats.txt file generated by a program compiled with Borland C++ 5.01A. Notice that the bytes allocated and deleted do not match, but the calls do.

```
Memory allocation statistics :
 (the numbers below should match)

Bytes Allocated : 600012
Bytes Deleted :   300024
Calls to new :    25001
Calls to new[] :  1
Calls to delete : 25001
Calls to delete[]:1
```

The following is a memstats.txt file generated by a program compiled with DJGPP using GCC 2.81:

```
Memory allocation statistics :
 (the numbers below should match)

Bytes Allocated : 600016
Bytes Deleted :   600016
Calls to new :    25001
Calls to new[] :  1
Calls to delete : 25001
Calls to delete[]:1
```

As you can see by the output of the programs, the compilers used in this case differed in how they handled the **delete** operators as well as how they handled the actual size of the **Sample_Data** class. The difference can be attributed to byte-alignment settings. The GNU compiler seems to default to 8-byte alignment (which is the fastest for Pentium and later processors) in this case, and the Borland compiler seems to default to 4-byte alignment.

However, the compilers seem to agree on array sizes, and align them on 8-byte boundaries.

Code Listings for Chapter 12

The following listing, ex1\newdel.cpp, overloads the **new** and **delete** operators:

```
// File: overnew.cpp
// Example for C++ How-To
// Shows how to overload new and delete to implement a simple memory
// statistics keeper.
// Copyright 1998, Jan Walter
// NO WARRANTY. If this code breaks you get to keep both pieces.

// Compiler verificiation:
// Borland C++ 5.01A:          Yes
// DJGPP 2.01 w. GCC 2.81 :    Yes
// Watcom 10.5:                     Not Tried
// Microsoft VC++ 5:               Not Tried
```

```
// GCC 2.7.2/Linux:            Not tried
// GCC/EGCS/Linux:             Not tried

#include <iostream.h>
#include <fstream.h>
#include <stddef.h>

#ifdef __BORLANDC__
#pragma hdrstop
#endif

#include <string>
#include <stdexcept>  // standard exception classes


using namespace std ;

//*********************************************************************
//                  Memory statistics class
//*********************************************************************

class MemStats
{
   private:

   unsigned    BytesAllocated ;
   unsigned BytesDeleted ;
   unsigned    CallsToNew ;
   unsigned    CallsToDel ;

   fstream    StatsFile;

   public:

   MemStats() :      BytesAllocated(0), BytesDeleted(0), CallsToNew(0),
                     CallsToDel(0)
   {
      StatsFile.open( "memstats.txt", ios::out ) ;
        if( !StatsFile )
           throw runtime_error( "Could not open memstats.txt" ) ;
   }

   MemStats( const string& filename ) : BytesAllocated(0), BytesDeleted(0),
                     CallsToNew(0), CallsToDel(0)
   {
      StatsFile.open( filename.c_str() , ios::out ) ;
        if( !StatsFile )
           throw runtime_error( "Could not open user-defined file." ) ;
    }

   // these functions can be expanded to do all sorts of other things,
   // like print more info into the output file, time and date, etc.
   // or keep track of the allocated chunks of memory in an associative
   // array.
```

```cpp
    void newcalled( size_t size )
    {
        CallsToNew++ ;
        BytesAllocated += size ;
    }

    void delcalled( size_t size )
    {
        CallsToDel++ ;
        BytesDeleted += size ;
    }

    ~MemStats()
    {
        StatsFile    << endl
                  << " Memory allocation statistics : " << endl
                  << "   (the numbers below should match)" << endl
                  << endl
                  << " Bytes Allocated : " << BytesAllocated << endl
                  << " Bytes Deleted :   " << BytesDeleted << endl
                  << " Calls to new :    " << CallsToNew << endl
                  << " Calls to delete : " << CallsToDel << endl
                  << endl ;
        StatsFile.close() ;    // explicitly close file to make
                               // doubly sure.
    }
} ;

//*********************************************************************

// an interesting side note:
// we cannot easily catch exceptions thrown by the constructor of
// a global object - above the constructor throws a runtime_error
// exception object if it cannot open the file in the constructor.
// If this is true, the program will abort with some message like
// "abnormal program termination" or "Abort!"

MemStats stats ;

//*********************************************************************
//          Sample Data class - nothing special, just an example
//*********************************************************************
class Sample_Data
{

    int    S_int ;
    double S_double ;

    public:

    Sample_Data() : S_int(0), S_double(0.0)
    { }

    Sample_Data( int a, double b = 0.0)
```

```
    {
        S_int = a ;
         S_double = b ;
    }

    Sample_Data( double b, int a = 0 )
    {
        S_double = b ;
        S_int = a ;
    }

    Sample_Data( Sample_Data& copyfrom )
    {
        S_int = copyfrom.S_int ;
        S_double = copyfrom.S_double ;
    }

    Sample_Data& operator=( const Sample_Data& copyfrom )
    {
        S_int = copyfrom.S_int ;
        S_double = copyfrom.S_double ;
        return *this ;
    }

    Sample_Data& operator++()
    {
        S_int++ ;
        return *this ;
    }

    void* operator new( size_t size )
    {
        stats.newcalled( size ) ;
        return (void*) ::new char[size] ; // allocate specified number of bytes
                                // with the actual new operator
    }

    void operator delete( void* mem, size_t size )
    {
        stats.delcalled( size );
        ::delete[] mem ;
    }

    // friend functions
    friend ostream& operator<<( ostream& s, const Sample_Data& data );

};

//*********************************************************************

ostream& operator<<( ostream& s, const Sample_Data& data )
    {
        s << data.S_int << ' ' << data.S_double ;
        return s ;
    }
```

```cpp
//*********************************************************************

int main( int, char** )
{
    const int array_size = 50000 ;

    // allocate our sample data
    cout << "Size of Sample_Data: " << sizeof(Sample_Data) << endl ;
    // declare one object
    Sample_Data a( 50 , 12.555 );

    // instantiate an object dynamically
    Sample_Data* p = new Sample_Data( 21 ) ;

    // declare an array
    Sample_Data* DataArray = new Sample_Data[array_size] ;

    // declare an array of pointers
    Sample_Data* PDataArray[array_size] ;

    // initialize the array
    for (int i = 0 ; i < array_size ; i++ )
        PDataArray[i] = new Sample_Data(i) ;


    // Now work with the data some

    DataArray[0] = a ;

    for( int i = 1; i < array_size ; i++ )
    {
        DataArray[i] = ++DataArray[i-1] ;
      //cout << DataArray[i] << endl ;
    }

    ++*p ;
    cout << *p << endl ;

    // and clean up dynamically allocated stuff.

    delete p ;
    delete[] DataArray ;
    for (int i = 0 ; i < array_size ; i++ )
        delete PDataArray[i] ;

    return 0;
}



// end of file
```

The following listing, ex2\newdel.cpp, is based on the previous listing, but has been extended to overload the new[] and delete[] operators as well:

```cpp
// File: overnew.cpp
// Example for C++ How-To
// Shows how to overload new and delete to implement a simple memory
// statistics keeper. This example also overloads new[] and delete[] operators.
// Copyright 1998, Jan Walter
// NO WARRANTY. If this code breaks you get to keep both pieces.

// Compiler verificiation:
// Borland C++ 5.01A:          Yes
// DJGPP 2.01 w. GCC 2.81 :   Yes
// Microsoft VC++ 5:            Not Tried
// GCC 2.7.2/Linux:            Yes
// GCC/EGCS/Linux:             Not tried

#include <iostream.h>
#include <fstream.h>
#include <stddef.h>

#ifdef __BORLANDC__
#pragma hdrstop
#endif

#include <string>
#include <stdexcept>  // standard exception classes


using namespace std ;

//*********************************************************************
//                 Memory statistics class
//*********************************************************************

class MemStats
{
    private:

    unsigned    BytesAllocated ;
    unsigned BytesDeleted ;
    unsigned    CallsToNew ;
    unsigned    CallsToDel ;
    unsigned CallsToNewArray ;
    unsigned CallsToDelArray ;

    fstream    StatsFile;

    public:

    MemStats() :    BytesAllocated(0), BytesDeleted(0), CallsToNew(0),
                    CallsToDel(0), CallsToNewArray(0), CallsToDelArray(0)
```

```
{
   StatsFile.open( "memstats.txt", ios::out ) ;
    if( !StatsFile )
       throw runtime_error( "Could not open memstats.txt" ) ;
}

MemStats( const string& filename ) : BytesAllocated(0), BytesDeleted(0),
                    CallsToNew(0), CallsToDel(0), CallsToNewArray(0),
               CallsToDelArray(0)
{
   StatsFile.open( filename.c_str() , ios::out ) ;
    if( !StatsFile )
       throw runtime_error( "Could not open user-defined file." ) ;
 }

// these functions can be expanded to do all sorts of other things,
// like print more info into the output file, time and date, etc.
// or keep track of the allocated chunks of memory in an associative
// array.

void newcalled( size_t size )
{
    CallsToNew++ ;
   BytesAllocated += size ;
}

void newarraycalled( size_t size )
{
    CallsToNewArray++ ;
   BytesAllocated += size ;
}

void delcalled( size_t size )
{
    CallsToDel++ ;
   BytesDeleted += size ;
}

void delarraycalled( size_t size )
{
    CallsToDelArray++ ;
   BytesDeleted += size ;
}

~MemStats()
{
    StatsFile     << endl
             << " Memory allocation statistics : " << endl
             << "  (the numbers below should match)" << endl
             << endl
             << " Bytes Allocated : " << BytesAllocated << endl
             << " Bytes Deleted :   " << BytesDeleted << endl
             << " Calls to new :    " << CallsToNew << endl
```

```
                            << " Calls to new[] :   " << CallsToNewArray << endl
                            << " Calls to delete : " << CallsToDel << endl
                            << " Calls to delete[]:" << CallsToDelArray << endl
                            << endl ;
            StatsFile.close() ;      // explicitly close file to make
                                     // doubly sure.
        }
    } ;

    //**********************************************************************

    // an interesting side note:
    // we cannot easily catch exceptions thrown by the constructor of
    // a global object - above the constructor throws a runtime_error
    // exception object if it cannot open the file in the constructor.
    // If this is true, the program will abort with some message like
    // "abnormal program termination" or "Abort!"

    MemStats stats ;

    //**********************************************************************
    //             Sample Data class - nothing special, just an example
    //**********************************************************************
    class Sample_Data
    {

        int    S_int ;
        double S_double ;

        public:

        Sample_Data() : S_int(0), S_double(0.0)
        { }

        Sample_Data( int a, double b = 0.0)
        {
            S_int = a ;
            S_double = b ;
        }

        Sample_Data( double b, int a = 0 )
        {
            S_double = b ;
            S_int = a ;
        }

        Sample_Data( Sample_Data& copyfrom )
        {
            S_int = copyfrom.S_int ;
            S_double = copyfrom.S_double ;
        }

        Sample_Data& operator=( const Sample_Data& copyfrom )
```

```cpp
    {
        S_int = copyfrom.S_int ;
        S_double = copyfrom.S_double ;
        return *this ;
    }

    Sample_Data& operator++()
    {
        S_int++ ;
        return *this ;
    }

    void* operator new( size_t size )
    {
        stats.newcalled( size ) ;
        return (void*) ::new char[size] ; // allocate specified number of bytes
                                // with the actual new operator
    }

    void* operator new[](size_t size )
    {
        stats.newarraycalled( size ) ;
        return (void*) ::new char[size] ;
    }

    void operator delete( void* mem, size_t size )
    {
        stats.delcalled( size );
        ::delete[] mem ;
    }

    void operator delete[]( void* mem, size_t size )
    {
        stats.delarraycalled( size ) ;
        ::delete[] mem ;
    }

    // friend functions
    friend ostream& operator<<( ostream& s, const Sample_Data& data );

};

//******************************************************************

ostream& operator<<( ostream& s, const Sample_Data& data )
    {
        s << data.S_int << ' ' << data.S_double ;
        return s ;
    }

//******************************************************************

int main( int, char** )
{
    const int array_size = 25000 ;
```

```cpp
    // allocate our sample data

    // declare one object
    Sample_Data a( 50 , 12.555 );

     // instantiate an object dynamically
    Sample_Data* p = new Sample_Data( 21 ) ;

    // declare an array
    Sample_Data* DataArray = new Sample_Data[array_size] ;

    // declare an array of pointers
    Sample_Data* PDataArray[array_size] ;

    // initialize the array
    for (int i = 0 ; i < array_size ; i++ )
        PDataArray[i] = new Sample_Data(i) ;


    // Now work with the data some

    DataArray[0] = a ;

    for( int i = 1; i < array_size ; i++ )
    {
        DataArray[i] = ++DataArray[i-1] ;
      //cout << DataArray[i] << endl ;
    }

    ++*p ;
    cout << *p << endl ;

    // and clean up dynamically allocated stuff.

    delete p ;
    delete[] DataArray ;
    for (int i = 0 ; i < array_size ; i++ )
        delete PDataArray[i] ;

     return 0;
}


// end of file
```

MEMORY MANAGEMENT TECHNIQUES USING CLASSES

MEMORY MANAGEMENT TECHNIQUES USING CLASSES

How do I...

13.1 Make a simple class to clean up dynamically allocated memory automatically?

13.2 Make a class that automatically cleans up objects allocated with new?

13.3 Make an object that deallocates itself when there is no more code referencing it?

Managing memory is something few programmers think about when designing a program, but wish they had when staring at debugger output. Although performance tuning of a program will often deal with memory management issues, memory management is more than just counting the bytes allocated and deallocated in a program.

Shuffling bytes around in main memory is one of the slowest operations on a computer, and although it's faster than accessing the hard disk or the video memory, things would go much faster if the only thing the processor had to fetch from main memory was code. Your operating system does a lot of shuffling of data in memory in its management of caches and other data areas, as well as handling things like virtual memory (which allows your computer to use free disk space as an extension to system RAM). This is a relatively fixed cost, but as a programmer you have control over how your program uses memory (how much, how often things are copied, and so on).

Another technique no programmer should be without is a basic understanding of how memory managers are implemented and their limitations. Easy-to-implement techniques are also covered because for most programs these produce excellent results with minimal effort.

13.1 Make a Simple Class to Clean Up Dynamically Allocated Memory Automatically

This How-To uses scope to automatically deallocate dynamically allocated memory. It is most useful in situations in which the new and `delete` operators aren't the most efficient. This allows experimentation with other allocation schemes, such as operating system API calls, to be done invisibly to the rest of the program.

13.2 Make a Class That Automatically Cleans Up Objects Allocated with new

This How-To uses a template for type-safe memory management to provide functionality similar to that of How-To 13.1, it underlines a different approach.

13.3 Make an Object That Deallocates Itself When There Is No More Code Referencing It

Counting the number of references to an object is useful in multithreaded programming environments because objects might not have finished being processed by other threads when the thread that allocated the object expires.

13.1 How do I...
Make a simple class to clean up dynamically allocated memory automatically?

Problem

You might want to do this for a number of reasons. The primary reason is so the user of the class does not need to remember to match up new calls with deletes because the scope mechanism and the class destructor will handle it automatically. This is not the only reason, though.

Some systems (Windows 3.1, most notably) do not lend themselves well to the use of new and delete operators (which, for the most part, eventually call malloc() or free()). Often this problem comes from the memory manager or the system's segmentation model. Under the 16-bit Windows operating systems, most data allocated using new and malloc() comes from the application's local heap, which is only 64KB in size. Although more memory can be had using global memory allocation functions, managing it is quite a hassle.

Operating system direct memory allocation functions are often quite complicated, with lots of arguments and so on. The use of these functions also makes porting the code difficult. Another reason might be that the operating system provides a more robust heap manager (OS/2 provides an extremely fast memory suballocation manager, for instance).

Encapsulating the process in a memory manager helps the process in a number of ways:

- It keeps the actual function calls to the operating system's memory allocation routines in one place. This makes porting the code easier because the memory allocations in the program need not change as long as the memory allocation object's interface remains the same.

- It's possible to experiment with different memory allocation techniques (which are not necessarily operating system–specific) without affecting the code that uses the memory management class.

- It is easy to keep statistics on the memory the program used.

- The memory-managing object can perform all the error checking, and even handle the problems in a way best suited to the operating system without the users' (that is, the other programmers) of the object knowing how it's done.

- A memory object can perform advanced functions such as reference counting, providing a copy-on-write scheme, and also calling operating system–optimized resizing functions to increase program performance and reliability.

- The memory object can automatically deallocate the memory after the object falls out of scope. This can reduce the occurrence of memory leaks tremendously. Just think of what could happen to an application if a delete call were missed in a function called one million times!

These techniques require some discipline to implement. It is sometimes difficult to unlearn the use of `new` and `delete` for one project, but these techniques can go a long way toward reducing the amount of debugging time for a project.

Steps

It is best to start out with code that is generic enough to be used everywhere in the program. After that, it's possible to use this code in overloaded `new` and `delete` operators, for example. In this example, the code will be modularized as well as object-oriented. It essentially entails keeping the code specific to memory management in one C++ file, which is compiled with the other code. Programmers get the definitions for the classes through a header file. Because this code is quite generic, placing it in a module makes it easier to reuse elsewhere.

This example will use only the `new` and `delete` functions because they are available in every C++ system to allow memory to be allocated dynamically that automatically deallocates itself when the object managing it falls out of scope. In this case, it will also be possible to implement operators to work on the memory if this functionality is desired, or, for instance, to set the memory contents to `0` before making it available for use.

There are as many approaches to this problem as there are C++ programmers. The example detailed here will allocate generic memory.

This code is best put into a header file to make it more reusable.

1. Create a header file to contain the class definition and the inline code for your class. This example uses `memclass.hpp`. The `.hpp` extension denotes a C++ header file, just to make keeping it apart from the C header files easier.

2. Set up `define`s to prevent the header from being included in a program more than once. This is vital because this header file might be included in several other header files that will finally be included in an actual `.cpp` file containing code. At best, the compiler will spit out an error message to the effect of `multiple definitions for the same symbol`, and at worst, your program will misbehave.

Enclosing the contents of your header files in pre-processor directives similar to the following will prevent errors like `multiple definitions for` or `multiple symbols`. Make sure to change the names for the #defines!

```
#ifndef __MEMCLASS_HPP
#define __MEMCLASS_HPP
// header file contents go here ...
#endif
```

3. Depending on the amount of allocating and deallocating memory your programs do, memory management can consume a substantial amount of your program's runtime. My advice: Keep it simple and keep it lean. Statistics are nice, but don't generally have a place in "production quality" code.

The following listing shows a simple pointer management class design to do this:

```
class MemPtr
{
   private:

   void*          data ;
   unsigned int   msize ;


   public:

   // constructor list
   MemPtr( const unsigned int size ) ;
   MemPtr( const MemPtr &copyfrom ) ;

   -MemPtr() ;

   // information functions
   unsigned int getsize() const { return msize ; }

   // the allocated storage is accessed using the
   // address of operator (&)

   void* operator& () ;

};
```

The preceding code is a pretty minimalist implementation, but it's relatively easy to extend it to provide for resizing and joining memory regions, for example.

4. Implement the shorter functions as inline. I tend to try to inline anything that's fewer than five statements and is used often in a program. Inlining functions that are too large tend to make your programs bloated.

There is another point: Even if you are inlining functions, it is best to separate the class member function definitions from their implementations to make the actual header file more readable. Consider data-access functions to be an exception if they are only one line. Larger functions are marked as "inlineable" by using the keyword `inline`. The following code snippet shows how implementation of inline functions goes in the header files from `memclass.hpp`:

```
inline
MemPtr::MemPtr( const unsigned int size )
{
   msize = size ;
   data = new char[size] ;
}

inline
MemPtr::MemPtr( const MemPtr &copyfrom )
{
   // this contructor copies over the data area
   msize = copyfrom.msize ;
   data = new char[copyfrom.msize] ;
   memcpy( data, copyfrom.data, msize ) ;
}

inline
void* MemPtr::operator&()
{
   return data ;
}

inline
MemPtr::~MemPtr()
{
   // with older C++ compilers (those that do not support
   // exceptions) it may be necessary to check to see if data is
   // NULL before calling delete.
   delete[] data ;
}
```

The core of the class is the overloading of the C++ address-of operator. Instead of the default behavior of returning the pointer to the actual object, it returns the pointer to the memory region it manages.

The only other remarkable function is the destructor. Definitions have changed for the **new** and **delete** operators. **delete** is now smarter in that it not deallocate memory that has already been deallocated. In previous versions, this behavior was undefined. Likewise, **new** no longer returns **null** if it fails, it now throws an **xalloc** exception. (Refer to Chapter 11, "Exception Handling in C++," for a detailed discussion of exceptions and exception handling.)

How It Works

The way this class works is extremely simple. Instead of calling **new** to alloca blocks of "raw" memory, a `MemPtr` object of the size required is declared. The address-of operator is used to get the pointer address, and then the pointer is used normally. The only difference is that the `MemPtr` object will **delete** the memory when it falls out of scope.

For example, the code

```
MemPtr hmem( strlen(test_string) + 1 );

char* chararray = (char*) &hmem ;
```

is all that is necessary—the memory will be **delete**d when `hmem` falls out of scope.

The strength of this technique is especially evident when portable code has to be written because using the **new** and **delete** included with the compiler might not be the most efficient way to do things. Instead of calling the **new** and **delete** operators, the class could call operating system functions, or implement its own suballocation scheme.

COMPLEXITY

ADVANCED

13.2 How do I...
Make a class that automatically cleans up objects allocated with new?

Problem

This is a different spin on the previous How-To. The previous How-To only allocated raw memory, leaving the host program to typecast the resulting pointer. The previous How-To is extremely useful if your program must use memory functions other than **new** or **delete**, for example, in 16-bit Windows programming. This How-To presents a better approach to dealing with objects allocated with **new**.

Technique

The Standard Template Library includes a class that is used as a self-managing pointer. It's the class I recommend using, but the purpose of this How-To is to implement our own to explain how it all works.

ous How-To, the memory management class handled the
deletion of memory. In this case, pointers will be submitted to
ge. This poses a problem: How does the class know if it being
to an array of objects, or a pointer to a single object? The truth
standard way to figure this out, so for the purpose of this
s's constructors will be made to take an additional, optional
ate that an array of objects is being managed.

problem is one of type safety. Dealing with **void*** data types is a
potentially hazardous endeavor because they must be typecast to prevent
compiler warnings, and can accidentally be assigned to the wrong data type.
The solution here is to make this a template class.

Steps

1. Start by creating a header file to contain your class definition. I called the
example **classm.hpp**, with the file extension denoting that this is a C++
header file.

2. Define your class. The example uses a template class to provide type
safety in addition to being able to use things such as overloaded
assignment functions internally. The following listing shows the definition
of a memory management class from **classm.hpp**:

```
template <class t>
class MemClass
{
   private :
   t     *_data ;
   int     array ;

   public:

   MemClass() : array(0) {} ;
   MemClass( t *data, int numitems ) ;

   // this constructor assumes the contained class's assigment
   // operator is overloaded.
   MemClass( const MemClass<t> &copyfrom ) ;

   // data access functions

   t*    GetPtr() {    return _data ; }

   MemClass<t>& operator=( const MemClass<t>& copyfrom ) ;

   ~MemClass() ;
} ;
```

Note again that even inline functions are not implemented within the
class definition to make this more readable. This is an especially
important point to remember if others have to read your code.

3. Implement the constructors and destructor. As a general rule, a copy constructor should always be defined to prevent little problems from cropping up. It's possible that some STL or library function might cause the copy constructor to be called, and in this case, the default would do exactly what you *don't* want it to. The following listing shows the constructors and destructor for the sample memory management class from `classm.hpp`:

```
template <class t>
inline
MemClass<t>::MemClass( t *data, int numitems = 1 )
{
    _data = data ;
    array = numitems ;
}

template <class t>
MemClass<t>::~MemClass()
{
    if( array == 1 )
        delete _data ;
    else
        delete[] _data ;
}

template <class t>
MemClass<t>::MemClass( const MemClass<t> &copyfrom )
{

    array = copyfrom.array ;

    if( copyfrom.array == 1 )
    {
      _data = new t ;
      *_dala = *copyfrom._data ;
    }
    else
    {
        _data = new t[array] ;
        for ( int i = 0; i < array ; i++ )
          _data[i] = copyfrom._data[i] ;
    }
}
```

Note how the class attempts to handle arrays. The class has no way of finding out (within the scope of the language anyway) whether the pointer it is given points to an array or to a single object. The second argument to the constructor allows the user of the class to indicate whether it is to manage an array.

The array size given needs to be accurate only if you are going to copy the class with the assignment operator or copy constructor. Otherwise, it is used only to tell which version of **delete** to call.

4. Implement a data access function. In this case, I chose not to use an overloaded operator because it is quite possible that the address-of operator will be used to deal with objects of this class for things such as function parameters. It is only one line, and so it is implemented in the class body:

```
t*    GetPtr() {    return _data ; }
```

5. Implement other functionality for the class. This is really up to the designer of the class (you). In this case, an assignment operator is normally very useful, and so this is provided. Plenty of things could also be added, such as a release function that deletes the contained object, which can be useful for handling objects that use a large amount of memory. This listing shows the overloaded assignment operator from `classm.hpp`:

```
template <class t>
MemClass<t>& MemClass<t>::operator=( const MemClass<t>
                                     ➡& copyfrom )
{
    if( &copyfrom == this ) // deal with possible self-assignment
        return *this ;

    if ( array == 1 )
        delete _data ;
    else if ( array > 1 )
        delete[] _data ;

    array = copyfrom.array ;

    if( copyfrom.array == 1 )
    {
        _data = new t ;
        *_data = *copyfrom._data ;
    }
    else
    {
        _data = new t[array] ;

        for( int i = 0 ; i < array ; i++ )
            _data[i] = copyfrom._data[i] ;
    }
    return *this ;
}
```

Note how self-assignment is handled in this operator. This is critical because assigning an object to itself is something that could possibly occur inside a library function, and not handling this possibility could be disastrous.

How It Works

The class essentially assumes ownership of a pointer to a class, and deallocates it when it falls out of scope. It also deals with one other problem that dealing with pointers creates: copying pointers by copying the object to which the pointer points. This eliminates program errors caused by forgetting to `delete` a pointer before assigning another value to it.

Comments

The Standard Template Library also includes a class that works like this one, called `auto_ptr`.

COMPLEXITY

ADVANCED

13.3 How do I...
Make an object that deallocates itself when there is no more code referencing it?

Problem

Programs that do not execute in an absolutely linear fashion can run into problems when one thread of execution tries to access an object that has already fallen out of scope in the thread that allocated it.

Operating system callback functions (in which the operating system calls a specified entry point in a user program, usually asynchronously) have similar problems to threads in that they might be accessing data deallocated by the program.

Operating systems provide shared data areas that handle this automatically. However, these operating system features usually are designed for C, not C++, so destructors are not called.

Technique

A great number of things relating to how threads share and lock memory are operating system–dependent. For the purpose of this How-To, code that is OS-dependent will be left out and replaced with comments indicating any issues with the code.

Because this is code that can quickly become complicated, it is critical that the class is designed (and viewed by the reader to be designed) to solve very specific problems.

Specifically, there are some issues specific to both multithreaded programming and programs that use OS callbacks: Multiple threads can reference the object at the same time. With OS callback functions, the reference count might get to zero before the callback function is executed. This means that handling an OS callback might require special rules for handling the contained data (such as deleting the contained object the *second* time the reference count arrives at zero). On the other hand, whether the callback function can execute at the same time as other code in the same program is operating system–dependent. Some (non-preemptive multitasking) operating systems will only execute a callback while a program is executing an API call to the system (for example, Windows 3.1 during the `GetMessage()` API call).

The memory management classes cannot take care of all thread-dependent issues. Much of the responsibility falls on the actual data that's being handled. This gives the code the most flexibility because the only rule that could really be enforced by a container class is to prevent more than one thread from using the contained data. Implementing this strategy is likely to be less efficient than letting the data class care for itself. All the container class needs to worry about is the protection of its own data used to manage the data class.

The sample implementation uses two classes. One object class will contain the data object (this is called the container object or class throughout this How-To), and another will abstract data access (referred to as the pointer class or object). The container keeps the reference count, and that is the actual number of data access objects currently instantiated. When a data access object falls out of scope, it notifies the container class of this event.

This technique is also an excellent candidate for using the C++ template mechanism to make this code applicable to many situations. This is best combined with a class library that has support classes that abstract thread control and management functions (these are usually portable to more than one operating system, and so make the classes here even more useful).

Steps

As mentioned above, memory management like this can become very complicated quickly. It requires very careful planning before beginning to implement the code.

1. Define the purpose of the memory management code. This is more than "to manage memory in the program." It should be specific and concise. For larger projects, several memory management implementations might be needed to provide specific behaviors or features required for specific parts of the program. At that point, consider using inheritance models to manage common functionality.

For this How-To, the criteria were as follows:

A. The container and pointer objects must be content-specific and type safe. Templates are used to accomplish this.

B. The container object must clean itself up in addition to the data object it owns. It will essentially **delete** itself when it is no longer referred to.

C. Criterion B would have disastrous effects if the object or container were not allocated with **new**. In the interest of keeping the code concise, it must be made a rule. Possible approaches that could be taken in production code are to overload the **new** operator, to cause it to set a flag in the container, and to throw an exception from the constructor if the object was not allocated with **new**.

D. The pointer objects should overload the member-of operator of the pointer (**operator->**) to make accessing the members of the contained object possible.

E. The object container class should be able to contain arrays of objects. To keep this How-To as brief as possible, the pointer class will not support arrays. Adding array support requires overloading the index-of operator, overloading the addition and subtraction operators, and maintenance of a pointer to the data within the pointer class. It's not as complicated as it sounds, but adding all this will likely cloud the basic techniques presented in this How-To.

F. The container must protect its own management data, but no more. Imagine one thread referencing an object while the object was cleaning itself up because its reference count arrived at zero in another. The program would have a deadlock at best, and an outright program crash would be a more likely result.

G. The container class will control the locking of the count variables though mutexes. This should allow the control of the restricted items to be kept in a central few member functions.

MULTITHREADED PROGRAMMING TERMINOLOGY

The multitasking and multithreaded operating system world has developed some terminology to describe the means to coordinate the actions of threads and processes, as well as the means of communicating between them. The general terms used to control execution in multithreaded programming are detailed in the following paragraphs.

continued on next page

continued from previous page

A *process* is defined as a program running with its own stack and data space on a computer. Processes are given a specific allocation of processor time by the host operating system. The scheme by which time is allocated varies from system to system.

A *thread* is a "mini process." All threads share the same data space as the process that starts them, but have their own stack space. All threads share the processor time of their process.

A *semaphore* is a generic term for a variable used to communicate between processes and/or threads.

A *mutual exclusion semaphore* (a *mutex* for short) is a semaphore intended to ensure only one thread can execute an area covered by the semaphore at one time. This is usually managed by the operating system. A program thread locks the semaphore, and while locked, any other thread attempting to lock the semaphore is blocked from continuing until the other code releases the semaphore. These are normally used to process data that does not fare well if another thread is working on it as well. This requires the code to attempt to lock the semaphore, and the system will not stop the program from working with the data in question without locking the semaphore. Because of the discipline required in working with mutexes, it is best to only work with a particular mutex in one or two sections of code.

2. Define the layout of the data container class. Depending on the purpose, it might be more useful to actually store the data object, rather than a pointer to it. The following code shows the object container class template (part of `memclass.hpp`):

```
template <class t>
class ObjectPtr ;

template <class t>
class ObjectContainer
{
   private:
   t*           _data ;
   unsigned int  ArraySize ;
   unsigned int  Refs ;
   friend        ObjectPtr<t> ;

   // for multithreaded environments, also include a mutex handle
   // to protect the reference counter and the pointer to data.

   public:

   ObjectContainer( t* data, int array_size ) ;
   ObjectContainer( const ObjectContainer<t> &copyfrom ) ;
```

```
ObjectContainer& operator=( const ObjectContainer<t>
                                    ➡ &copyfrom ) ;

    // reference handlers

    void reference() ;
    void dereference() ;

    // inspection functions
    unsigned int getrefs() const { return Refs ; }

    ~ObjectContainer() ;
} ;
// end ObjectContainer class definition
```

Note the forward declaration of the `ObjectPtr` template class. This must be defined in order to allow the `ObjectContainer` class to have it as a friend class.

The remainder of the listing implements a memory management class as implemented in How-To 13.2. The number of references to the object contained is in the `Refs` variable.

3. Fill out the declaration of the pointer class. The class as implemented in the sample code assumes its pointer to the `ObjectContainer` object is always valid. If you're paranoid, feel free to add code that checks the validity of the pointer whenever referenced, and perhaps throw an exception to provide feedback during the debugging cycle. An invalid pointer could indicate a bug in the reference handling code somewhere. The following listing shows the filled-out `ObjectPtr` class (from `memclass.hpp`):

```
template <class t>
class ObjectPtr
{
    ObjectContainer<t>    *PointTo ;
    public:

    ObjectPtr( ObjectContainer<t> *source ) ;
    ObjectPtr( const ObjectPtr<t> &copyfrom ) ;

    ObjectPtr<t>& operator=( const ObjectPtr<t> &copyfrom ) ;

    ~ObjectPtr() ;

    // data access
    t*              operator->(){ return PointTo->_data ; }
    t&              operator* (){ return *(PointTo->_data) ; }
} ;
// end class definition
```

4. Implement the inline functions. In How-To 13.2, functions that could not
be inlined by the compiler were left in the header file for the sake of
brevity. In this case, the two functions are broken out and put into their
own header file to demonstrate the difference (and to get rid of the
annoying warning messages `cannot pre-compile headers ... code
in header` that some compilers spit out).

Generally, compilers cannot inline functions that contain loops; there are
other general rules about what compilers can and can't inline, but some
are compiler dependent. Let the compiler worry about whether it can
inline something or not because many things a compiler can (and will, if
you tell it to) inline have a negative performance impact on your
program. Rather, concentrate on making sure code you know should not
be inlined (because of length, generally) is not declared inline. The
following listing shows the inline functions for the `ObjectContainer` and
`ObjectPtr` classes from `memclass.hpp`:

```
//--------------------------------------------------------------
//         In-line functions for ObjectContainer
//--------------------------------------------------------------

template <class t>
inline
ObjectContainer<t>::ObjectContainer( t* data, int array_size )
{
    _data = data ;
    ArraySize = array_size ;
    Refs = 0 ;
}

// these two functions are the core functionality of the code,
// and because they deal with the actual management of the data
// must be protected from other threads

template <class t>
inline
void ObjectContainer<t>::reference()
{
    // lock mutex here
    Refs++ ;
    // and release mutex
}

template <class t>
inline
void ObjectContainer<t>::dereference()
{
    // lock mutex here
    Refs-- ;

    // copy mutex to local variable
```

```
   if( Refs == 0 ) delete this ;

   // release mutex though local variable (this has been
   // destroyed, and so the mutex data member is no longer valid
}

template <class t>
inline
ObjectContainer<t>::~ObjectContainer()
{
   if( ArraySize > 1 ) delete[] _data ;
   else delete _data ;

   // now throw an exception if we still have objects referring to
us...
    if( Refs ) throw logic_error( "ObjectContainer destructor
called while \
referenced.") ;
}

//-------------------------------------------------------------
//        In-line functions for ObjectPtr
//-------------------------------------------------------------

template <class t>
inline
ObjectPtr<t>::ObjectPtr( ObjectContainer<t> *source )
{
   source->reference() ;
    PointTo = source ;
}

template <class t>
inline
ObjectPtr<t>::ObjectPtr( const ObjectPtr<t> &copyfrom )
{
    copyfrom.PointTo->reference() ;
    PointTo = copyfrom.PointTo ;
}

template <class t>
inline
ObjectPtr<t>& ObjectPtr<t>::operator=( const ObjectPtr<t>
                                  ➥&copyfrom )
{
   // handle possible self-assignment
    if( this == &copyfrom ) return *this ;

    PointTo->dereference() ;

   copyfrom.PointTo->reference() ;
   PointTo = copyfrom.PointTo ;

    return *this ;
}
```

```
template <class t>
inline
ObjectPtr<t>::~ObjectPtr()
{
    PointTo->dereference() ;
}
```

The noteworthy items in the code are the **reference()** and
dereference() member functions. These require mutexes when running
in multithreaded programs to prevent an object from referencing the
object while it is in the process of being deleted.

5. Implement the out of line functions. Because these are template functions,
they cannot be placed into a separate **.cpp** module; the compiler will
need them to generate code for programs that use this class. The
following code lists the out of line functions defined in **memclass.hpp**:

```
// copy constructor and assignment operator are not inlined,
// and for non-template implementations should be in a
// separate module if used with a compiler that supports
// pre-compiled headers

template <class t>
ObjectContainer<t>::ObjectContainer( ObjectContainer<t>
                                        ➥&copyfrom )
{
    ArraySize = copyfrom.ArraySize ;
    Refs = 0 ; // we are making a copy of the contained object
        // and therefore have no references.

    if( ArraySize > 1 )
    {
        // deal with an array
      _data = new t[ArraySize] ;

        for( int i = 0 ; i < ArraySize ; i++ )
            _data[i] = copyfrom._data[i] ;
    }
    else
    {
        _data = new t ;
      *_data = *copyfrom._data ;
    }
}

template <class t>
ObjectContainer<t>& ObjectContainer<t>::operator=
                        ( ObjectContainer<t> &copyfrom )
{
    if( this == &copyfrom ) return *this ;
```

```
        if( Refs ) // error condition: cannot assign to container
                   // that isbeing referred to
            throw logic_error("Tried to assign object container
                               ➥with Refs.");

        // prevent copyfrom from being deleted while we're copying it
        copyfrom.reference() ;

        if( ArraySize > 1 )
            delete[] _data ;
        else
            delete _data ;

        ArraySize = copyfrom.ArraySize ;

        if ( ArraySize > 1 )
        {
            _data = new t[ArraySize] ;

            for( int i = 0 ; i < ArraySize ; i++ )
                _data[i] = copyfrom._data[i] ;
        }
        else
        {
            _data = new t ;
            *_data = *copyfrom._data ;
        }

        copyfrom.dereference() ;

        return *this ;

}

// end of file
```

Notable items in this file are the calls to reference() and dereference() in the assignment operator and copy constructor. The object references the other object while it is working on it to prevent a dereference() call in another thread from destroying the object while the copying is in progress.

There is one problem with this code. Can you spot it? (Feel free to skip the rest of this paragraph until you have played with the code.) The process of copying can destroy an object with no other references. Because a newly created object has a reference count of 0, referencing and then dereferencing the object in any way will cause the object to self-destruct. To fix it, make the copy constructor or assignment operator grab the mutex that protects the reference count variable, increment copyfrom. Refs, and free the mutex. Decrement the Refs variable at the end of the function, remembering the mutexes. This has the effect of bypassing the self-destruct code in the dereference() function.

6. Implement a program to test the classes. This program reads 200 words from a file (I chose the source file for the test program), and writes them back to the screen as just words with line wrapping, and then counts the lines as it goes. This is something I wish every email editor could do with quoted text. Here is the listing for the test program for our class, `refcount.cpp`:

```cpp
// File: refcount.cpp
// A program that uses our reference counting class.
// Copyright 1998, Jan Walter
// NO WARRANTY. If this code breaks you get to keep both pieces.

// Compiler verificiation:
// Borland C++ 5.01A:          Yes
// DJGPP 2.01 w. GCC 2.81 :    Yes
// Microsoft VC++ 5:              Not Tried
// GCC 2.7.2/Linux:              Not tried
// GCC/EGCS/Linux:             Yes

#include <iostream>
#include <fstream>

#ifdef __BORLANDC__
#pragma hdrstop
#endif

#include "memclass.hpp"

typedef ObjectContainer<string> StringC ;
typedef ObjectPtr<string>       StringP ;

const int numstrings = 200 ;
StringC* stringlist[ numstrings ] ;

int main( int, char** )
{
    ifstream infile( "refcount.cpp", ios::in | ios::nocreate ) ;

    for ( int i = 0 ; i < numstrings ; i++ )
    {
        string temp ;
        infile >> temp ; // grab a word from our file
        stringlist[i] = new StringC( new string(temp), 1 ) ;

    }

    int lines = 0, width = 3 ;

    cout << (lines + 1) << " :" ;

    for ( int i = 0 ; i < numstrings ; i++ )
    {
        StringP ourstring( stringlist[i] ) ;
```

```
            // determine how far along on the line we are ...
        width += ourstring->length() + 1 ;

        if( width > 75 )
        {
            lines ++ ;
            cout << endl << (lines + 1) << " :";
            width = ( ourstring->length() + 3 ) ;
        }
        else
            cout << ' ' ;

        cout << *ourstring ;

    }

    cout    << endl
            << endl
            << "Statistics: " << endl
            << "Total lines output: " << (lines + 1) << endl ;

    return 0;
}
// end of file
```

The program file shows the use of **typedef**s to make the use of template classes a bit easier on the reader and the keyboard. The objects contained in the renamed **ObjectContainer** are **delete**d at the end of the second **for** loop, one at a time, as the program traverses the array.

How It Works

The trick with the classes as they are presented is to determine when to count references. The easiest way to accomplish this is to make a pointer class to encapsulate pointer functionality.

The pointer objects can be created and fall out of scope ad nauseum, and the data will be valid until the last pointer object is deleted. At that point, the container object will self-destruct.

The classes effectively deal with a number of problem areas:

- Automatic cleanup of objects external to the scope in which they are being accessed (essentially primitive garbage collection).

- With mutexes implemented, provide thread safe access to dynamically allocated memory.

- Prevent the overwriting of memory currently being referred to elsewhere. The assignment operator of the **ObjectContainer** class will throw a **logic_error** exception if this is the case.

Comments

It is possible to accidentally grab a pointer to the data contained that's not accounted for through the overloaded operators of the `ObjectPtr` class. This is difficult to prevent. Having said this, it is not likely to happen if the programmer using the class understands the implications of the code. After all, it is possible to access private data members of classes from outside a class, too (by typecasting the object to an array of `char`, and then reading it as an array).

Also, the data object being encapsulated within the `ObjectContainer` might need mutex protection for the data it contains. Because this is a data issue, I recommend that the data class handle this and not the container class.

PART VI

I/O

14

UNDERSTANDING THE I/O STREAMS LIBRARY

How do I...

14.1 Use the C Standard I/O Library with the C++ I/O streams library?

14.2 Make my own classes compatible with cin and cout?

14.3 Perform complex formatting with cout or another ostream object?

14.4 Make my own stream manipulators?

So many programmers have difficulty with the C++ I/O streams library that it is quite common to see C++ code still using old C **stdio** functions to handle program I/O. Although some programmers might consider this approach practical, or even superior, the C **stdio** library does not do much to help good programming practice or catch oversights made by the programmer.

Consider the following points:

- The C++ I/O streams library implements type checking, whereas the **stdio** library's I/O is primarily done through void pointers.

- The C++ I/O streams library uses overloaded functions to make handling all built-in data types simple and identical.

- It is easy to extend the I/O streams library to allow the input and output operators to operate on user-defined classes.

14.1 Use the C Standard I/O Library with the C++ I/O Streams Library

At some time, every C++ programmer will have to work with existing C code or very old C++, and either integrate this code with new C++ code or use libraries that contain C-style I/O. Some issues regarding this are discussed in this How-To.

14.2 Make My Own Classes Compatible with `cin` and `cout`

This How-To shows the technique for overloading the stream insertion and extraction operators.

14.3 Perform Complex Formatting with `cout` or Another `ostream` Object

Basic output with `cout` might not always produce the desired results. Another header file contains advanced stream manipulators that can provide additional output formatting options.

14.4 Make My Own Stream Manipulators

It is often inconvenient to repeatedly use the in-stream formatting manipulators. This How-To demonstrates how to create an in-stream manipulator to combine the effects of several pre-defined manipulators.

COMPLEXITY
INTERMEDIATE

14.1 How do I...
Use the C Standard I/O Library with the C++ I/O streams library?

Problem

Using both the C Standard I/O Library and the C++ I/O streams library is a bad idea, and should be avoided whenever possible because the problems that can occur are difficult to diagnose. However, there are reasons you might want to use both libraries:

- To use or maintain existing C code with C++

• To use a prewritten C library with your C++ programs

The point is that you should only employ this technique if there is no other way, and if the program is experiencing irregular problems related to I/O.

The problem with using both libraries for I/O is that both libraries allocate their own buffers to increase the performance of I/O. Buffering also implies there is no guarantee that output will occur during the `printf()` or `cout.write()` call. It is likely to happen sometime afterward, when the buffer has been filled completely with other data to write. If you have two buffering systems, they will likely fill at different times, and output will appear out of order unless the buffers are synchronized.

This technique incurs a fairly high price for compatibility with old C code. File operations, such as writing and seeking, begin to incur a significant performance penalty because the output stream has to check continuously whether it's synchronized with the C library's buffers.

Also, the latest GNU development system's `stdio` implementation in the `libio` library on Linux and other UNIX-like operating systems is inherently compatible with GNU's `IOStreams` implementation. On GNU systems, this technique is unnecessary unless complete code compatibility between the GNU and other systems is desired.

NOTE

The GNU project, started by the Free Software Foundation, creates free software (now called "Open Source Software") for use by everyone, and all GNU projects make the source code available for anyone to modify. Systems like Linux, as well as a number of C and C++ development tools, are fruits of the Open Source movement. GNU stands for "GNU's Not UNIX." You can find out more about the GNU project at `http://www.gnu.org`.

Technique

For each `IOStreams` base class, call its inherited `sync_with_stdio()` function. It is possible to turn synchronization off again by passing `0` as the argument to the function. Incidentally, the default argument is `1`, meaning to turn on compatibility.

WARNING

Each class based on `IOStreams` must execute this call individually to ensure it is synchronized with the `Stdio` library.

Steps

1. Identify each class that is based on either `istream` or `ostream` by using a class viewer or the utility `grep`. Consult your development environment documentation if you're not sure how to do this.

2. Determine whether the class performs any file I/O (note that output and input from `stdout` and `stdin` are also file I/O).

3. After each class is identified, the class's constructor is the best place to implement this for each class in a way that it is not left out. If that is not possible—for instance, if the class is to be employed in situations in which this technique is not necessary or if you don't have access to the source code—add a call to the class's `sync_with_stdio()` after each class is instantiated.

Comments

Depending on how the classes are instantiated in your program, it might be possible to wrap the instantiation into a macro to ensure that the function is added for every class.

Macros are leftovers from the C language, but still have some usefulness in this case. To review this quickly, macros have no type checking at all. Therefore, one needs a great deal of discipline to get macros to work in a production environment.

A macro like this would instantiate a class, and call its `sync_with_stdio()` function. It's not possible to restrict the macro to `iostreams` classes only.

```
#define SYNCED_IOSTREAM_CLASS(classname, varname ) \
        classname varname ; \
        varname.sync_with_stdio()
```

Note that the last comma is not there. Most programmers put one there by habit, and the designer (me, in this case) figured that it would be best to leave that habit in place. The compiler will generate an error if the semicolon is left out when the macro is used in code.

The preceding example does not take into account any arguments that must be passed to the stream constructor. In your code, this macro would be used like this:

```
// Code above
SYNCED_IOSTREAM_CLASS( ostream, myOstream ) ;
// code below
```

If the source library with the class can be edited, it might be worthwhile to make the code optional, or allow it to be enabled by using a `#define` statement.

COMPLEXITY

INTERMEDIATE

14.2 How do I...
Make my own classes compatible with cin and cout?

Problem

It would substantially simplify code to use the `istream` and `ostream` operators >> and << to perform the custom output, rather than to individually output the public data members each time, or to output protected and private members via member access functions.

Technique

After a class is made compatible with the standard `istream` and `ostream` classes, I/O for the class will be much more consistent. The best way is to overload the << or >> operators for your class.

The extraction and insertion operators for C++ take the following format:

For output:

```
ostream& operator<<
(ostream& outstream, <insert your data type here>& data)
```

For input:

```
istream& operator>>
(istream& instream, <insert your data type here>& data)
```

The code in these functions is dependent on the contents of your data type. For classes, it might be necessary to declare the function a friend of the class to allow it access to private and protected data members.

Steps

1. Determine the best way to get data into or out of your class—either by the friend declaration or some other means, such as an overloaded = operator.

2. Create the declaration of the function. Be sure the `iostream.h` header file is included before the declaration, or the `ostream` or `istream` data types will not be visible and result in a compile-time error.

The easy way is to make the overloaded operators for your class friends to your class if you have to handle protected or private data members. However, this is not recommended because it circumvents any validity checking imposed by the functions that would validate this input. With some modifications, it is possible to make this reasonably safe, but the safest (the fewest possible side-effects) way is to not use the friend mechanism unless you absolutely have to.

You can use the following code as a template (it's taken from the `iostreams\ex3` directory on the CD-ROM):

```
istream& operator>>(istream&, RowProcessor&);
ostream& operator<<(ostream&, RowProcessor&);
```

3. Handle the data input and output. When processing is finished, return the `istream` or `ostream` object.

How It Works

Using the operator overloading mechanism, the C++ streams libraries "chain" what are in essence procedure calls for stream operations. Because the overloading mechanism depends entirely on the argument types passed to a function, this system is easily extendable for user-defined types.

Comments

Because file handling in the streams library is also based on the same mechanism, extending a class for console I/O will automatically support streaming to files and character arrays as well.

COMPLEXITY

ADVANCED

14.3 How do I...
Perform complex formatting with cout or another ostream object?

Problem

Although formatting with C++ is simpler than formatting with the `printf` family of functions from the C `stdio` library, it still has its pitfalls. On some systems, a lot of in-stream formatting needs to have an additional header file included to give access to the additional member functions used to perform advanced formatting.

Technique

In-stream formatting operators tend to be underrated, and unlike the `printf` series of functions, are type-safe and easily extended to fit the needs of your programs. Although some of the functionality is visible with the stock header file, `iostream.h`, most of the functionality of the stream modifiers is in `iomanip.h`.

Extending the system with your own manipulators is rather easy as well, and will be covered later. Normally, they will work with string-based and file-based streams as well.

The predefined manipulator library is by no means complete, however, and only encompasses some of the actual functionality included in the streams classes. Additional functionality can be accessed through each stream's `setf()` function and by passing the appropriate constant to it.

Standard Manipulators

Explaining standard manipulators is best done with a sample program. There are many possibilities for combining standard manipulators, and others might have been added in your development environment that are specific to your compiler vendor. Check your documentation for any of the nonstandard manipulators.

Setting Output Width with `setw()`

The `setw()` manipulator takes an integer argument and defines the default width of each item given to the output stream. The manipulator is in effect until changed again, and setting it to **0** will reset it to defaults. Using this manipulator will not cause output to be truncated; if the width of the item sent into the stream is wider than the given `setw()` value, the width of the item will determine the space given to the item.

The code

```
cout << "double d1 = " << setw(9) <<  d1 << '.' << endl ;
```

will cause the value to be shown in a field exactly nine characters wide. The following file, `setw.cpp`, demonstrates application for the `setw` manipulator:

```
// File: setw.cpp
// Example for C++ How-To
// Example file 1 for using io manipulators
// Using setw to set output width
// Copyright 1998, Jan Walter
// NO WARRANTY. If this code breaks you get to keep both pieces.
```

```
// Compiler verificiation:
// Borland C++ 5.01A:              Yes
// DJGPP 2.01 w. GCC 2.81 :    Yes
// Watcom 10.5:                         Not Tried
// Microsoft VC++ 5:                    Not Tried
// GCC 2.7.2/Linux:                   Not tried
// GCC/EGCS/Linux:                    Not tried


#include <iostream.h>
#include <iomanip.h>

#ifdef __BORLANDC__
#pragma hdrstop
#endif


int main()
{
    // the names are not the best  -sorry

    double     d1, d2;
    int        i1, i2;


      // note that there are functions to do both of these in the math.h
    // library, but since this is so simple this is easier to do.
      d1 = 22.0 / 7.0 ; // this approximates pi
    d2 = d1 * d1 ;

      i1 = d1 * 100 ;
    i2 = d2 * 1000 ;

// Using setwidth()

    cout       << endl
         << "Using the setw() example:" << endl
         << endl
         << "Numbers before setw():" << endl
         << "double d1 = " << d1 << '.' << endl
         << "double d2 = " << d2 << '.' << endl
         << "int i1 =    " << i1 << '.' << endl
         // note the spaces align things here.
         << "int i2 =    " << i2 << '.' << endl
         << endl
         << "Note how the output looks after using setw(9):" << endl

         // setw does not need to be called every time, it's just
         // this way for clarity.

         << "double d1 = " << setw(9) <<  d1 << '.' << endl
         << "double d2 = " << setw(9) << d2 << '.' << endl
         << "int i1 =    " << setw(9) << i1 << '.' << endl
```

```
        << "int i2 =    " << setw(9) << i2 << '.' << endl
        << endl
   << "Note how the numbers by default are right-aligned, and text" << endl
   << "is left-aligned." << endl;

// wait for keypress routine to prevent os windows from closing when the
// program has completed.

// non-dos (or Windows or OS/2) platforms use the '\r' char
// for the enter key. Sorry, no Mac definition here. You'll have to experiment.
   cout << endl << "Press enter key to continue ..." << endl;
   int c1;
   while( cin && (c1 = cin.get())  != '\n' ) ;


   return 0;
}

// end of file
```

Setting the Whitespace Character with `setfill()`

The `setfill()` manipulator selects what the stream considers to be whitespace. By default, this is the space (" ") character, and can be changed to suit the application's needs. Check-printing routines would normally use the * character, for instance. This setting stays in effect until changed again by another call to `setfill()`.

The following code (given that **i2** has a value of **10250**)

```
cout << "int i2 = " << setw(11) << setfill('*')<< i2 << '.' << endl;
```

will produce output that looks like this:

```
int i2 =******10250.
```

Setting the Number of Decimal Points with `setprecision()`

The `setprecision()` modifier affects only floating-point numbers such as **float** and **double** types. It sets the number of digits of precision used when displaying the number, and stays in effect until changed again. Note that the behavior is as expected—the decimal point is not counted as a digit when the output stream calculates the precision.

For example, if the **double d1** had a value of **44.123456789**, the code

```
cout    << setprecision(9)
        << "double d1 = " << setw(11) << setfill('*') << d1 << '.' << endl ;
```

would print like this on the screen:

```
double d1 = **44.1234568.
```

Whether the last number rounds up depends somewhat on your compiler's `iostreams` implementation, and could possibly be affected by other precision-related rules because this is a double-precision floating-point number. The following file, `precisn.cpp`, demonstrates the uses of `setfill` and `setprecision` I/O manipulators:

```cpp
// File: precisn.cpp
// Example for C++ How-To
// This file demonstrates the setprecision and setfill io manipulators.
// Copyright 1998, Jan Walter
// NO WARRANTY. If this code breaks you get to keep both pieces.

// Compiler verificiation:
// Borland C++ 5.01A:              Yes
// DJGPP 2.01 w. GCC 2.81 :     Yes
// Watcom 10.5:                      Not Tried
// Microsoft VC++ 5:                 Not Tried
// GCC 2.7.2/Linux:                Not tried
// GCC/EGCS/Linux:                 Not tried

#include <iostream.h>
#include <iomanip.h>

#ifdef __BORLANDC__
#pragma hdrstop
#endif



int main()
{

    double      d1, d2;
    int       i1, i2;


    // note that there are functions to do both of these in the math.h
    // library, but since this is so simple this is easier to do.
     d1 = 22.0 / 7.0 ; // this approximates pi
    d2 = d1 * d1 ;

     i1 = d1 * 100 ;
    i2 = d2 * 1000 ;

// Using setprecision()

    cout       << endl
           << "The setprecision() call affects all floating point" << endl
       << "output after the call. The default precision is 6." << endl
```

```
                << "Also note that setprecision does not include the decimal" << endl
                << "point in the precision." << endl
                << setprecision(9)
                << "double d1 = " << setw(11) << setfill('*') << d1 << '.' << endl
                << "double d2 = " << setw(11) << setfill('*')<< d2 << '.' << endl
                << "int i1 =    " << setw(11) << setfill('*')<< i1 << '.' << endl
                << "int i2 =    " << setw(11) << setfill('*')<< i2 << '.' << endl;


// wait for keypress routine to prevent os windows from closing when the
// program has completed.

// non-dos (or Windows or OS/2) platforms use the '\r' char
// for the enter key. Sorry, no Mac definition here. You'll have to experiment.
   cout << endl << "Press enter key to continue ..." << endl;
   int c1;
   while( cin && (c1 = cin.get())  != '\n' ) ;


     return 0;
}
// end of file
```

Conversion Bases

Conversion bases cause numerical output to be given in something other than decimal. Octal and hexadecimal output are most commonly used for debug messages and other computer- or system-related output.

For incoming data, the manipulator tells its stream what type of numerical data to expect by default. Base prefixes, such as the **0x** prefix, are normally used to determine the base of the number. On some platforms, such as some older UNIX compilers, prefixing the input number with something like a **0x** will cause the stream to read only the first number (that's the **0**), and leave the rest in the stream.

For instance, the following code will read an octal number from the user and write it back to the screen:

```
cout      << endl
          << "Enter an octal number: ";
cin       >> oct >> i2;
cout      << endl
     << "The number was: " << oct << i2 << " Base 10: " << dec << i2 << endl;
```

Note that unlike the modifiers in the previous examples, these do not take any arguments. The following file, **setbase.cpp**, shows how to use some of the manipulators used to set the base of the number read:

```
// File: setbase.cpp
// Example for C++ How-To
// This program demonstrates IO using base manipulators.
```

```cpp
// Copyright 1998, Jan Walter
// NO WARRANTY. If this code breaks you get to keep both pieces.

// Compiler verificiation:
// Borland C++ 5.01A:            Yes
// DJGPP 2.01 w. GCC 2.81 :   Yes
// Watcom 10.5:                    Not Tried
// Microsoft VC++ 5:               Not Tried
// GCC 2.7.2/Linux:              Not tried
// GCC/EGCS/Linux:                 Not tried

#include <iostream.h>
#include <iomanip.h>

#ifdef __BORLANDC__
#pragma hdrstop
#endif

int main ()
{

    double      d1, d2;
    int      i1, i2;


      // note that there are functions to do both of these in the math.h
    // library, but since this is so simple this is easier to do.
      d1 = 22.0 / 7.0 ; // this approximates pi
    d2 = d1 * d1 ;

      i1 = d1 * 100 ;
    i2 = d2 * 1000 ;

    // Setting the base for reading and writing numbers

      cout      << endl
          << "Using the base modifiers affects all integers inserted" << endl
          << "into the stream from that point onwards, like" << endl
          << "setprecision() does for floating point numbers." << endl
          << "double d1 = " << setw(11) << setfill('*') << d1 << '.' << endl
          << "double d2 = " << setw(11) << setfill('*')<< d2 << '.' << endl
          << "int i1 = " << setw(11) << setfill('*') << i1 << '.' << endl
          << "int i1 as hexadecimal = " << setw(11) << hex << i1 << '.' << endl
          << "int i2 = " << setw(11) << dec << i2 << '.' << endl;


      // demonstrate input - different compiler systems' iostreams
    // classes handle this somewhat differently

    cout      << endl
              << "Enter an octal number: ";
    cin     >> oct >> i2;
    cout      << endl
          << "The number was: " << oct << i2 << " Base 10: " << dec << i2 << endl;
```

```
    cin.ignore(3, '\n'); // gets rid of any left over newlines in the input
                         // stream

// wait for keypress routine to prevent os windows from closing when the
// program has completed.

// non-dos (or Windows or OS/2) platforms use the '\r' char
// for the enter key. Sorry, no Mac definition here. You'll have to experiment.
    cout << endl << "Press enter key to continue ..." << endl;
    int c1;
    while( cin && (c1 = cin.get())  != '\n' ) ;


    return 0;
}
// end of file
```

Manipulations Using setf()

Although the other manipulators are inline, that is, placed between <<
operators, the modifications done using **setf()** and **unsetf()** are performed
using these member functions to the stream object.

Good programming practice dictates that all flags should be unset after the
output is completed because other routines, possibly in other people's code,
might assume the flags to be left as defaults.

Alignment

Although on some systems it is possible to set the alignment of text in a field
defined with **setw()**, this is not guaranteed to work on all compilers. It is
confirmed not to work with the GNU and DJGPP **iostreams** libraries, which
are essentially the same. Alignment of numbers is what the alignment setting
was intended for, and it is likely that most library authors will only support
this. Borland's implementation is the notable exception to this case.

The call to set right alignment (which is the default) is shown for the **cout**
class:

```
cout.setf( ios::right )
```

and

```
cout.setf( ios::left )
```

to set numbers to left align in their fields, just as text is by default.

Showing Positive Numbers with a + Sign

By default, only negative numbers are prefixed with a – on output to indicate
they are negative numbers. If desired, this flag can be set to cause the system to
mark positive numbers with a + also.

To get the system to denote positive numbers, use a call like this:

```
cout.setf( ios::showpos )
```

Showing Floating-Point Numbers in Scientific Notation

Scientific notation as displayed on a computer screen is not exactly the way humans would write it on paper—most systems lack superscript, for example. Instead, the significant digits are shown, and then usually a lowercase *e*, and a positive or negative exponent sign. This is particularly useful for showing numbers with most of their significant digits more than six places away from the decimal point by reducing the amount of space used when printing the numbers on the console.

To set the output class to use scientific notation to output floating-point numbers, use the call

```
cout.setf( ios::scientific ) ;
```

Following is the code listing for **setf.cpp**, from the CD-ROM. The code demonstrates some common uses of the **setf()** member function of the **ostream** classes (such as **cout** and the file streams) and shows some common **setf()** calls and their effects.

```
// File: setf.cpp
// Example for C++ How-To
// This program demonstrates using the setf() and unsetf() member functions
// with the iostreams classes.
// Copyright 1998, Jan Walter
// NO WARRANTY. If this code breaks you get to keep both pieces.

// Compiler verificiation:
// Borland C++ 5.01A:            Yes
// DJGPP 2.01 w. GCC 2.81 :    Yes - right align text does not work
// Watcom 10.5:                  Not Tried
// Microsoft VC++ 5:             Not Tried
// GCC 2.7.2/Linux:               Yes - right align text does not work
// GCC/EGCS/Linux:                Yes - right align text does not work

#include <iostream.h>
#include <iomanip.h>

#ifdef __BORLANDC__
#pragma hdrstop
#endif

#include <string> // string includes code with some libraries
                            // this prevents precomiled headers from
                  // being used, and slower compilations.
using namespace std ;
```

```
int main ()
{

    double      d1, d2;
    int      i1, i2;
      string   s1, s2;

      // note that there are functions to do both of these in the math.h
      // library, but since this is so simple this is easier to do.
      d1 = 22.0 / 7.0 ; // this approximates pi
    d2 = d1 * 1000 ;

      i1 = d1 * 100 ;
    i2 = d2 * 1000 ;

// setting text or number alignment

      s1 = "This text is right aligned.";

    cout.setf( ios::right );
      cout      << endl
            << "Width will be set to: " << (s1.size() + 10) << endl
          << setw(s1.size() + 10 ) << s1
          << setw(0) << "." << endl ;


      // unset the right-alignment flag
    cout.unsetf( ios::right ) ;
    s2 = "This text is left aligned.";
    cout      << endl
            << setw(s2.size() + 10) << setfill('x') << s2 << endl
          << endl << setw(0) << setfill(0)
          << setw(10) << i2 << setw(0) << endl ;


      // Showing the base of a number on output.

    cout.setf( ios::showbase ) ;
    cout      << endl
            << "Using setf( ios::showbase ) for numeric output:" << endl
          << "i1 as base10: " << i1 << " Octal: " << oct << i1 << dec << endl
          << "i2 as base10: " << i2 << " Hex:    " << hex << i2 << dec << endl;

      // reset the flag
    cout.unsetf( ios::showbase ) ;

      // show positive sign

    cout.setf( ios::showpos ) ;
    cout      << endl
            << "Using setf( ios::showpos ) for numeric output:" << endl
          << "i1 as base10: " << i1 << " Octal: " << oct << i1 << dec << endl
          << "i2 as base10: " << i2 << " Hex:    " << hex << i2 << dec << endl;
```

```
        cout.unsetf( ios::showpos ) ;

        // using scientific notation for floating point output

        cout.setf( ios::scientific ) ;
        cout        << endl
                    << "Using setf( ios::scientific ) to produce scientific" << endl
              << "notation floating point output." << endl
              << "d1 in scientific notation: " << d1 << endl
              << "d2 in scientific notation: " << d2 << endl;

        cout.unsetf( ios::scientific ) ;

// wait for keypress routine to prevent os windows from closing when the
// program has completed.

// non-dos (or Windows or OS/2) platforms use the '\r' char
// for the enter key. Sorry, no Mac definition here. You'll have to experiment.
    cout << endl << "Press enter key to continue ..." << endl;
    int c1;
    while( cin && (c1 = cin.get())  != '\n' ) ;


    return 0;
}
// end of file
```

Steps

In order to use I/O manipulators, include **iomanip.h** in your source file or common header file. The individual steps depend on the intended format of output.

It's important that you leave your output streams in the default state when your code is finished. This might not matter in the simple examples shown here, but it will come back to bite you if you have to work in conjunction with other programmers or use other people's code.

How It Works

Stream manipulators take a stream reference and possibly some other arguments, perform processing or output into the stream, and then return the stream reference. This has the effect of allowing stream operations to be chained onto each other. In reality, the compiler sees this as a set of nested function calls, rather than a chain of events.

Comments

Probably the most important point is to remember to reset any manipulators you change. Code that comes after yours, either in your functions, library functions, or third-party code, might depend on the flags being set to the defaults. Short programs probably make an exception here, if resetting everything could make up a significant percentage of the lines in the program.

COMPLEXITY

ADVANCED

14.4 How do I...
Make my own stream manipulators?

Problem

Often a specific series of manipulations to the input or output streams is required to be repeated in a program. While this can be accomplished using a regular function (by passing the stream by reference and performing the manipulations there), it is much more convenient to actually write a manipulator. This can be worked into the insertion or extraction operation with a minimum of fuss.

Technique

The technique is similar to overloading the stream insertion and extraction operators—all manipulators take a stream reference as the first argument and return a stream reference. All operations normally done on streams are valid, and it is possible to add characters and other data to the stream as well as manipulate the stream properties themselves.

> **NOTE**
>
> Remember that stream manipulators do have lasting effects, and it is good practice to return the stream to its original state when all operations are complete. This is especially important if the work your code is doing is in a function and part of a larger project—you could affect other programmers' work (or your own) in adverse ways.
>
> The best approach is to have one modify the stream, and another manipulator undo the modifications.

Steps

1. Determine the operations necessary on the stream to get the data into or out of the stream in the way you want.

2. Create a function taking a stream (input or output, depending on the operation) as a reference argument, and returning one.

```
ostream& setfmt( ostream& output )
```

3. In that function, perform all the modifications that need to be done—that is, setting widths, precision, numerical base, and adding any characters or other data to the stream.

```
ostream& setfmt( ostream& output )
{
    output << setw( 9 ) ;
  output.setf( ios:: right ) ;

    return output ;
}
```

4. Create another function to undo the modifications to the stream. This is not necessary if all that happened was that the manipulator inserted some formatting characters into the stream (tabs, dollar signs, or ANSI control sequences).

```
ostream& unsetfmt( ostream& output )
{
    output << setw( 0 ) ;
    output.unsetf( ios:: right ) ;
    output << " degrees." ;

    return output ;
}
```

5. Use the manipulator and the unmanipulator in your code:

```
os << setfmt << write.val() << unsetfmt ;
```

How It Works

Stream operations get their relatively easy-to-learn syntax from the fact that they return stream objects themselves (whose functions can be called, and so on). Manipulators use this syntax too, and that makes it possible to easily hook in in-stream formatting style manipulators when convenient.

The advantages of this technique are

- Reduced chance of formatting errors because some stream manipulator was left out or was not unset.

- Easier-to-understand syntax to the reader or maintainer of the program, provided the manipulators are aptly named.

- More consistent formatting—to change the input or output style of the data, only one function needs to be changed.

The following code listing, `usrmanip.cpp`, shows how to use non-parameterized manipulators:

```
// File: usrmanip.cpp
// Example for C++ How-To
// Writing your own stream manipulators
// Copyright 1998, Jan Walter
// NO WARRANTY. If this code breaks you get to keep both pieces.

// Compiler verificiation:
// Borland C++ 5.01A:          Yes
// DJGPP 2.01 w. GCC 2.81 :   Yes
// Watcom 10.5:              Not Tried
// Microsoft VC++ 5:         Not Tried
// GCC 2.7.2/Linux:          Not tried
// GCC/EGCS/Linux:           Not tried

// This sample program details how to write your own streams manipulators.
// While it is only possible to write manipulators that don't take parameters
// without modifying the actual streams source code (which is beyond the
// scope of this book), the advantages of having only one function to set
// a stream to the way it's needed (and another to return it to its original
// state) are many: it's easier, more clearer for others to understand, and
// less likely to result in program bugs or undesired behavior.

// In this example we will use non-parameterized IO manipulators to set the
// width of numerical output and the alignment of numerical output in one
// operation. This technique can be combined with overloaded insertion and
// extraction operators to make code more readable and less susceptible to
// oversights (i.e. bugs and side effects).

// What the program itself does:
// This program reads standard input for numbers as fractions, numerator and
// then denominator, interpreted as fractions of the angle of full circle
// (i.e. 360 degrees) and converts those to the angle in degrees. For example,
// 25 100 (meaning the fraction of 25 over 100) would be 90 degrees.
//
// The best way to feed data to a program of this type is to put all of the
// numbers into a text file, and then redirect the file into the program's
// standard input using the operating system shell's redirection symbol.
// i.e. usrmanip < angles.txt
//
//     If you choose to enter fractions manually, the letter Ctrl-Z is the
// end-of-file character and will denote to the program that you're finished
// entering data.
```

```cpp
#include <iostream.h>
#include <iomanip.h>

#ifdef __BORLANDC__
#pragma hdrstop
#endif

#include <string>

// The program will define 2 manipulators - one that configures the stream
// to the way we want it for output, and the other one to append some text and
// set it back to the way it was.

ostream& setfmt( ostream& output )
{
    output << setw( 9 ) ;
    output.setf( ios:: right ) ;

    return output ;
}

ostream& unsetfmt( ostream& output )
{
    output << setw( 0 ) ;
    output.unsetf( ios:: right ) ;
    output << " degrees." ;

    return output ;
}


// the class degree abstracts the io and error handling for the reading,
// writing, and calculations of this program.

    // degrees in a full circle.
    const double maxdegrees = 360 ;


class degree
{
    private:

        double      numerator ;
        double      denominator ;

    public:

    // constructors: the default constructor, an initialized constructor,
    // and a copy constructor

    degree() : numerator(0), denominator(0)
    {}
```

```
degree( double num, double dem )
{
    numerator = num ;
  denominator = dem ;
}


// technically, a copy constructor is not required in this case, since
// compilers will generate a memberwise copy constructor in cases like this.
// However, anytime arrays are involved, a copy constructor must be defined,
// since assignment of one array to another actually only copies the address
// of the array, and not the contents. Then it becomes a race to see which
// instance of the class deallocates the memory for the array first - the
// second time the now invalid array gets deallocated the operating system
// will terminate the program with a GPF (Windows, Win32, OS/2) or a
// segmentation fault (UNIX, Linux).
//
// This being said, it's good practice to include one anyway.
degree ( degree& copyfrom )
{
    numerator = copyfrom.numerator ;
  denominator = copyfrom.denominator ;
}

// overloaded assignment operator
degree& operator=( const degree& copyfrom )
{
    numerator = copyfrom.numerator ;
  denominator = copyfrom.denominator ;
  return *this ;
}

// validity operator ! - dividing by zero is an illegal operation from the
// computer's point of view, so we check for this possibility using the
// NOT operator

bool operator!() const
{
    if( denominator == 0.0 ) return true ;
  return false ;
}

// this returns the actual degrees
  double val() const
{
    if( !*this ) // check to see if our data is valid
      return 0.0 ;

  return numerator / denominator * maxdegrees ;
}

};

  // overloaded stream extraction and insertion operators
```

```cpp
istream& operator>>( istream& is, degree& read )
{
     double a, b ;
   is >> a >> b ;
   read = degree(a, b);

   return is ;
}

// decision time: we could put the io manipulators into the output stream
// instead, if we wanted to.

ostream& operator<<( ostream& os, const degree& write )
{
    if( !write ) // data is not valid
         os << "Error!" ;
    else
        os << setfmt << write.val() << unsetfmt ;

    return os ;
}


// the main function actually does the IO handling and printing of the
// copyright.


int main( int, char** )
{

    // the cerr output stream does not get redirected by default,
    // so it's used to print messages that have to make it though to the user

    cerr      << " Fraction to angle calculator." << endl
              << " (c) Jan Walter, 1998. NO WARRANTY." << endl ;

    degree mydegree ;
    int count = 1 ;

    cin >> mydegree ;

    while( cin )
    {
        cout << " Reading " << count++ << " : " <<  mydegree << endl ;
      cin >> mydegree ;
    }

}
// end of file
```

Comments

Using custom I/O manipulators can make code more readable, more trouble-free, and also more maintainable. This is probably one of the least-exploited features of the **iostreams** library. Another advantage is that your program's output will be more consistent.

The criteria I use is that if I have to repeat a formatting sequence more than three times for a given type of data, it's worth my time to put the sequence into a custom modifier to ensure that the output of the program will be more consistent.

15

FILE I/O

How do I...

15.1 Open a file stream?

15.2 Continually read data until the end of file?

15.3 Handle stream errors?

15.4 Read and write binary files?

15.5 Read from or write to different positions in a file?

A great strength of C++ is that stream processing is identical whether the stream is a console, a file, or a memory area. This design was intentional, and along with the inheritance structure of the **IOStreams** library, allows code to be written independent of whether the target stream deals with a file, console, or memory area.

This chapter covers **IOStreams** with a focus on file streams because some issues affect them more visibly. It's not that these issues don't exist with the other streams, but rather that these features are most often used when dealing with files. For instance, **cin** does not need to deal with end-of-file notifications very often because consoles generally do not suddenly end. **cin** would have to account for this, however, if it were fed a redirected file through the shell (consult your operating system or shell manual for information on pipes and redirection).

15.1 Open a File Stream

Console streams `cin` and `cout` are defined automatically in your program. This How-To shows how to work with files in the same way, using the same techniques.

15.2 Continually Read Data Until the End of File

Some sample code in the previous chapter hinted at how this works. This How-To describes how to read data from a file without the last piece appearing twice and other pesky "off-by-one" errors.

15.3 Handle Stream Errors

Errors when handling file streams are much more common than when working with `cout` and `cin`. Most of the techniques here are useful when dealing with other streams as well, but are in highest demand when working with data files.

15.4 Read and Write Binary Files

Binary files are different to deal with than text files. The main reason is that the entire `IOStreams` library is based on converting from human-readable values to machine-readable ones. In this How-To, techniques to bypass this difficulty are discussed, and the advantages of doing so are also covered.

15.5 Read from or Write to Different Positions in a File

Binary data is mainly used for things that need to be accessed quickly, such as databases and other file types. Binary data also has the advantage of having a calculable size. This is ideal for retrieving records using random file access techniques.

COMPLEXITY
BEGINNING

15.1 How do I...
Open a file stream?

Problem

There are lots of options when opening a file stream. What's the best way to open one?

Technique

The `IOStreams` library provides two classes to handle file I/O for your programs. The thing to remember is that the streams `cout`, `cerr`, and `cin` are also technically file streams, as most operating systems treat consoles as regular files. Although this does not usually affect programs, it can be an important point if your program has its input or output redirected.

The Classes

The class that handles writing to a file is called `ofstream`. It is declared like a normal variable, and its most commonly used constructor looks like this:

```
ofstream::ofstream( const char* filename, int openmode = ios::out,
➥int prot = filebuf::openprot);
```

The counterpart to read from a file is `ifstream`. Its constructor looks identical, but operates on different assumptions:

```
ifstream::ifstream( const char* filename, int openmode = ios::in ,
➥int prot = filebuf::openprot);
```

Finally, there is the class that can both read and write to a file. Most C++ systems make this stream for input only by default. It's an `fstream`, and its constructor looks like this:

```
fstream::fstream( const char* filename, int openmode = ios::in,
➥int prot = filebuf::openprot);
```

`filename` is the name of the file you wish to open. Note that even on MS-DOS and related systems, the forward-slash character should be used for directory names, for example `"c:/config.sys"`. The reason is that the backslash character, when followed by certain characters, has special meaning in strings. For instance, the string `"c:\newfile.txt"` will not open that file; the \n sequence translates to a newline sequence. If your program does use the backslash character, denote that by using two backslashes, like `"c:\\newfile"`.

`openmode` is the stream mode, which is defined by the base of all **IOStreams** classes, `ios`. The default (which is probably correct for most uses) is `ios::in`, meaning that the stream should refuse to be written to. Additional values need to be bitwise **or**ed together.

Options include the following:

- `ios::app` will seek to the end of file and assume to be ready to append. This really makes little sense for input streams.

- `ios::ate` will seek to the end of the file when it's open. Again, this usually does not make sense for file streams that will be read from.

- `ios::binary` will open the stream in binary mode. This makes things somewhat different to work with, in that the stream is not parsed by whitespace anymore. This will be covered in a later How-To.

- `ios::trunc` will truncate a file if it exists. This is the default for opening files for writing if neither `ios::app` nor `ios::ate` is specified.

- `ios::nocreate` will cause the stream to fail if the file does not exist. This is implied in most `ofstream` implementations.

- `ios::noreplace` will cause the stream to fail if the file already exists. Use this if you don't want to overwrite anything. This is implied with `ifstreams`.

The constructor's `prot` argument is the file's opening mode. Which modes are supported depends on your operating system (and therefore varies from compiler to compiler). The `IOStreams` library does its best to accommodate everybody, but systems are diverse, so your system might support modes that are not in the stock library. To find out more about the modes that your operating system and compiler support, look at the documentation for `open()` function in `io.h`. By default, all file streams classes open the file in read-write mode, without sharing.

Now that the constructors are covered, a few other things need to be explained:

- A file stream object can be reused by using the `open` and `close` member functions (note that these are different from the `open` and `close` discussed above). The `open` member function takes the same argument as the constructor, and `close` takes no arguments.

- File stream classes automatically close the file they are associated with when they fall out of scope.

Steps

To use file stream classes in your programs:

1. Include the header file `fstream`. The latest compilers (ANSI C++ 3) no longer require the `.h` extension.

```
#include <fstream>
```

2. Declare one of the classes, and open a file either in the constructor or by using the `open` method.

3. Use the class just as you would use `cin` or `cout` objects.

How It Works

These classes share the same base classes as the classes `cin` and `cout`, meaning they have the same functionality with a bit extra added. Because of this, your overloaded insertion and extraction operators should work fine with file streams as well. Just make sure that your overloaded operators work with `istream` and `ostream` objects.

15.2 How do I...
Continually read data until the end of file?

Problem

The program seems to read from the file one more time than it is supposed to. Things such as counters are off by one, and the last item is processed twice.

Technique

This is a common problem for programmers. This particular "off-by-one" error is usually caused by the way the stream is read.

Problem 1: The Reading Loop and Stream Errors

All **IOStreams** overloaded operators return a reference to the stream that can be checked for validity after the attempt to read from the stream. The problem is that most programmers don't realize that reading to the end of the stream is not an error condition. However, attempting to read *past* the end of the stream will cause the stream to go to an "end of file" condition. This is important to remember in processing loops dealing with streams, and it might be necessary to add other conditions to ensure that the loop does not iterate once more than it should.

For instance, the code

```
while ( !inputfile.eof() )
{
    inputfile >> myString ;
    wordcount++ ;
}
```

will definitely cause the loop to execute once more than it should. Even if the last word is read from the file, the `eof()` member function will not return **true** because there is no error condition. The `eof()` function will return **true** on the next iteration because the extraction operator tried to read past the end of the file.

Problem 2: Differing Implementation of the STL and Other Methods of Extracting Data

Because the C++ 3 Standard is so new, it is possible to run into implementations of the STL that are not 100 percent compliant with the standard. For instance, when extracting to a **string** object, these implementations might use different methods of reading from the stream, and possibly reset error conditions.

The sample code provided for this How-To provides two programs that accomplish the same thing: both open a file as a stream, read each line, count the words, lines, and characters, and print statistics at the end of it all including average word lengths. One implementation (**fileread.cpp**) uses STL strings, and the other (**filerea2.cpp**) uses a plain character array and the library function **strlen()** to determine the length. The second example runs identically on all platforms tested, but the first behaves quite differently. The following code is the read processing loop from **fileread.cpp**:

```
while( infile.getline( temp, 128 ) )
   {
        strstream buffer ;
      int pwords = words ;
      lines ++ ;
      buffer << temp << " " << ends ;

      while( buffer >> tmpstring && tmpstring.length() )
      {
         words ++ ;
         totallen += tmpstring.length() ;
         tmpstring = "" ;
      }
   cout << words - pwords << ": " << temp << endl ;
   }
```

The outer **while** loop reads from the input file, line by line. After that, the **infile** object is checked for validity. Because the program counts lines, it was not feasible to pull words directly from the file stream.

Immediately inside the loop, an in-memory stream is declared into which the line is fed. **strstreams** work the same as all other streams, but work on memory areas. The **ends** stream modifier adds the terminating **NULL** byte to denote the end of the stream. The interesting thing here is that Borland C++'s STL string class will generate correct output if the line is terminated with a space before the **ends** modifier, while this throws the STL included with GNU and EGCS compilers off. The code compiles and executes fine, but code compiled by the Borland and GNU compilers does not match.

The inner `while` loop pulls all the individual words out of the in-memory stream, and then sizes and counts them. The additional check for string length and the assignment of an empty string to `tmpstring` are actually unnecessary, but are left there to make absolutely sure the code is not processing an empty string. The following code shows the processing loop from `filerea2.cpp`:

```
while( infile.getline( temp, 128 ) )
    {
        strstream buffer ;
        int pwords = words ;
        lines ++ ;
        buffer << temp << ends ;

        while( buffer >> tmpstring && strlen( tmpstring ))
        {
            words ++ ;
            totallen += strlen( tmpstring ) ;
        }
        cout << words - pwords << ": " << temp << endl ;
    }
```

The preceding code does the same thing as the read processing loop from `fileread.cpp`, except it uses an array of `char` and string functions instead of the `string` class.

The preceding code produces correct code with all compilers I have tested it with. The lesson here is that if time permits, experiment (that is, replace character strings with `string` class objects) when getting results that don't look right from code. Personally, I am surprised at the different output. If you want to compare the output from different compilers, I left the batch file used to compile, link, and execute the two programs using Borland C++ and DJGPP in the same directory as the source file. I used the source files as input for the program, with the output redirected to a file for easy comparison.

Steps

The steps presented are generic rules for ensuring that your code will behave as expected:

1. When reading from a stream with a loop, use code such as

```
while ( infile >> variable )
```

Because the input stream is checked for validity each time the variable is extracted, the condition for the loop will be **false** as soon as it attempts to read past the end of the stream.

2. When reading data from a stream whose format you're not familiar with, use a character array. Until the behavior differences are sorted out between the STL implementations (which should be soon), it is better to read an array of characters from a stream, and use it to initialize a string object to work with.

3. Be aware that one stream error condition is not getting data of the type expected from the stream. If you try to extract an `int` from a stream when the next item in a stream is a set of non-numerical characters, the stream will stop reading there. If you want to handle this in your program instead, read to a temporary character array, and work with that (`strstreams` and STL strings have internal conversion functions, in addition to the runtime library functions).

How It Works

Streams typically only set error conditions if the stream cannot convert the next item in the stream to the type requested, or if an attempt is made to read past the end of the stream. Reading up to the end of a stream will not set the error condition.

COMPLEXITY

INTERMEDIATE

15.3   How do I...
Handle stream errors?

Problem

A stream processing loop stops reading from a file when it encounters an error. This How-To details a way to handle stream errors gracefully.

Technique

In the previous How-To, it was explained that streams only set error conditions when reading unexpected input, or when trying to read past the end of a stream.

The goal now is to deal with the error if it is expected, handle it, and then continue processing.

Stream Error Conditions

IOStreams classes define only three error conditions:

eof: The stream has arrived at the end of the file. This is only set for streams that read.

fail: This is the catch-all error. This can be caused by something as simple as bad input to a hard failure.

bad: The stream had a hard failure. This is usually something beyond the program's control, such as the operating system returning an error, or the file no longer being available (for example, a network connection through which the file was accessed was lost). When writing to a file, this error could mean that the drive the file is on ran out of disk space.

How these errors are handled varies from program to program. Usually handling the bad error state is pretty involved, and varies from operating system to operating system. When dealing with the operating system directly, getting the file descriptor might be useful. This can be done (for file streams) by calling the <filestream name>.rdbuf()->fd() function to get the file descriptor held by the underlying buffer object.

Steps

An effective method for handling streams errors is one that does not affect the readability of the code. The idea is to keep the stream processing as clear as possible to anyone else reading the code and handle the error elsewhere. I tend to put this into a function to keep the potentially ugly code from polluting an otherwise transparent processing loop.

These steps assume that an error condition is handled within a reading loop, but the technique is applicable everywhere.

1. Create a function definition at the beginning of your C++ program file, or in another module, if that is what you prefer.

The prototype should look like this:

```
bool handle_stream_error( istream& );
```

If your code deals with an output stream, use an ostream reference instead.

2. In the file, find the area where the stream is being read from.

Where the code is

```
while( infile >> indata)
```

change it to

```
while(handle_stream_error( infile >> indata ) )
```

The effect of adding a function here minimizes the impact of the error handling code on overall readability.

3. Implement the `handle_stream_error` function as you see fit. For this example, the class handles the three error types, and issues messages on the ones it either can't or should not recover from. The following code shows the implemented `handle_stream_error()` function from `qread2.cpp`:

```
bool handle_stream_error( istream& strm )
{
    // handle our favorite error condition, which is
    // "No error" :)

    if ( strm.good() ) return true ;
     else if ( strm.eof() )
    {
        // handle end of file condition
       cerr << "\nEnd of file reached\n" ;
       // note that endl is not used, as potentially the
       // calling code could want to output something nicely
       // formatted before this message appears on the screen
       return false ;
    }
    else if ( strm.fail() )
    {
      // encompasses the bad condition, so we need to distinguish
      if ( strm.bad() )
      {
          cerr << "\nUnrecoverable Failure.\n" ;
         return false ;
      }

      // we can assume that the error state is invalid input, so
      // we'll handle this by resetting the stream, and pulling
      // one character out and returning ok.
      strm.clear() ;
      while( !isdigit( strm.peek()) && strm )
          int useless = strm.get() ;

      return true ;
    }
    // we fell though the loop for some reason, and some compilers
    // spit out a warning if the following is not there:
     return false ;
}
```

4. Change the processing loop slightly. The preceding error handling function is designed to ignore all characters from the stream. However, when the stream gets an invalid character, it fails first, causing nothing to be read, and leaving the numeric value untouched. This means the processing loop might need to deal with repetitive input. The function could be made to deal with that, but it would detract from the function's inherent reusability (reusable except for one line). The following code shows the reworked processing loop from `qread2.cpp`:

```
if( indata != -1 )
   {
      cout << indata << " " ;
    indata = -1 ;
   }
```

In this case, it was easiest to invalidate the data read from the file and check to see whether the value was changed. Depending on the data, it might be easier to keep the previous value and compare the two. Note that this change does introduce one possible problem: Should a -1 value be read from the file, it will not be processed.

How It Works

In the sample code, the error handling decisions are nicely isolated from the rest of the program. The function receives the `ostream` object after the extraction operation has completed (or been attempted, at least), and can then query the object for its status, handle any predicted errors, and decide whether the loop should continue based on its findings.

In general, file streams differ from other streams in that they have an underlying buffer class that holds file-related things such as the file descriptor. This class is called `filebuf`, and is returned by the file stream's member function `rdbuf()`. This is important for getting further error information from the operating system.

Some systems, such as Win32, might also have some information available though a function that stores the last error encountered. In the case of Win32 specifically, the `GetLastError()` function can be useful.

Comments

The C++ streams classes only perform minimal error handling for the programs that use them. This is simply because handling specific errors in a portable and operating system–independent way is difficult to do well, and the programmer (you) looking for the error knows best the types of error to expect.

To know more about ways to handle specific errors, consult your operating system or compiler documentation.

15.4 How do I...
Read and write binary files?

Problem

The human representations of data in a computer are essentially text. However, this file format is not the most efficient. An eight-digit number will take 8 bytes, plus delimiting spaces, when stored as text, whereas the binary representation is only 4 bytes, with no delimiter required.

Accuracy is also a concern. Floating-point numbers run the risk of losing accuracy every time they are converted to text and back. The default precision of streams output for floating-point numbers is 6, but **double** and **long double** precision floating-point numbers have a much higher degree of accuracy. Again, space is also a concern (standard **float**s in binary form take 4 bytes, **doubles** take 8, and **long doubles** take 10), but it is accuracy that's the bigger concern.

The final concern is performance. Converting text to and from formats that a computer can use for calculations is time-consuming, and this can significantly affect program performance when dealing with large amounts of data. Binary access bypasses all of this, so that in-memory structures can be filled from disk files with a minimum of processing.

Technique

To open a file for writing, open an **ofstream** like this:

```
ofstream myoutfile( "output.dat", ios::out ¦ ios::binary ) ;
```

The key here is the **ios::binary** open mode. Similarly, to read a binary file, an **ifstream** will work with the correct modifier:

```
ifstream myinfile( "input.dat", ios::in ¦ ios::binary ) ;
```

Opening the files, however, is the easiest part. At issue is the core design philosophy of the **IOStreams** library. Its insertion and extraction operators are entirely designed to convert data to and from human representations to something that can be used in the program. Suppose you have the **ofstream** object open, and your code does the following:

```
int myInt = 234, myOtherInt = 556 ;

myoutfile << myInt << myOtherInt ;
```

Both numbers would still be written to the file as text, and it would look like the following if you looked at the contents with the DOS **type** command or the UNIX **cat** command (depending on your system).

```
C:\TEMP> type output.dat
234556
C:\TEMP>
```

If you were to attempt to read the numbers back, you would get only one number, and that would be **234556**. The way to deal with this is to cast the data you want to write to the file to the most fundamental of all data types, the **char**. A **char** is essentially a byte on the machine, and that is what to write to the file.

The **read** and **write** member functions (which the insertion and extraction operators ultimately call) are the easiest way to write simple data types in a binary format. Overloading the insertion and extraction operators is a technique better suited to classes.

The prototypes of the **read** and **write** methods of the streams classes are as follows:

```
istream::read( const char* data, int size ) ;

ostream::write( const char* data, int size ) ;
```

where **data** is a pointer to the data you want to write, and **size** is the size of the data. The **sizeof()** operator would be used to get the size.

The revised example of writing to the binary file (assuming the stream is open, and so on) is

```
int myInt = 234, myOtherInt = 556 ;

myoutfile.write( (char*) &myInt, sizeof(int) ) ;
myoutfile.write( (char*) &myOtherInt, sizeof(int) ) ;
```

To read the data back (again, assuming the stream is open, and so on):

```
int myInt, myOtherInt ;

myinfile.read( (char*) &myInt, sizeof(int) ) ;
myinfile.read( (char*) &myOtherInt, sizeof(int) ) ;
```

The key things here are that the address of the variable is cast to a **char***, and that the size of the data type is the second argument. Some programmers prefer to use the actual variable name rather than the type. Beware of dealing with strings (that is, **null**-terminated character arrays) or other arrays in this manner. **sizeof(myArray)** would be **4** on most systems, regardless of the actual size of the array because **myArray** is just a pointer.

Binary I/O of classes, **struct**s, and other types work exactly the same way.

Steps

The sample code is shared between this How-To and How-To 15.5. Note that these techniques cannot just be applied to an existing program. The choice of how to store data is so fundamental to how a program operates that this decision must be made very early in the design process.

1. Take stock of the stream options available, and open the file stream in binary mode:

```
inline
PhoneDatabase::PhoneDatabase( const char* filename )
    : Datafile( filename, ios::in ¦ ios::out ¦ ios::binary ¦
                ➥ ios::app),
    CurrentRecord(0), current(-1)
{
}
```

The preceding options state to open the file for reading and writing and not to erase the contents. Each operation after the file is opened will seek to the position it needs, so starting at the end of the file is acceptable. It is possible to add a `Datafile.seekg(0)` into the constructor, but the downside is that the code will have to seek to the end again to add new records.

2. For most applications, it is best to isolate complicated I/O operations to a few functions per class. This keeps the code in one place, where it is easier to maintain and troubleshoot. In the sample code, isolate the operations **AddRecord** and **GetRecord**. The following is The implementation of the **AddRecord**, **GetRecord**, and **UpdateRecord** functions in **phone.cpp**:

```
void PhoneDatabase::GetRecord( PhoneRecord& record, int recnum )
{
    if( recnum != current )
    {
        Datafile.seekg( (recnum * sizeof(PhoneRecord)) ) ;
        CurrentRecord = ++recnum ;
    }
    else
        CurrentRecord++ ;

    Datafile.read( (char*) &record, sizeof(PhoneRecord)) ;
}

void PhoneDatabase::UpdateRecord( const PhoneRecord& record,
                                  ➥int recnum )
{
    if( recnum != current )
    {
```

```
        Datafile.seekp( (recnum * sizeof(PhoneRecord)) ) ;
          CurrentRecord = recnum++ ;
   }
   else
     CurrentRecord++ ;

   Datafile.write( (char*) &record, sizeof(PhoneRecord)) ;
}

void PhoneDatabase::AddRecord( const PhoneRecord& record )
{
    Datafile.seekp( 0, ios::end ) ;
    CurrentRecord = Datafile.tellp() / sizeof(PhoneRecord) + 1 ;
    Datafile.write( (char*) &record, sizeof(PhoneRecord) ) ;
}
```

In the preceding code, the class keeps track of the record to which the
database is currently pointing. This will be used to facilitate sequential
processing (using the overloaded >> and << operators).

3. Build surrounding I/O functions as you see fit. In the case of the example,
the class managing the database was given stream-like operators for linear
processing of records. The following code shows higher-level I/O
operations for the data in **phone.cpp**:

```
// Overloaded operators for sequential reading

PhoneDatabase& operator<<( PhoneDatabase& strm,
                          ⇒const PhoneRecord& data )
{
    strm.AddRecord( data ) ;
  return strm ;
}

PhoneDatabase& operator>>( PhoneDatabase& strm,
                          ⇒ PhoneRecord& data )
{
    strm.GetRecord( data, strm.current );
    return strm ;
}
```

These functions are designed to behave identically to the functions used
in regular stream processing from the user's point of view. Other functions
were implemented to facilitate importing data from a text file and printing
data to the screen. Because these are based on true streams, they deal with
the text mode **istream** and **ostream** objects. These functions are there to
be used in importing and exporting data from text. Note in the following
code the extra processing required to work with the same data in text
mode.

```
// overloaded operators for the record structure

inline
ostream& operator<< (ostream& strm, const PhoneRecord& data )
{
    strm            << data.FirstName << " "
                 << data.LastName << " "
            << data.AreaCode << " "
            << data.PhoneNumber << " ";
    if( !strlen( data.Extension ) )
        strm  << "0 ";
    else
        strm  << data.Extension << " " ;

    return strm;
}

inline
istream& operator>> (istream& strm, PhoneRecord& data )
{
    strm            >> data.FirstName
            >> data.LastName
            >> data.AreaCode
            >> data.PhoneNumber
            >> data.Extension ;
    if( !strcmp( "0", data.Extension ) )
            data.Extension[0] = '\0' ;

    return strm ;
}
```

These functions do more processing than their binary counterparts, and are slower to execute.

4. Implement error checking. There should be some way for the program using your class to see whether there has been a problem, and to deal with it. Functions to overload the typecasting of the managing class to a **boolean** type can make possible syntax such as **while(db >> records)** for use in processing data. Alternately, your class can internalize error handling completely. This can be difficult because the class created could be used in ways that were not initially accounted for in the design. The following code shows the error reporting and handling functions for the **PhoneDatabase** class in **phone.cpp**:

```
bool operator!() ;
    bool bad() { return Datafile.bad() ; }
    bool good() { return Datafile.good() ; }
    bool fail() { return Datafile.fail() ; }
    void clear() { Datafile.clear() ; }
```

```
    // overloaded typecasts to allow while( dbname >> record )
    // style code
    operator bool() { return Datafile.good(); }
...
inline
bool PhoneDatabase::operator!()
{
    if( !Datafile ) return false ;
    return true ;
}
```

Most of the functions query the **fstream** object that the object contains. The idea was to emulate the error functions of a true stream class. The overloaded typecast operator is very useful for loops (as indicated by the comments).

How It Works

Reading and writing binary data is more straightforward than text in many ways. There is no need to worry about parsing the data at all—it is ready to be used as soon as it has been read from disk. The complexities arise more from the format chosen to write to disk with than from the actual operation. Database files for commercial programs add much more than the raw data into headers, such as lists of free blocks in the files, which blocks are taken, and perhaps even the structure of the data or the data type in the file.

The key points when dealing with reading and writing binary data are

- Remember not to use the built-in stream extraction and insertion operators. They are designed specifically for text. Overload your own if you must.

- A binary stream will never receive invalid data. As long as the bytes are coming, they are valid. If you need some sort of error check for validity, consider adding some set value to the structure and checking it to make sure the read alignment is on.

- Try to keep the reading and writing of binary data confined to a few functions. This will make troubleshooting easier, as well as maintenance.

- Byte alignment settings will affect the size of the structures written to disk. This can be a problem to deal with when making different versions of a program interact, as well as different operating system platforms.

- Byte ordering is also something to consider when moving data between platforms. Because the program is dealing with binary data, it is vulnerable to differences in the in-memory representation of that data. This is not necessarily the same for all processors, or even all operating systems.

Comments

There are fewer rules for working with raw binary data, but also more things to watch for. This puts the responsibility for an effective implementation more on the programmer. One useful strategy is emulating the streaming functionality and error handling because they are easy to understand for C++ programmers.

COMPLEXITY
INTERMEDIATE

15.5 How do I...
Read from or write to different positions in a file?

Problem

Without the ability to move arbitrarily to different locations in a file, data would have to be read in the same order it was written. This is inconvenient, and all streams objects contain the functionality to move to different locations in the stream.

Technique

IOStreams classes implement two functions to facilitate moving around in a stream. An internal representation of a read/write stream (such as an **fstream**) contains both a read location and a write location (which are not guaranteed to be pointing at the same location in the stream).

Another thing to keep in mind when working with file streams (and streams in general) is that they are essentially like arrays. An array has an index, and the index moves ahead as your code extracts data from the stream. When code inserts items into a stream, it is like appending data to the array. Seeking is just a matter of repositioning the index in the array. Some streams don't have a meaningful beginning; for instance, seeking to the beginning to the **cout** stream does nothing useful. File streams, however, do have a distinct beginning and an end, and that is what makes seeking in these streams worthwhile.

The difference between an array and a stream is that a stream is self-managing. The stream knows where the data is supposed to go, and does its best to make sure everything you feed to the stream gets to where you told the stream to put it.

Stream Position Functions

The following function prototypes are available for working with streams:

Table 15.1 Position-Related Stream Member Functions

`streampos istream::tellg()`	Returns the current position of the input stream.
`streampos ostream::tellp()`	Returns the current position of the output stream.
`istream& istream::seekg` `( streampos position )`	Moves to the absolute position given by position in the stream.
`istream& istream::seekg` `( streamoff offset, seek` `_dir direction )`	Moves a set number of bytes based on the current position. `seek_dir` is an `enum` that's declared in the `ios` base class. `ios::beg` means to seek from the beginning of the file, `ios::cur` means seek forward from the current position (if `offset` is negative, it means backward), and `ios::end` seeks from the end of the file (which means a negative `offset` should be specified because the stream cannot go further forward).
`ostream& ostream::seekp` `( streampos position )`	Moves to the absolute position in the output stream.
`ostream& ostream::seekp` `( streamoff offset, seek` `_dir direction )`	Moves to a relative position in the stream. See istream::seekg earlier in this table.

The preceding positioning member functions are present in any stream, but vary somewhat in implementation. The positional arguments (`offset` and `position` for the preceding functions) are usually `long` values (hence, the common operating system limitation of a 2GB maximum file size), but this is highly compiler dependent. Most compilers use a defined type that the compiler can easily cast to from a `long` value, but might support larger numbers. Unless your program needs to work with files larger than 2GB, you are safe in believing that these parameters are `long` values. Beyond that, it is time to delve into your compiler documentation.

Seeking Strategies

Using the seek function is usually only useful when dealing with binary streams. It is most commonly used for database or database-like operations in which records are fetched from a data file. To get to a certain record stored in a binary file, the location of the record must be calculated. This calculation is usually a multiple of the record size; for example, `sizeof(myRecord)*2` would be the start position of the third record in the file. The following function (from `file.cpp`) demonstrates random record access for the data file:

```
void PhoneDatabase::GetRecord( PhoneRecord& record, int recnum )
{
    if( recnum != current )
    {
        Datafile.seekg( (recnum * sizeof(PhoneRecord)) ) ;
        CurrentRecord = ++recnum ;
    }
    else
        CurrentRecord++ ;

    Datafile.read( (char*) &record, sizeof(PhoneRecord)) ;
}
```

What's the best way to work with data in files? It depends on the data. It is possible to abstract this any number of ways. For some kinds of data, it's possible to overload the array index `operator[]` to implement random access. This can be implemented either by accessing a function like the preceding code (to keep the code that actually fetches things in one place for easy maintainability), or by directly accessing the file stream object. For sequential access, your database file management class can be given a stream-like interface, but records can be streamed instead of streaming fundamental data types.

Using overloading, it's possible to stream objects out of a database and to an output stream using code that looks very familiar:

```
cout << rec << endl ;

    while( db >> rec )
    {
        cout << rec << endl ;
    }
```

This technique is useful any time anything sequential needs to be done. This does not necessary reflect that the *underlying* data has to be sequential. For instance, a SQL query class might allow the returned result records to be accessed sequentially using this method.

Steps

Using the ability to seek in a stream is very data dependent. The details of these techniques are used in the sample phonebook program, `sample.cpp`. Using the ability to seek should never be added to an existing program because it's so fundamental to the way data is handled.

1. Seek functions see the data file as an array of bytes, and it's up to your program to determine from what point to start interpreting data. Usually, it will be some multiple of the size of the data type in the file, or some offset (for any leading information) plus some multiple of the record stored.

2. Seek functions for reading use the `seekg` member function, as demonstrated in the following code:

```cpp
void PhoneDatabase::GetRecord( PhoneRecord& record, int recnum )
{
   if( recnum != current )
   {
      Datafile.seekg( (recnum * sizeof(PhoneRecord)) ) ;
      CurrentRecord = ++recnum ;
   }
   else
      CurrentRecord++ ;

   Datafile.read( (char*) &record, sizeof(PhoneRecord)) ;
}
```

3. When seeking to write to a location to a file, use the `seekp` member function, as shown in the following:

```cpp
void PhoneDatabase::UpdateRecord( const PhoneRecord& record,
                                  ➡ int recnum )
{
   if( recnum != current )
   {
       Datafile.seekp( (recnum * sizeof(PhoneRecord)) ) ;
       CurrentRecord = recnum++ ;
   }
   else
     CurrentRecord++ ;

   Datafile.write( (char*) &record, sizeof(PhoneRecord)) ;
}
```

4. Seeking from the current position accepts both positive and negative values, the following code demonstrates using `tellp()` and a relative `seekp()` function.

```
void PhoneDatabase::AddRecord( const PhoneRecord& record )
{
    Datafile.seekp( 0, ios::end ) ;
    CurrentRecord = Datafile.tellp() / sizeof(PhoneRecord) + 1 ;
    Datafile.write( (char*) &record, sizeof(PhoneRecord) ) ;
}
```

The technique for finding the current record index based on the file position is also shown in the preceding code.

How It Works

As mentioned earlier, seek methods view a binary data file as an array of bytes. This gives the programmer the freedom to implement any required sort of structure in the disk file. Some file formats become quite elaborate. Complexity is the flip side of the coin—the more complex the file format, the more complex the code to read data from the file, and the greater the chance of a programming error.

Comments

When working with binary files, and especially when designing your own file format, simplicity is the goal to keep in mind. Many subtle errors can be introduced into a program when code that works with binary data miscalculates the offset in the file it is to read from. Another thing to keep in mind is that most binary data, such as floating-point numbers and integers, is not human-readable in binary form, which makes debugging of subtle file format errors even more difficult.

PART VII
APPENDIXES

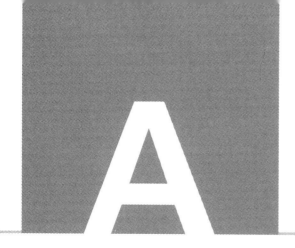

NAMESPACES

Being a member of the C++ standardization committee, it's not hard to guess what my opinion is. Seriously, Java and C++ differ radically from one another in many respects. One of them is compiler writing. Bjarne Stroustrup addresses this issue: "the overall principle [is] that where there is a choice between inconveniencing compiler writers and annoying users, the compiler writers should be inconvenienced" (*The Evolution of C++*, ISBN 026273107x, page 50). My experience with Java has led me to conclude that its designers adopted the opposite approach: simple compiler writing at the cost of programmer's drudgery. Some examples of this are the exclusion of operator overloading, **enum** types, and default arguments. They do not incur overhead of any kind, and no one doubts their importance and usefulness. Yet they make a compiler writer's work more difficult.

Namespaces are very different from packages. Both provide a mechanism for name clashing prevention, but remember that namespaces allow a fine-grained control on the extent to which declarations are injected to a scope. A using-declaration enables the user to inject only a single constituent, and a fully qualified name is even finer. Koenig lookup is also meat to ease the life of a programmer. No equivalents exist in Java.

Namespaces were introduced to the C++ Standard in 1995. This appendix will explain what namespaces are, how and when they should be used, and why they were added to the language. Finally, this appendix will discuss the way namespaces interact with other language features.

THE RATIONALE BEHIND NAMESPACES

To understand why namespaces were added to the language in the first place, let's use an analogy. Imagine that the file system on your computer didn't have directories and subdirectories at all. All files would be stored in a flat repository, visible all the time to every user and application. As a consequence, extreme difficulties would arise. Filenames would clash (with some systems limiting a filename to 8 characters and 3 more characters for the extension, this is likely to happen); simple actions such as listing, copying, and searching files would be much more difficult. In addition, security and authorization restrictions would be severely compromised.

Namespaces in C++ are equivalent to directories. They can be nested easily, they protect your code from name clashes, they allow you to hide declarations, and they do not incur any runtime or memory overhead. Most of the components of the C++ Standard Library are grouped under namespace `std`. Namespace `std` is subdivided into additional namespaces such as `std::rel_ops`, which contains the definitions of STL's overloaded operators.

A BRIEF HISTORICAL BACKGROUND

In the early 1990s, when C++ was making its way as a general-purpose programming language, many vendors were shipping proprietary implementations of various component classes. Class libraries for string manipulations, mathematical functions, and containers were integral parts of frameworks such as MFC, STL, OWL, and others. The proliferation of reusable components caused a name clashing problem—a class named `vector`, for instance, could appear both in a mathematical library and a separate container library that were used at the same time. It was impossible for the compiler and the linker to distinguish between the identical names of two different classes.

LARGE-SCALE PROJECTS ARE SUSCEPTIBLE TO NAME CLASHES

Name clashes are not confined to vendors' frameworks. In large-scale software projects, short and elegant names for types and functions can also cause name conflicts because the same name might be used more than once to denote different entities. In the pre-namespace era, the only workaround was to use various affixes in identifiers' names. This practice, however, is tedious and error prone:

```
class string { // short but dangerous. someone else may have
picked this name already...
        //...
};

class excelSoftCompany_string { // a long name is safer but
tedious. A nightmare if company changes its name...
        //...
}
```

Namespaces allow you to use convenient, short, and intelligible names safely. Instead of repeating the unwieldy affixes time after time, you can group your classes and functions in a namespace and factor out the recurring affix like this:

```
//file excelSoftCompany.h
namespace excelSoftCompany { // a namespace definition

        class string {/*..*/};
        class vector {/*..*/};
}
```

PROPERTIES OF NAMESPACES

Namespaces are more than just name containers. They were designed to allow fast, simple, and efficient migration of legacy code without inflicting overhead of any kind. Namespaces have several properties that facilitate their usage.

A FULLY QUALIFIED NAME

A namespace is a scope in which declarations and definitions are grouped together. In order to refer to any of these from another scope, a fully qualified name is required. The fully qualified name of an identifier consists of its namespaces(s), followed by scope resolution operator, then its class name, and finally, the identifier itself. Because both namespaces and classes can be nested, the resulting name can be rather long, yet it ensures unique identification:

```
size_t maxPossibleLength =
  std::string::npos;  //a fully qualified name. npos is a member
of string; string  belongs to namespace std
```

However, repeating the fully qualified name is tedious and less readable. In general, a **using**-declaration or a **using**-directive is preferred.

A USING-DECLARATION AND A USING-DIRECTIVE

A **using**-declaration consists of the keyword **using** followed by *namespace::member*. It instructs the compiler to locate every occurrence of a certain identifier (type, operator, function, constant, and so on) in the specified namespace, as if the fully qualified name were supplied:

```
#include <vector>  //STL vector; belongs to namespace std
void main()
{
   using std::vector;  //using declaration; every occurrence of
vector is looked up in std
   vector <int> vi; // instead of std::vector<int>
}
```

A using-directive, on the other hand, instructs the compiler to recognize all members of a namespace and not just one. It consists of the following sequence: using namespace followed by a *namespace-name*. For example:

```
#include <vector>    // belongs to namespace std
#include <iostream> // iostream classes and operators are also in
namespace std
void main()
{
  using namespace std; // a using-directive; all <iostream> and
<vector> declarations  now accessible
  vector  <int> vi;
  vi.push_back(10);
  cout<<vi[0];
}
```

Let's look back at the string class example (the code is repeated here for convenience).

```
//file excelSoftCompany.h
namespace excelSoftCompany {

        class string {/*..*/};
        class vector {/*..*/};
}
```

You can access your own string class as well as the ANSI string class in the same program now.

```
#include <string> //ANSI string class
#include "excelSoftCompany.h"

void main()
{
using namespace excelSoftCompany;
string s; //referring to class excelSoftCompany::string

std::string standardstr; //now instantiate an ANSI string object
}
```

NAMESPACES ARE OPEN

The C++ standardization committee was well aware of the fact that related declarations can span across several translation units. Therefore, a namespace can be defined in parts. For example:

```
  //file proj_const.h
namespace MyProj {
  enum NetProtocols {
             TCP_IP,
             HTTP,
             UDP
             }; // enum
}
```

```
//file proj_classes.h
namespace MyProj { //now extending MyProj namespace
        class RealTimeEncoder{ public: NetProtocols detect()
{return UDP;}
                                        //other class members
                        };

        class NetworkLink {};

        class UserInterface {};
}
```

In a separate file, the same namespace can be extended with additional declarations.

The complete namespace can be extracted from both files like this:

```
//file app.cpp

#include "proj_const.h"
#include "proj_classes.h"

void main() {
    using namespace MyProj;
    RealTimeEncoder encoder;
    NetProtocols protocol = encoder.detect();

}//end main
```

NAMESPACE ALIASES

Choosing a short name for a namespace can eventually lead to a name clash. Yet very long namespaces are not easy to use. For this purpose, namespace aliases can be used. The following sample defines an alias, **ESC**, of the unwieldy Excel_Software_Company namespace.

```
//file decl.h
namespace Excel_Software_Company {
class Date {/*..*/};
class Time {/*..*/};
}

//file calendar.cpp
#include "decl.h"
void main()
{
namespace ESC = Excel_Software_Company; //ESC is an alias for
Excel_Software_Company
ESC::Date date;
ESC::Time time;
}
```

KOENIG LOOKUP

Andrew Koenig, one of the forefathers of C++, devised an algorithm for resolving namespace members' lookup. This algorithm is used in all Standard-conforming compilers to handle cases like the following:

```
namespace MINE {
  class C {};
  void func(C);
}

MINE::C c; // global object of type MINE::C

void main() {
  func( c ); // OK, MINE::f called
}
```

No using-declaration or using-directive exists in the program. Still, the compiler did the right thing by applying Koenig lookup. How does Koenig lookup work?

Koenig lookup instructs the compiler to look not just at the usual places such as the local scope, but also at the namespace that contains the argument's type. Thus, in the following source line the compiler detects that the object c, which is the argument of the function f, belongs to namespace MINE. Consequently, the compiler looks at namespace MINE to locate the declaration of f.

```
func( c ); // OK, MINE::f called
```

NAMESPACES DO NOT INCUR ADDITIONAL OVERHEAD

The underlying implementation of namespaces is by means of name mangling. The compiler incorporates the function name with its list of arguments, class name, and namespace in order to create a unique name for it. Therefore, namespaces do not incur runtime or memory overhead.

THE INTERACTION OF NAMESPACES WITH OTHER LANGUAGE FEATURES

Namespaces affect other features of the language as well as programming techniques. For example, namespaces make some features superfluous or undesirable.

:: OPERATOR SHOULD NOT BE USED TO DESIGNATE A GLOBAL FUNCTION

In some frameworks (MFC, for instance), it is customary to add the scope resolution operator, ::, before a global function's name to mark it explicitly as a function that is not a class member. For example:

```
void String::operator = (const String& other)
{
 ::strcpy (this->buffer, &other); // strcpy is preceded by ::
operator, not a good idea
}
```

This practice is not recommended anymore. Many of the standard functions that used to be global are now grouped under namespaces. For example, strcpy now belongs to namespace std, as do most of the Standard library's functions. Preceding these functions with the scope resolution operator will stymie the lookup algorithm of the compiler, resulting in compilation errors. Therefore, it's advisable to use the function's name without the scope resolution operator.

TURNING AN EXTERNAL FUNCTION INTO A FILE-LOCAL FUNCTION

In standard C, a function declared as static has an internal linkage; it is accessible only from within the translation unit (source file) in which it is declared. This technique is used to support information hiding, such as in the following sample:

```
//File hidden.c

static void decipher(FILE *f);//function accessible only from
within this file

//now use this function in the current source file

decipher ("passwords.bin");

//end of file
```

Though still supported in C++, this convention is now considered a deprecated feature, which means that future releases of your compiler might issue a warning message when finding a static function that is not a member of a class. To make a function accessible only from within the translation unit in which it is declared, you should use a nameless namespace instead. You might do that, for instance, when you migrate C code. The following example demonstrates this technique:

```
//File hidden.cpp

namespace { //nameless
  void decipher(FILE *f); //accessible only from within this file
}

  //now use the function in the current source file. No 'using'
declarations or directives are needed.
decipher ("passwords.bin");
```

It is guaranteed that nameless namespaces in different source files are unique. If you declare another function with the same name in a nameless namespace of another file, the two functions are hidden from one another and their names do not clash.

STANDARD HEADERS NAMES

All Standard C++ header files now have to be #included in the following way:

```
#include <iostream> //note: no ".h" extension
```

That is, the .h extension is omitted. This convention applies to the Standard C header files as well, with the addition of the letter c affixed to their name. A C Standard header formerly named <xxx.h> is now <cxxx>. For example:

```
#include <cassert> //formerly: <assert.h>  note the prefix 'c'
and the omission of  ".h"
```

The older convention for C headers, <xxx.h>, is still supported, but is now considered deprecated and should not be used in new C++ code. The reason is that C <xxx.h> headers would inject their declarations into the global namespace. In C++, most standard declarations are grouped under namespace std, and so are the <cxxx> Standard C headers. No inference should be drawn from the actual name convention used on the physical location of a header file or its underlying name. In fact, most implementations share a single physical file for both the <xxx.h> and its corresponding <cxxx> notation. This is feasible due to some under-the-hood preprocessor tricks. This convention eliminates name conflicts that might occur when global declarations are used. Remember that you must have a using-declaration, a using-directive, or a fully qualified name in order to access the declarations in the new-style standard headers:

```
#include <cstdio>
using namespace std; //using directive

void f(){
      printf ("Hello World\n");
}
```

RESTRICTIONS ON NAMESPACES

The C++ Standard defines several restrictions on the use of namespaces. These restrictions are meant to avert anomalies or ambiguities that would create havoc in the language.

NAMESPACE STD MAY NOT BE MODIFIED

Generally, namespaces are open. It is perfectly legal to expand existing namespaces with additional declarations and definitions across several files. The only exception to the rule is namespace **std**. According to the Standard, the result of modifying namespace **std** with additional declarations—let alone a removal of existing ones—yields undefined behavior and should therefore be avoided. This restriction might seem arbitrary, but it's just common sense—any attempt to tamper with namespace **std** undermines the very concept of a namespace dedicated exclusively to standard declarations.

USER-DEFINED NEW AND DELETE CANNOT BE DECLARED IN A NAMESPACE

The Standard prohibits declarations of **new** and **delete** operators in a namespace. To see why, consider the following example:

```
char *pc; //global
namespace A {
  void operator new ( size_t );
  void operator delete ( void * );

  void func ()
  {
    pc = new char ( 'a'); //using A::new
  }
}

void f() { delete pc; } // which version of delete to call,
A::delete or standard delete?
```

Some programmers expect the operator `A::delete` to be selected because it matches the operator **new** that was used to allocate the storage. Others expect the standard operator **delete** to be called because `A::delete` is not visible in function **f**. By prohibiting declarations of **new** and **delete** in a namespace, this hassle is avoided.

COMMENTS

Namespaces were the latest addition to the C++ Standard. Therefore, not all existing compilers support this feature yet. However, all compiler vendors will provide namespace-supporting compilers in the near future. The importance of namespaces cannot be over-emphasized. As you have seen, any non-trivial C++ program uses components of the Standard Template Library, the `iostream` library, and other standard header files—all of which are now declared in namespace `std`.

C++ offers three methods for injecting a namespace constituent into the current scope. The first is a `using`-directive, which injects all of the members of a namespace into the current scope. The second is a `using`-declaration, which is more selective and enables the injection of a single component from a namespace. Finally, a fully qualified name uniquely identifies a namespace member. However, namespaces provide more than a mechanism for the prevention of name clashing; they can streamline the process of version control by assigning different namespaces to a namespace alias. In addition, the argument-dependent lookup, or Koenig lookup, captures the programmer's intention without forcing him or her to use explicit references to a namespace.

RUNTIME TYPE INFORMATION

One of the fundamental principles of object-oriented programming is *polymorphism*, which is the ability of different objects to react in an individual manner to the same message. Polymorphism is widely used in natural languages. Consider the verb "to close." It means different things when applied to different objects. Closing a door, closing a bank account, and closing a program's window are all different actions; the exact meaning of closing depends on the object on which the action is performed. Similarly, polymorphism in object-oriented programming means that the interpretation of a message depends on its object. In C++, polymorphism is implemented via static and dynamic binding. Dynamic binding is a delayed resolution of which function is invoked. The resolution in dynamic binding is delayed until runtime. Static binding, on the other hand, resolves function calls at compile-time.

STATIC BINDING

C++ has two mechanisms for implementing static polymorphism:

- *Operator overloading.* Applying operator +=, for example, to an `int` or a `string` is interpreted by each of these objects in an individual manner. But the results can be predicted intuitively, and some similarities can be found between the two.

- *Templates.* A `vector<int>` and a `vector<string>` react differently; that is, they execute a different set of instructions when they receive the same message. However, close behaviors can be expected. For example:

```
vector < int > vi;  vector < string > names;
string name("Bjarne");
vi.push_back( 5 ); // add an integer at the end of the vector
names.push_back (name); //add a string at the end of the vector
```

DYNAMIC BINDING

Dynamic binding takes the notion of polymorphism one step further. In dynamic binding, the meaning of a message depends on the object, but the exact type of the object can be determined only at runtime. Virtual member functions are a good example of that. The specific version of a virtual function is unknown at compile time. Therefore, the call resolution is delayed until runtime. Here is an example:

```
#include <iostream>
using namespace std;

class base{
  public: virtual void f() { cout<< "base"<<endl;}
};

class derived : public base{
  public: void f() { cout<< "derived"<<endl;} //overrides base::f
};

void identify(base & b) { // the argument can be an instance of base or any
                          // object derived from it
  b.f(); // which f should be invoked base::f or derived::f? resolution is
         // delayed to runtime
}
void main()
{
  derived d;
  identify(d); // argument is an object derived from base
}
```

Please note that the function **identify** can receive any object derived from class **base**, even objects of subclasses that were defined after **identify** was compiled.

Dynamic binding has enormous advantages. In this example, it enables the user to extend the functionality of **base** without modifying **identify** in any way. In procedural programming, such flexibility is impossible. Furthermore, the underlying mechanism of dynamic binding is automatic. The programmer doesn't need to implement the code for runtime lookup and dispatch of a virtual function, nor does he or she need to check the dynamic type of the object. Still, under some circumstances, detecting of the dynamic type of an object is unavoidable. In this appendix, you will learn when and how runtime type information (RTTI) is used.

Virtual Functions

Suppose you have to develop a file manager application that is a component of a GUI-based operating system. The files in the system are represented as icons that respond to a right-click of a mouse, and display a menu with options such as open, close, read, and so on. The underlying implementation of the file system relies on a class hierarchy that represents files of various types. A well-designed class hierarchy usually has an abstract class serving as an interface:

```
class File { //abstract
  public: virtual void open() =0; //pure virtual member function
  public: virtual void read() =0;
  public: virtual void write() =0;
  public: virtual ~File () =0;
};
```

At a lower level in the hierarchy is a set of derived classes that implement the common interface. Each of these classes represents a different family of files. To simplify the discussion, let's assume there are only two file types in the system: binary .exe files and text files.

```
class BinaryFile : public File {
public:
  void open () { OS_execute(this); }  //implement the pure virtual function
  //...other member functions
};
class TextFile : public File {
public:
 void open () { Activate_word_processor (); } //implement pure virtual function
 //other member functions of File are implemented here
 void virtual print();  // an additional member function
};
```

The pure virtual function **open** is implemented in every derived class according to the type of the file. Therefore, a **TextFile** object activates a word processor, whereas a **BinaryFile** object invokes the operating system's API function **OS_execute**, which in turn executes the program stored in the binary file.

There are several differences between a binary file and a text file. For example, a text file can be printed directly on a screen or a printer because it consists of a sequence of printable characters. Conversely, a binary file with an .exe extension contains a stream of bits. Therefore, such a file cannot be printed or displayed on a screen directly. It must be converted to a text file first, usually by a utility that translates the binary data into its symbolic representations. For instance, the sequence **0110010** can be replaced by a corresponding *move esp, ebp* assembly directive. Therefore, the member function **print** is declared only in class **TextFile**.

In this file manager, a right-click of a mouse on a file icon opens a menu of messages (options) to which the object can respond. For that purpose, the operating system has a function that takes a reference to a **File**:

```
OnRightClick (File & file); //operating system's API function
```

Obviously, no object of class **File** can be instantiated because **File** is an abstract class. However, the function **OnRightClick** can accept any object *derived* from **File**. For instance, when the user right-clicks on a file icon and chooses the Open option, **OnRightClick** invokes the virtual member function **open** of its argument, and the appropriate member function is called.

```
OnRightClick (File & file) //operating system's API function
{
  switch (message){
  //...
  case m_open:
    file.open();
  break;
  }
}
```

So far, so good. You have implemented a polymorphic class hierarchy and a generic function that does not depend on the dynamic type of its argument. In this case, the language support for virtual functions was sufficient for the purpose; no explicit RTTI was required. Well, not exactly. You might have noticed that file printing was not addressed. Let's look at the definition of class **TextFile** again:

```
class TextFile : public File {
public:
  void open () { Activate_word_processor (); } //implement the pure virtual
                                               //function
  void virtual print();
};
```

The member function **print** is not a part of the common interface implemented by all files in this system. It would be a design error to move it to the abstract class **File** because binary files are nonprintable and cannot define a meaningful operation for it. Then again, **OnRightClick** has to support file printing when it handles a text file. In this case, ordinary polymorphism in the form of virtual member functions is insufficient. All that **OnRightClick** knows about its argument is that the argument is derived from `File`, which isn't enough to tell whether the actual object is printable or not. Clearly, `OnRightClick` needs more information about the dynamic type of its argument to handle file printing properly. This is where the need for runtime type information arises.

HISTORICAL BACKGROUND

Originally, C++ did not support RTTI. Furthermore, its creators balked at the idea of adding RTTI support to C++ for at least two reasons. First, they wanted to preserve backward compatibility with C. Second, they were concerned about efficiency. Other RTTI-enabled languages, such as Smalltalk and LISP were characterized by sluggish performance. C++ designers attempted to preserve the efficiency of C. Still, it became apparent that under some circumstances, static type checking alone was insufficient. The addition of multiple inheritance (and consequently, virtual inheritance) to C++ in 1989 gave overwhelming ammunition to the proponents of RTTI.

> **NOTE**
>
> Multiple inheritance will not be discussed here. Nonetheless, it is important to note that RTTI is required when virtual inheritance is used.

Eventually, the C++ standardization committee approved the addition of RTTI to the language. Two new operators, `dynamic_cast<>` and `typeid`, were added to C++ to support RTTI. In addition, the class `type_info` was added to the Standard Library.

RTTI CONSTITUENTS

RTTI Is Applicable to Polymorphic Objects Exclusively

It is important to realize that RTTI is applicable to polymorphic objects solely. A class must have at least one virtual member function in order to have RTTI support for its objects. C++ does not offer RTTI support for non-polymorphic classes and primitive types. This restriction is just common sense—a `double` or a `string` cannot change its type at runtime. Therefore, there is no point in detecting its dynamic type—it is identical to the static type anyway. But there is another reason for confining RTTI support to polymorphic classes. As you probably know, every object that has at least one virtual member function also contains a special data member added by the compiler. This member is a pointer to the virtual function table. The runtime type information is stored in this table as a pointer to a `const type_info` object.

Class `type_info`

For every distinct polymorphic type, C++ instantiates a corresponding RTTI object that contains the necessary runtime type information. The RTTI object is an instance of the standard class `type_info` (defined in the standard header `<typeinfo>`). The `type_info` object is owned by C++, and may not be altered in any way by the programmer. The implementation-independent part of `type_info` looks like the following (source: *ANSI/ISO Final Draft International Standard of the C++ Programming Language*, ISO/IEC 14882: 1998):

```
namespace std { //class type_info is declared in namespace std
  class type_info {
  public:
    virtual ~type_info(); //may be subclassed
    bool operator==(const type_info&  rhs ) const; // comparison; return true
                                                   // if *this == rhs
    bool operator!=(const type_info&  rhs ) const; // return !( *this == rhs)
    bool before(const type_info&  rhs ) const; // ordering
    const char* name() const; //return a const null terminated string
                              // containing the type's name
  private:
    //objects of this type cannot be copied
        type_info(const type_info&  rhs );
        type_info& operator=(const type_info&  rhs );
  }; //type_info
}
```

In general, all instances of the same type share a single **type_info** object. The most widely used member functions of **type_info** are **name** and **operator==**. But before you can invoke these member functions, you have to access the **type_info** object itself. How is it done?

Operator `typeid`

Operator **typeid** takes either an object or a class name as its argument and returns a matching **const type_info** object. The dynamic type of an object can be examined like this:

```
OnRightClick (File & file) //operating system's API function
{
  if ( typeid( file)  == typeid( TextFile ) )
  {
    //we received a TextFile object; printing should be enabled
  }
  else
  {
    //not a TextFile object, printing is not supported
  }
}
```

To understand how it works, let's look at the highlighted source line

```
if ( typeid( file)  == typeid( TextFile ) ).
```

The `if` statement tests whether the dynamic type of the argument `file` is `TextFile` (the static type of `file` is `File`, of course). The leftmost expression `typeid(file)` returns a `type_info` object that holds the necessary runtime type information associated with the object `file`. The rightmost expression `typeid(TextFile)` returns the type information associated with class `TextFile`. Of course, when `typeid` is applied to a class name (rather than an object) it always returns the `type_info` object that corresponds to that class name. As you saw earlier, `type_info` overloads the operator ==. Therefore, the `type_info` object returned by the leftmost `typeid` expression is compared to the `type_info` object returned by the rightmost `typeid` expression. If indeed `file` is an instance of `TextFile`, the `if` statement evaluates to `true`. In this case, `OnRightClick` displays an additional option in the menu: `print`. If, on the other hand, `file` is not a `TextFile`, the `if` statement evaluates to `false`, and the `print` option will not be displayed.

This is all nice and well, but a `typeid`-based solution incurs a drawback. Suppose you want to add support for a new type of file, say an HTML file. What happens when the file manager application has to be extended? HTML files are essentially text files. They can be read and printed. However, they differ from plain text files in some respects. An `open` message applied to an HTML file launches a browser rather than a word processor. In addition, HTML files have to be converted to a printable format before they can be printed. The need to extend a system's functionality at a minimal cost is an everyday challenge that software developers face. Object-oriented programming and design can facilitate the task. By subclassing `TextFile`, you can reuse its existing behavior and implement only the additional functionality required for HTML files:

```
class HTMLFile : public TextFile {
  void open () { Launch_Browser (); } //override TextFile::open
  void virtual print();  // perform the necessary conversions to a printable
                         // format and then print file
};
```

This is only half of the story. `OnRightClick` will fail badly when it receives an object of type `HTMLFile`. Let's look at it again to see why:

```
OnRightClick (File & file) //operating system's API function
{
  if ( typeid( file)  == typeid( TextFile ) )
  {
    //we received a TextFile object; printing should be enabled
  }
```

```
else //OOPS! we get here when file is of type HTMLFile
  {
  }
}
```

typeid returns the *exact* type information of its argument. Therefore, the if statement in OnRightClick will evaluate to false when the argument is an HTMLFile. However, a false value implies a binary file. Consequently, no support for printing is available. This onerous bug is likely to occur every time support is added for a new file type. Fortunately, C++ offers a better way to handle this situation.

Operator dynamic_cast<>

It is a mistake to let OnRightClick take care of every conceivable class type. By doing that, you are forced to modify it whenever you add a new file class or modify an existing class. In software design in general, and object-oriented design in particular, such dependencies should be minimized. If you examine OnRightClick closely, you will realize that it shouldn't really know whether its argument is an instance of class TextFile (or any other class for that matter). Rather, all OnRightClick needs to know is whether its argument *is a* TextFile. There is a big difference between the two; OnRightClick has to know whether its argument is a TextFile object or an instance of a class *derived* from TextFile. However, typeid is incapable of examining the derivation hierarchy of an object. For this purpose, you have to use the operator dynamic_cast<>. dynamic_cast<> takes two arguments. The first is a type name. The second argument is a polymorphic object, which dynamic_cast<> attempts to cast at runtime to the desired type. For example:

```
dynamic_cast <TextFile &> (file); //attempt to cast file to a reference to an
                                  // object of type TextFile
```

If the attempted cast succeeds, either the second argument is an instance of the class name that appears as the second argument, or it is an object derived from it. The dynamic_cast<> expression above will succeed if file is a TextFile. This is exactly what OnRightClick needs to know to operate properly. How do you know whether dynamic_cast<> was successful?

There are two flavors of dynamic_cast<>. One uses pointers and the other uses references. Accordingly, dynamic_cast<> returns a pointer or a reference of the desired type when it succeeds. When dynamic_cast<> cannot perform the cast, it returns a null pointer, or in the case of a reference, dynamic_cast<> throws an exception of type std::bad_cast. Let's look at a pointer cast example:

```
TextFile * pTest = dynamic_cast < TextFile *> (&f); //attempt to cast file
                                                    // address to a pointer to
                                                    // TextFile

if (pTest) //dynamic_cast succeeded, file is-a TextFile
```

```
{
}
else // file is not a TextFile;  pTest has a NULL value
{
}
```

C++ does not have **null** references. Therefore, when a reference dynamic_cast<> fails, it throws an exception of type std::bad_cast . That is why you should always place a reference dynamic_cast<> expression within a try block and include a suitable catch statement to handle std::bad_cast exceptions.

```
try {
 TextFile  tf = dynamic_cast < TextFile &> (f); //attempt to cast file to a
                                              // reference to TextFile
//use tf safely,
}
catch (std::bad_cast) { //we get here when dynamic_cast<> fails
//
}
```

Now you can revise OnRightClick to handle HTMLFile objects properly:

```
OnRightClick (File & file) //operating system's API function
{
  try
  {
    TextFile temp = dynamic_cast<TextFile&> (file);
    //display options, including "print"
    switch (message){
    case m_open:
      temp.open();  //virtual; either TextFile::open or HTMLFile::open is executed
    break;
    case m_print:
      temp.print();//virtual; either TextFile::print or HTMLFile::print is
                   //executed
    break;
    }//switch
  }//try
  catch (std::bad_cast& noTextFile)
  {
    // treat file as a BinaryFile; exclude"print"
  }
}// OnRightClick
```

The revised version of OnRightClick handles an object of type HTMLFile appropriately because an object of type HTMLFile is a TextFile. When the user clicks on the **open** message in the file manager application, the function OnRightClick invokes the member function **open** of its argument, which behaves as expected because it was overridden in class HTMLFile. Likewise, when OnRightClick detects that its argument is a TextFile, it displays a **print** option. If the user clicks on this option, OnRightClick will send the message **print** to its argument, which is supposed to react as expected.

COMMENTS

The RTTI mechanism of C++ consists of three components: operators `typeid`, operator `dynamic_cast<>`, and class `type_info`. RTTI is relatively new in C++. Some existing compilers do not support it yet. Furthermore, even compilers that support it can usually be configured to disable RTTI support. The reason is that RTTI adds a moderate overhead in terms of memory usage, execution speed, and the size of the executable. Even when there is no explicit usage of RTTI constructs in a program, the compiler automatically adds the necessary "scaffolding" to polymorphic objects. To avoid this, you should consult your compiler's manual to check how you can toggle its RTTI support.

From the object-oriented design point of view, operator `dynamic_cast<>` is preferable to `typeid` because it enables more flexibility and robustness, as you have seen. However, `dynamic_cast<>` can be slower than `typeid` because it might traverse through the entire derivation tree of an object to decide whether the object can be cast to the desired type. When complex derivational hierarchies are used, the incurred performance penalty can be noticeable. Therefore, it is advisable to use RTTI judiciously. In many cases, a virtual member function is sufficient to achieve the necessary polymorphic behavior. Only when virtual member functions are insufficient, should RTTI be considered.

When using RTTI, please note the following:

- In order to enable RTTI support, an object must have at least one virtual member function. In addition, you should switch on your compiler's RTTI support (please consult your user's manual for further information).

- Make sure your program has a `catch` statement to handle `std::bad_cast` exception whenever you are using `dynamic_cast<>` with a reference.

- When using `dynamic_cast<>` with a pointer, always check the returned value.

INDEX

Symbols

#include directive, 14
>> operator, 20
* operator, purpose of, 34
<< operator, 15
= (assignment) operator, 116
== operator, 328

A

abort function, 375, 391-393
abstraction, 56
access
    elements (built-in arrays), 254
    encapsulated data, 109
        classes, 144-148
    variables, 169-174
access control (keywords), 121
access functions, 132
access specifiers, 76
accessor member functions, 90
accessors (member functions), 77
accumulate algorithm, 346-351
accumulated sums (container elements), 319, 345-351
actions (container ranges, repeating), 318, 333-337
addition operator (+), overloading, 134
addRecord function, 377
addRecord method, 379-380
algorithms
    accumulate, 346-351
    count, 329
    equal, 318, 338-341
    find, 329
    for each, 333-337
    functionality, increasing, 333
    legacy code, 287
    member functions, 316
    mismatch, 318, 338-341
    mutating, 362
    mutation operations, 316
    nonmutating operations, 316
    nonmutative, 334
    numeric operations, 316-318
    partial sum, 346-351
    predicates (power), 333
    search, 342-345

sort (vectors), 358
sorting operations, 316-317
Standard C Library, 287-312
STL algorithms, 288, 316
unique, 320, 325, 329
aliases (namespaces), 553
alignment, 511
allocation
    containers, automatic, 268-273
    embedded allocators (STL containers), 253
    memory, 376
        dynamic, 475-479
        at runtime, 41
analyzing source code, 13-15
    allocating and deallocating memory
        program, 39-41
    calculations program, 18-19
    derived data types program, 31-36
    exception handling program, 44-49
    loop statements, 22-23
angle brackets (templates), 252
ANSI C macros (runtime error handling), 383
appending arrays, 248
applications, terminating, 375, 391-393
arguments
    char *argv[], 16
    int argc, 16
    prot, 528
    qsort function, 292
    unique algorithm, 325
    value, 32
array allocation statement, 40
arrays, 35
    appending, 248
    built-in
        element access, 254
        pointers, 273
    characters, 119
    compound data types, 220
    declaring, 100
    delete operator, overloading, 455-469
    deleting, memory leaks and, 450-451
    double values (template classes), 232
    elements, locating, 289, 298-305
    for each algorithm, 334-337
    new operator, overloading, 455-469
    programs, writing, 29-36
    qsort function, 288

sorting, 288-297
    qsort function, 289-292
    strings, 296
  stacks as, 119
  template classes, 229-231
assert function, 385-386
assert utility, 374
assignment operator, 116
asterisk (*) in function pointers, 294
at( ) member function, 249
atexit function, 375, 393-395
attributes, 55
  hiding, 90

B

bad alloc class, 45
bad error, 533
base classes, 57, 60-61
  inheritance, declaration, 194
  member functions (subclasses), 256
binary files, 526, 536-542
binary operators, overloading, 134-139
BinaryFile object, 561
binding
  dynamic binding, 293, 560-563
  late binding, 293
  static binding, 559
block comments, 14
block style, 15
blocks
  catch, 46-48
  try, 46-48, 416-417
bool data type, 20, 73
braces in loops, 24
bsearch function, 289, 298-301
buffers
  dynamically creating, 128
  I/O libraries, 501
  size, adjusting automatically, 250
built-in arrays
  elements, accessing, 254
  pointers, 273
byte alignment settings, 448
byte padding structures, 449

C

C comments, 288
Calc( ) member function, 183
calculations, writing, 17-20
callback functions, 292-295
calloc function, 376
cast operator, 288
catch block, 46-48
catch clause, 416-425
catch constructs, 410

CATCH directory, 419
catch ordering, 419-425
changing references, 32
char *argv[] argument, 16
char data type, 20
characters, 119
cin object, 20
  class compatibility, 500, 503-504
  console stream, 526
class keyword, 76
classes, 55, 109, 169
  access (encapsulated data), 144-148
  bad alloc, 45
  base classes, 57, 60-61
  cin (compatibility), 500, 503-504
  constructors, 76, 121
  containers
    sequential, 318-328
    see also *container classes*
  cout (compatibility), 500, 503-504
  creating, 72-80
  declaration, 73, 120, 123
    header line, 196
    overloaded operators, 141
    writing, 131
  deconstructors, 121
  defining, 73
  delete operator, overriding, 451-455
  derived, 195
    member functions, 94
    variables, 201
  destructors, 77
  dynamically allocated memory clean up,
    475-479
  encapsulated data access, 109
  errors (runtime), 376
  exception, 410, 425-429
  file stream, 528
  friend, 147-148
  fstream, reading/writing to files, 527
  functions, coding, 122
  ifstream, reading files, 527
  implementation, 73, 124
    constructor functions, 131
    destructor functions, 131
  inheritance, 56-62
  instantiation (macros), 502
  interfaces, 77
  internal information, hiding, 118
  IOStreams
    base classes, 501
    error conditions, 533
  linked list, 151
  members (static), 72, 97-101
  memory management, 473-495
  memory use, 447-450

new operator, overriding, 451-455
object clean up, 479-483
ofstream, writing to files, 527-528
runtime errors, 400-405
Shape, 186-190
size, 450
sort order, 361
SStack (data members), 120
stack, defining, 123
string, 264
structures comparison, 108, 151-155
templates, 220, 252
testing, 124, 133
TSimple, 227-228
type_info, 564
variables, access, 169-174
views, 89-91
virtual, 161, 206-216
when to use, 128, 151-155
clean up (classes), 479-483
code
   access functions, 132
   modular, 128
   source
     compiling, 13
     described, 12
     linking, 13
   try block, 416-417
code pointers, 292-295
CodeGuard (Borland), 450
coding class functions, 122
comments
   block, 14
   C, 288
   line, 14
   styles, 14-17, 20, 24, 37, 41, 49
compare callback function, 295
comparison functions, 356
comparisons
   lexicographical, 297
   sequences, 318, 337-341
compilers
   DJGPP, 75
   function of, 13
compiling
   source code, 13
   statements, troubleshooting, 16
compound data types (template classes), 220, 228-232
compound statements, 19
conflicts in naming, *see* namespaces
console streams
   cin, 526
   cout, 526
const keyword, 20
const modifier, 77
const variable, 20

constructor functions, class implementation, 131
constructors, 121
   class instances, 181
   classes, 76
   defining (template classes), 222
   inline member functions, 99
   memory allocation, 78
   names, 186
   overloaded (signatures), 189
   private variables, 173
   selecting, 161, 186-190
   signatures, 186
   SStack, 124
container classes, 247-284
container objects, 249-254
containers
   accumulated sums, 319
   allocation/reallocation, 268-273
     automatic, 249, 268-273
     memory allocation scheme, 268
   deque, 320
   elements, 250
     accumulated sums, 345-351
     accumulating, 319
     displaying all, 273-278
     modifying, 249, 257-260
     order, 319, 362-368
     reading, 249, 254-256
     sorting, 319
   ranges, repeating actions, 318, 333-337
   sequential (classes), 318-328
   sorting, 351-361
   stack, 261-268
   STL, 248-250
     embedded allocators, 253
   values
     searching for sequences, 319
     sequences, searching for, 341-345
   vector, 320
conversion bases, 509-511
count algorithm, 329
cout, 36, 423
   class compatibility, 500, 503-504
   console stream, 526
   formatting with, 500, 504-515
creating
   data types, 108
   loop statements, 21-25
   programs
     to allocate and deallocate memory, 37-41
     with derived data types, 29-36
     exception handling, 41-50
     without knowing C++, 12-17
     with one or more functions, 25-28
     to perform calculations, 17-20
CurrentElement variable, 124

D

data, hiding from external programs, 118-128

data declaration, 130

data extraction (STL), 530-531

data hiding, *see* encapsulation

data members, 121
 encapsulation, 87
 SStack class, 120
 see also variables

data models
 LIFO, 249, 261-268
 queue, 250, 278-281

data operations (declaration), 352

data pointers, 292-295

data types, 108
 bool, 20, 73
 char, 20
 compound (template classes), 220, 228-232
 creating, 110-117, 129
 derived (programs)
 writing, 29-33, 35-50
 double, 20
 fields, 129
 float, 20, 136
 int, 14, 20
 long, 20
 template classes
  simple data types, 221-225
  undefined, 220, 233-238
 unknown, 222
  TSimple class, 227-228
 variables, 110

databases, initialization, 415

dbClose( ) function, 418

dbCloseEH( ) function, 416

dbGetDat( ) function, 417

dbGetDataEH( ) function, 416

dbInit( ) function, 415-417

dbInitEH( ) function, 416

dbOpen( ) function, 415-417

dbOpenEH( ) function, 416

DDate type, 113

deallocation (self deallocation), 483-494

debugging
 assert function, 385-386
 assert utility, 374
 inheritance and, 161
 memory management, 451

decimal points, setting, 507-509

declaration, 62-63
 arrays, 100
 classes, 73, 120, 123
  header line, 196
  writing, 131
 constructors, 76

data, 130

error handlers, 436

inheritance, 194-195

linked list classes, 152

main (optional), 16

member functions, 77

namespaces, 551

overloaded operators, 140

relational operations, 352

struct, 32-33

declarative languages, 58

deconstructors, 121

deference operator, 34

defining
 classes, 73
 constructors (template classes), 222
 enumeration types, 76
 pointers, 294
 variables (template classes), 235-236

definitions
 errorCode, 45
 member functions, 196
 namespaces, 552-553
 stack classes, 123

delete expression, 40

delete operator, 444
 free( ) routines and, 445-446
 malloc( ) routines and, 445-446
 overloading for arrays, 455-469
 overriding for classes, 451-455
 user-defined, namespaces, 557

delete[ ], 450-451

deleting arrays, memory leaks and, 450-451

deque container, 320-321

derived classes
 creating, 195
 member functions, 94
 variables, 201

derived data types (programs, writing), 29-50

destructor functions (class implementation), 131

destructors, 77-78

directives
 #include, 14
 preprocessor, 14
 using, 75, 252
  described, 14
  namespaces, 552

directories
 CATCH, 419
 EXCEPTH, 411
 EXCLASS, 426
 UNEXPECT, 434

DisplayDate function, 116

displaying container elements, 273-278

divide( ) function, 428

DJGPP compiler, 75

do-while loop, 23
dot notation (member functions), 160, 181-186
dot operators, 79
    structures, 117
double data type, 20
dynamic binding, 293, 560-563
dynamically allocated memory (clean up),
    475-479
dynamic_cast operator, 563, 566-567

E

ed as text editor, 12
EH string, 414
elements
    arrays
        locating, 298-305
        location, 289
    container ranges, repeating actions, 333-337
    containers, 250
        accumulated sums, 345-351
        accumulating, 319
        displaying all, 273-278
        modifying, 249, 257-260
        order, 319, 362-368
        reading, 249, 254-256
        sorting, 319
    vectors
        inserting, 250-254
        modifying, 257-260
        reading, 254-256
ellipsis in catch clause, 424
embedded allocators (STL containers), 253
encapsulation, 54, 56, 62-63, 72, 87-91, 108, 122,
    128-134
    accessing data, 144-148
    data access, 109
    friend functions and, 148
    security and, 134
enumeration types, 76
EOF (end of file), 526
    eof error, 533
    reading files, 529-532
equal algorithm, 318, 338-341
Equal( ) function, 163
equality operators, overloading, 109, 139-144
errno variable, clearing, 382
error conditions (IOStreams classes), 533
error detection
    reading files, 375, 395-397
    writing to files, 375
error handlers, declaration, 436
error handling, 374-407
    function error values, 400
    maintaining state, 397-399
    programs, writing, 41-50

    raise function, 387-391
    runtime errors, 374
    signal function, 387-391
    stream errors, 526
    streams, 532-535
ErrorClass, 400, 402, 405
errorCode definition, 45
errors
    bad, 533
    eof, 533
    fail, 533
    off-by-one, 529-532
    one-off, 35
    potential, exception handling, 411-418
    run time (classes), 400-405
    runtime, reporting, 381-385
    runtime errors, 376-381
    stream errors, reading loop, 529
examining source code
    allocating and deallocating memory
        program, 39-41
    calculations program, 18-19
    derived data types program, 31-36
    exception handling program, 44-49
    first C++ program, 13-15
    loop statements, 22-23
EXCEPTH directory, 411
exception classes, 410
    implementation, 425-429
exception handling, 409-439
    LIFO data model, 261
    potential error conditions, 411-418
    programs, writing, 41-50
    rethrowing exceptions, 410
exception specification, 45
exceptions
    functions, specifying, 410
    rethrowing, 410, 419-425
    specifying for functions, 430-434
    unexpected, 434-437
EXCLASS directory, 426
exit function, 375, 393-395
ExitCurrentScope, 267
exiting functions, forcing, 267
expressions
    delete, 40
    initializer, 40
    new, 39-40, 79
    return, 15
    validity testing, 385
external functions (file-local function), 555-556
external programs, hiding data, 118-128
extracting data (STL implementations), 530-531
extraction operator
    described, 20
    overloading, 242

F

fail error, 533
ferror function, 375, 396
fields (data types), 129
FIFO (first-in-first-out), 279
file I/O, 525-547
file stream classes, 528
file streams, opening, 526-529
file-local functions (external functions), 555-556
files
    binary, reading/writing, 536-542
    header files, 76, 288
    iostream, 16
    opening, writing to, 536
    reading
        different positions, 542-546
        error detection, 375, 395-397
        ifstream class, 527
    reading from (different positions), 526
    reading/writing to (ifstream class), 527
    stack.h, 123
    writing to
        different positions, 526, 542-546
        error detection, 395-397
        ofstream class, 527-528
find algorithm, 329
float data type, 20, 136
float values (Transaction float), 347
floating-point numbers, 192, 512-514, 536
for each algorithm, 333-337
for loop, 24-25, 100
forcing function exit, 267
formatting
    alignment, 511
    comments, 14-17, 20, 24, 37, 41, 49
    conversion bases, 509-511
    cout, 500, 504-515
    decimal points, 507-509
    floating-point numbers (scientific notation),
      512-514
    ostream objects, 500, 504-515
    positive numbers, 511
    whitespace, 507
free( ) function, 444-469
    deleting operator and, 445-446
    new operator and, 445-446
friend classes, 147-148
friend functions, 145-148
fstream class, reading/writing to files, 527
function calls, results, 415
function members, 121
function overloading, implementing, 161
function pointers, 293
functions
    abort, 375, 391-393
    access functions, 132

addRecord, 377
assert, 385-386
atexit, 375, 393-395
bsearch, 298-301
callback functions, 292, 295
calloc, 376
class functions, coding, 122
comparison functions, 356
constructor, class implementation, 131
dbClose( ), 418
dbCloseEH( ), 416
dbGetData( ), 417
dbGetDataEH( ), 416
dbInit( ), 415, 417
dbInitEH( ), 416
dbOpen( ), 415, 417
dbOpenEH( ), 416
destructor, class implementation, 131
Display Date, 116
divide( ), 428
Equal( ), 163
error values, 400
exception throwing, specifying exceptions,
  430-434
exceptions, specifying, 410
exit, 375, 393-395
ferror, 375, 396
forcing exit, 267
free( ), 444-469
friend, 145-148
GetDate, 116
getValue, 32-36
identify, 560
inlining, 477
InterruptHandler, 388
IsEmpty, 119
IsFull, 119
lfind, 289
long, 31-32
longjmp, 375, 397-399
lookup functions, 302-309
lsearch, 289
main
    described, 14
    optional declarations, 16
malloc( ), 376, 444-469
member functions, 121
    accessors, 90
    at( ), 249
    declaration, 77
    dot notation, 160
    inline, 99
    overloading, 76
    overloading addition operator, 134
    set( ), 173
    SStack class, 120
    static, 100-101

memcpy( ), 446-447
memmove, 446-447
multiply, 32
mutator, 77
NameExists, 326
names, 191
new, 376
nonvirtual, 207
overloading, implementing, 191-194
perror, 374, 381-385
Pop, 119
PrintM, 334
program, writing with one or more, 25-28
Push, 119
qsort, 288-292, 298
raise, 375, 387-391
rand, 309-311
RemoveDuplicates, 325
Result( ), 163
rethrowFunc( ), 421-422
return values, 49
setjmp, 375, 397-399
signal, 375, 387-391
srand, 309-311
SStack( ), 121
stdio functions, 499
stdio.h file, 288
strerror, 374, 381-385
sync_with_stdio( ), 501
terminate( ), 417
TerminateHandler, 388
throwFunc( ), 421-422
unary functions (predicates), 329
validation code, 132
virtual, 206-207, 561-563

G

Gather( ) member function, 183
generating random numbers, 289, 309-311
get( ) member function, 173
GetDate function, 116
getValue function, 32-36
global data, 109, 148-151
global functions, scope resolution (::) operator,
    555
global variables, 169-174
GNU projects, 501

H

handling errors, *see* error handling
header files, 76, 556, 288
hiding data from external programs, 118-128
hierarchies, inheritance, 81
hierarchy, 59

I

I/O
    file I/O, 525-547
    operations, 288
    streams library, 499-521
identify function, 560
ifstream class, reading files, 527
if_else statements, 415
implementation, 56
    classes, 73, 124
        constructor functions, 131
        destructor functions, 131
    encapsulation, 87
    exception classes, 425-429
    print manager, 281
    static polymorphism, 559
implementations (STL), 530-531
implementing, overloading functions, 191-194
include statements (containers), 252
indented block style, 15
indexes, sorting indexes, 351-361
inheritance, 54-62, 72, 80-87, 161, 194-199
    debugging and, 161
    declaring, 195
    hierarchies, 81
    member variables, 202
    model, 209-210, 214-216
    multiple, 563
    parameter passing, 161, 200-206
    properties, 200
    templates, 256
initialization
    databases, 415
    instances (constructors), 76
initializer expression, 40
initializer list, 78
inline functions, 477
inline member functions (constructors), 99
inserting elements in vectors, 250-254
insertion operator, 15
    overloading, 238, 242
instances
    initializing (constructors), 76
    objects, 186
instantiation (classes), 502
int argc argument, 16
int data type, 14, 20
integer values
    int data type, 14
    private variables, 184
integers, 192
interface, 56, 77, 87
interpreting source code
    allocating and deallocating memory
        program, 39-41
    calculations program, 18-19

derived data types program, 31-36
exception handling program, 44-49
first C++ program, 13-15
loop statements, 22-23
InterruptHandler function, 388
iostream file, 16
iostream member functions, 173
IOStreams base classes, 501
IOStreams classes, 533
IOStreams library, 525-547
is-a relationships, 57
ISAM (Indexed Sequential Access Methods) C
  libraries, 414
IsEmpty function, 119
IsFull function, 119
istream operators (>>), 503-504
iterators, 250, 277
    container elements, 274
    list items (pointers), 326
    pattern vector, 339
iVal variable, 35-36

J-K

jumps (non-local), 375

K&R style, 15
keywords
    access control, 121
    class, 76
    const, 20
    namespace, troubleshooting, 16
    private, 121
    public, 121
    static, 97-101
    struct, 110
        DDate type, 113
        described, 32
    try, 416
    virtual, 94
Koenig loookup, 554

L

languages
    declarative, 58
    typed, 219
late binding, 293
leaks, memory, preventing, 450-451
legacy code, algorithms and, 287
lexicographical comparison, 297
lfind function, 289, 302-309
libraries
    I/O streams library, 499-521
    IOStreams, 525-547
    stdio, 499

LIFO (last-in-first-out) data model, 249, 261-268
line comments, 14
linked list classes, 151-152
linkers, 13
linking source code, 13
lists
    linked list classes, 151
    sequential containers, 321
long data type, 20
long function, 31-32
longjmp function, 375, 397-399
lookup functions
    lfind, 302-309
    lsearch, 302-309
loop statements, writing, 21-25
loops
    braces, 24
    do-while, 23
    for, 24-25
    for loops, 100
    reading loop, stream errors, 529
    while, 23
    while loops, 184
lsearch function, 289, 302-309

M

macros, 502
main function, 14-16
malloc( ) function, 376, 444
    delete operator and, 445-446
    new operator and, 445-446
manipulators
    setf( ), 511
    setfill( ), 507
    setw( ), 505-507
    stream manipulators, 515-521
    unsetf( ), 511
MAX ELEMENTS constant, 39
member functions, 121
    accessors, 77, 90
    algorithms, 316
    at( ), 249
    base classes (subclasses), 256
    Cal( ), 183
    declaration, 77
    definitions, 196
    derived classes, 94
    dot notation, 160, 181-186
    duplicate names, 179
    Gather( ), 183
    inline (constructors), 99
    invoking, 183
    iostream, 173
    message( ), 427
    methods, 179

overloading, 76
public visibility classes, 77
set( ), 173
Show( ), 183
SStack class, 120
static, 100-101
streams, 543
template classes, 222, 226
unique, 320
virtual, 206
virtuality, 94
visibility, 90
member variables, inheritance, 202
members (classes), 72
memcpy( ) function, 446-447
memmove( ) function, 446-447
memory
    allocation and deallocation, 376
        at runtime, 41
        desructors, 78
        operating systems, 475
        programs
    dynamically allocated, clean up, 475-479
    leaks
        deleting arrays and, 450-451
        preventing, 450-451
    object use, 447-450
    structure use, 447-450
    virtual classes, 216
    writing, 37-41
memory management
    classes, 473-495
    debugging, 451
memory manipulation functions, 446
mem( ) routines, 446-447
MemPtr object, 479
message( ) member function, 427
messages, 15
methods, 121
    addRecord, 379-380
    member functions, 179
    predicates (count algorithm), 329
mismatch algorithm, 318, 338-341
modifiers (const), 77
modifying
    elements
        containers, 257-260
        containters, 249
        vectors, 257-260
    namespaces (std), 557
    references, 32
modular code, 128
modules (global data), 109
multiple inheritance, 563
multiply function, 32
multithreaded programming, 485-486

mutating algorithms, 362
mutating operations, 316
mutator functions, 77
mutex (mutliple exclusion semaphore), 486
MyChar, 448
MyLongInt, 448

N

name conflicts, 550-551
NameExists function, 326
names
    constructors, 186
    functions, 191
namespace keyword, troubleshooting, 16
namespaces, 549-558
    aliases, 553
    definition, 552-553
    delete operator, user-defined, 557
    described, 14
    external functions, 555-556
    file-local functions, 555-556
    header files, 556
    interaction with other language features, 554
    Koenig lookup, 554
    new operator, user-defined, 557
    properties, 551
    restrictions, 557
    std, 550, 557
    using-declaration, 551-552
    using-directive, 552
new expression
    described, 39-40
    object creation, 79
new function, 376
new operator, 444
    free( ) routines and, 445-446
    malloc( ) routines and, 445-446
    objects (clean up), 479-483
    overloading for arrays, 455-469
    overriding for classes, 451-455
    user-defined (namespaces), 557
non-local jumps, 375
nonmutating operations (algorithms), 316
nonmutative algorithms, 334
nonvirtual functions, 207
nonvirtual inheritance model, 210, 214-216
Notepad as text editor, 12
numbers, (random, generating), 289, 309-311
numeric operations (algorithms), 318

O

object-oriented approach vs procedural, 160-162,
    165-169
object-oriented paradigm, 55-56

object-oriented programming, *see* OOP
objects, 55
 BinaryFile, 561
 cin, 20
 clean up, 479-483
 container, 249-254
 creating
  dot notation, 183
  new expression, 79
 instances, 186
 member functions, invoking, 183
 memory use, 447-450
 MemPtr, 479
 ostream, formatting with, 500, 504-515
 polymorphic (RTTI), 563
 proxy, 37
 references, 32
 self-deallocating, 483-494
 size, 450
 TextFile, 561
ofstream class
 opening files, 536
 writing to files, 527-528
Ohm's law, 207
one-off error, 35
OOP (object-oriented programming), 53, 159
 basics, 54
 encapsulation, 54
 inheritance, 54, 57-62
 polymorphism, 54
 return two letters, 168
opening
 file streams, 526-529
 files, writing to, 536
operating systems, memory allocation, 475
operations
 algorithms, 316
 sequence (predicates), 318, 328-333
operator overload, 134-139
 declaration, 140
 equality operators, 139-144
 relational operators, 139-144
 testing, 143
operators, 109
 ==, 328
 assignment operator, 116
 binary, overloading, 134-139
 cast, 288
 creating, 134-139
 deference, 34
 delete, 444-469
  overloading for arrays, 455-469
  overriding for classes, 451-455
 dot operator, 79, 117
 dynamic_cast, 563, 566-567

extraction
 described, 20
 overloading, 242
insertion
 described, 15
 overloading, 242
 istream (>>), 503-504
 new, 444-469
  overloading for arrays, 455-457, 459-469
  overriding for classes, 451-455
 ostream (<<), 503-504
 overloading, 109
 scope resolution, 124, 160
 scope resolution (::) operator, 175-180, 55
 sizeof( ), 450
 typeid, 97, 564-566
 unary, overloading, 138
order of container elements, 319, 362-368
ostream objects, formatting, 500, 504-515
ostream (<<) operators, 503-504
output
 setw( ) manipulator, 505-507
 described, 15
overloading
 constructors, 186, 189
 deleting operator, 455-469
 functions
  implementing, 191-194
  implementing overload, 161
  member functions, 76
 insertion operator, 238, 242
 new operator (arrays), 455-469
 operator overloading, 134
 operators, 109
  binary, 134-139
  testing, 143
  unary, 138
 subscript operator, 254
overriding operators, 451-455

P

parameters, passing to parent classes through
 inheritance, 161, 200-206
partial sum algorithm, 346-351
passing parameters to parent classes through
 inheritance, 161, 200-206
pattern vector, 338-339
perror function, 374, 381-385
pointer variables, 294
pointers
 arrays (built-in), 273
 code pointers, 292-295
 data pointers, 292-295
 defining, 294

described, 32
function pointers, 293
programs, writing, 29-36
references, changing, 32
values, storing, 32
polymorphism, 54-56, 64-67, 72, 91-97, 559
static, implementing, 559
type_info class, 564
Pop function, 119
position-related stream member functions, 543
positive numbers, 511
predicates
algorithms, 333
methods (count algorithm), 329
sequence operations, 318, 328-333
preprocessor directives, 14
preventing memory leaks, 450-451
print manager, implementation, 281
printing to screen, 202
PrintM function, 334
private keyword, 121
private variables, 169-174
constructors, 173
integer values, 184
procedural approach versus object-oriented, 160-169
procedural programs, returning two letters, 167
programs
creating to perform calculations, 17-20
external, hiding data, 118-128
writing
to allocate and deallocate memory, 37-41
with derived data types, 29-36
exception handling, 41-50
without knowing C++, 12-17
loop statements, 21-25
with one or more functions, 25-28
properties
inheritance, 200
namespaces, 551
prot argument, 528
proxy objects, 37
pseudorandom numbers, 310
public keyword, 121
public variables, 169-174
public visibility, member functions, 77
Push function, 119
pushing data into stacks, 119

Q

qsort function, 288-292, 298
callback function, 294
queue data model, 250, 278-281

R

raise function, 375, 387-391
rand function, 309-311
random numbers
generating, 289, 309-311
pseudorandom, 310
ranges (containers), repeating actions, 318, 333-337
rational operators, overloading, 109
reading
binary files, 526, 536-542
container elements, 254-256
elements
containers, 249
vectors, 254-256
files
different positions, 526, 542-546
ifstream class, 527
reading files
EOF, 526, 529-532
error detection, 375, 395, 397
errors (off-by-one), 529-532
reading loop (stream errors), 529
reading/writing files (ofstream class), 527
reallocating containers, automatic, 249, 268-273
references
changing, 32
values, storing, 32
relational operations
declaration, 352
overloading, 139-144
RemoveDuplicates function, 325
restrictions on namespaces, 557
Result( ) function, 163
rethrowFunc( ) function, 421-422
rethrowing exceptions, 410, 419-425
return statement
calculations program, 19
described, 15
return values, 49
reviewing source code
allocating and deallocating memory
program, 39-41
calculations program, 18-19
derived data types program, 31-36
exception handling program, 44-49
first C++ program, 13-15
loop statements, 22-23
rotating sequences, 362
RTTI (runtime type information), 563
runtime, allocating, 41
runtime errors, 374-381
classes, 376, 400-405
reporting, 381-385
runtime type information, 559-568
see also RTTI

S

satellite data, 154
scientific notation (floating-point numbers),
  512-514
scope (namespaces), 551
scope resolution (::) operator, 124, 160, 175-180
  global functions, 555
search algorithm, 342-345
searches (containers)
  value sequences, 319
  values, 341-345
security, encapsulation and, 134
seeking in streams, 545
semaphores, 486
sequence operations (predicates), 318, 328-333
sequences
  accumulated sums (container elements),
    345-351
  comparing, 318, 337-341
  container values, searching for, 341-345
sequeneces
  rotating, 362
sequential containers
  classes, 318-328
  deques, 321
  lists, 321
  vectors, 321
services, 59
set( ) member function, 173
setf( ) manipulator, 511
setfill( ) manipulator, 507
setjmp function, 375, 397-399
setprecision( ) modifier, 507-509
setw( ) manipulator, 505-507
Shape class, 186-190
sharing data, 148
  see also global data
Show( ) member function, 183
signal function, 375, 387-391
signals, 389-390
signatures (constructors), 186, 189
size
  buffers, adjusting automatically, 250
  containter objects, 250-254
  vectors, 252
sizeof( ) operator, 450
sort order (classes), 361
sorting
  arrays, 288-297
    qsort function, 289-292
    strings, 296
  container elements, 319, 351-361
  indexes (containers), 351-361
  vectors (sort algorithm), 358

sorting operations (algorithms), 316-317
source code
  analyzing
    allocating and deallocating memory
      program, 39-41
    calculations program, 18-19
    derived data types program, 31-36
    exception handling program, 44-49
    first C++ program, 13-15
    loop statements, 22-23
  comments, 14-17, 20, 24, 37, 41, 49
  compiling, 13
  described, 12
  linking, 13
specialization, 252
specifications (exception), 45
srand function, 309-311
SStack class, 120
SStack constructor, 124
SStack( ) function, 121
stack classes, defining, 123
stack container, 261-268
stack.h file, 123
stacks
  as arrays, 119
  characters, 119
  pushing data into, 119
Standard C Library algorithms, 287-315
standard header files (namespaces), 556
standard output messages, 15
Standard Template Library (self-managing pointer
  class), 479
Standard Template Library, *see* STL
starting point in C++ programs, 14
statements
  array allocation, 40
  compiling, troubleshooting, 16
  compound, 19
  cout, 36, 423
  if_else, 415
  loop, writing, 21-25
  return
    calculations program, 19
    described, 15
  throw, 418
  try block, 416
static binding, 559
static class members, 97-101
  implementing, 72
static keyword, 97-101
static member functions, 100-101
static polymorphism, implementing, 559
std namespace, 550, 557
stdio (GNU), 501
stdio functions, 499

stdio library, 499
stdio.h file functions, 288
STL (Standard Template Library), 316, 479
  algorithms, 288, 316
  containers, 248-250, 253
  implementations, 530-531
storing
  values, 32
  variables, 165
stream errors, reading loop, 529
stream manipulators, 500, 515-521
streams
  data extraction, 530
  error handling, 532-535
  error handling , 526
  files streams, opening, 526-529
  member functions (position-related), 543
  seeking in, 545
strerror function, 374, 381-385
string class, 264
strings
  array, sorting, 296
  EH, 414
  lexicographical comparison, 297
Stroustrup, Bjarne, 120
struct declaration, 32-33
struct keyword, 110
  DDate type, 113
  described, 32
structure members, 117
structures, 108-109
  byte padding, 449
  classes comparison, 108, 151-155
  memory use, 447-450
  settings, working with all, 449
  size, 450
  template classes, 221, 238-243
  variables, 117
  when to use, 128, 151-155
styles
  block, 15
  comments, 14-17, 20, 24, 37, 41, 49
  indented block, 15
  K&R, 15
subscript operator, overloading, 254
sync_with_stdio( ) function, 501

T

template classes
  arrays, 229
    double values, 232
    simple data types, 231
  compound data types, 220, 228-232
  constructors, defining, 222

data types
  simple, 221-225
  undefined, 220, 233-238
  member functions, 222, 226
  reading in data, 220, 225-228
  structures, 221, 238-243
  variables, defining, 235-236
templates
  angle brackets, 252
  class, 252
  inheritance, 256
terminate( ) function, 417
TerminateHandler function, 388
terminating applications, 375, 391-393
testing
  classes, 124, 133
  operator overload, 143
text editors
  ed, 12
  Notepad, 12
  vi, 12
TextFile object, 561
threads, 486
throw statement, 418
throwFunc( ) function, 421-422
Transaction vector float values, 347
troubleshooting
  keywords (namespace), 16
  statements (compiled), 16
try block, 417
  described, 46-48
  exception classes, 428
  statements, 416
try keyword, 416
TSimple class, 227-228
typed languages, 219
typedef (error handler declaration), 436
typeed operator, 564-566
typeid operator, 97
types
  classes, 55
  declaring, 76
type_info class, 564

U

unary functions (predicates), 329
unary operators, overloading, 138
undefined data types (template classes), 220, 233-238
UNEXPECT directory, 434
unique algorithm, 320, 329
unique member function, 320
UNIX text editors, 12
unknown data types, 222
  TSimple class, 227-228

unsetf( ) manipulator, 511
user-defined operators (namespaces), 557
using directive, 14, 75, 252, 552
using-declaration (namespaces), 551-552

V

validation code (functions), 132
validity testing (expressions), 385
value argument, 32
values
    containers, 319, 341-345
    integer (int data type)
    described, 14
    pointers, storing, 32
    references, storing, 32
    return, 49
    variables (function cal results), 415
variables
    access, 169-174
    const, 20
    CurrentElement, 124
    data members, 160
    data types, combining into, 110
    derived classes, 201
    global, 169-174
    iVal, 35-36
    pointer variables, 294
    private, 169-174, 184
    protected, 201
    public, 169-174
    reading in data (template classes), 220,
      225-228
    specifying, 111
    storage (main), 165
    structures, 117
    template classes, defining, 235-236
    values (function call result), 415
vector container, 320
vectors
    class template, 252
    elements
      inserting, 250-254
      modifying, 257-260
      reading, 254-256

pattern vector, 338
sequential containers, 321
size, 252
sorting (sort algorithm), 358
Transaction (float values), 347
vi text editor, 12
views (classes), 89-91
virtual classes, 161, 206-216
    memory, 216
    model, converting to nonvirtual inheritance
      model, 214-216
virtual functions, 206-207
    dynamic binding, 561-563
virtual keyword, 94
virtual member functions, 94, 206
visibility (member functions), 90
void pointer (bsearch function), 300

W-Z

while loop, 23, 184
whitespace, setting, 507
writing
    binary files, 526, 536-542
    loop statements, 21-25
    programs
      to allocate and deallocate memory, 37-41
      with derived data types, 29-36
      exception handling, 41-50
      without knowing C++, 12-17
      with one or more functions, 25-28
      to perform calculations, 17-20
writing to files
    different positions, 526, 542-546
    error detection, 375, 395-397
    fstream class, 527
    ofstream class, 527-528
    opening, 536

Other Related Titles

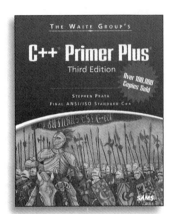

**The Waite Group's
C++ Primer Plus,
Third Edition**
Stephen Prata
1-57169-162-6
$35.00 USA/$50.95 CAN

C++ Unleashed
Jesse Liberty, et al.
ISBN: 0-672-31239-5
$39.99 USA/$57.95 CAN

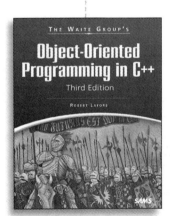

**The Waite Group's
Object-Oriented
Programming in C++,
Third Edition**
Robert Lafore
ISBN: 1-57169-160-X
$34.99 USA/$50.95 CAN

Using C++
Rob McGregor
ISBN: 0-7897-1667-4
$29.99 USA/$42.95 CAN

SAMS

www.samspublishing.com

All prices are subject to change.

WHAT'S ON THE
CD-ROM

The companion CD-ROM contains all the authors' source code, samples from the book, and some third-party software products.

WINDOWS 3.1 AND WINDOWS NT 3.51 INSTALLATION INSTRUCTIONS

1. Insert the CD-ROM disc into your CD-ROM drive.

2. From Program Group or File Manager, select File, Run.

3. Type in *DRIVE*:\SETUP.EXE to run the installation program, where *DRIVE* is the drive letter associated with your CD-ROM drive. For example, if your CD-ROM is assigned the drive letter D, you would type D:\SETUP.EXE and select OK.

4. Follow the onscreen instructions to finish the installation.

WINDOWS 95, WINDOWS 98, AND WINDOWS NT 4 INSTALLATION INSTRUCTIONS

1. Insert the CD-ROM disc into your CD-ROM drive.

2. From the desktop, double-click the My Computer icon.

3. Double-click the icon representing your CD-ROM drive.

4. Double-click the icon titled START.EXE to run the installation program.

5. Follow the onscreen instructions to finish the installation.

UNIX INSTALLATION INSTRUCTIONS

Because each flavor of UNIX has its own method of mounting a CD-ROM, I will only outline the most common method of mounting a CD-ROM on a UNIX workstation. If you need additional instructions, consult the man pages for mounting a CD-ROM, a UNIX book, or your system administrator.

1. Insert the CD-ROM disc into your CD-ROM drive.

2. Issue the appropriate mount instruction to mount the CD-ROM, such as

```
mount [options] [device] [mountpoint]
```

where [*options*] is the parameters for mounting the CD-ROM, [*device*] is the device associated with your CD-ROM, and [*mountpoint*] is where the CD-ROM will be mounted onto the file system. The mount point must exist before you issue the **mount** command. For example, a typical **mount** command for a Red Hat Linux workstation would be

```
mount -tiso9660 /dev/cdrom /mnt/cdrom
```

3. The file UNIX.TXT at the root level of the CD-ROM contains specific information on copying and installing the UNIX-specific software on your computer.

NOTE

If Windows 95, Windows 98, or Windows NT 4 is installed on your computer and you have the AutoPlay feature enabled, the START.EXE program starts automatically whenever you insert the disc into your CD-ROM drive.
